DATE DUE

DEMCO 38-296

CONTEMPORARY MUSICIANS

ISSN 1044-2197

CONTEMPORARY MUSICIANS

PROFILES OF THE PEOPLE IN MUSIC

MICHAEL L. LaBLANC,
Editor

VOLUME 6

Includes Cumulated Indexes

 Gale Research Inc. · DETROIT · LONDON

STAFF

Michael L. LaBlanc, *Editor*

Julia M. Rubiner, *Associate Editor*

Suzanne M. Bourgoin, *Assistant Editor*

David Bianco, Barbara Carlisle Bigelow, Marjorie Burgess, David Collins, Margaret Escobar, Christine Ferran, Simon Glickman, Joan Goldsworthy, Anne Janette Johnson, Kyle Kevorkian, Jeanne M. Lesinski, Meg Mac Donald, Louise Mooney, Michael E. Mueller, Rob Nagel, Nancy Pear, Nancy Rampson, Heather Rhodes, Megan Rubiner, Calen D. Stone, B. Kimberly Taylor, Elizabeth Wenning, *Contributing Editors*

Peter M. Gareffa, *Senior Editor*

Jeanne Gough, *Permissions Manager*
Margaret A. Chamberlain, *Permissions Supervisor (Pictures)*
Pamela A. Hayes, *Permissions Associate*
Karla L. Kulkis, Nancy M. Rattenbury, Keith Reed, *Permissions Assistants*

Mary Beth Trimper, *Production Manager*
Shanna Philpott Heilveil, *External Production Assistant*
Arthur Chartow, *Art Director*
Cynthia Baldwin, *Graphic Designer*
C.J. Jonik, *Keyliner*

Special thanks to the Biography Division Research staff

Cover Illustration by John Kleber

The paper used in this publication meets the minimum requirements of American National Standard for Information Sciences—Permanence Paper for Printed Library Materials, ANSI Z39.48-1984. ∞™

ISBN 0-8103-2216-1
ISSN 1044-2197

Contents

Introduction   ix

Photo Credits   xi

Cumulative Subject Index   269

Cumulative Musicians Index   279

Introduction

Fills the Information Gap on Today's Musicians

Contemporary Musicians profiles the colorful personalities in the music industry who create or influence the music we hear today. Prior to Contemporary Musicians, no quality reference series provided comprehensive information on such a wide range of artists despite keen and ongoing public interest. To find biographical and critical coverage, an information seeker had little choice but to wade through the offerings of the popular press, scan television "infotainment" programs, and search for the occasional published biography or expose. Contemporary Musicians is designed to serve that information seeker, providing in one ongoing source in-depth coverage of the important figures on the modern music scene in a format that is both informative and entertaining. Students, researchers, and casual browsers alike can use Contemporary Musicians to fill their needs for personal information about the artists, find a selected discography of the musician's recordings, and read an insightful essay offering biographical and critical information.

Provides Broad Coverage

Single-volume biographical sources on musicians are limited in scope, focusing on a handful of performers from a specific musical genre or era. In contrast, Contemporary Musicians offers researchers and music devotees a comprehensive, informative, and entertaining alternative. Contemporary Musicians is published twice yearly, with each volume providing information on 80 to 100 musical artists from all the genres that form the broad spectrum of contemporary music—pop, rock, jazz, blues, country, new wave, New Age, folk, rhythm and blues, gospel, bluegrass, rap, and reggae, to name a few, as well as selected classical artists who have achieved "crossover" success with the general public. Contemporary Musicians will occasionally include profiles of influential nonperforming members of the music industry, including producers, promoters, and record company executives.

Includes Popular Features

In Contemporary Musicians you'll find popular features that users value:

- **Easy-to-locate data sections**—Vital personal statistics, chronological career summaries, listings of major awards, and mailing addresses, when available, are prominently displayed in a clearly marked box on the second page of each entry.

- **Biographical/critical essays**—Colorful and informative essays trace each personality's personal and professional life, offer representative examples of critical response to each artist's work, and provide entertaining personal sidelights.

- **Selected discographies**—Each entry provides a comprehensive listing of the artist's major recorded works.

- **Photographs**—Most entries include portraits of the artists.

- **Sources for additional information**—This invaluable feature directs the user to selected books, magazines, and newspapers where more information on listees can be obtained.

Helpful Indexes Make It Easy to Find the Information You Need

Contemporary Musicians features a Musicians Index, listing names of individual performers and musical groups, and a Subject Index that provides the user with a breakdown by primary musical instruments played and by musical genre.

We Welcome Your Suggestions

The editors welcome your comments and suggestions for enhancing and improving *Contemporary Musicians*. If you would like to suggest musicians or composers to be covered in the future, please submit these names to the editors. Mail comments or suggestions to:

The Editor
Contemporary Musicians
Gale Research Inc.
835 Penobscot Bldg.
Detroit MI 48226-4094
Phone : (800) 347-4253
Fax: (313) 961-6241

Photo Credits

CONTEMPORARY MUSICIANS

The Allman Brothers

Rock band

Duane and Gregg Allman were born one year apart in Nashville, Tennessee, in 1946 and 1947, respectively. Their father died when they were young, and when Duane was 12, their mother moved the family to Daytona, Florida. They grew up listening to the great blues artists on southern radio stations and were soon playing music themselves. After Gregg received a guitar for Christmas he taught Duane some basics that he had picked up, and then switched to keyboards. By the time they were in their mid-teens, both were members of local groups like the House Rockers and the Untils.

In 1965 they formed a four-piece unit, the Allman Joys, and recorded a rendition of Willie Dixon's classic, "Spoonful." A year later they were brought to Hollywood by Bill McEuen but the group only lasted until 1967. The brothers formed another band, Hourglass, but the results were less than spectacular. "They handed us a boxful of demos and said pick out your album," Gregg said in *Rock 100*. Their label wouldn't even let the band play in clubs and eventually the group folded.

For the Record. . .

Group has included **Howard Duane Allman,** born November 20, 1946, Nashville, TN, died in a motorcycle accident October 29, 1971; **Gregg Allman,** born December 8, 1947, Nashville; Duane and Gregg's mother's name was Geraldine Allman; **Dicky Betts** (guitar); **Warren Haynes** (guitar); **Jai Johanny Johanson** (drums); **Chuck Leavell** (piano); **Johnny Neel** (harmonica and keyboards); **Berry Oakley** (bass), deceased, 1972; **Dan Toller** (guitar); **Butch Trucks** (drums); **Lamar Williams** (bass); **Allen Woody** (bass).

Band formed c. 1968.

Addresses: *Record company*—Epic (Sony Music Distribution), Sony Music Entertainment, P.O. Box 4450, New York, NY 10101.

The brothers' brief recordings from this period can be heard on the LPs *Early Allman* and *Power of Love.*

Gregg stayed in California to honor the remainder of the Hourglass contract, while Duane headed back south where he latched on to a highly lucrative but artistically unsatisfying job as a studio sideman. "Oh man! Studios—that's a terrible thing! You just lay around and you get your money, man," Duane once said in *Guitar Player.* He added tasteful guitar lines to songs by Wilson Pickett, Aretha Franklin, Delaney and Bonnie, King Curtis, Boz Scaggs, Clarence Carter, and others while helping to establish Rick Hall's Muscle Shoals as one of the nation's recording capitals.

Band Formed After Stunning Session

At the same time Duane was hanging out with Butch Trucks and his band, 31st of February. Gregg, who had been writing tunes out west, was convinced by Duane to come home and play. Upon his return the brothers recorded some demos with Truck's outfit before hooking up with The Second Coming, a progressive Jefferson Airplane-style band headed by Dicky Betts and Berry Oakley. The unit became the Allman Brothers Band and from their first jam together, Duane knew he had a hot group. "It lasted two-and-a-half hours," he told *Guitar Player.* "When we finally quit, nobody ever said a word man. Everybody was speechless. Nobody'd ever done anything like that before."

Duane eventually quit his studio work as the band went to New York to record their debut LP. *The Allman Brothers Band,* released in 1969, was mainly blues as

the brothers were allowed the freedom that their Hourglass sessions prohibited. "Before we went into the studio to record our first album, we had a very clear idea of what we were all trying to do musically and that it was unique—a style totally different from anything else anyone was playing," Dicky Betts told *Guitar World.* "It wasn't that we got *lucky* as we went along; from the earliest rehearsals, we had the same mindset."

Twin Guitars: An Allman Trademark

The unique aspect of the Allman Brothers was the unison counterpoint guitar lines that Duane and Betts played so brilliantly together. This approach reached its peak on their *Live at the Fillmore East* LP, released in 1971 after their second studio album, *Idlewild South.* The band was building a reputation on their four-hour live sets that transformed the blues in much the same way as Eric Clapton's trio, Cream. Recorded on March 12 and 13, 1971, three of the double LP's seven songs totalled 54 minutes, creating one of the most stunning live albums in rock history.

The two guitarists stretched classics like "Statesboro Blues" and "Stormy Monday" into new forms while creating beautiful and blistering originals like "Hot 'Lanta" and "In Memory of Elizabeth Reed." With Gregg on keyboards and vocals, Oakley on bass, and Butch Trucks and Jai Johanny Johanson both pounding on the drums, the Allman Brothers were a very high-powered machine. "The Allmans simply plowed straight ahead, unrelenting, not content to stop until both themselves and the audience were dizzy from exhaustion," *Rock 100* stated.

Sparked Generation of Southern Rockers

The new formula of two guitars and two drums spawned an entire school of southern rock bands: Wet Willie, the Outlaws, .38 Special, Molly Hatchet, Marshall Tucker, Charlie Daniels, Black Oak Arkansas, and the three-guitar attack of Lynyrd Skynyrd. With the exception of the latter, most of these bands just seemed like imitations, mainly because none of them included a guitar genius like Duane Allman.

"Duane was the father of the band," said Gregg in *Guitar Player.* "He had a lot to do with the spontaneity of the whole thing. He was like the mother ship. Somehow he had this real magic about him that would lock us all in, and we'd take off." Although he is hardly ever mentioned in the same breath as his contemporaries, Duane was as equally inventive and skillful as Jeff Beck, Jimi Hendrix, or Jimmy Page. His work on Clapton's

Layla LP prodded the Englishman to new heights and created one of the finest rock albums of all time.

The Allman Brothers band took a devastating blow on October 29, 1971 when Duane was killed in a motorcycle crash at the age of 24. A tight-knit family, the Allman Brothers band continued on without replacing Duane and issued *Eat a Peach* in 1972. One half of the LP consisted of live cuts from their Fillmore dates and the studio side included the hit "Melissa." Betts took control of the band's direction and continued in his instrumental vein with "Jessica" on their next album, *Brothers and Sisters*. They had their biggest hit, "Ramblin' Man," but were also struck again by tragedy when Berry Oakley died just 13 months after Duane in an eerily similar accident.

Survived Breakups and Reunions

By 1974 the media began to focus more on the group's personal lives than their music as Gregg's solo tour, drug bust, and marriage to singer Cher took the spotlight while the group's financial situation worsened. *Win, Lose or Draw* saw the band continuing but breaking no new ground in 1975, the same year Capricorn issued a compilation LP, *The Road Goes On Forever*. *Wipe the Windows, Check the Oil, Dollar Gas* was released a year later and consisted of outtakes from 1972-75 sessions as the band began to disintegrate.

The final straw came when Gregg testified against their road manager, Scooter Herring, who eventually got 75 years in jail on a drug conviction. "He threw Scooter away just because he didn't need him anymore," Betts told *Rolling Stone,* "and there's not one person in this band who won't tell you anything different than that. That's why there's no Allman Brothers band. . . There is no way we can work with Gregg again ever."

Betts left to form Great Southern while Johanson organized Sea Level with pianist Chuck Leavell and bassist Lamar Williams. By 1979 the wounds were healed, however, as Gregg, Trucks, and Johanson jammed with Great Southern in New York's Central Park, sparking the first Allman Brothers reunion. Their comeback LP, *Enlightened Rogues,* was controlled by Betts as he again explored the dual guitar approach with Dan Toler. "Whatever *Enlightened Rogues* lacks in virtuosity, it makes up for in emotional intensity," stated *Rolling Stone*. Jas Obrecht in *Guitar Player* called it their "strongest album since *Eat a Peach*. It's good to see them back."

They followed with *Reach for the Sky,* which seemed hollow compared to *Rogues*. "We had a bad experience with (recording executive) Clive Davis," Betts told

Guitar Player. "We did two albums with him—one of them was a real good album, and one of them was a real bad one. . . . The last album we did wasn't worth a. . .you know." The reunited Allmans lasted only one more album longer, *Brothers Of The Road,* before disbanding. Gregg hooked up with Toler and produced a major hit thereafter with *I'm No Angel* in 1987.

Launched 20th-Anniversary Tour

In the late 1980s, Mike Caplan of Epic Records had signed both Betts and Allman to separate contracts in hopes of getting them back together. By 1989 his strategy paid off and the Allman Brothers 20th Anniversary Tour, their first tour in eight years, was on the road playing their classic tunes. "We're just taking it easy and seeing what happens from here," Butch Trucks told the *Detroit Free Press*. Though enthusiastic, Betts expressed caution, joking in *Rolling Stone* that the folks from Epic "were afraid we would *break up* again before we ever finished the tour." The tour was a success as it coincided with the release of *Dreams,* a retrospective multi-disk box set containing several previously unreleased tracks.

After the tour the band members were back in the studios working once again with producer Tom Dowd on *Seven Turns*. Released in 1990, the album was praised as an encouraging return to the vintage sound of the Allman Brothers of old,. and the single "Good Clean Fun" received considerable air play. Any doubts about the new incarnation of the pioneers of southern rock were removed in 1991 when the Allman Brothers released *Shades of Two Worlds*. "Charged by top-flight performances from Dickey Betts and Gregg Allman, the band summons up both the spirit and the musical resonance of the original group," remarked John Swenson in *Rolling Stone*. Swenson joined other reviewers in applauding the addition on these two albums of Warren Haynes, a slide guitarist who has done more than a creditable job of filling Duane's shoes: "He references Allman's tone and signature techniques yet animates his presentation with his own distinctive personality."

Now in their third decade together, Allman, Betts, Trucks, and Johanson have run the full gamut of emotions, yet they continue to produce an enduring, distinctive brand of rock and roll. "They've gone through a lot of peaks and valleys," producer Tom Dowd told the *Free Press,* "but now they're enjoying each other's company again, and they realize how valuable they are to each other."

Selected discography

The Allman Brothers Band, Atco, 1969.
Idlewild South, Atco, 1970.
Live at the Fillmore East, Capricorn, 1971.
Eat a Peach, Capricorn, 1972.
Brothers and Sisters, Capricorn, 1973.
Win, Lose or Draw, Capricorn, 1975.
The Road Goes on Forever, Capricorn, 1975.
Wipe The Windows, Check the Oil, Dollar Gas, Capricorn, 1976.
Enlightened Rogues, Capricorn, 1979.
Reach for the Sky, Arista, 1980.
Brothers of the Road.
Dreams (retrospective box set), Polydor, 1989.
Seven Turns, Epic, 1990.
Live At Ludlow Garage, Polygram, 1990.
Shades of Two Worlds, Epic, 1991.

Also released *Power of Love* under band name Hourglass and *Early Allman,* Dial Records, 1973, under band name Allman Joys.

Duane Allman

An Anthology, Capricorn, 1972.
An Anthology, Volume II, Capricorn, 1974.
Best Of, Polydor.

Gregg Allman

Laid Back, Capricorn, 1973.
Gregg Allman Tour, Capricorn, 1974.
Playin' Up a Storm, Capricorn, 1977.
I'm No Angel, Epic, 1987.
Just Before the Bullets Fly, Epic, 1988.

Dickey Betts

Highway Call, Capricorn, 1975.
Great Southern, Arista, 1977.
Atlanta Burning Down, Arista, 1978.

Pattern Disruptive, Epic, 1989.

Sea Level

Sea Level, Capricorn, 1977.
Cats on the Coast, Capricorn, 1978.
On the Edge, Capricorn, 1978.
Long Walk on a Short Pier, Capricorn, 1979.
Ballroom, Arista, 1980.

Sources

Books

Christgau, Robert, *Christgau's Record Guide,* Ticknor & Fields, 1981.
The Rolling Stone Record Guide, edited by Dave Marsh with John Swenson, Random House/Rolling Stone Press, 1979.
Dalton, David, and Lenny Kaye, *Rock 100,* Grosset & Dunlap, 1977.
Logan, Nick, and Bob Woffinden, *The Illustrated Encyclopedia of Rock,* Harmony, 1977.
The Rolling Stone Illustrated History of Rock & Roll, edited by Jim Miller, Random House/Rolling Stone Press, 1976.
The Guitar Player Book, by the editors of *Guitar Player* magazine, Grove Press, 1979.

Periodicals

Detroit Free Press, July 11, 1989.
Guitar for the Practicing Musician, September 1987.
Guitar Player, July 1979; October 1984; January 1987; August 1989; November 1990.
Guitar World, February 1989; March 1989; September 1989.
Rolling Stone, November 6, 1975; August 26, 1976; November 4, 1976; March 10, 1977; May 31, 1979; October 16, 1980; August 9, 1990; October 18, 1990; August 8, 1991.

—Calen D. Stone

Kathleen Battle

Opera singer

"**S**he won't do Tosca or Mimi, but concentrates on the coquettish '-ettas' and '-inas' of the opera repertoire. Next to those like Jessye Norman's, her voice sounds small. But that sound is so ravishing, the intonations so true, the voice so flexible, and the timbre so pure, that Kathleen Battle is one of our most adored divas, reigning as the finest coloratura soprano of her generation," wrote Michael Kimmelman in a *Vogue* profile of the diminutive, black opera star in 1986. An attractive woman dubbed "the undisputed best-dressed concert performer in the business" by *Time*, Battle confines her roles to the soubrette and coloratura repertoires which accommodate her range. "I won't stretch or pull my voice beyond its capacity and capability," the renowned artist with numerous Grammy nominations said to Heidi Waleson in *Opera News*. "And I know what the limit is."

Battle was born August 13, 1948, in Portsmouth, Ohio. The daughter of a steelworker, originally from Alabama, and the youngest of seven children, she was reared in a musical household. "I learned to sing listening to my father," Battle told Bernard Holland in a *New York Times Magazine* interview. "He was a singer in a gospel quartet. My sister taught me how to read music. . . . The piano I kind of picked up, getting a fingering here, a chord there, looking over people's shoulders." Her first audience was the African Methodist Episcopal Church, where Battle sang from a tabletop at civic functions, banquets, and church affairs. Charles Varney, a Portsmouth High School music teacher and mentor to the adolescent Battle, related to *Time* reporter Michael Walsh his wonder at first hearing "this tiny little thing singing so beautifully," referring to the eight-year-old Battle. "I went to her later," Varney recalled, "and told her God had blessed her, and she must always sing."

Considered a Career in Mathematics

Battle was an excellent student in school, and wavered between a career in math or music. Pressure from Varney persuaded her to pursue music after her graduation from Portsmouth High School in 1966. The winner of a National Achievement Scholarship, she enrolled at the College-Conservatory of Music of the University of Cincinnati, but hesitated to get a degree in performance. She opted for a more secure route in music education, where she took a B.A. in 1970 and an M.A. in 1971. "I never would have dreamed of being a performance major," Battle explained in *Opera News*. "Still, I was feeling my way in college. I took art, dance, piano, and languages. I kept promising myself I'd take more math. It gives me a comfortable feeling to keep my options open."

For the Record. . .

Born August 13, 1948, in Portsmouth, OH; daughter of a steel worker, the youngest of seven children. *Education:* University of Cincinnati College-Conservatory, B.A., 1970, M.A., 1971.

Former inner-city elementary school music teacher. Opera and concert singer. Has toured and recorded extensively, and appeared on Grammy Awards shows. Debuted with the Michigan Opera Theatre, 1976; has since appeared in major festivals, including Festival of Two Worlds, Spoleto, Italy, 1972; May Festival, Cincinnati, OH, 1974; New York City Opera, 1976; Metropolitan Opera, New York City, 1978—; Salzburg Festival, 1984; has appeared with major orchestras, including the New York Philharmonic, Cleveland Orchestra, and Los Angeles Philharmonic.

Awards: National Achievement Scholarship; numerous awards and Grammy nominations, including one for *Salzburg Recital;* honorary doctorate, University of Cincinnati College-Conservatory, 1983.

The next two years after graduation Battle taught music to inner-city elementary students while taking private voice studies at the College-Conservatory. In 1972 she auditioned for Thomas Schippers, the conductor of the Cincinnati Symphony. Schippers chose Battle to perform Brahm's *Ein Deutsches Requiem* at the Festival of Two Worlds in Spoleto, Italy, that year. By 1973 Battle had resigned her teaching position to concentrate on performing music full-time, and soon was introduced to James Levine. The music director and principal conductor of New York's Metropolitan Opera, Levine was a native of Cincinnati who had come home to be the visiting director at the orchestra's renowned May Festival. He auditioned Battle. "Blown away" by what he heard, he related to Holland, he chose Battle to sing a short soprano role in Mahler's *Eighth Symphony* at the festival the following year. "Some singers have little instinct but do have the intellect to balance technical and musical issues. Some have instinct and a beautiful voice but less intellect," Levine told Holland. "I had never come across a more complete talent than hers."

Debuted at Michigan Opera Theatre

Levine became Battle's career mentor, encouraging her to develop a repertoire which included sacred music and emphasized Mozart. With performances throughout the United States enhancing her reputation,

Battle went to New York when she was offered an understudy part in Scott Joplin's opera *Treemonisha.* After making her operatic debut at the Michigan Opera Theatre in 1976, she was summoned back quickly to the Big Apple that same year to debut as Susanna in *The Marriage of Figaro* with the New York City Opera. Then came an audition at the Metropolitan Opera where, two years later on September 18, 1978, she made her debut under Levine's direction as the shepherd in Wagner's *Tannhauser.*

Critical response to Battle's performances has rarely varied throughout the ensuing years following her debut. *Time* magazine, among others, pronounced her "the best lyric coloratura soprano in the world" in 1985. Restricting her lyric fare to the Adinas, Despinas, Norinas, Zerlinas, Paminas, and Rosinas typical of coloratura opera singers, Battle has also added spirituals and suitable works by Schubert, Duparc, Brahms, Haydn, Mahler, and Bach. Her recital at Alice Tully Hall in New York was sold out months in advance in 1986. Averaging sixty performances a year, the artist whose most memorable roles have been the young servants (soubrettes) and heroines of Mozart is not dismayed by the few critics who lament her limitations. The consensus among many critics is akin to Holland who wrote that her "relatively confined set of roles may actually concentrate her talents." Terry Teachout in *High Fidelity* was baffled by the criticism of the soprano's voice as "a vocal fragment" in 1987. In his review of her album *Salzburg Recital,* he stated, "Artists like Battle should be cherished, and not dismissed with a vulgar sneer."

"Difficult" Reputation

"Those who have found her occasionally difficult," noted Holland in his response to the tag "temperamental" attached to Battle's reputation, "usually agree that her skirmishes are fought in the name of the music rather than personal aggrandizement." Battle first earned the tag during rehearsals with opera diva Kiri Te Kawana. They were appearing together in Strauss's *Arabella* in 1983 when Battle objected to cuts to her part as Zdenka. Acting on the advice of members of the production staff, she requested her part be restored, but Te Kawana denied her request. The relationship between the two stars subsequently deteriorated, and Battle's image as "difficult" has persisted to the present. Matthew A. Epstein gave his perspective of the singer in the *New York Times Magazine.* The producer of Handel's *Semele* at Carnegie Hall—in which Battle starred to huge success—said, "She is not a pushover; she's a professional liberated woman."

Unmarried, Battle keeps a home in Quogue, Long

Island. Eventually, she would like to teach at the conservatory level, or commission music composed for soprano and small orchestra. Performances in all the great opera houses of the world still await the stellar vocalist who has not bent to pressures placed upon her by prestigious conductors to take roles beyond her range. "I've accepted my reality," she declared to Holland. "I was meant to sound the way I do."

Selected discography

Lulu Suite, 1983.
Symphony no. 2 in C "Resurrection," 1983.
A German Requiem, 1984.
Arias (Mozart), 1986.
Kathleen Battle Sings Mozart, 1986.
Papst Johannes Paul II, 1986.
Salzburg Recital, 1986.
Pleasures of Their Company, 1986.
A Christmas Celebration, 1986.
Ariadne auf Naxos, op. 60, 1987.
Lieder (Schubert), 1988.
Live in Tokyo 1988, 1989.
Symphony no. 4 (Mahler), 1989.
Arias (Handel), 1990.

Sources

High Fidelity, November 1987.
Jet, February 1, 1988.
New York Times, January 26, 1986.
New York Times Magazine, November 17, 1985.
Opera News, March 13, 1982; February 14, 1987.
People, March 7, 1983.
Stereo Review, November 1986.
Time, November 11, 1985.
Vogue, February 1986.

—*Marjorie Burgess*

Regina Belle

Singer

Singer Regina Belle has dazzled critics and fans alike since her debut album, *All by Myself,* was released in 1987. Acclaimed as one of the most exciting new singers to emerge on the rhythm and blues scene, the New Jersey songstress boasts a style that recalls some of the most successful black pop female singers in the industry, yet is nonetheless distinctive. Jim Miller in *Newsweek* heralded Belle's entry onto the music scene in 1987: "Move over, Anita Baker—and make way for Regina Belle, who may be the most electrifying new soul singer since Baker herself. . . . Imagine a singer who simultaneously recalls Aretha Franklin, Sade and Anita Baker, and you'll get a fair idea of Belle's singular style."

Dazzled Reviewers with Impressive Range

Belle's wide vocal range has particularly impressed reviewers. "She has a strong, expressive voice and she's versatile, dealing well with sultry ballads ('Baby Come to Me') or sassy jump-ups ('When Will You Be Mine')," wrote David Hiltbrand in *People* of *Stay With Me,* Belle's follow-up to *All by Myself.* Steve Bloom commented in *Rolling Stone* that Belle's "full-throated, pop-gospel vocal style brings to mind Anita Baker, Patti LaBelle, and Stephanie Mills." A number of critics have similarly compared Belle's vocals to those of soul-jazz phenomenon Baker. Hiltbrand noted that, like Baker, Belle "displays a voice of tantalizing quality. . . . She can sound both promisingly intimate and world-weary without sacrificing vibrancy."

Belle has remarked, however, that comparisons to Baker are off-target. She told Bloom: "Because Anita Baker is prominent right now, Regina Belle sounds like Anita Baker. . . . I've been singing since I was three years old. By the time [Baker's 1986 album] *Rapture* came out, my style was already developed. People say I got certain inflections from Anita, but I got them from Phyllis Hyman. *That* was my girl." In addition to Hyman, Belle lists other musical influences as Billie Holiday, Donny Hathaway, and Nancy Wilson; she refers to the latter as her "show business mother." Belle met famous song stylist Wilson at a music convention in Los Angeles. "When I met her she told me that Billie Holiday did it for Dinah [Washington], Dinah did it for her and she has to do it for me," Belle was quoted as saying in *Jet.*

Grew Up with Gospel and R & B

Belle's musical roots are in gospel, which she grew up singing in church with her family. She told an *Ebony* contributor that she was raised in a house where music was "something . . . involuntary." Her mother's special-

For the Record. . .

Born in 1963; native of Englewood, NJ; daughter of Eugene and Lois Belle; formerly married to Horace A. Young III; children: Tiy Chreigna (daughter). *Education:* Attended Rutgers State University.

Singer and recording artist, 1987—.

Awards: Nomination for best rhythm and blues female singer, American Music Awards, 1991.

Addresses: *Record company*—Columbia Records, 51 West 52nd St., New York, NY 10019.

ty was gospel, and she learned rhythm and blues from her father. "The music was the same, just the message was different," she told Bloom. Belle sang during high school and on weekends attended classes at New York City's Manhattan School of Music, where she studied opera and classical music. Belle did not study jazz until college, when she enrolled in the Jazz Ensemble at Rutgers University. Belle told Bloom that with jazz she learned "to listen for colors, as opposed to trying to sing just notes. For the longest time, I couldn't figure out what that meant."

Not sure that music would be her career, Belle majored in accounting and history at Rutgers. Her big break as a singer came when disc jockey Vaughn Harper heard her open a concert on the Rutgers campus. Impressed, Harper introduced Belle to the manager of the singing group The Manhattans, who were looking for a female backup singer. Shortly thereafter Belle was touring with the group; a recording contract from the group's label, Columbia, soon followed.

All by Myself Sent Career Soaring

Belle's 1987 debut, *All by Myself,* was an instant success; *Stay With Me,* her 1989 effort, established Belle as a major singer on the rhythm and blues scene. Both albums generated a string of solo hits, including "Show Me the Way," "Make It Like It Was," and "When Will You Be Mine." Belle has been primarily popular on the black charts, something she would like to see eventually change. "It's insulting to me when somebody says, 'You're Number One on the *black* charts.' It suggests that nobody appreciates my music but black people," she told Bloom. "I'd love to have a Number One pop single, but I'm not at the point where I *have* to. It doesn't plague me."

In addition to receiving acclaim as a recording artist, Belle is also considered an outstanding live performer who is not afraid to take chances musically. "Her gifted voice and stage presence make her a tough 'opening' act," noted *Ebony.* "She is said to hold her own on any given night, and on others make the 'headliner' acts sweat for their star-status." Peter Watrous of the *New York Times* reviewed a show-stealing opener by Belle in 1989, noting that "Ms. Belle, who has an extraordinary voice, dug deep into gospel and blues melodies, letting the grit of her voice show, often tearing apart the original impulse of a song." The following year Watrous reviewed Belle as a headliner at New York's Avery Fisher Hall, commenting that "though she's not working as a jazz singer, she is an exceptional improviser." Belle's shows, Watrous continued, are "expansive and improvisatory, old-fashioned qualities that make her one of the most exciting pop singers working."

Selected discography

All by Myself, Columbia, 1987.
Stay with Me, Columbia, 1989.

Sources

Ebony, June 1990.
Essence, May 1990.
Jet, May 14, 1990.
Newsweek, June 22, 1987.
New York Times, September 16, 1989; June 30, 1990.
People, June 22, 1987; October 2, 1989.
Rolling Stone, April 5, 1990.

—*Michael E. Mueller*

Yefim Bronfman

Pianist

Yefim Bronfman, an American pianist of Russian descent, has performed with most of the major orchestras in the United States and Europe and in chamber music collaborations with many celebrated musicians. He is known for his virtuosity of technique, clarity and beauty of tone, and soulful interpretations of the world's great piano literature. Violinist Isaac Stern, the mentor of many young musicians, told Eugenia Zuckerman of *CBS Sunday Morning,* "I think that he is probably one of the two or three greatest talents to come along in this part of our time. And it's a career that I see growing steadily and enriching himself and everybody around him for the next fifty years."

Bronfman was born into a musical family on April 10, 1958 in Tashkent, Soviet Union, a city of over one million not far from the Chinese and Afghan borders. Because his father was a violinist and mother a pianist, it was assumed that Bronfman would become a musician. At age seven Bronfman began music lessons with his mother and continued his studies at a music school for gifted children in Tashkent. In 1969 he made his debut with the school orchestra, and in 1970 he performed Rachmaninoff's *Concerto No. 1.*

In 1973, at age fifteen, Bronfman emigrated with his family to Israel. That same year, he auditioned for Eugene Istomin, who had him play for Zubin Mehta, conductor of the Israel Philharmonic. The following December he performed with the Israel Philharmonic in Tel Aviv. In 1974 the young pianist also won a scholarship from the America-Israel Cultural Foundation (AICF) in a competition chaired by Isaac Stern. The award enabled Bronfman to study privately with pianist Arie Vardi, the head of the Rubin Academy of music at Tel Aviv University, and brought him to the attention of philanthropist Frederick Mann, who gave Bronfman his first piano.

In 1975 Bronfman made his North American debut with the Montreal Symphony under the baton of Zubin Mehta. In September 1976, he toured the United States with the Israel Philharmonic, performing the Rachmaninoff *Concerto No. 3.* In 1976 Bronfman emigrated to the United States and in 1989 became a U.S. citizen. With the aid of the AICF, he participated in the Marlboro Music Festival and was quickly invited for numerous orchestral and recital engagements. Bronfman also studied at the Curtis Institute in Philadelphia, and in Vermont with Rudolph Serkin. In 1978 he entered New York's famous Juilliard School of Music. That same year he made his debut with the New York Philharmonic, performing the Beethoven *Triple Concerto* with violinist Shlomo Mintz and cellist Yo-Yo Ma.

Since then Bronfman has appeared numerous times with orchestras worldwide in solo and recital concerts.

Born April 10, 1958, in Tashkent, U.S.S.R.; naturalized U.S. citizen; father was a violinist, mother, a pianist. *Education:* Attended Juilliard School of Music, beginning 1978, and Curtis Institute, Philadelphia; studied privately with Rudolf Serkin, Arie Vardi, Leon Fleisher, and Rudolf Firkusny.

Made professional debut with the Israel Philharmonic, 1974; soloist with orchestras in North America, Europe, and Israel.

Awards: American-Israel Cultural Foundation Scholarship, 1974; Avery Fisher Prize, 1991; Edison Prize (Netherlands) for best recording, for *Franck, Debussy and Ravel Violin Sonatas,* recorded with Shlomo Mintz.

Addresses: *Manager*—ICM Artists, 40 West 57th St., New York, NY 10019. *Publicist*—Audry Michaels Public Relations, 122 East 76th St., New York, NY 10021.

A sensitive and dedicated chamber music performer, he has collaborated with the Emerson, Guarneri, Juilliard, and Cleveland Quartets. He is a regular at the Marlboro Music Festival in Vermont, the Mostly Mozart Festival in New York, and the Spoleto Festivals in the United States and Italy.

"Everything you do in life is reflected in your playing," Bronfman told Tom Strini of the *Milwaukee Journal.* "The kind of life you lead is more important than practicing twenty-four hours a day. Once you try to get out of yourself, you can overcome self-consciousness and play more purely and honestly. You should always be ready to stop and ask yourself what you're doing it for. The great people I've heard are completely dedicated to the cause of music." In 1991 Bronfman's talent and dedication were recognized concretely when he was awarded the Avery Fisher Prize in recognition of outstanding achievement and excellence in music. One of the primary purposes of this prize, which includes a monetary award of $25,000, is to recognize solo instrumentalists who are United States citizens and who have clearly demonstrated outstanding professional ability and have contributed significantly to the world of music.

Bronfman's discography includes solo piano works and recital performances. With violinist Shlomo Mintz he recorded *Franck, Debussy and Ravel Violin Sonatas,* which was nominated for a Grammy Award and the *Ovation* Chamber Music Record of the Year, and which won the Netherlands' Edison Prize for Best Recording. Again with Mintz, Bronfman was awarded the Grand Priz National du Disque in 1988 for the recording of Gabriel Faure's *Violin Sonatas.*

Bronfman lives on the Upper West Side of Manhattan. His interests include swimming, stamp collecting, and African art, particularly statues and musical instruments.

Selected discography

Brahms: Sonata in F minor/Scherzo, Op. No. 4, Musicmasters.
Faure: Violin Sonatas (with violinist Shlomo Mintz), Deutsche Grammophon.
Franck, Debussy and Ravel Violin Sonatas (with Mintz), Deutsche Grammophon.
Mozart: Sonatas for Piano and Violin (with pianist Robert Mann), Musicmasters.
Mussorgsky: Pictures at an Exhibition, Sony Classical.
Prokofiev: Violin Sonatas Nos. 7 and 8 (with Mintz), CBS Masterworks.
Prokofiev: Violin Sonatas (with Mintz), Deutsche Grammophon.
Rachmaninoff: Piano Concert Nos. 2 & 3., Sony Classical.

Sources

CBS Sunday Morning, CBS-TV, aired August 1990.
Dallas Morning News, July 10, 1990.
Milwaukee Journal, September 18, 1988.
New York Times, August 6, 1988.

—*Jeanne M. Lesinski*

Buckwheat Zydeco

Buckwheat Zydeco has been instrumental in the rise to popularity of zydeco music, a mixture of danceable black and Cajun French stylings originating in Louisiana. With his accordion and his band *Ils sont partis*—which, as Andrew Abrahams in *People* noted, "loosely translated, means 'They're off!'" in French—he burst on the music scene in 1987 with his first major-label album, *On a Night Like This*. Though Zydeco has yet to have a Top 40 hit, his first and subsequent albums have proved successful with both critics and fans; his records are especially loved by college dance crowds. As reviewer Michael Tearson of *Audio* explained, "Buckwheat Zydeco's music is sweat, joy, spirit and fun."

Zydeco was not, however, always a fan of the music from which he takes his stage name. Born Stanley Dural, Jr., in 1947 in Lafayette, Louisiana, he rebelled when his father suggested he learn to play the accordion, the traditional lead instrument of zydeco music. He told Abrahams: "I was just like kids are now. They get up and leave the room as soon as you say the word 'accordion.' To them, that's for polkas." Instead, Zydeco learned the piano at the age of four, playing for family reunions. By the time he was nine, he was playing professionally. He also received the first half of his recording name when he was a child; he was nicknamed by friends and family after the "Little Rascals" character Buckwheat.

In 1971, Zydeco formed a rhythm-and-blues band called Buckwheat and the Hitchhikers. The fifteen-piece group was fairly successful on the local level, because, he told Abrahams, it played "what everybody was listening to." After four years with the Hitchhikers, however, Zydeco decided to take a year off from the music business, "to get [his] mind back," as he said to Abrahams.

When he resurfaced, it was as the organist for zydeco great Clifton Chenier's band. At the hands of Chenier, he learned the value not only of the traditional music of his black-Cajun ancestors, but of the previously despised accordion. By 1979, he had left Chenier to form his own zydeco group, for which he played the squeezebox himself. The band, which he called *Ils sont partis*, also featured the traditional zydeco instrument called a rub board. Zydeco explained the uninitiated audience's response to the instrument for Abrahams: "Before the show they look at this thing on stage that looks like a steel T-shirt . . . then a guy puts this thing over his chest, grabs two spoons, and the folks say, 'Now what in the hell is he going to do with *those*?'"

Some years passed before Buckwheat Zydeco came to the attention of a major record label, but by the mid-1980s New York music writer Ted Fox had become a

For the Record. . .

Born Stanley Dural, Jr., c. 1947 in Lafayette, LA; son of Stanley Dural (an automobile mechanic); married and divorced; children: four.

Singer, accordion, organ, and piano player. Began playing piano and organ professionally at the age of nine; formed and led Buckwheat and the Hitchhikers, 1971-75; played organ with Clifton Chenier c. 1977-78; solo performer, 1979—.

Addresses: *Record company*—Island, 14 East Fourth St., New York, NY 10012.

fan, and gave some of Zydeco's tapes to Island Records founder Chris Blackwell. Blackwell was extremely impressed and signed Zydeco to a contract, making him the first zydeco act recruited by a major label. Island released his first album, *On a Night Like This*, in 1987.

On a Night Like This is "lively enough to get the dead to dance," proclaimed Tearson. In addition to Zydeco's original compositions like "Ma 'Tit Fille" (contracted French for "my little girl") and "Buckwheat's Special," he also covers songs by Booker T and the MG's, the Blasters, and Bob Dylan—"Time is Tight," "Marie, Marie," and the title track—on the album. Also included is Chenier's zydeco classic, "Hot Tamale Baby."

Though many critics considered *On a Night Like This* a good introduction to the genre of zydeco music, Tearson considered it "pop-oriented" compared to the "much more down-home album" *Taking It Home,* which Zydeco released the following year. Jeff Hannusch of *Rolling Stone* disagreed, however, claiming that "the producers . . . try to steer Buckwheat in the direction of contemporary rock and roll" on *Taking It Home*. Both reviewers, though, praised Zydeco's version of Eric Clapton's "Why Does Love Got to Be So Sad" (on which Clapton provides guest guitar work) and the accordion instrumental "Drivin' Old Gray." Tearson also had kind words for the title track and "Creole Country," and

concluded: "what else is there to do but take Buckwheat home . . . turn the record player up loud, and disturb the neighbors?"

Where There's Smoke, There's Fire, Zydeco's third album on Island Records, was released in 1990. "It's a good-time party music album that works best when it sticks closest to the party music that zydeco traditionally is," according to Tearson. Though Larry Birnbaum of *Down Beat* suggested that by the release of this album "Buckwheat's sound has congealed into a formula," he asserted that *Where There's Smoke, There's Fire* throbs with raw energy." Tearson lauded the tracks "What You Gonna Do" and the instrumental "Buck's Hot Rod," while Birnbaum favored Zydeco's covers of "Beast of Burden" and "Route 66." The latter critic concluded that Zydeco's music "is unfailingly soulful."

Selected discography

Waitin' for My Ya Ya, Rounder, 1986.
On a Night Like This (includes "Ma 'Tit Fille," "Buckwheat's Special," "Time Is Tight," "Marie, Marie," "On a Night Like This," and "Hot Tamale Baby"), Island, 1987.
Zydeco Party, Rounder, 1988.
Taking It Home (includes "Taking It Home," "Why Does Love Got to Be So Sad," "Drivin' Old Gray," "Creole Country," and "Down Dallas Alley"), Island, 1988.
Where There's Smoke, There's Fire (includes "Where There's Smoke, There's Fire," "Hey, Good Lookin'," "We're Having a Party," "Maybe I Will," "Beast of Burden," "Route 66," "What You Gonna Do?," "Buck's Hot Rod," and "Pour Tout Quelqu'un"), Island, 1990.

Also released *100 Percent Fortified Zydeco,* Black Top, and *Turning Point,* Rounder.

Sources

Audio, December 1987; January 1989; November 1990.
Down Beat, July 1990.
People, December 7, 1987.
Rolling Stone, November 17, 1988.

—Elizabeth Wenning

Carol Burnett

Actress, comedienne, singer

Carol Burnett's contributions to musical theater have been eclipsed by her longstanding career as a comedienne, but music helped to make her the star she is today. Burnett launched her zany career with a parody song, "I Made a Fool of Myself over John Foster Dulles," and made a hit of the Off-Broadway musical "Once upon a Mattress" well before she found herself starring on a perennially popular television variety show. A *People* magazine contributor called Burnett "Fanny Brice in a noisebox, an all-purpose funny girl with sexy legs who could hoof it, belt it, swing the slapstick and then with terrifying tenderness tear the heart out of some chuckleheaded caricature and lay it in your startled hands."

A number of critics have noted that Burnett's fierce, satirical comedic style is a reflection of her difficult childhood. She was born in San Antonio, Texas, the daughter of two alcoholics. Her father deserted the family when she was eight, and she moved with her mother and grandmother to Los Angeles. There they lived on welfare in a boarding house. As she grew up, Burnett spent more and more time with her grandmother, who was strict and deeply religious. Needless to say, her troubled childhood left emotional scars that trouble her even today. "I couldn't understand what my parents were going through," she told *Newsweek* magazine. "I thought it was something *I* had done. So I tried to be as quiet and as cooperative as I could be. Just a little caretaker."

First Thought About Journalism

That urge to be a "people pleaser" led Burnett through busy, productive high school years to study at the University of California, Los Angeles, which she attended on scholarship. She had originally intended to major in journalism, but when she took a playwrighting class that required acting, she discovered that she loved the stage. She promptly changed her major to theater and studied voice, acting, and dancing.

Burnett was a member of UCLA's opera workshop during her junior year. Under that aegis, she and a partner, Don Saroyan, performed a duet from "Annie Get Your Gun" for a private party. The act so impressed one of the wealthy guests that he staked the two young entertainers $1000 each to travel to New York and find work in show business. Burnett pocketed the grant and made her way to New York City in the summer of 1954.

A part-time job as a hat checker in a club helped to pay the bills while Burnett made the audition rounds in Manhattan. She lived at the famed Rehearsal Club, a hotel for aspiring actresses, and she quickly became

For the Record. . .

Born April 26, 1936 (some sources say 1934), in San Antonio, TX; daughter of Jody (a theater manager) and Louise (Creighton) Burnett; married Don Saroyan (an actor), 1955 (divorced); married Joe Hamilton (a producer), 1963 (divorced); children: Carrie Louise, Jody Ann, Erin Kate. *Education:* Attended the University of California, Los Angeles, 1953-55.

Comedienne, 1955—. Began career as singer in cabarets and musical comedies; achieved national recognition with parody song "I Made a Fool of Myself over John Foster Dulles," 1957. Guest performer on numerous television shows, including the *Ed Sullivan Show*, the *Dinah Shore Show*, and the *Tonight Show*. Regular performer on the *Garry Moore Show*, 1959-62. Star of the *Carol Burnett Show*, 1967-78, and *Carol & Company*, 1990—.

Performer in musical comedies for stage, including *Once Upon a Mattress*, 1959, *Fade Out, Fade In*, 1964, and *I Do, I Do*, 1974. Performer in nonmusical comedies on stage, including *Plaza Suite*, 1970, and *Same Time Next Year*, 1977.

Principal film work includes *Pete 'n' Tillie*, 1972, *Front Page*, 1974, *A Wedding*, 1977, *Health*, 1979, *The Four Seasons*, 1981, and *Annie*, 1982. Television films include *Friendly Fire*, 1978, *The Grass Is Always Greener over the Septic Tank*, 1979, *The Tenth Month*, 1979, *Life of the Party*, 1982, *Between Friends*, 1983, and *Hostage*, 1988.

Awards: Five Emmy Awards, Academy of Television Arts and Sciences, for comedy.

popular enough there to be elected president of the club. Under Burnett's supervision, a number of young women in the club pooled their resources, rented a hall, and staged a revue for all the agents and theater reviewers they could cajole into coming. Burnett's contribution to the revue was a spoof of Eartha Kitt's sexy "Monotonous," performed in ragged bathrobe and curlers. The performance won her an agent who secured her employment in summer stock and in nightclubs.

Burnett broke into television on Paul Winchell's children's show for NBC, and by 1956 she was making semi-regular appearances on Garry Moore's daytime variety program. Much of the early television work she did was in the musical-comedy vein, and in 1957 she made a national name for herself with a send-up of teenage love songs called "I Made a Fool of Myself over John Foster Dulles." The silly song became such a hit that Burnett eventually quit performing it—she was afraid the public would identify her too strongly with that one number.

Became a Regular on *Garry Moore*

In 1959 Burnett became a regular on the nighttime version of the *Garry Moore Show*. She also starred in an Off-Broadway musical, *Once Upon a Mattress*. The show, based on the fairy tale *The Princess and the Pea*, featured Burnett as a gawky, tomboy princess named Fred. *Once Upon a Mattress* ran for 460 performances, moving from Off-Broadway to the Winter Garden and the St. James Theatre before closing in 1960. Burnett stayed with the show throughout its entire run, even though the simultaneous work for the *Garry Moore Show* brought her to the point of exhaustion.

Burnett loved musical comedy, but as her fame grew her work as a singer diminished rapidly. In the early 1960s she was still working elegant bookings such as New York's Persian Room at the Plaza Hotel, and in 1962 she co-starred with Julie Andrews in a television special, *Julie and Carol at Carnegie Hall*. By the time she signed as the star of her own comedy show, however, Burnett had accumulated a cornucopia of comic characters, few of which ever belted out a tune. Her wildly popular *Carol Burnett Show* featured far more skits than songs, a reflection of the American viewer's growing boredom with the musical-variety format.

Carol Burnett Show

The *Carol Burnett Show* allowed its star to inhabit a limitless range of characters, from charwomen and downtrodden housewives to the snobbiest bluebloods and royalty. Few politician's wives escaped her scathing parodies, and she specialized in wacky spoofs of great Hollywood movies. The *People* reviewer noted: "Like a jellyfish, she flowed from one outlandish shape into another. Unlike jellyfish, she never stung. The harder we laughed at her characters, the more we loved them. The crudest were killingly funny, the subtlest wonderfully touching cameos of the human predicament."

In the 1980s Burnett appeared in some straight dramatic roles on television and in films, and she won the coveted role of the greedy orphanage superintendent in the film version of *Annie*. That part brought her back into her first love—musical comedy—but by 1990 she was back at what she did best, comedy-variety. The executives at NBC were quite pleased when her *Carol & Company* show became a sleeper hit, moving into the Nielsen top twenty in the spring of the year. In fact, Burnett's new show survived its first season and was renewed for 1991—no small feat for a woman entertainer nearing 60.

Burnett has not been spared her share of tabloid headlines over the years. Twice divorced, she has undergone therapy herself and has relived the nightmare of substance abuse and addiction through the suffering of her oldest daughter, Carrie. *Newsweek* reporter Harry F. Waters noted that the comedienne "has used therapy to confront some personal demons, including her rage toward her alcoholic parents and a resultant urge to hide her anger behind a mask of perennial good cheer."

Her personal tragedies notwithstanding, Burnett has staged a comeback at an age when even the best actresses and singers often struggle for recognition. Waters observes that even though Burnett's comedy "has taken on a dark (and daring) new edge," American audiences continue to find the redheaded star endearing. "Loving Carol Burnett is a national habit," the reporter concluded. "Just when we forget we're hooked, it all comes back."

Sources

Esquire, June 1972.
Newsweek, June 18, 1990.
People, Summer 1989.

—*Anne Janette Johnson*

Cab Calloway

Singer, bandleader

Cab Calloway was a famous singer and bandleader in 1930, and some 60 years later, he is still going strong. At an age when most people retire and rest on old laurels, Calloway keeps a full schedule of touring with a band and singing his signature song, "Minnie the Moocher." Long ago dubbed the "Dean of American Jive," Calloway has brought the joys of the jazzy big band sound to the under-40 generations, helping to preserve the very style he helped to create.

Calloway was born Cabell Calloway III, in Rochester, New York. When he was six his family moved to Baltimore, Maryland, where his father practiced law and sold real estate. Although young Cab enjoyed singing solos at the Bethlehem Methodist Episcopal Church, it was assumed that he would follow in his father's footsteps and study law. Cab had other ideas, however. His older sister had found work singing with a show in Chicago, and he appealed to her for advice. Her "advice" was substantial—she sent him a train ticket, and when he arrived in Chicago, she set him up as a singer with a quartet. He was still in his teens.

Calloway himself gives 1925 as the year his career began. By that time he had become a talented drummer, and he secured a position with the Sunset Cafe orchestra in Chicago. He did not hide behind a drum set for long, however. Within two years—or by his twentieth birthday—he had organized his own orchestra and was singing lead vocals again. The group, "Cab Calloway and his Alabamians," became quite popular in Chicago and eventually took a booking at the Savoy Ballroom in New York City. That engagement did not go well, and Calloway dissolved the band. He was about to return to Chicago when he landed a part in a Broadway comedy, *Connie's Hot Chocolates*. The show was an all-black revue, and Calloway brought the house down with his rendition of "Ain't Misbehavin'."

Invited to the Cotton Club

Broadway manager Irving Mills encouraged Calloway to form another band, so the young musician gathered another orchestra and immediately found work in the well-attended Harlem speakeasies and nightclubs. In 1929 he was invited to fill in for Duke Ellington at the Cotton Club, and thereafter the two band leaders alternated engagements at the prestigious venue. It was during his years at the Cotton Club that Calloway developed his crisp, jazzy song-and-dance style, and it was there that he composed and debuted "Minnie the Moocher."

Calloway was one of the first performers to make deliberate use of scat singing in his act. As with so many

For the Record. . .

Born Cabell Calloway III December 25, 1907, in Rochester, NY; son of Cabell (a lawyer and real estate broker) and Eulalia (Reed) Calloway; children: Constance, Chris. *Education:* Attended Crane College, Chicago, IL.

Singer, songwriter, bandleader, 1925—. Drummer with the Sunset Cafe orchestra, Chicago, 1925; formed his own band, Cab Calloway and His Alabamians, c. 1927; moved to New York City for appearances at the Savoy Ballroom. Formed and became leader of the Cab Calloway Orchestra, which performed regularly at the Cotton Club, New York City, 1929. Has toured extensively in the United States and Europe since 1935; entertained American and Canadian troops during World War II.

Principal film work includes *Hi De Ho, Cab's Jitterbug Party,* c. 1932; *The Big Broadcast,* 1932; *International House,* 1933; *Roadshow,* 1941; *Stormy Weather,* 1943; *Sensations of 1944,* 1944; and *The Blues Brothers,* 1980. Appeared on Broadway as Sportin' Life in *Porgy and Bess* and as Horace Vandergelder in *Hello, Dolly!*

Addresses: *Home*—White Plains, NY.

others, he began scat singing—random use of nonsense syllables—when he forgot a song's lyrics. Audiences loved the sound, however, so he began to write tunes with scat choruses. "Minnie the Moocher," his best-known song, is one such composition. Its refrain—"hi de hi de hi de ho"—invites the audience to sing along in the old call-and-response style. Recordings of "Minnie the Moocher" have sold in the millions worldwide, and at least one version is still available in record stores.

Hepster's Dictionary

Calloway's fame soared in the 1930s and 1940s. He appeared in such films as *International House* and *Stormy Weather,* he helped to popularize the jitterbug with tunes like "Jumpin' Jive," "Reefer Man," "It Ain't Necessarily So," and "If This Isn't Love," and he even wrote a popular book, *Hepster's Dictionary,* which sold two million copies and ran into six editions. Although Calloway's name does not spring to mind in association with the big band era, he actually fronted a fine ensemble during the period. His ability to pay top salaries attracted a group of brilliant musicians, including sax players Chu Berry, Ben Webster, and Hilton Jefferson, trumpeters Dizzy Gillespie and Jonah Jones, bassist Milt Hinton, and drummer Cozy Cole. In his book *The Big Bands,* George T. Simon noted: "the *esprit de corps* of the Calloway band was tremendous, and the great pride that the musicians possessed as individuals and as a group paid off handsomely in the music they created."

The years of World War II found Calloway entertaining troops in the United States and Canada. After the war he returned to club work and to the Broadway stage, most notably as Sportin' Life in the George Gershwin operetta *Porgy and Bess.* In the late 1960s he took another important Broadway role, that of Horace Vandergelder in the all-black version of *Hello, Dolly!* His work with Pearl Bailey in that show was the culmination of a long friendship—he had helped Bailey get a start in show business in 1945 by hiring her to help him with vocals. Even though he was 60 when he appeared in *Hello, Dolly!,* Calloway never missed a step in the strenuous show. In fact, he was just hitting his stride.

Shone in *The Blues Brothers*

The energetic performer's career received an enormous boost when he was asked to star in a 1980 film, *The Blues Brothers.* The movie, which also starred John Belushi and Dan Aykroyd, gave Calloway the opportunity to perform "Minnie the Moocher" for an audience young enough to be his grandchildren—and, clad in a snazzy white zoot suit with tails, he made the number the highlight of the film. Critics who otherwise panned *The Blues Brothers* singled Calloway out for praise, and his popularity soared.

Today Calloway is still on the road most of the time, sometimes performing with his daughter Chris. *Philadelphia Inquirer* correspondent John Rogers observed that, even in his 80s, Calloway struts around the stage "like some nimble tightrope walker." Rogers added: "[His] moves have slowed a bit since the '30s, a time when Calloway could have danced Michael Jackson or Mick Jagger into the ground. The hair is white and thinner now, the midsection thicker, and that classically handsome face lined and puffy after eight decades of full-throttle living. But every bit of his voice is still there—and every bit of the style and grace that made the legend."

Asked if he has any heroes in the music business, Calloway scoffs at the very idea. It is easy to understand why he might not idolize Ellington or Webster or Gillespie—he simply ranks right up there with them, on the fine edge where new music is made. "I'll tell you who my heroes are," he said. "My heroes are the notes, man. The music itself. You understand what I'm saying? I love the music. The music is my hero."

Selected discography

Jumpin' Five, Zeta.
Live 1944 (with Ike Quebec), Magnetic.
Live 1945 (with Quebec), Magnetic.
Best of the Big Bands: Cab Calloway, Columbia.
Cab Calloway, *Glendale*.
The Hi-De Ho Man, Columbia.
Mr. Hi-De-Ho, MCA.
(Contributor) *The Blues Brothers*, 1980.

Sources

Books

Calloway, Cab, *Of Minnie the Moocher and Me*, Crowell, 1976.
Simon, George T., *The Big Bands*, Macmillan, 1967.
Simon, George T., *Best of the Music Makers*, Doubleday, 1979.

Periodicals

Philadelphia Inquirer, August 16, 1990.

—Anne Janette Johnson

Mariah Carey

Singer, songwriter

Pop vocalist and songwriter Mariah Carey set the music world ablaze when her self-titled debut album was released in 1990. Featuring the hit single "Vision of Love," the disc provoked critics to rave over Carey's seven-octave vocal range and gospel-toned voice, and eventually sold more than seven million copies worldwide. She has been compared to the late pop soprano Minnie Riperton, the Peruvian singer Yma Sumac, and, most often, to superstar Whitney Houston. As reviewer Ralph Novak asserted in *People,* Carey "sings with extraordinary control, driving power, lovely pitch, and wide range."

Carey was born to a mother who had sung with the New York City Opera and remained a vocal coach throughout Carey's childhood. Carey's mother influenced her a great deal, the singer revealed in *Seventeen.* "I knew from watching and listening to my mom that singing could and would be my profession." She recounted further that her mother "had to tear me away from the radio each night just to get me to go to sleep." Carey also enjoyed listening to the record collection of her older brother and sister, especially albums by Gladys Knight, Aretha Franklin, and Stevie Wonder.

When Carey was 17 she left her family home on Long Island, New York, to live in New York City. Sharing an apartment with another aspiring musician, she waited on tables to earn her living while making demo tapes of original songs to give to music executives. Carey eventually got a job as a backup singer for a small record label. One of the vocalists she sang for, Brenda K. Starr, was sufficiently impressed with her abilities to introduce her to Tommy Mottola of Columbia Records. At Starr's insistence Carey gave him one of her demo tapes. Mottola listened to it in his car on the way home from the party where the meeting had taken place; he called Carey to sign her the next day.

Carey worked on recording her debut album for the next two years. *Mariah Carey* was released by the time the singer turned 20. Carey co-wrote and arranged all of the songs on the album, though critics have not been particularly impressed by her non-vocal efforts. Novak called the tunes "uniformly forgettable, both melodically and lyrically"; Alanna Nash of *Stereo Review* commented that "none of the ten songs sticks in the mind." Nevertheless, Carey's single "Vision of Love," raced up the pop and adult contemporary charts, eventually reaching Number One. She gained further exposure on national television by singing "America, the Beautiful" before the first game of the National Basketball Association finals at Michigan's Palace of Auburn Hills. Carey's debut album also contained the tracks "Someday" and "There's Got to Be a Way," which Nash described as "social-consciousness raising."

For the Record. . .

Born c. 1970; daughter of a vocal coach and former opera singer.

Worked as a waitress and backup singer c. 1987. Recording artist, 1988—.

Awards: Two Grammy Awards; one for best new artist, 1991.

Addresses: *Record company*—Columbia/CBS Records, 51 West 52nd St., New York, NY 10019.

"What you remember" about Carey, however, said David Gates in *Newsweek,* "is the voice—all seven octaves or so of it, from purring alto to stratospheric shriek." Likewise, in spite of her criticism of Carey's songwriting, Nash did affirm that *Mariah Carey* "is as exhilarating as a ride on the World's Tallest Roller Coaster." Amusement parks came to the mind of a *Seventeen* reporter as well, who noted that the "lissome diva carries the listener away on a riveting . . . roller coaster of sound." Not surprisingly, in light of such comments, Carey's efforts on the album garnered her a Grammy Award for best new artist 1991. As Novak concluded, "She is just about a lock to become pop music's biggest sensation since Whitney Houston."

Selected discography

Mariah Carey (includes "Vision of Love," "There's Got to Be a Way," "I Don't Wanna Cry," "Someday," "Vanishing," and "All in Your Mind"), Columbia, 1990.

Sources

Glamour, October 1990.
Newsweek, August 6, 1990.
People, July 16, 1990.
Rolling Stone, August 23, 1990.
Seventeen, October 1990.
Stereo Review, October 1990.

—*Elizabeth Wenning*

Mary-Chapin Carpenter

Singer, songwriter

Mary-Chapin Carpenter is a Nashville artist who is stretching the boundaries of country music to embrace contemporary folk and rock. Carpenter's intensely personal songs about rocky relationships and self-identity have earned a strong following on college and alternative radio stations, but they have also found their way into the country market and even onto the country top-forty charts. *Richmond Times-Dispatch* correspondent Gordon Ely noted that Carpenter, who writes her own material, "has a style that manages to combine the literariness of her Ivy League education with the emotional honesty and self-revelation that is the stock in trade of country music. In the process, she's managed to dodge the glitz-and-glamour boys and maintain an air of unpretentiousness."

Sequined suits and cowboy boots are not part of Carpenter's act. Nor does she often rely on the standard stock of country instruments as backup for her songs. Instead she performs in well-worn, comfortable clothing, with her own acoustic guitar work complimenting her arresting low-range vocals. "I don't think of myself as country," Carpenter told the *Wichita Eagle-Beacon*. But, she added, "The truth is I was never really comfortable about being labeled as a folkie. For me, folk music means playing something traditional, or ethnic music. But when I played my music in clubs for years, I played contemporary music."

Mary-Chapin, whose name is a double moniker like Mary Jane, was born in Princeton, New Jersey. Her father was a prominent executive with *Life* magazine, so she grew up in comfortable circumstances. When she was still young the family moved to Washington, D.C., a city that has embraced her as one of its own. There she picked up the guitar and learned to play, influenced by her older sisters' Beatles, Mamas and Papas, and Judy Collins albums.

Launched Performing Career

After she graduated from high school, Carpenter became very serious about music, spending long hours strumming her guitar and composing songs in the privacy of her room. She told the *San Jose Mercury News* that she never considered a career in music until her father prodded her in that direction. "He said, 'There's a bar down the street; they have open-mike sessions; why don't you go out and play at one of those things?'" she remembered. "That was the first time it occurred to me, frankly."

Carpenter attended Brown University, where she earned a bachelor's degree in American civilization. On the weekends and in the summers she performed, simply as a hobby to earn spending money. Her repertory at the time was standard bar fare: top forty hits and oldies, with only an occasional original tune thrown in. Carpenter recalls these years as difficult ones—the late nights in pub settings led to excessive drinking. "I had a big problem," she told the *San Jose Mercury News.* "It was awful. I had to make a lifestyle change in a drastic way. . . . It's still so painful to me to think about how I was."

Eventually Carpenter decided to play only in those places that would allow her to do her own material. She was fortunately situated in Washington, D.C., a stronghold for bluegrass, folk, and innovative acoustic music. By 1986 Carpenter was a local star, very much in demand in Washington's busy clubs. With the help of sideman John Jennings, she assembled enough songs for a demo tape and secured a manager who would try to find her a recording contract in Nashville. A CBS executive liked the tape, signed Carpenter to the label, and allowed her a large measure of creative freedom in the studio.

Carpenter's first album, *Hometown Girl,* was released in 1988. Her work was quickly—if somewhat dubiously—categorized as "contemporary country," similar in style and substance to the music of Lyle Lovett and Nanci Griffith. Carpenter remembered in the *Wichita Eagle-Beacon* that although *Hometown Girl* received positive reviews, it did not sell well. "If it weren't for public radio, it wouldn't have seen the light of day," she said. Even public radio provided her with a fan following, however, especially on college campuses.

Won Popular and Critical Acclaim

The breakthrough album for Carpenter was *State of the Heart,* released in 1989. Somewhat to her surprise, two cuts from the album—"Quittin' Time" and "You Never Had It So Good"—shot up the country charts, and she was named best new female vocalist by the Academy of Country Music in 1990. Carpenter made these strides without condescending to the so-called "traditional" country female vocalist sound. "The people in the country community made me feel accepted that you can be different," she told the *Wichita Eagle-Beacon.* "Outside Nashville, there's a notion that country music is all cheating songs and beehive hairdos and they don't allow you to be anything else. But you can see that they're reaching out."

A Mary-Chapin Carpenter album may contain a wide variety of songs and styles, from Cajun-country to simple acoustic folk ballads to blue laments about love gone wrong. *San Jose Mercury News* correspondent Eliza Wing called Carpenter's voice "a strong, straight-ahead instrument that sounds as though it's used to talking out problems late into the night." The critic added that the artist's songs, "whether they're mournful, contemplative or angry, rely on country idioms even as they bend the genre."

Music Offers Woman's Perspective

Carpenter admits that she uses songwriting as "self-therapy" to help expel her own personal melancholy over broken relationships and sundered friendships. Her music certainly offers a woman's perspective on deep emotional issues, but her appeal cuts neatly across the gender gap. "I never set out to write songs to appeal to only one kind of person or gender," she told the *Orlando Sentinel.* "My characters tend to be single women—a lot of the songs I write are about me . . .— but the feelings I feel are feelings I know I share with a lot of men my age, too."

The acceptance in Nashville is particularly gratifying to Carpenter, since it has come on her own terms. "Country music is not what you wear or what kind of instruments are on your record," she told the *Orlando Sentinel.* "It's a state of mind having to do with substance, not style."

Selected discography

Hometown Girl, CBS, 1988.
State of the Heart (includes "Quittin' Time" and "You Never Had It So Good"), CBS, 1989.

Shooting Straight in the Dark, CBS, 1991.

Sources

Books

Vaughan, Andrew, *Who's Who in New Country Music*, St. Martin's, 1989.

Periodicals

Orlando Sentinel, November 23, 1990.
Philadelphia Inquirer, October 3, 1990.
Richmond Times-Dispatch, June 8, 1990.
San Jose Mercury News, March 22, 1991.
Wichita Eagle-Beacon, April 30, 1991.

—*Anne Janette Johnson*

Betty Carter

Singer

"'I don't hear anybody out there now who really scares me, who makes me think, 'Betty, you got to push a little harder,'" Betty Carter once told the *Daily News Magazine.* "So many of the good ones straddle the line between jazz and commercial. They think they can do both. But when I see someone straddling, I know I got nothin' to worry about."

"Straddling" has no place in Carter's aesthetic. While many of her contemporaries went the commercial route over the years, striving for the money and fame that a hit record might bring, Carter stuck to what she set out to do as a teenager—sing jazz, her way. In the end her perseverance and talent paid off. Though she's self-taught and considers herself not a "true" singer, she's earned a place alongside such jazz divas as Billie Holiday, Ella Fitzgerald, and Sarah Vaughan. In jazz, after all, what matters is not so much training and technique as originality—which she has plenty of.

As noted in the *New York Post,* she's a "singer who can take a standard and—without relying on facile 'shoo-be-doo-be' scat—reinvent it on the spot by reharmonizing the melody, changing the emphasis of the lyrics, and toying with the tempo and rhythm." (Older-generation critics have accused her of losing the theme in the complexity of her interpretations; younger ones are usually floored by her inventions.) Each time she performs, whether standards or originals, she seems to stretch the concept of improvisation to a new limit. She's known for taking ballads at tempos that are impossibly and mesmerizingly slow. Then there's her inimitable contralto—deep, sensuous, and husky. And she has a character whose strength underlies the power of her voice. Throughout her four-decade-plus career she's done things her way from start to finish, even though it meant struggling for many years. "A lot of people don't like dealing with an independent black female, who takes care of her own business and holds her head high," she told AP writer Mary Campbell. "But I've never thought about quitting. I've been discouraged maybe but something would always happen to make you think you'd be a star in the next six months."

Tuned in to Bebop

Carter was born Lillie Mae Jones on May 16, 1930, in Flint, Michigan. She grew up in Detroit and as a high school student studied piano at the Detroit Conservatory of Music. It was a time when a brilliant and bold new music was sweeping the country—bebop, the postwar jazz style that was being pioneered by the great saxophonist Charlie "Bird" Parker, and horn player Dizzy Gillespie. Lillie Mae was immediately turned on to it. She often "played hookey at the soda joint across the

For the Record. . .

Born Lillie Mae Jones, May 16, 1930, in Flint, MI; children: two sons.

Studied piano as a teenager at the Detroit Conservatory of Music; won a talent show at Detroit's Paradise Theater, 1946; while still in high school, sat in on gigs with Charlie Parker, Dizzy Gillespie, and other bebop musicians visiting Detroit. Toured with Lionel Hampton's band, 1948-51, Miles Davis, 1960, and Ray Charles, 1960-63; performed in Japan, 1963, London, 1964, and France, 1968. In 1969, began to work with her own trio and founded her own record company, Bet-Car Productions. In 1975, appeared in Howard Moore's musical *Don't Call Me Man.* Continues to perform and record with her trio.

Awards: Earned Grammy nominations for the albums *The Audience With Betty Carter, Whatever Happened to Love?,* and *Look What I Got!* In 1981, Bet-Car Productions won an Indy Award as the nation's best independent label.

Addresses: *Home*—Brooklyn, New York. *Media information*—Polygram Classics, 810 Seventh Ave., New York, NY 10019.

street from my high school and listened to the jukebox, which was filled with bebop singles," she told *Pulse!* "We would sit around and learn the solos, and go to see them whenever they came to town—we met Bird and Dizzy when they came to our school." Soon she was singing Sunday afternoon cabaret gigs; by the age of 18 she had sat in with Bird, Dizzy, trumpeter Miles Davis, and other greats. Her first employer, though, was not a bebopper but a veteran of swing music—the vibraphonist and bandleader Lionel Hampton. In a 1988 interview with AP writer Campbell, Carter recounted their first meeting: "I went with some classmates to hear Lionel's band. We were standing in front of the bandstand. A guy said, 'Why don't you let Lillie Mae sing?' That was my name then. He said, 'Can you sing, Gates?' I said yes. He said, 'Then come on up, Gates.'"

Toured With Lionel Hampton

The impromptu audition landed her a job. From 1948 to 1951 she toured with Hampton, standing in front of his big band and scatting (improvising with nonsense syllables) segments of the tunes they played. "I didn't get a chance to sing too many songs because Hamp had a lot of other singers at the same time; but I took care of the bebop division, you might say," she told *Pulse!* with a chuckle. "He'd stick me into songs they were already doing, so I was singing a chorus here, a chorus there; I didn't realize at the time what good training that was. And I had the late Bobby Plater teach me to orchestrate and transpose, which I really needed later on." While she was learning from Hampton she was also learning from his wife. "I had this role model of Gladys Hampton to emulate. She took care of the band, saw to it that everything ran smoothly, that everybody got paid and such. That was the first time I'd ever experienced dealing with a woman who was the boss—and she was a black woman. It was very unusual at that time, and still is."

Lorraine Carter, as the young singer had begun calling herself, made quite a stir at New York's Apollo Theater. Jack Schiffman, son of the late Apollo owner Frank Schiffman, recalled his impressions for the *Daily News Magazine:* "Lionel Hampton introduced a small girl, hair bobbed short, eyes seemingly larger than her face, who burst out on stage, took a deep breath, and sang bebop riffs, a whole machine-gun load of them that turned the house upside down. I never saw an audience turned on so quickly to a new sound." Hampton began calling her Betty Bebop (which evolved into Betty Carter). But the relationship between the two was a stormy one; Hampton allegedly fired her half a dozen times for mouthing off to him. "I wanted to be with a hipper band—the guys playing bebop, not swing," Carter told Polygram. "But in retrospect I was right where I needed to be." She elaborated in the *Daily News Magazine,* "I couldn't see the advantage of his making me go out there and improvise every night. But without that training, I might not know how to be spontaneous now." "And suppose I *had* been with Dizzy's band," she told *Pulse!,* "The things that were going on there"—the use of heroin among the musicians—"were things I didn't need to come in contact with. But I didn't know that then."

Paid Dues in New York City

In 1952, after two and a half years of "doing what Hamp wanted me to," as she told AP writer Campbell, "I struck out to find out what more I could do with myself. I came to New York and got work right away at the Apollo Bar, a couple of doors from the Apollo Theater." Thus began a grueling period of dues-paying. "I did the usual, playing dives and joints, wherever I could," she told *Pulse!* "There were a lot of places around to do the hustling then. . . . Besides all the clubs that were in New York, we had Philadelphia to work with, and Boston, and Washington, D.C.; all up and down the East Coast there were lots of places to work. And Detroit was still good then, and Chicago." It was a golden time of opportunity. "There was a big, beautiful music world for us in the '50s," she told the *Daily News Magazine.* "We played and learned together, because we all loved music and musicianship. It wasn't about money—we weren't making any of that—it was about a whole community. No one had to dominate. We liked each other. I'd hang around clubs with Sarah Vaughan or Ruth Brown. I played on bills with Sonny Til and the Orioles, the Temptations, Muddy Waters, Bo Diddley, Miles Davis. It didn't matter what you did; you just had to be good at it. At the Apollo, you could play classical music if you did it well. . . . Someone should write a book about those days. There was such *joy*. We thought that world would never end."

Recorded With Ray Charles

Carter's hard work led to a theater tour with Miles Davis, which led to a tour with the famed gospel pianist and singer Ray Charles. In the midst of the latter, Charles asked Carter to do a record with him. "He asked me in Baltimore, in the hallway by the dressing rooms," she recalled in *Pulse!* "After he asked me, it got silent; I mean, he had 'Georgia' going, a bi-iii-ig hit record; he didn't need me. . . . I went to his house to work on the tunes, and then went back to the hotel numb because I was really gonna do it. I learned the tunes by thinking about it more than practicing them; we didn't go over anything more than one time, because I was capable of understanding everything he said to me about what to do and how to do it." The result was the 1961 classic *Ray Charles and Betty Carter,* which has been reissued by Dunhill on CD. "It was the one thing that kept my name out in front of people, because I didn't have any records of my own."

Changing Times for Jazz

During the sixties jazz got undercut by rock music, and the industry pressured jazz musicians to commercialize. As Carter told the *Daily News Magazine,* "the business became about money. Lots of money. And when some jazz players see that, they want some of it. Instead of $500 a night, they think they can make $4,000 in the commercial world. And some do, for a while. But the commercial world is a trap. You have one hit, they want number two, and number three. If you don't get it, they drop you." Carter stuck by her own bebop-rooted music and tried to convince her peers to do the same. But as she told *Pulse!,* "nobody in jazz paid me any attention because I was female and a singer. Had it been a male who said what I said, we might have made a dent—the way [trumpeter] Wynton Marsalis is making a dent now, saying a lot of the things that I said a long time ago. I think we might have

stopped a lot of jazz artists from switching to commercial stuff."

Refusing to change her style, Carter found herself shut out by record labels. "What do you do after you've tried to sell yourself and nobody wants to buy? That hurts, it really does. Anyway, I decided if I was ever going to record again I should do it myself." In 1969 she founded her own label, Bet-Car Productions, and, along with a female business partner, assumed control of not only the recording and producing but also the financing, manufacturing, and distribution ends of the business. "I had to do everything myself only because I could not be controlled," she told *Jam Sessions.* "I could not be produced by somebody else, telling me what to do; telling me how to be, how to think and how to move."

Discovered by a New Audience

As Carter recorded for Bet-Car in the 1970s and continued to perform, her audience grew. But as she told the *New York Post,* "I realized I was bottling up my

---

When I improvise, I don't want a note. I want the note.

---

musicianship, trying to accommodate, trying not to be too extreme. Because a lot of my peers were talking about, 'Why don't you stop doing the bebop? . . . Why don't you get a hit record?' But why should I deal with something that was making me feel bad? . . . I decided to just stick with my music, to try to improve it, and suddenly I started going to colleges and discovered that there was a whole new audience. And the more interesting it got, the more the audience liked it."

It seems appropriate that Carter began playing colleges, as she has always been an educator of jazz music. As *Cash Box* observed, she has been "one of the most eloquent drum-beaters for jazz. She sits on panels, she makes speeches, she has been very vocal in her opinion about what is jazz, what isn't jazz, and what's happening in this art form." What motivates her, as she told *Cash Box,* is her own "black culture. I want to make these young kids realize that it was the black people who started this wonderful music of jazz, and not Dave Brubeck." Since the 1970s, her most powerful tool as an educator has been to perform with young sidepeople, often kids straight out of college. "There's something about having young people play for young people that makes a better impact than, say, five old men," she told *Mother Jones*. "So it's three young musicians and this old person, Grandma, if you want to say, and we get on stage and we work together. The energy is there, the enthusiasm, the fun, the charisma—everything that youth wants. See, without that, there's no way I can compete with the hip-hoppers."

Thrived on Musicians' Suggestions

Carter's band members receive an education of their own. Drummer Kenny Washington, who played with Carter from 1978 to 1980, told the *Christian Science Monitor* that "you have to watch Betty all the time. She has it completely in her mind what she wants. But she doesn't say you do it my way or not at all. She thrives on suggestions. She wants you to speak what you feel and think. The minute you don't have any ideas and suggestions, you're gone." Carter probably wouldn't deny that. "I want my musicians to think all the time," she told the *Daily News Magazine*, "If somebody plays the same thing 10, 12 times, I'll say, 'Hey, I'm *tired* of that. What else you got?' The other day I gave my drummer some 7/4. He'd never played it before. It'll give him new tools. . . . When I improvise, I don't want *a* note. I want *the* note. My piano player is 18. *Eighteen*. And he knows how to get *the* note. My bass player sometimes hits *a* note. But he'll get it together. I may be the only musician today who'll tell somebody if I hear a mistake. That's the way it used to be. You told the truth and no one's feelings were hurt, because you did it in a positive way. You see potential, you help develop it."

Named "Jazz Legend"

In 1988, after nearly two decades of running her own label, Carter signed a deal with Polygram's Verve for both new recordings and reissues of Bet-Car titles. *Look What I Got!*, her first release on Verve, topped Billboard's jazz chart and earned her a Grammy nomination. Her latest release is 1990's *Droppin' Things*. She continues to play both the club and college circuits. In the spring of 1991, having been named "Jazz Legend" by the Southern Arts Federation, she lectured and performed at 11 southeastern colleges.

"There's no describing the joy of getting up on stage and doing your thing and having an audience respond to it," Carter told the *Boston Globe Magazine*. "No one has told you what to do. You haven't been produced by anybody. You're on stage because you have talent and you know what to do. And you do it, and the audience is out of their heads. That's what jazz allows you to do. It's the only art form that allows you to do that. Most commercial art forms are produced. Popular music is produced by someone who tells some kid how to sing the song. Not jazz. You're free. That's the difference."

Selected discography

The Betty Carter Album, Verve, originally released 1976.
The Audience With Betty Carter, Verve, 1981.
Look What I Got!, Verve, 1988.
Ray Charles and Betty Carter, Dunhill, 1988.
The Carmen McRae-Betty Carter Album, Great American Music Hall Records/Fantasy, 1988.
Whatever Happened to Love?, Verve, 1989.
Droppin' Things, Verve, 1990.

Sources

Boston Globe, August 21, 1988.
Cash Box, February 13, 1988.
Christian Science Monitor, October 6, 1988.
Daily News Magazine, January 24, 1988.
Jam Sessions, March 1988.
"Jazz South" (newsletter of the Southern Arts Federation), Spring 1990.
London Times, 1985.
Mother Jones, January/February 1991.
Nation, July 30/August 6, 1988.
New York Post, January 26, 1988.
Polygram Jazz publicity biography, 1990.
Pulse!, August 1988.

—Kyle Kevorkian

June Carter Cash

Singer, songwriter, autoharpist

June Carter Cash followed her mother, Maybelle Carter, into country music and has been performing virtually nonstop since she was ten years old. A second-generation member of the famous Carter Family, June has won a worldwide following for the traditional folk-oriented Appalachian sound of her forebears. By virtue of her marriage to country superstar Johnny Cash, she has brought mountain music to country and even blues and rock fans, thus assuring a continued interest in a rich musical heritage.

Two years before June was born in 1929, her mother, aunt, and uncle journeyed to Bristol, Virginia, to audition for record producer Ralph Peer. Peer, who also produced country legend Jimmie Rodgers, signed the trio to a contract, and the original Carter Family began to release songs on the Victor label. The Carter Family's repertoire consisted primarily of Blue Ridge Mountain ballads, sung in three-part harmony with sophisticated acoustic accompaniment. Maybelle Carter, known to country fans as Mother Maybelle, took the alto part in most of the recordings, and she picked both guitar and autoharp. Throughout the 1930s the Carter Family recorded together regularly, even though its members had to supplement their musicians' incomes by working in factories and on farms.

June was born and raised in her father's hometown of Maces Springs, Virginia. Her father, Ezra Carter, was a farmer. The success of the Carter Family occasioned frequent travel, and by the time she was ten June was no stranger to the road. She began to perform with her famous family in Texas on a powerful border radio station in 1939. By the time June joined the Carter Family on the airwaves, several other second-generation Carters were already included in the group. The younger Carters—June, her sisters Helen and Anita, and a cousin, Janette Carter—often performed novelty songs and popular 1930s hits in their portion of the radio show, while their parents adhered to the traditional Appalachian folk music that had brought them renown.

The original Carter Family disbanded in 1943. Maybelle, arguably the most talented picker in the group, recruited her daughters and formed a new act, the Carter Sisters and Mother Maybelle. This reconstituted Carter Family played both traditional and novelty songs, and soon they earned a spot on WRVA's Old Dominion Barn Dance in Richmond, Virginia. From there they moved to WSM in Nashville, becoming regulars on the Grand Ole Opry. In an essay for *Stars of Country Music,* John Atkins wrote: "Where the original [Carter] family had never veered from their own tradition, Maybelle and the girls made every effort to keep up with the many changes and developments in Nashville and in country music generally. In short, they were shrewd enough to always retain a number of the family's original songs in their program, and yet at the same time they were prepared to compete with anyone around to gain their share of success and fame.''

By the mid-1950s, June Carter was an established figure in Nashville. Most critics agree that her sister Anita showed more vocal talent, but June sometimes stole the show with her comedy, her picking ability on autoharp, guitar, and banjo, and her vivacious good looks. Eventually she decided to pursue a solo career in dramatics. She studied acting in New York City briefly, and she won guest appearances on such television shows as *Jim Bowie* and *Gunsmoke*. Having married Nashville crooner Carl Smith, she returned to singing by the late 1950s and worked as a solo act or with her family.

In the 1960s the Carter Sisters and Mother Maybelle joined the entourage of superstar Johnny Cash. The group travelled across the nation with Cash, opening for him and occasionally joining him onstage for encores. June was particularly drawn to the troubled young star who was struggling with drug abuse and antisocial behavior. She wrote or co-wrote songs for him, providing him hits in ''Happy to Be with You,'' ''Jackson,'' and ''Guitar Pickin' Man.'' In turn Cash featured June and her sisters on his television variety show, a favor that widened the women's audience

considerably. June Carter married Johnny Cash in 1968 after Cash underwent rehabilitation for his substance abuse. They have been together ever since and have a son, John Carter Cash.

Johnny and June Carter Cash still perform as a duo, but they also continue to pursue separate careers. Even after her marriage, June teamed with her sisters for numerous tours in America and Europe. On one such tour, in 1986, June's daughter from her first marriage, Carlene, stood in for Anita Carter in a London concert. Thereafter, Carlene Carter joined the family group. June is particularly proud that her daughter has shown an interest in the traditional Carter Family music and a desire to incorporate that style into her own work.

Singer, songwriter, and—some say—savior of the willful Johnny Cash, June Carter Cash is a reigning queen of country music. The dedication June and her sisters have shown to the original Carter Family music has kept a valuable national resource—Appalachian balladry—in the public eye. Although she is equally at home with standard country fare, and is even an engaging comedienne, June has earned significant praise for keeping faith with tradition—and for passing it on to those who follow her.

Selected discography

The Carter Family on Border Radio, John Edwards Memorial Foundation.
Keep on the Sunny Side, Columbia.
Three Generations of the Carter Family, Columbia.
Wildwood Flower, Columbia.

With Johnny Cash

Jackson, Columbia, 1970.
Give My Love to Rose, Harmony, 1972.
Johnny Cash and His Woman, Columbia, 1973.

Sources

Books

Malone, Bill C., *Country Music U.S.A.,* revised edition, University of Texas Press, 1985.
Malone, Bill C., and Judith McCulloh, editors, *Stars of Country Music,* University of Illinois Press, 1975.
Stambler, Irwin, and Grelun Landon, *The Encyclopedia of Folk, Country, and Western Music,* St. Martin's, 1969.

Periodicals

People, November 12, 1990.

—Anne Janette Johnson

Carol Channing

Singer, actress

Carol Channing is a *grande dame* of stage comedy, an enduring figure on Broadway, in nightclubs and in concert halls. Channing's unique grin and wide-eyed stare—and her deep, raspy voice—have been imitated by a whole generation of impersonators and have made her recognizable worldwide. *Charlotte Observer* correspondent Natalie Shelpuk noted that the former Tony Award-winner "has lost none of her spunk and originality," even though she is nearing seventy. Shelpuk concluded: "Even though the trademark husky flutter of her voice has matured to a prominent warble, Channing still has that spindly-legged, knob-kneed innocence that rocketed her to stardom."

Channing forged her fame on the Broadway stage in such classic musicals as *Gentlemen Prefer Blondes* and *Hello, Dolly!* While many of her contemporaries moved on to film and television, the energetic Channing chose to work primarily as a live performer. Today, as she tours the country with a one-woman show, she is literally a throwback to the golden era of nightclub acts and touring Broadway hits. She told the Orlando *News and Sun-Sentinel* that she started out as a revue artist and she still prefers the variety show. "If you have enough bright spotlights and good-enough acoustics," she said, "it's like blowing the performer up like a close-up. It makes a tremendous difference."

Channing was born in Seattle, Washington in 1923, the only child of a prominent newspaper editor. Her father was actively involved in the Christian Science movement, and he taught his daughter how to reach an audience with music and oratory. She was thus "performing" in church activities from an early age, and she learned to amuse her schoolmates by clowning and mimicking other students.

Began Acting Career

Most of Channing's childhood was spent in San Francisco, a town still dear to her heart. She went east for higher education, matriculating at the prestigious Bennington College. There she majored in drama and dance, supplementing her school work by taking parts in summer stock in the nearby Pocono resorts. During a winter recess in 1941 she landed her first role in a New York show, a walk-on in Marc Blitzstein's *No for an Answer*. The show only ran for three days, but Channing decided not to return to college anyway. Between 1941 and 1946 she eked out a precarious living as an understudy for Eve Arden in *Let's Face It* and as a straight dramatic actress.

Channing returned to San Francisco in 1946, but she did not give up the idea of a career in show business.

The following year she moved south to Los Angeles and supported herself by doing one-night stands for lodge and benefit groups. Eventually she earned a place in a show called *Lend an Ear,* a musical revue directed by Gower Champion. The revue was a hit in Los Angeles, and it moved to New York for a Broadway run in 1948. There Channing earned her first attention from the critics for her "silly blonde" routine.

Starred in Broadway Hit

The work with *Lend an Ear* brought Channing to the attention of Herman Levin and Oliver Smith, who were preparing a musical called *Gentlemen Prefer Blondes.* Channing won the lead in that Broadway show and made her name as the gold-digging Lorelei Lee. To this day she still performs the principal song from that show, "Diamonds Are a Girl's Best Friend." *Gentlemen Prefer Blondes* ran for nearly two years on Broadway, and then Channing went with the show for a national tour. She returned to New York in 1953 for another well-received role, that of Ruth in *Wonderful Town.*

A few appearances in film and on television convinced Channing that she did her best work on stage. Late in the 1950s she prepared a nightclub act and went on national tour, beginning in Las Vegas. The show included dancing, impersonations, and songs from several Broadway musicals. Channing revised and enriched the act over time and brought it to Broadway in 1961 as *Show Girl.* The following year she teamed with George Burns for a series of musical comedy performances. Their last show together was a command performance for President and Mrs. John F. Kennedy.

On January 16, 1964, Channing opened her biggest show ever—the immensely successful *Hello, Dolly!* Channing gave the signature performance of Dolly Gallagher Levi, the witty, manipulative widow intent upon finding a wealthy second husband. The musical won ten Tony awards in 1964, including Channing's for best actress in a comedy, and it ran on Broadway for years. Channing has never been far from *Dolly* since. She has appeared in numerous revivals and road tours of the play, and she includes numbers from it in her other live performances.

Channing told the *Phoenix Gazette* that she has always been grateful for the opportunity to work in her two greatest hits, *Gentlemen Prefer Blondes* and *Hello, Dolly!* "It's lucky when you have a character or a song that's identified with you," she said. "I'm doubly lucky because I have two of them. People know who you are!"

Age Didn't Slow Her Down

Age has not slowed Carol Channing down at all. In 1985 she returned to the stage with another hit comedy, *Legends,* about two feuding stars who must work together in a show. She also keeps a hectic schedule of live appearances in a one-woman revue, playing larger halls in every major American city. In order to enliven her revue she even learned how to conduct a symphony orchestra, and she often takes the podium when she is backed by a large ensemble. "I'm a stage hog," she told the *News and Sun-Sentinel.* "I mean, the longer you're out there the easier it is to communicate."

Channing's future plans are many and varied. She is constantly searching for the right vehicle to bring to Broadway, and she especially hopes to revive *Hello, Dolly!* one more time. Channing told *People* magazine that her favorite project is always "the one I'm doing at the moment, and that's the dead-on truth." She added: "You know why? It's like asking a woman who is madly in love, 'Which man did you love the most?' Well, my God, you don't remember anybody but the man you're in love with right now."

Selected discography

Gentlemen Prefer Blondes, original Broadway cast, 1949.
Hello, Dolly!, original Broadway cast, RCA, 1964.

Sources

Charlotte Observer, January 22, 1989.
Look, May 19, 1964.
News and Sun-Sentinel (Orlando, FL), December 8, 1989.
New York Times, January 8, 1961.
People, December 16, 1985.
Phoenix Gazette, January 30, 1991.

—*Anne Janette Johnson*

Harry Chapin

Singer, songwriter

Singer-songwriter Harry Chapin is best remembered musically for his famous folk-story songs, especially "Taxi" and "Cat's in the Cradle," the latter of which garnered him a Grammy nomination. During his career, however, he also became deeply involved in helping charitable organizations, particularly those concerned with hunger issues. In addition to lobbying Congress and then President Jimmy Carter to take stands to defeat U.S. and worldwide malnutrition, Chapin himself donated large sums from the proceeds of his live concerts to a wide variety of charities. When he was killed in a car crash in 1981, the world was not only deprived of his artistic talents but of one of its most valiant fighters on behalf of the poor.

Chapin was born December 7, 1944, in Greenwich Village, New York, to a musical family. His father was big-band drummer James Chapin, who had played with the bands of Tommy Dorsey and Woody Herman. As a child Harry Chapin sang in the Brooklyn Heights Boys Choir. Later he learned to play first the trumpet and then the guitar and banjo. His brothers were musical also, and when he was fifteen, they formed their own folk band. Calling themselves the Chapin Brothers, they played off and on at local clubs on the Greenwich Village folk scene while Harry pursued his education, first at the Air Force Academy and then at Cornell University.

First Pursued Film

By the time he dropped out of Cornell in 1964, Chapin had become more interested in film than music. He began working in filmmaking, working his way up to editor and eventually writing and making the boxing documentary *The Legendary Champions* with his associate Jim Jacobs in 1969. Chapin's screen effort took first prizes at film festivals in New York and Atlanta, Georgia, and even received an Academy Award nomination. But he continued to work at his music as well, and when his songs were used in yet another documentary, *Blue Water, White Death,* Chapin returned his concentration to composition. In 1970 his brothers Steve and Tom reformed their group, and Harry provided them with songs, but did not sing and play with them.

The following year, however, Chapin was ready to go back to the music business in full force. He rented the Village Gate in New York for the summer, and, backed by his brothers, began attracting local fans in large numbers. By the end of the year, Chapin had been signed to a recording contract by Elektra Records. His debut album, *Heads and Tales,* released in 1972, contained the single "Taxi"—a story song about a taxi driver meeting up with his old flame who is now married to a wealthy man; they both have regrets. "Taxi" was well received by fans, and the hit was responsible for Chapin's first Grammy nomination for best new artist of 1972.

Chapin followed "Taxi" with albums such as *Sniper and Other Love Songs, Short Stories,* and *Verities and Balderdash,* and singles such as "W*O*L*D," about a disc jockey talking to his ex-wife on the phone, and the smash "Cat's in the Cradle," about a father too busy with business to watch his son grow up. The latter song netted Chapin a Grammy nomination for best male vocal performance of 1975. But while fans responded well to the singer-songwriter's music, many critics did not, complaining of the didactic moral tone of many of his efforts. Dave Marsh of *Rolling Stone* explained further that reviewers felt that Chapin was "preachy . . . a simplistic and woeful singer, a careless craftsman in the studio, [and] emotionally overwrought onstage." But Marsh added: "If the ungainly accents and sputtering diction of some of Chapin's songs can't kill their power, that is because more important things than simple aesthetics are at work in those tunes, and because Chapin wasn't working in a pop context of craftsmanship and cool but from the folk-music tradi-

tions of the American left." Despite Chapin's critical reputation, "The Night That Made America Famous," the Broadway musical for which he composed and wrote lyrics, garnered two Tony Awards in 1975.

Committed to Charity

While Chapin worked steadily on his musical career, he also became involved with many charitable causes, especially those set up to aid famine victims. With his friend Bill Ayres he founded World Hunger Year in 1974, "an educational organization devoted to eradicating starvation," in the words of Giola Diliberto in *People.* Also concerned with the artistic enrichment of his fellow man, Chapin gave some of his efforts to charities involving music and dance companies. All in all, he gave almost half of his concert proceeds—roughly five million dollars—to causes he felt were worthy. Not only did Chapin contribute personally, but he interested others, like singers Gordon Lightfoot, John Denver, and Kenny Rogers, in doing benefits for hunger. He also continually lobbied in Washington, D.C., for hunger causes, and was instrumental in President Jimmy Carter's 1978 decision to set up the President's Committee on International, Domestic, and World Hunger.

Though Chapin did not have much in the way of hits during the late 1970s, as Marsh reported, he "toured a great deal and his concerts were always well attended." In addition to his standard story-songs, Chapin added numbers such as "Circle" and "Remember When the Music," which Marsh praised as "simple folk songs appropriate to any gathering of the faithful, whether sung around a campfire or at a mass rally." Chapin also encouraged audience participation in his songs during concerts, and, especially when playing a benefit, was often willing to talk with his fans and sign autographs after a performance. His brothers Steve and Tom continued to be regular features of his backup band, and occasionally his father would open for them with a Dixieland jazz group that the senior Chapin had formed.

Killed in Auto Accident

In 1980, Chapin released another hit, "Sequel." As the title implies, it revisits the characters of one of his previous story songs, "Taxi." This time, the former taxi driver has become a successful musician and the woman has divorced her wealthy husband. "Sequel" remained on the charts until 1981. Tragically, later that year, Chapin, who had several tickets for speeding and moving violations, and had his driver's license revoked, was driving illegally and was involved in a fatal crash on Long Island. His oldest brother, James, told Diliberto in *People:* "Ironically, I don't think this accident was Harry's fault." Chapin's death was mourned not only by his fans, but by the U.S. politicians he had badgered into acting on hunger legislation. As Marsh reported, "No other singer—not Bing Crosby, nor Elvis Presley, nor John Lennon—has ever been so widely honored by the nation's legislators. Nine senators and thirty congressmen paid tribute to Harry Chapin on the floor." The Harry Chapin Memorial Fund was founded by his family to help continue his charitable works.

Selected discography

Heads and Tales (includes "Taxi"), Elektra, 1972.
Sniper and Other Love Songs, Elektra, 1972.
Short Stories (includes "W*O*L*D"), Elektra, 1973.
Verities and Balderdash (includes "Cat's in the Cradle"), Elektra, 1974.
Portrait Gallery, Elektra, 1975.

On the Road to Kingdom Come, Elektra, 1976.
Greatest Stories Live (includes "Circle" and "30,000 Pounds of Bananas"), Elektra, 1976.
Dance Band on the Titanic, Elektra, 1977.
Living Room Suite, Elektra, 1978.
Legends of the Lost and Found, Elektra, 1980.
Sequel (includes "Sequel"), Boardwalk, 1980.

Sources

Books

Contemporary Authors, Volume 105, Gale, 1982.
Stambler, Irwin, and Grelun Landon, *The Encyclopedia of Folk, Country, and Western Music,* St. Martin's, 1984.

Periodicals

People, March 15, 1982.
Rolling Stone, April 6, 1978; September 3, 1981.

—*Elizabeth Wenning*

Clifton Chenier

Singer, accordionist

Clifton Chenier has been eulogized in magazines as diverse as *Nation* and *Rolling Stone* as "the King of Zydeco." He began recording in the 1950s, when zydeco—described by Jeff Hannusch in *Rolling Stone* as "the primitive R & B-oriented dance music of the black French-speaking Creoles of southwest Louisiana"—like other forms of regional American music, was dying out. Chenier both enjoyed and was a large factor in the genre's resurgence during the 1970s and 1980s. In addition to contributing his own live performances and recordings such as the Grammy Award-winning album *I'm Here,* Chenier was a formative influence on other zydeco artists, including Buckwheat Zydeco, Rockin' Sidney, and Queen Ida.

Chenier was born June 25, 1925, in the small town of Opelousas, Louisiana. His father was a sharecropper who played the accordion, a staple of zydeco music, at country dances. Chenier also enjoyed listening to the records of zydeco pioneer accordion player Amadie Ardoin, and had learned the instrument himself by the time he was sixteen, practicing with his older brother Cleveland, who played another featured device of zydeco, the rub board. But like many of the rural youngsters of their generation, rather than continue working in the local rice and sugar fields, the Chenier brothers left the countryside for better jobs in more urban areas; they drove oil refinery trucks in Port Arthur, Texas, during the late 1940s and early 1950s.

The two young men continued playing their music, however, performing nights for some of their fellow refinery workers. While doing this, Chenier was discovered by talent scout J. R. Fulbright, who signed him to the small Elko record label in 1954. Chenier cut the singles "Louisiana Stomp" and "Clifton's Blues" before moving to Specialty Records the following year. With that label, and with his band, the Zydeco Ramblers, he cut his first real hit, "Ay, 'Tit Fille"—Hannusch translates the contracted French as "Hey, Little Girl." The single did well on the rhythm and blues charts, especially in the South. Hannusch quoted latter-day zydeco artist Rockin' Sidney's recollections of Chenier's first heyday: "At that time Cliff was as big as Elvis Presley in Louisiana. . . . When he came to town, it was a big event. People would be talking about his dances a month in advance. . . . I thought he was the biggest star in the world."

Nevertheless, Chenier did not attain much renown beyond the Gulf Coast area, and as zydeco continued to slip into the region's past, he supplemented his small-label recordings with more blues and rhythm and blues numbers. During the early 1960s, Chenier relocated to Houston, Texas, playing small clubs in the section of that city called Frenchtown. There he was gigs as often as he could. "The last time I saw Clifton Chenier perform," recounted Wolff, "he was too sick to stand up. But from a folding chair . . . he played a set of bluesy, rocking accordion solos that made it almost impossible for the audience to stay seated." Chenier died December 12, 1987, in Lafayette, Louisiana; he had been scheduled to play in a local club that day.

discovered by the head of Arhoolie Records, Chris Strachwitz. Strachwitz was interested in preserving some of the dying forms of regional music, and he signed Chenier to a contract in 1963, releasing his first album the following year, *Louisiana Blues and Zydeco*.

Notwithstanding the title of Chenier's Arhoolie debut, Strachwitz kept something of a tight rein on the artist, limiting his work in other genres to the benefit of zydeco music. The record executive recalled for Daniel Wolff in *Nation:* "It was . . . a battle to get Clifton to record the older French material. . . . He'd tell me, 'That isn't what the kids like!'" But Chenier persisted with zydeco long enough to enjoy its resurgence during the 1970s and 1980s, both in his native Louisiana and on college campuses throughout the United States. In 1973, Chenier and what Frank-John Hadley of *Down Beat* praised as his "jazzy, waggish-yet-wailful piano accordion and granular blues singing" were featured in the documentary film *Hot Pepper;* before his life and career ended, Chenier had toured the United States, Canada, and Europe.

In his later years, Chenier was beset by health problems. One of his feet had to be amputated because of diabetes, and he frequently required kidney dialysis. But he continued singing and playing at fairs and other

Selected discography

Singles

"Louisiana Stomp," Elko, 1954.
"Clifton's Blues," Elko, 1954.
"Ay, 'Tit Fille," Specialty, c. 1955.
"Ay, Ai, Ai," Arhoolie, 1963.
"Why Did You Go Last Night," Arhoolie, 1963.

Also recorded single "Squeeze Box Boogie."

LPs

Louisiana Blues and Zydeco, Arhoolie, 1964.
Live at the San Francisco Blues Festival, Arhoolie, 1982.
I'm Here, Alligator, 1984.
Clifton Chenier Sings the Blues, Arhoolie, 1987.

Also recorded the albums *Black Snake Blues* and *Bon Ton Roulet,* both Arhoolie.

Sources

Down Beat, March 1988; December 1989.
High Fidelity, May 1988.
Nation, March 19, 1988.
Rolling Stone, January 28, 1988.

—Elizabeth Wenning

Maurice Chevalier

Singer, actor, comedian

Even two decades after his death, Maurice Chevalier reigns as the most popular entertainer France has produced in the twentieth century. Through films, television, and especially live revues, the jaunty Chevalier charmed audiences for 70 years. He managed to age gracefully and slide without effort from romantic leading man roles to the part of a charming, witty grandfather—all with a voice one *New York Times* reporter deemed "no great shakes."

Arthur Cooper described Chevalier in a *Newsweek* obituary: "As effervescent as vintage champagne, as durable as the Eiffel Tower (which he predated by one year), he was a sophisticated Gallic charmer who easily lived up to his billing as The Most Popular Frenchman in the World. In movies, on television and, above all, on stage, his elegantly relaxed style conjured up memories of a simpler time, of liveried attendants and horse-drawn carriages parked along the Champs-Elysees."

That burnished and elegant persona, however, was quite at odds with Chevalier's upbringing. The ninth child of an itinerant house painter, he was born in 1888 in the Menilmontant section of Paris. His father was a heavy drinker who abused the family before deserting entirely when Maurice was eight. The singer's mother—whom he adored—had to support her children as best she could by making lace. Chevalier even spent some time in a government-run almshouse while his mother was too ill to work.

Singing Safer Than Acrobatics

Chevalier left school at the age of ten, determined to be an acrobat. He apprenticed at the metal-engraving company where his brother worked, but all of his spare time was spent practicing and planning routines. He was given an audition at the Cirque d'Hiver, but during a rehearsal he slipped and fell. After that his mother decreed that he would have to find suitable employment in a "safe" trade.

He drifted through a succession of jobs, including that of carpenter and store clerk, but still yearned for the stage. Finally, he decided to be a singer. At the tender age of 12 he persuaded a cafe owner to allow him to sing on Amateur Night; his debut was a disaster—he stood stiffly in front of the crowd and sang off-key—and he was laughed off the stage. With grim determination he mastered his nerves and returned, honing an act that played upon his extreme youth.

Chevalier became a professional performer in December of 1901, when he played a week's engagement at the Casino de Tourelles, billed as "Little Chevalier, miniature comic." The routine included clownish make-up and some obscene gestures and language; it was a hit with the music-hall clientele, but more fashionable audiences found it revolting. Gradually, as he grew into a slender and handsome young man, Chevalier refined his style. As Cooper put it, "he transformed himself from a *titi*—boulevard smart aleck—into a suave *seducteur.*"

At 21 Chevalier was hired by France's premier revue, the Folies-Bergere. He signed a three-year contract and by his second year was earning top billing as partner to the famous and beautiful Mistinguett. The two performers sang romantic love ballads onstage and were linked romantically offstage as well; Chevalier's career was launched.

Learned English in P.O.W. Camp

In 1913 Chevalier was drafted and the next year found himself on the front lines when Germany invaded France at the start of World War I. He suffered a serious shrapnel wound to the lung at Cutry and was captured and sent to Alten Grabow, a prisoner-of-war camp. He spent 26 months in the camp, during which time he learned English from a fellow prisoner. Released in 1916, he returned to the stage, and eventually to the Folies-Bergere.

Chevalier decided to become a solo performer in 1919, after years spent in the shadow of Mistinguett. During a short engagement in London he noticed a dapper Englishman in formal dress with a straw hat on his head. The singer told the *New York Times:* "He looked so smart that I thought, 'I do not need to look farther. There is my hat. It's a man's hat. It's a gay hat. It's the hat to go with a tuxedo.' From that moment I was never without a straw boater if I could help it, even when those hats went out of fashion."

With his trademark straw hat and his half-singing, half-talking vocal delivery, Chevalier took France, and then America, by storm. He told the *New York Times:* "Thank God, it was my good luck not to have any voice. If I had, I would have tried to be a singer who sings ballads in a voice like a velvet fog, but since I am barely able to half-talk and half-sing a song, it made me look for something to make me different from a hundred other crooners who are neither good nor bad. If I had any voice, I would have been content to rest on my voice and learn nothing else. Since I had no voice, I had to find something that would hold the interest of the public."

Made His Fortune in Films

Chevalier was exaggerating, of course, but he did develop a delightful, affably seductive persona that proved popular through a string of Paramount movies in the early 1930s. His leading ladies in Hollywood included Jeanette MacDonald in *Love Me Tonight,* Norma Shearer in *The Merry Widow,* and Claudette Colbert in *The Smiling Lieutenant.* At the height of the Great Depression Chevalier was earning $20,000 a week as a contract player with Paramount. He moved to MGM in 1935, but no amount of money or success could persuade him to remain in Hollywood after a dispute with MGM production chief Irving Thalberg. Chevalier returned to Paris—to the live stage—and did not make another movie in America for more than a dozen years.

During World War II Chevalier kept a low profile, principally because his companion, Nita Raya, was Jewish. Accusations of collaboration with the Nazi occupation, leveled at him during the war, were quickly withdrawn afterwards and his popularity continued undiminished. When he returned to American films in the 1950s, Chevalier projected a new image—that of the gracefully aging *bon vivant,* a man of the world who could offer sage advice to distraught young lovers. With his 1958 rendition of "Thank Heaven for Little Girls" in MGM's *Gigi,* Chevalier effectively stole that big-budget musical from its stars. He was awarded an honorary Academy Award the following year.

Theater Was His True Love

Although he starred in several television specials and appeared on numerous other shows, Chevalier always felt most comfortable in front of a live audience. In his later years he traveled extensively, bringing his one-man show to audiences on every continent. "Maurice knew the secret of aging gracefully," Cooper wrote. "He seemed really to mean it when he sang 'I'm Glad I'm Not Young Any More.' He had a voice like a broken promise; indeed, the tireless troubadour freely admitted that 'I walk tightrope on the mere thread of a voice.'"

Chevalier died of heart failure on the first day of 1972.

Throughout his life he had battled depression, finding strength in the adoration he earned from audiences. "I believe in the rosy side of life," he once told the *New York Times.* "I know that life has many, many dark sides for everybody. It has been for me at many moments of my life. But I believe in bringing to the people the encouragement of living, and I think I am lasting so long in the interest of the people through something that comes out of my personality and my work, which is to be sort of a sunshine person, see."

Selected writings

The Man in the Straw Hat (autobiography), 1949.
With Love (autobiography), 1960.
I Remember It Well (memoirs), 1970.

Sources

Newsweek, January 10, 1972.
New York Times, January 2, 1972.

—Anne Janette Johnson

Rory Cooney

Liturgist

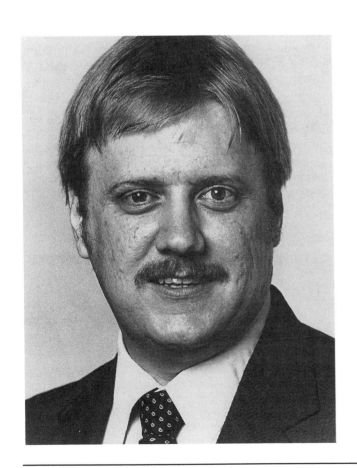

American liturgist Rory Cooney is in the vanguard of church music composition in the United States. His songs, which employ popular instrumentation, are used in worship services at Catholic parishes nationwide. One of seven children, Rory was born on May 29, 1952, in Delaware, Ohio, to Patrick and Martha Cooney, both U.S. postal service employees. When Rory was five years old, the family moved to Phoenix, Arizona, where he attended the St. Vincent de Paul Catholic grade school. As a boy he sang in the choir, and the Daughters of Charity taught him Gregorian chant. He was privileged to sing with the David Windsor Boys' choir, and his love for church music grew.

Cooney later attended the St. Vincent Seminary, in Montebello, California for his high school studies and taught himself to play the piano. He then spent a year at St. Mary's Seminary, a preparatory seminary in Santa Barbara, before enrolling at St. Mary's Seminary in Perryville, Missouri. Cooney studied philosophy and languages, among other subjects, intending to enter the priesthood. However, while many of his classmates went on to become ordained priests, Cooney left the seminary during his junior year to pursue other interests. He was eventually granted a bachelor of arts in liberal studies from St. Mary's Seminary.

After serving as the music director at St. Mary's Seminary Church from 1972 to 1973, Cooney became the assistant music director at the St. Vincent de Paul Catholic Church in Phoenix, Arizona, a position he held until 1977. From 1978 to 1983 he directed the choirs at Saint Simon and Saint Jude cathedrals and the folk ensemble of St. Augustine Catholic Church. During these years Cooney spent his weeks working as a travel agent. He also served as the assistant director of the Phoenix Diocesan Chorale from 1981 to 1983, becoming the chorale's director in 1986 and 1987.

Largely self-taught, Cooney has composed over 250 songs, many of them based on lyrics paraphrased from the Psalms. And several of these works have been published by North American Liturgy Resources in collections used for worship in Catholic churches nationwide. While through his music Cooney tries to help modern listeners understand Biblical concepts that date back centuries, his instrumentation is representative of modern popular idioms and includes synthesizers, electric guitars, and trap drums, as well as acoustic instruments: piano, trumpets, and saxophone. Cooney sings some of his songs and recruits colleagues to sing others. Soprano Theresa Donohoo, who appears on several of Cooney's albums and has performed in concert with the composer, describes his music as cutting "across all lines." She told Joseph Kenny of the *St. Louis Review,* "He writes intelligent, prayerful lyrics.

The theme is just as important as the music. It has a lot of meaning."

From 1985 to 1987 Cooney attended the Corpus Christi Center for Advanced Liturgical Studies where he completed the Directors' Certification Program. Cooney is part of a group of Catholic musicians who visit other parishes in many states to teach church leaders how to better use music in their worship services. He has also designed or assisted in designing and performing music at several regional and national conferences, including the Johannes Hofinger Conference, The East Coast Religious Education Conference, the LACCD (Los Angeles Religious Education Conference), the North American Conference on Worship, the Southwest Liturgical Conference, the Conference of Major Superiors of Men Religious, and conventions of the National Association of Pastoral Musicians and the Long Beach California Association of Pastoral Musicians. In addition, Cooney writes articles on music for worship for such magazines as *Today's Parish*, *Pastoral Music*, and *Modern Liturgy*.

In 1987 the Missionary Oblates of Mary Immaculate and the National Shrine of Our Lady of the Snows in Belleville, Illinois commissioned a musical based on the Biblical parable of the prodigal son. Cooney collaborated with Jody Serey, whom he had met in liturgy classes at the seminary, eventually composing the lyrics and the music for the book, *Lost and Found: A Musical Parable*.

In Luke's gospel (15:11-32), Jesus tells a crowd about a father and his two sons. The younger son asks for his inheritance and leaves for a distant country, where he squanders his money on a life of debauchery. In poverty, the son becomes a hired hand, feeding the pigs on a farm. Eventually he decides to return home to beg his father's forgiveness and work there as a servant. Upon his return, the son is greeted with great joy by his family, except his older brother, who has worked diligently but in his own self-interest. The father's "prodigal love," that is, "love beyond reason," in this parable represents the generous and unending love of God for all people.

Cooney added several characters to his retelling of this parable—including a mother and daughter—to make the story apply to the family as a whole. The distant country became the Distant Land Bar and Grill, populated with barflies and floozies, and the farm where the son worked in his poverty become the Hog Heaven Bar, replete with pig bikers and "pig floozies." The language is forthright and comic relief abounds. *Lost and Found* was first performed on June 20, 1987 at Youth Sing Praise, a week-long gathering of high school students from throughout the country. After its debut performance, Cooney rewrote the script, and subsequent performances have been followed by further alterations.

Music has also played an important role in Cooney's personal life, for it was through his musical activities that he met his wife, Therese. They were married in 1974 and have five children. Cooney's hobbies include writing, stamp collecting, fishing with his children, attending movies and theater, and traveling.

Selected discography

You Alone, North American Liturgy Resources, 1984.
Do Not Fear to Hope, North American Liturgy Resources, 1986.
Mystery, North American Liturgy Resources, 1987.
Missa America, North American Liturgy Resources, 1987.
Lost and Found: A Musical Parable, North American Liturgy Resources, 1989.
Safety Harbor, GIA Publications, 1990.
Psalms for the Church Year IV, GIA Publications, 1991.
Cries of the Spirit: Psalms for Liturgy, North American Liturgy Resources, 1991.

Sources

Arizona Republic, April 18, 1987.
Mustard Seed (Kingston, RI), Winter 1991.
St. Louis Post Dispatch, June 18, 1987.
St. Louis Review, June 21, 1987.
St. Petersburg Times, June 2, 1990.

—Jeanne M. Lesinski

Chick Corea

Keyboardist

"At the very least, music is a soothing thing . . . but, at best, it can be an expanding thing," Chick Corea, jazz and crossover keyboardist extraordinaire, disclosed to Josef Woodard in *Down Beat.* Corea's mix of Mozart with Moog synthesizers spans a wide musical range which coincides with his personal philosophy. The many-time Grammy Award-winning composer and arranger helped pioneer jazz away from the domains of small, intimate clubs to sell-out rock concert halls. Whether electric or acoustic, Corea remains enormously popular fusing jazz and rock impulses at earsplitting decibels, or amps, performing mini-sonatas on a quiet classical stage.

Anthony Armando Corea was born in Chelsea, Massachusetts, on June 12, 1941, to Armando and Anna (Zaccone) Corea. He received his nickname Chick from one of his aunts, who called him "Cheeky" whenever she pinched his cheek. His father, a second-generation Italian, played trumpet and bass in the society and Dixieland bands he led around Boston. "He wrote out arrangements of popular songs for me," Corea recalled to Len Lyons in *High Fidelity.* "He always kept them to my level, so the language of music became familiar to me." Corea was taught piano at home as a four-year-old, and drums later as an eight-year-old. His only formal lessons were in classical piano with local instructor Salvatore Sullo. The adolescent Corea played piano at weddings, bar mitzvahs, and area functions before his graduation from Chelsea High School in 1959. Moving to New York City the same year, Corea entered Columbia University, but dropped out after one month. The next ten months he practiced piano eight hours a day to audition at the Juilliard School of Music. Accepted at Juilliard as a piano major, he remained two months. Corea left when he realized a conventional education was not for him.

Teamed With Miles Davis

During the sixties Corea joined the ensemble Mongo Santamaria and the Willie Bobo combo. He worked as a sideman for Blue Mitchell, Herbie Mann, and Stan Getz. Subsequently, his debut albums, including *Tones for Miss Bones* (1966) and *The Song of Singing,* appeared. In 1968 he was an accompanist for Sarah Vaughan when keyboardist Herbie Hancock called him. Hancock was on his honeymoon and needed Corea to replace him for a Baltimore date with jazz's hottest star, Miles Davis. When he joined his childhood idol's band replacing Hancock in 1969, Corea got acquainted with the electric piano through Davis. Chick put the instrument to use during his two years with Davis making albums, including *Bitches Brew,* which became the paradigm album of jazz-rock fusion.

In 1970 Corea converted to the Church of Scientology, whose founder, the late L. Ron Hubbard, practiced a method of unblocking the mind he called "dianetics." Though Corea did not consider himself religious, he followed Scientology's approach to pare off the mind's emotional baggage and discovered artistic impetus. Later the same year he formed the group Circle with Davis's former bassist Dave Holland, drummer Barry Altschul, and reed player Anthony Braxton. Together they recorded the albums *Circling In* and *Circulus,* among others, but audiences did not find the group accessible. "Not enough people could relate to us. . .," Corea stated in *The Pleasures of Jazz.* "They were pleased by the technical brilliance of the performance, though the content and feeling would be a mystery to them." Corea learned his lesson and began to pursue "namely the simple desire to reach out and communicate."

Popularized Jazz-Rock Fusion

The winner of nine best keyboardist polls from 1973 to 1979, Corea has since solved his communication prob-lems. His popularity soared as a solo artist with three volumes of *Piano Improvisations* in the seventies. He began his on-going duos with vibraharpist Gary Burton at the same time, recording *Crystal Silence* and *Duet.* From 1972 until 1976, Corea let loose the decibels with his energized fusion band Return to Forever. The group, whose most memorable members were drummer Lenny White and guitarists Bill Connors and Al DiMeola, recorded eight albums, including 1975 Grammy Award winner *No Mystery.* Composing and arranging his own suites, Corea received two more Grammy Awards the next year with the solo album *The Leprechaun.* In 1977 the Latin-element album *My Spanish Heart* sold 170,000 copies, an unprecedented number for a jazz recording. The following year *People* reported the critical concordance that "together the two friends have created what many jazz critics consider the tour of the decade" when Corea and Herbie Hancock improvised Bela Bartok, George Gershwin, and Miles Davis in duets on acoustic grand pianos. The album *Herbie Hancock & Chick Corea in Concert 1978* proved that fusion master Corea was just as comfortable concertizing. Corea met his second wife, vocalist and composer Gayle Moran, in the seventies, when she began her musical collaboration with him on several of his albums, and she was featured prominently as part of Corea's group Return to Forever.

Eye of the Beholder Won Raves

From the eighties to the present, Corea has been just as successful. In 1982 he won an additional Grammy Award for further work with Gary Burton on *Chick Corea and Gary Burton in Concert.* Continuing his solo work, he also collaborated with various musicians from jazz, crossover, and classical fields, including Michael Brecker, Freddie Hubbard, Keith Jarrett, Eddie Gomez, Miroslav Vitous, violinist Ida Kavafian, and cellist Fred Sherry. In 1986 he emulated Mozart at a performance of his own concerto with the Philharmonia Virtuosi in New York. While forming his Elektric Band in 1985, Corea began to fuse an acoustic piano with an electric keyboard. Finding the balance of instruments that had eluded him previously, Corea produced the album many critics viewed as the best jazz-rock record of 1988 with *Eye of the Beholder.*

In 1990 Chick Corea and his Elektric Band—bassist John Patitucci, drummer Dave Weckl, guitarist Frank Gambale, and saxophonist Eric Marienthal—put together "more of a musician's album" with *Inside Out* wrote Ricardo Silveira in *Playboy.* Though some critics dubbed him "Mr. Scientology" and have not always been receptive, the consensus opinion was stated by Silveira: "Just remember that there's an intellectual bent to Chick's music making—he does that sort of thing as well as it can be done."

Corea lives in Hollywood Hills with Gayle Moran. His first wife remained in Boston to raise his two (now adult) children, Thaddeus and Liana. A workaholic who tours in a bus that once belonged to country star Merle Haggard, Chick Corea wants to compose more orchestral and chamber pieces in the future. Rendering a fitting homage to the jazz leader, Woodward wrote, "Corea's mission of mind-expansion barrels forward, with signposts in the subconscious, the fingers, and the airwaves."

Selected discography

Tones for Miss Bones, 1966.
The Song of Singing.
Chick Corea, Blue Note.
Piano Improvisations, Vol. 1 & 2, ECM, 1971.
No Mystery, 1975.
The Leprechaun, Polydor, 1976.
My Spanish Heart, Polydor, 1977.
The Mad Hatter, Polydor, 1979.
Three Quartets, Warner Brothers, 1980.
Elektric Band, GRP, 1986.
Light Years, GRP.
Eye of the Beholder, GRP, 1988.
Beneath the Mask, GRP, 1991.
Akoustic Band, GRP.
Inside Out.
Thunder from Down Under.

With Gary Burton

Crystal Silence, ECM, 1972.

Duet, ECM.
Corea/Burton, 1982.

With Herbie Hancock

Corea/Hancock, Polydor.
An Evening With. . ., Columbia, 1978.

With Return to Forever

Return to Forever, ECM, 1973.
Light As A Feather, Polydor, 1973.
Musicmagic, Columbia.

With Circle

Circling In, Blue Note, 1968.
Circulus, Blue Note, 1970.
Paris Concert, ECM.

With Miles Davis

Bitches Brew, Columbia, 1970.

Sources

Books

Feather, Leonard, *The Pleasures of Jazz*, Horizon, 1976.
Lyons, Len, *The Great Jazz Pianists*, Morrow, 1983.

Periodicals

Down Beat, March 9, 1978; June 1981; January 1986; June 1986; September 1988.
High Fidelity, February 1979.
People, March 13, 1978; May 15, 1989.
Playboy, July 1990.

—Marjorie Burgess

Bing Crosby

Singer, actor

B ing Crosby was one of the most popular singing stars in the history of show business and one of the best-selling musicians of all time. In the course of a career spanning more than 50 years, Crosby produced over 1,600 recordings, of which he sold half a billion copies; his honeyed baritone revolutionized crooning and won him a worldwide audience. "Bing Crosby [was] probably the most-loved character in the world apart from the creations of Walt Disney," wrote Charles Thompson in *Bing: The Authorized Biography*. "He has dispensed much joy and much entertainment for the benefit of millions who were never ever to meet him but felt that they knew him and in him had a friend. A colossal, enveloping warmth of affection has justly come his way through the years."

During the glory days of the big Hollywood studios, Crosby was under contract to Paramount Pictures. He often appeared in as many as three full-length features per year and won an Academy Award for portraying a priest in *Going My Way*. It was radio, however, that made Crosby a star. His exceptional voice and casual, relaxed demeanor projected well over the airwaves, and his innovative, jazzy style of singing won the hearts of younger fans and the envy of his peers. In the midst of the Great Depression, Bing Crosby became a millionaire, and by his death in 1977 he was estimated to be worth more than $80 million, most of it invested in industry and real estate. His success is all the more phenomenal in that it came long before the inflated salaries and lucrative endorsement contracts earned by today's popular singers.

Comic Strip Spawned Nickname

Crosby always gave the year of his birth as 1904, but some sources say he was born on May 2, 1903 in Tacoma, Washington. He was one of seven children of a bookkeeper and a pious, ambitious mother. When Crosby was still a young child, his family moved to Spokane, where his father took a job with the Inland Brewery. Young Crosby attended Catholic schools and earned the nickname "Bing" from his fondness for a newspaper comic strip called the "Bingville Bugle."

Residents of Spokane remembered Bing Crosby as a child who loved to sing and who sang to himself everywhere he went. Ironically, he never learned to read music, and he quit his only formal singing lessons after a few weeks. Entirely self-taught as a singer, Crosby gravitated to the kind of music he heard on his parents' gramophone—popular songs, ragtime, and show numbers.

Crosby attended Gonzaga High School, a Jesuit school,

For the Record. . .

Born Harry Lillis Crosby, May 2, 1903 (some sources say 1904), in Tacoma, WA; died of a heart attack October 14, 1977, in Madrid, Spain; son of Harry Lowe (a bookkeeper) and Catherine Helen (Harrigan) Crosby; married Dixie Lee (an actress), September 29, 1930 (died, 1952); married Kathryn Grant (an actress), October 24, 1957; children: (first marriage) Dennis, Gary, Philip, Lindsay; (second marriage) Harry, Mary Frances, Nathaniel. *Education:* Attended Gonzaga University, 1921-24. *Religion:* Roman Catholic.

Singer, 1921-77. With James Heaton, Miles Rinker, Bob Pritchard, Clair Pritchard, and Alton "Al" Rinker, formed group The Musicaladers, 1921, group disbanded, 1925; with Al Rinker, moved to Los Angeles, 1925, and performed as duo Two Boys and a Piano on West Coast vaudeville circuit; with Rinker, joined Paul Whiteman Orchestra, 1926; with Rinker and Harry Barris, formed trio The Rhythm Boys, 1927, group cut first single, "Side by Side," for Victor label, 1927; baritone and front man for The Rhythm Boys, 1927-31, playing on vaudeville circuit and with the Gus Arnheim Orchestra at the Coconut Grove, Los Angeles.

Solo artist, 1931-77. Appeared on musical variety radio shows, on CBS, 1931-35 and 1949-52; NBC, *The Kraft Music Hall,* 1935-46; and ABC, 1946-49, and on numerous television specials, 1952-77, including *The Bing Crosby Show* (sitcom), 1964-65. Recording artist, 1927-77, for RCA Victor, Columbia, Decca, MCA, and numerous other labels. Star of films for Paramount and other studios.

Awards: Academy Award for best actor, 1945, for *Going My Way.*

In 1925 the two decided to take a chance at the big time; they pooled their resources and set off for Los Angeles in a beat-up Model T Ford. They were nothing less than an overnight success. Rinker's sister was Mildred Bailey, herself a successful vaudevillian, and she was able to help the boys secure a contract for West Coast vaudeville work. Billing themselves as Two Boys and a Piano, Crosby and Rinker sang popular numbers in a jazzy style that has since become the signature sound of crooning.

According to Donald Shepherd and Robert F. Slatzer in *Bing Crosby: The Hollow Man,* Crosby and Rinker had seized upon a formula that set them apart from the many duos playing vaudeville at the time. "Al and Bing would soon learn that while they had great appeal to everyone, they were even more enthusiastically received by members of the younger generation, who were caught up in what Easterners were calling hot jazz," the authors wrote. "And since Crosby and Rinker had culled the best from the wide range of music being recorded in New Orleans, Chicago, and New York and had fashioned and presented it in a style uniquely their own, they were destined to become show-stoppers in the West. There was nothing quite like them, even in the East."

Late in 1926 the duo received a lucrative—and flattering—offer from Paul Whiteman, one of the nation's most famous orchestra leaders. They joined Whiteman in Chicago, then moved with him to New York City. There, for some reason, Crosby and Rinker failed to make a hit. Shepherd and Slatzer suggested that Manhattan's mainstream audiences were not quite ready for Bing's scat singing and off-beat presentation. Whatever the case, Crosby and Rinker separated from Whiteman's act and added a third partner, Harry Barris. With Barris and Rinker both at piano and Crosby as front man, the group became known as The Rhythm Boys.

Rhythm Boys Tackled Recording and Film

As The Rhythm Boys, Crosby and his partners regained their professional standing quickly. They cut several singles, including "Mississippi Mud," "From Monday On," and "Side by Side," and after a vaudeville tour on their own, rejoined Whiteman for a highly successful West Coast run. In 1930 they appeared in their first feature film, which starred Whiteman and was called *The King of Jazz.* When the movie was completed, they struck out on their own again, signing a contract to appear with the Gus Arnheim Orchestra at the prestigious Coconut Grove nightclub in Los Angeles.

Much has been written about Crosby's irresponsible

earning above-average grades and participating in numerous sports. After high school he enrolled in Gonzaga University with the intention of becoming a lawyer. Other interests intervened, however; with a group of his Spokane buddies, he formed a small band, The Musicaladers, which performed at school functions and private parties. Crosby was the group's vocalist and drummer—his only work as an instrumentalist. The Musicaladers were surprisingly successful for a band staffed principally by teenagers; before long they found themselves entertaining audiences between films at a Spokane movie house.

Overnight Success

Even after the Musicaladers disbanded, Crosby and a friend, Al Rinker, continued to work together as a duo.

behavior during his early career. He did indeed miss performances occasionally because of drinking binges, only his fantastic popularity with audiences saving his career. After 1930, however, he began to take a more serious attitude toward his work—to see singing as a way to make money as well as entertain. In September of 1930 he married starlet Dixie Lee. Shortly thereafter he made his first two-reel short film, *I Surrender, Dear,* using a song Barris had written for him as the movie's title. Crosby's performance of "I Surrender, Dear" brought him to the attention of William Paley, the owner of CBS. Paley offered Crosby his own radio show, and—after some nasty legal wrangling—Crosby left both the Coconut Grove and The Rhythm Boys.

Radio Cemented Career

On September 2, 1931, Crosby opened his first radio show with a new theme song: "Where the Blue of the Night Meets the Gold of the Day." The rest, as they say, is history. He performed live for an unprecedented 20 weeks at Manhattan's Paramount Theatre, signed a movie contract with Paramount Pictures, and began recording regularly with a new label, Decca Records. Throughout the Great Depression and on into the years of World War II, Bing Crosby was the nation's most beloved crooner and one of its favorite stars. Thompson attested: "Even if the image of the casual, lazy pipe-smoking crooner was not completely true it would not matter. He was Bing, Mr. Family Man, Mr. Clean. . . . The clean image [was] a great asset to him in his career, but he had to be extremely careful to maintain great dignity in public, particularly after he became so closely associated with the Father O'Malley character of *Going My Way.*"

Crosby's voice and delivery were surprisingly adaptable; over the years he sang every type of popular song, from cowboy ditties to blues, ballads, and patriotic numbers. He was initially reluctant to sing hymns, but he eventually overcame this reticence, and today his Christmas carols—especially "White Christmas"—are his most treasured recordings. For many years Crosby's rendition of "White Christmas" was the best-selling recording in history.

Made "Road" Pictures With Hope

In 1935 Crosby moved from CBS radio to NBC, where he starred on the popular *Kraft Music Hall.* He worked on that show—live—for nearly a dozen years, leaving only when ABC radio allowed him to pre-record his programs on audiotape. In the meantime, he starred or appeared in some one hundred films, including the highly popular "Road" series—"The Road to Singapore," "The Road to Zanzibar," "The Road to Morocco"—with Bob Hope and Dorothy Lamour; Hope and Crosby played off one another perfectly, often ad-libbing dialogue and flip comments in these essentially silly pictures.

Crosby returned to CBS radio in 1949 and made the transition to television easily—if reluctantly—in the early 1950s. His television forte was the variety special. Beginning in 1966 he hosted a yearly Christmas show that featured his second wife, Kathryn, and their children. Crosby's only regular weekly television show was a situation comedy, *The Bing Crosby Show,* which ran for two seasons in the mid-1960s.

Rock and Roll Proved No Competition

Even the advent of rock and roll did little to erode Crosby's popularity. His fans had aged along with him and saw him as a wholesome, relaxing alternative to the rhythms of the new generation. Nor did Crosby disappoint them; his voice held its clarity as he aged, and he continued to perform—live and on television—right up to his death in 1977. In his later years he indulged his lifelong passion for golf by founding a tournament in his name.

In October of 1977, Crosby collapsed from a massive heart attack on a golf course outside Madrid, Spain. He is survived by his second wife and seven children—four sons from his first marriage, and two sons and a daughter from his second. Several of his older sons had performed with him during the 1940s, and his second family often appeared with him on his television specials.

The persistence of Crosby's fame is evident in the number of his recordings still in print and in the rebroadcast of his many films. His Irish good looks and inimitable baritone stand as one of the strongest testaments of radio's golden age and one of the crowning achievements of the Hollywood film. Shepherd and Slatzer concluded that at the peak of his popularity, Crosby's "musical ability knew no bounds, and [he] continually nudged at—and often broke through—the very limits of contemporary music of the day. . . . In Bing's later years, one remembers the bubbly *b*s and rippling, rhythmic cadence of his conversational voice, reminiscent of the vibrant tones of a soft, laid-back string bass."

Selected discography

Singles

(With Al Rinker) "I've Got the Girl," Columbia, 1926.
(With Rinker) "Wistful and Blue," Victor, 1926.
"Muddy Water," Victor, 1927.
(With Rinker and Harry Barris) "Side by Side," Victor, 1927.
"I Surrender, Dear," Victor, 1931.
"Out of Nowhere," Victor, 1931.
"I Love You Truly," Decca, 1934.
(With wife, Dixie Lee) "A Fine Romance," Decca, 1936.
(With son, Gary Crosby) "Sam's Song," Decca, 1950.

Albums

A Crosby Christmas, Decca, 1950.
The Best of Bing, MCA, 1965.
Seasons, Polydor, 1977.
The Radio Years, Volumes 1-4, GNP Crescendo, 1985-88.
Christmas Songs, MCA, 1986.
Bing Sings Again, MCA, 1986.
(With Bob Hope) *Bing & Bob*, Spokane, 1986.
(With Trudy Erwin) *Bing & Trudy: On The Air*, Spokane, 1986.
Merry Christmas, MCA, 1987.
Crosby Classics, Columbia, 1988.
Greatest Hits, 1939-1947, MCA, 1988.
Holiday Inn, MCA, 1988.

Bing in the '30s, Volumes 1-6, Spokane.
Der Bingle, Volumes 1-3, Spokane.
A Christmas Sing With Bing, MCA.
The Crooner: The Columbia Years, 1928-1934, Columbia.
Distinctively Bing—Volume 1, Sunbeam.
Hey Bing!, MCA.
Holiday Inn/Bells of St. Mary's, Spokane.
Kraft Music Hall Highlights, Spokane.
Bing Crosby on the Air: 1934 & 1938, Spokane.
Rare 1930-31 Brunswick Recordings, MCA.
Shillelaghs & Shamrocks, MCA.
That Christmas Feeling, MCA.
The Small One/The Happy Prince, MCA.
When Irish Eyes Are Smiling, MCA.
(With Louis Armstrong) *Havin' Fun!*, Sounds Rare.
(With Armstrong) *More Fun!*, Sounds Rare.
(With Al Jolson) *Bing & Al*, Volumes 1-6, Totem.

Sources

Shepherd, Donald and Robert F. Slatzer, *Bing Crosby: The Hollow Man*, St. Martin's, 1981.
Thompson, Charles, *Bing: The Authorized Biography*, McKay, 1975.

—Anne Janette Johnson

Charlie Daniels

Singer, songwriter

Charlie Daniels is one of the best known band leaders in the rowdy, hard-stomping Southern rock style. Throughout his 35-year career, Daniels has resisted labels and rebelled against everything ordinary and middle-of-the-road. His unusual blend of styles from bluegrass to boogie has found its way where country never trod before, into big-city arenas in every part of the nation. *Newsweek* contributor Barbara Graustark described Daniels as "more like a fiddle-playing grizzly bear than a rock star," a riveting singer and instrumentalist who "cooks up a stew of Southern-fried country and hard-edged rock."

One of Daniels's central themes is a Southern rock favorite—pride in home, country, and region. Songs such as "In America," "The South's Gonna Do It," and "The Devil Went Down to Georgia" pay homage to the strength and courage of rural folk, especially the Dixie longhairs who supported Daniels early in his career. While his sentiments are sometimes simple, however, Daniels's music is an energetic, complicated fusion of styles—bluegrass fiddle may compete with a rock beat, or a single number may veer from Texas swing to pure jazz. "Our music represents wide-open spaces and a free-wheelin' attitude," Daniels told *Stereo Review.* "Maybe the people who don't get a chance to live like that a whole lot—especially the people in big cities like Chicago and New York—can live that kind of life vicariously, for a few minutes anyway, by comin' to one of our concerts."

Learned Guitar Elvis-Style

Many country pickers master their instruments at very young ages. Daniels is the exception to that rule. He never touched a guitar or a fiddle until he was in his teens. Daniels was born in Wilmington, North Carolina, in 1937. As a child he moved frequently, following his father, who purchased and cut timber. Attending as many as three schools a year, Daniels had little enthusiasm for education. He discovered his life's passion at 15, when he bought his first guitar. He taught himself to play by listening to early Elvis Presley and tunes he heard on a black station, WLAC. At seventeen he began listening to Nashville's WSM, where he heard the riotous bluegrass of Bill Monroe.

His interest in bluegrass led Daniels to try his talents on the fiddle. "I like to run my parents crazy when I first started playin' fiddle," he told *Stereo Review.* "One of the guys I went to school with said it sounded like somebody stepped on a cat every time I started playin'." The young, would-be performer did not lose faith, though. He kept practicing until he had mastered both the fiddle and the guitar. Then he founded a band called the Jaguars and set out to perform in "every honky-tonk between Raleigh and Texas, or at least quite a few of 'em."

During a gig in Fort Worth, Texas, Daniels met producer Bob Johnston. Together Daniels and Johnston wrote a song, "It Hurts Me," that found its way onto the B side of one of Elvis Presley's singles. In 1963 Johnston produced Daniels's first album, an Epic release that did not sell well. Johnston had some clout in Nashville, however, and he was able to find Daniels work in the lucrative session music business. With his flair for jazz and rock, Daniels earned credits on some of the most unconventional country recordings of the late 1960s, including Ringo Starr's *Beaucoups of Blues* and Bob Dylan's *Nashville Skyline*.

Formed Charlie Daniels Band

"I never was a real hot-shot session musician," Daniels remembered in *Stereo Review,* "and I never really had that many friends in the studios in Nashville. I like to have fun when I play, and I didn't really have that much fun playin'. I never really had a handle on playin' the Nashville type of sound, and I never was really accepted that much by those guys. I guess I was a little too rowdy for them, or at least my music was." In a daring move, Daniels gave up his niche as a session musician to return to live performance. He formed a new band,

the Charlie Daniels Band, and hit the road for as many as 250 live shows each year.

Between 1971 and 1980 Daniels and his band released ten albums for the Kama Sutra and Epic labels. The act was not long in earning its first top ten hits, making the country charts in 1973 with "Uneasy Rider" and in 1975 with "The South's Gonna Do It." One of the Charlie Daniels Band's biggest fans during the period was the governor of Georgia, Jimmy Carter. When Carter decided to run for president, Daniels hosted not one but three fundraising concerts for the candidate. Interestingly enough, Carter's arrival in the White House coincided with Daniels's rise to the pinnacle of fame in the ranks of country music.

Daniels's tenth album, *Million Mile Reflections,* went double platinum in 1980, with more than two million units sold. The work also yielded Daniels's biggest hit, a rip-roaring fiddle explosion called "The Devil Went Down to Georgia." The song, which featured a now-classic duel between the devil and a proud Georgia fiddler, won both the Grammy Award and the Country Music Association award for best country single of the year. That same year Daniels won two other prestigious CMA awards, best instrumentalist and best instrumental group. The Charlie Daniels Band has been a favorite country act ever since.

Disdains Labels

Charlie Daniels and his associates continue to pursue their own joyful brand of music, never mindful of the fashionable trends other artists follow. "I don't see why everything has to be pigeonholed, categorized, and computerized," Daniels told *Stereo Review.* "I don't think about what *kind* of music we play. I think about what *quality* of music we play. Our music has definitely got some country influence on it, but it's definitely not what's known as traditional country music. We just play the music and let other people put titles on it. Some reviewer from up the way called it 'Southern twang, Northern bang, and city gang.' I thought that was pretty apt. But if people want to call me a hillbilly, hell, that's all right. If they want to call me a rock-'n'-roller, I don't care about that, either. It don't make no difference."

In recent years Daniels has gained added notoriety for his annual Volunteer Jams, concerts that regularly turn staid Nashville inside out. With his six-foot-one-inch, 250-pound frame and woolly beard, Daniels remains a noticeable figure among country-rock superstars—middle age and the rigors of touring have done little to blunt his enthusiasm for his audiences. "I can't see myself as nothin' but a lucky, blessed musician," Daniels told *People* magazine. "Someone once asked me how happy I was on a scale of one to 10. I had to say '11.'"

Selected discography

Honey in the Rock, Kama Sutra.
Fire on the Mountain, Kama Sutra.
Nightrider, Kama Sutra, reissued, Epic.
Charlie Daniels, Capitol.
Saddle Tramp, Epic.
High Lonesome, Epic.
Uneasy Rider, Epic.
The Essential Charlie Daniels, Kama Sutra.
Million Mile Reflections, Epic.
A Decade of Hits, Epic.
Full Moon, Epic.
Midnight Wind, Epic.
Windows, Epic.
Volunteer Jam VII, Epic.
Me and the Boys, Epic, 1985.

Powder Keg, Epic, 1987.
Homesick Heroes, Epic, 1988.
Simple Man, Epic, 1990.
Renegade, Epic, 1991.

Sources

Books

Brown, Charles T., *Music U.S.A.: America's Country and Western Tradition*, Prentice-Hall, 1986.
The Illustrated Encyclopedia of Country Music, Harmony, 1977.

Periodicals

Down Beat, May 1985.
Newsweek, September 15, 1980.
People, October 29, 1979.
Stereo Review, January 1980.
Time, May 10, 1982.

—*Anne Janette Johnson*

Alex de Grassi

Guitarist

The praiseworthy beginning of Windham Hill Records is losing focus behind the increasingly discordant view of new age music. Early recordings on the label feature some of the finest steel-string guitar work in the recent rebirth of acoustic music. The label, responsible in great part for this renaissance, offered the voicings of Will Ackerman, Michael Hedges, and Alex de Grassi. While Ackerman is known for his lyrical guitar work and business acumen (he is founder and CEO of Windham Hill Records), and Hedges for his innovative, other-worldly interpretation of guitar playing, de Grassi is, Lee Underwood asserted in *Down Beat,* one of the "most original, technically advanced, and musically captivating steel-string pickers to emerge from this genre. . ., bringing to three- and four-finger folk picking the fiery spirit of improvisation and personal exploration."

Born in 1952, de Grassi began playing guitar at the age of thirteen. At twenty-one, the self-taught guitarist drifted around Europe playing in folk clubs and subways. Not considering music as a career, de Grassi returned to the United States to study carpentry under his cousin Will Ackerman at Windham Hill Builders from 1974 to 1977. Working as a carpenter and attending school at the University of California at Berkeley, de Grassi continued to play his guitar, but, like his cousin, played only for friends and at private gatherings. Finally, upon the strong urging of these friends, Ackerman founded Windham Hill Records and began recording. De Grassi entered the studio to record for what was originally to be an anthology of fingerstyle guitarists for the label, but the resulting sessions brought forth his 1978 debut, *Turning: Turning Back.*

"His *Turning: Turning Back* LP is a classic of the genre," Underwood lauded. "Initially, one might think de Grassi has overdubbed two or more tracks—not so: one man, two hands, one guitar." In *Folk Scene,* critic Mark Leviton proclaimed de Grassi's first album "as fine a solo guitar disc as I've heard. He slips in and out of rhythms effortlessly. . . . When he casually throws in harmonics in difficult places, as in 'Window,' he is truly breathtaking." Underwood defined the style that culminated in such moments: "De Grassi has mastered the art of playing melodies, countermelodies, harmonies, and intricate rhythms simultaneously. His touch is as exquisite as his lyricism, and his improvisational/compositional musical consciousness is as intricate and subtle as sparkling crystal."

De Grassi continued this linear, almost meditative style on his follow-up album, *Slow Circle,* which received warm reviews. This time, however, there were detractors like *Down Beat* contributor Elaine Guregian, who wrote, "De Grassi's music irritated me (but gently) with

For the Record. . .

Born February 13, 1952, in Yokosuka, Japan; raised near San Francisco; father was a classical pianist. *Education:* University of California, Berkeley, A.B. in urban geography, 1979.

Guitarist; played subways and folk clubs throughout Europe, 1973; apprenticed as a carpenter under Will Ackerman at Windham Hill Builders, 1974-77; recorded first album for Windham Hill in 1978.

Addresses: *Record company*—Wihdham Hill, P.O. Box 9388, Stanford, CA 94305.

its complacency." After her self-confessed "cavilling," Guregian conceded that de Grassi "plays beautifully, sometimes awesomely facile with his inventive lines. This guitarist has the ability—which many others lack—to use the device of repeated fragments without becoming derivative. There are many moments of achievement on this recording."

Despite such accolades, de Grassi never fully offered this style of playing again. On his 1981 release, *Clockwork,* most tracks feature the guitar in combination with piano, percussion, bass, violin, saxophone, and other instruments. "I wrote a lot of the pieces for *Clockwork* with specific instruments in mind," de Grassi explained to Dan Forte in *Guitar Player.* "I used the guitar more as a compositional tool." He also began experimenting with different musical styles—such as South American music—that have informed his work since.

In his last album on the Windham Hill label, *Southern Exposure,* de Grassi returned to the solo acoustic guitar, but also moved further away from his original compositional technique. He described the evolution to Forte: "On the first two albums, the tuning really determines a lot about how the music is. By the time of *Southern Exposure,* where I'm using both open and standard tuning equally, the musical idea dictates the tuning more." Forte felt the album signaled the maturation of the artist and was "possibly de Grassi's most realized work as a composer and guitarist. The songs are less stream-of-consciousness, more melodic; the playing is cleaner in execution and clearer in tone."

As illustrated in the title of his fifth album, *Altiplano,* de Grassi continued to seek direction and influence from South American music, as well as other sources. Jas Obrecht, writing in *Guitar Player,* observed that the "project features an eclectic array of instrumentalists . . . and often couches the guitar in a supporting role. While a couple of tracks are reminiscent of his earlier work, de Grassi ventures into jazz, Brazilian, Middle Eastern, and pop flavors." Trying to expand on his compositional abilities, de Grassi pointed out to Obrecht, "I want to feature the guitar, but not necessarily have it dominate each piece." A concert appearance in support of this album, however, failed to convince a reviewer from the *New York Times* of the validity of de Grassi's explorations. Jon Pareles felt de Grassi's group "showed that eclecticism doesn't guarantee musical substance" and that as de Grassi "blended in with the band, a listener half expected a soloist to come on stage and do something against the pretty backdrop."

Selected discography

Turning: Turning Back, Windham Hill, 1978.
Slow Circle, Windham Hill, 1979.
Clockwork, Windham Hill, 1981.
Southern Exposure, Windham Hill, 1984.
Altiplano, Novus/RCA, 1987.
Deep at Night, Windham Hill, 1991.

Sources

Down Beat, October 1979; August 1980.
Folk Scene, January 1979.
Guitar Player, February 1985; June 1987.
Musician, September 1987.
New York Times, June 24, 1987.
Rolling Stone, June 10, 1982.

—Rob Nagel

Enya

Singer, songwriter, composer

After performing in the folk group Clannad and doing solo soundtrack work for a few years, Irish vocalist, composer, and musician Enya rushed up the British charts with the album *Watermark* in 1988. The following year she achieved success in the United States, most notably with her hit single "Orinoco Flow." Enya's sound combines the spiritual qualities of New Age music with traditional Celtic sounds in a way that ultimately "transcends the category of Celtic New Age," asserted Helena Mulkerns in *Rolling Stone*. Enya was born Eithne Ni Bhraonain in Gweedore, County Donegal, Ireland, to a musical family in the early 1960s. Her first language, as well as her name, is Gaelic; Enya is an English spelling of the pronunciation of her first name. She and several of her eight siblings inherited their parents' musical abilities and were involved in the Irish folk group, Clannad. In 1982 though, Enya left the group to find follow her own inspiration. To pursue this goal she traveled to Dublin, where she rented a room in the home of former Clannad manager Nicky Ryan. She struck up a working relationship with Ryan's wife, Roma, who began providing Enya with lyrics for her compositions. Eventually, in 1985, Enya was contracted to score a film for David Puttnam entitled *The Frog Prince*. This opportunity led to her real breakthrough, recording the soundtrack of the BBC television series "The Celts." Music from this project was released on the album *Enya* by Atlantic Records. Though critic Michael Tearson of *Audio* pointed out that *Enya* "is not as elaborate" as the artist's later *Watermark,* he recommended it "as a fitting companion" to the more popular album.

When *Watermark* was released in Great Britain, the single "Orinoco Flow"—described variously as "a moody tale of traveling down Venezuela's Orinoco River" in *People,* and as "genuinely upbeat" by Tearson—became England's biggest seller during the autumn of 1988. When "Orinoco Flow" found its way to the United States the following year, it received a great deal of airplay on adult contemporary radio stations and thus became popular with American fans as well. As Lucy O'Brien noted in the *New Statesman,* some of the song's success can be credited to "the 'Orinoco Flow' video, a video montage of nature, maritime and wildlife footage sealed with a high speed painted effect." This creative effort was aired frequently on the video cable channel VH-1.

Enya's style on *Watermark* has been favorably analyzed by many critics. One unusual feature of the album is the composer's use of three different languages—English, Latin, and Gaelic. One *Watermark* track, "Cursum Perficio," was labeled by O'Brien as a "hymn-like Latin . . . tribute to Marilyn Monroe." And Mulkerns declared that "the ethnic touches throughout tend to enrich without dominating, as with the Gaelic lyrics on

B orn Eithne (pronounced Enya) Ni Bhraonain c. 1962 in Gweedore, County Donegal, Ireland; daughter of musicians.

Member of folk group Clannad prior to 1982; composed score for film *The Frog Prince*, 1985; performed soundtrack of the BBC series *The Celts;* music has also been featured in the films *Green Card* and *L.A. Story;* solo recording artist, c. 1986—.

Addresses: *Record company*—Geffen (UNI Distribution Corp.), 70 Universal City Plaza, Universal City, CA 91608.

. . . 'Na Laetha Gael M'Oige.'" Though Enya uses English on "Storms in Africa" as well as on "Orinoco Flow," O'Brien noted the engaging use of African hand drums and the "muted percussive threat" of the former cut.

Reviewers seem to agree that *Watermark*'s best effects come from the use of Enya's remarkable voice on many different tracks of particular songs. As Mulkerns reported, Enya's manager and producer Nicky Ryan "overdubbed up to 100 voice tracks to create a chorus of Latin-chanting Enyas" on "Cursum Perficio." Tearson asserted that by overdubbing on songs like "Orinoco Flow," and "The Longships" the artist "creates vast aural sweeps that are at once astonishing and lovely."

One critic who was not so keen on the overdubbing, Tish Hamilton of *Seventeen,* nonetheless praised Enya's singing abilities, rejoicing that in "On Your Shore," her "pure, bell-tone voice is . . . unencumbered by layered production." Tearson concluded that "the ethereal beauty" of Enya's "sounds" raise *Watermark* "way beyond most so-called New Age music. It makes the difference between background and foreground music."

Selected discography

Enya (includes music from "The Celts"), Atlantic, c. 1986.
Watermark (includes "Orinoco Flow," "Cursum Perficio," "The Longships," "On Your Shore," "Na Laetha Gael M'Oige," and "Storms in Africa"), Geffen, 1989.

Sources

Periodicals

Audio, May 1989.
New Statesman, November 18, 1988.
People, March 27, 1989.
Rolling Stone, March 23, 1989.
Seventeen, May 1989.

—Elizabeth Wenning

Eurythmics

Rock duo

One of the most successful pop acts to emerge in the 1980s, the British group Eurythmics combines the strong, often brooding, vocals and lyrics of Annie Lennox with the pop instrumentation and scoring talents of guitarist Dave Stewart. The duo burst onto the music scene in 1983 with their international hit-debut album, *Sweet Dreams (Are Made of This)*. And over the next nine years they released a string of hit recordings that demonstrated their trademark fine line between themes of passion and disdain, optimism and angst, and a music style which eventually nestled itself somewhere between New Wave synthesizer pop and American soul. Eurythmics' compelling, almost at-odds, sound was complemented by their diverse stage and music video personalities, with the dynamic Lennox sporting a chameleon-like array of gender-bending image transformations, and Stewart often off to the side in the role of aloof and absorbed musician. Both the music and image of Eurythmics are reflected in the origins of their name, derived from the Greek term for the art of harmonious body movement, through an

For the Record. . .

Group formed in 1980, in London, England; members include **Annie Lennox** (born December 25, 1954, in Aberdeen, Scotland) and **Dave Stewart** (born c. 1952, in Sunderland, England). Lennox married Radha Rohnfeld, March 14, 1984 (divorced, 1985); married Uri Fruchtman (a filmmaker); one child from second marriage, and a daughter, Lola. Stewart's first wife named Pam; currently married to Siobhan Fahey (a singer). *Education:* Lennox attended the Royal Academy of Music, London, early 1970s.

Lennox and Stewart formed group, The Tourists, 1978. Lennox appeared in film, *Revolution,* 1985.

Awards: Grammy Award nominations for best new artist, 1984, and for best rock performance by a duo or group, 1986.

Addresses: *Record company*—Arista, 6 West 57th St., New York, NY 10019.

expressive and synchronized response to improvised music.

Lennox's and Stewart's musical and personal partnership (they were lovers before Eurythmics) is belied by very different backgrounds. Born in the northern Scottish seaport of Aberdeen, Lennox was the daughter of a boilermaker who played the bagpipes, and grew up an only child in a small two-room tenement house. She played both piano and flute as a girl, and at seventeen was proficient enough to study flute at London's Royal Academy of Music. Lennox became exasperated with the academy, however, and left before graduating. "I'd been taught that there was a perfect phrasing, a perfect sound, a perfect dynamics," she told Freff in *Musician.* "But there is no perfect. The most perfecting this is to express *yourself,* totally, but nobody teaches you that." To offset the academy's rigors, Lennox began composing songs on a reed organ in her London flat and practiced singing. Already fond of the Scottish folk songs of her youth, Lennox discovered singer-songwriter Joni Mitchell and the soul music of Stevie Wonder. Once she listened to Wonder's music under the effects of marijuana. "It was such a revelation to me to listen with very heightened senses to the music; it touched me," she told Barbara Pepe in *Ms.* "It was something that in the future I wanted to aspire to, that depth of subtlety and profound statement through music."

Dave Stewart, on the other hand, was born into a prosperous family in Sunderland, England, the son of an accountant and a bohemian mother who left her husband to become a writer and, eventually married a French Zen Buddhist. Stewart's pre-Eurythmics music career was varied—to say the least. His early interests were medieval ballads and the songs of Bob Dylan, and at the age of fifteen, he stowed away in the van of the folk-rock group Amazing Blondels, travelling with the band for a time. He later worked as a guitarist for an off-shoot of the black African group, Osibisa, and as a composer-arranger for the Sadista Sisters (leaving his first wife to run off with one of the group members). In 1969, he was a guitarist for the group Longdancer, which obtained a contract with Elton John's Rocket Records, only to break up after squandering most of their advance money on drugs. Stewart himself checked out on a year-long affair with LSD and was nearly fatally injured in a car crash in West Germany, surviving a major operation on a collapsed lung. He eventually cleaned up his act, ran a record store for a time, and teamed up with a singer-songwriter named Peet Coombs, who was looking for work in London. By the age of 25, as a *Rolling Stone* contributor writes, "Stewart was a walking jukebox with a past."

From Tourists to Eurythmics

In the mid-1970s, Stewart and Coombs were dining in a London restaurant, where their waitress was Lennox, who was about to chuck her ambitions to be a singer-songwriter for a career as a music teacher. She invited them to her place, and the three struck up an immediate musical kinship; Stewart and Lennox soon after became lovers. The trio formed a group called Catch, which by 1978 came to be called The Tourists, a folk-pop group. The Tourists released three moderately successful albums, and had a British top-five single with their cover of an old Dusty Springfield record, "I Only Want to Be with You." Disputes with their recording label, however, led The Tourists to break up in the 1980s, and Lennox and Stewart likewise dissolved their personal relationship. The two decided to continue working together as musicians, however, and named themselves Eurythmics. Stewart remarked to a *Rolling Stone* interviewer: "We *are* the only couple I know that lived together and then virtually on the week we stop living together we form Eurythmics and become famous as a couple. Usually it is the other way around."

Eurythmics' first album, *In the Garden,* was recorded in a West German studio. Further troubles with record management, however, led Stewart and Lennox to construct their own studio, which they installed in a warehouse attic and eventually moved to a sixteenth-century church in the Crouch End section of London. "The Church," as it was known, became a meeting place for local musicians, and Stewart began experimenting with recording equipment, synthesizers, various instruments, and an array of unlikely musical sounds. Eurythmics' second album, *Sweet Dreams (Are Made of This)*, was entirely recorded and mixed in their private studio, and incorporated such sounds as the roar of a subway train, voices of people in their neighborhood, and musical pitches from water-filled milk bottles. Two singles off the album, "Sweet Dreams (Are Made of This)" and "Love Is a Stranger," became international hits, and Eurythmics were on their way to becoming pop superstars. The title track, bolstered by its video, combined an alternating husky and piercing Lennox vocal and ruminating lyrics, with a catchy New Wave-pop and funk-influenced score by Stewart. The song displayed what would become vintage Eurythmics. As Stewart explained to Stephen Holden in the *New York Times:* "In our music we like to have the sense of two things battling at once. You have to have something that sounds nice on the surface, but underneath there's an ominous side." Lennox concurred, adding that "most really inspired music has a kind of friction about it. There's an element of danger, of roughness and crudeness that goes along with something very melodic."

Launched World Tour

1984 was a busy year for Eurythmics. Their second album, *Touch,* was released and had more hit singles, including "Here Comes the Rain Again," "Right By Your Side," and "Who's That Girl?" On an extensive world tour in early 1984, Lennox developed what would become a recurring problem with nodes on her vocal cords, and had to rest her voice as much as possible. The same year, Lennox startled many when she performed on the 1984 Grammy Awards—Eurythmics were nominated for Best New Artist—and sang "Sweet Dreams" dressed in Elvis Presley garb, complete with sideburns. Coupled with their music videos, in which Lennox sported short-cropped, orange-dyed hair, a haughty demeanor, and mannish clothes, Eurythmics became as famous for their music as for what Holden described as a look of "elegant transvestitism." Lennox explained to *Rolling Stone* that her androgynous look was intended to "detract from what people had come to expect from women singers. . . . Ironically, a different kind of sexuality emerged from that. I wasn't particularly concerned with bending genders. I simply wanted to get away from wearing cutesy-pie miniskirts and tacky cutaway push-ups."

Influenced by Lennox's Scottish "Soul"

Future Eurythmics' albums showed an increasing influence of soul. 1985's *Be Yourself Tonight* included a feminist anthem duet with "queen of soul" Aretha Franklin, entitled "Sisters Are Doin' It for Themselves," while another track, "There Must Be an Angel," featured Stevie Wonder on a harmonica solo. Although many reviewers in the past commented on an iciness in Eurythmics' music, particularly Lennox's vocals, their music on *Be Yourself Tonight* and subsequent albums displays a continual warming up of styles, and a confidence in approach. Regarding 1986's *Revenge*, Jon Young in *Musician* wrote that Eurythmics have an ability "to make records sound good." Stewart "uses studio smarts to construct tracks that are models of streamlined efficiency," while Lennox "takes firm command of a melody from the very first line." Commenting on the 1988 album *Savage*, Ken Richardson wrote in *High Fidelity:* "The tick-tock of technology remains, but Dave Stewart works a lot of human touches into the mix. . . . And Annie Lennox, though still showing off her impeccable vocal technique, gives warmth a chance and, equally welcome, sings bare for a spell."

Lennox's wide-ranging and expressive voice has often been singled out as one of the strong points of the Eurythmics' sound. Describing herself as coming from an "earthy" working-class Scottish family, Lennox commented to *Rolling Stone* on the "soul" of her music. "I suppose it's all to do with people who have some knowledge of poverty—the struggle. . . . I can't say that I really know the black experience, but there's something in knowing about the rich and poor and the differences in class and not being able to get this and that." Reviewers have noted a Scottish strain of melancholia permeating Lennox's lyrics as well, even in her most upbeat moments. Stewart commented in *Rolling Stone* that "certain people have the feeling—it's a kind of angst. And Annie has it. It's the way they approach things. That is soul, and there's a lot of soul in Scottish folk songs. It's very passionate stuff."

Parted But Not Disbanded

Eurythmics' 1990 album, *We Too Are One,* turned out to be their last, at least temporarily, as the following year Lennox and Stewart took a break from working together. "We just need to go away and do something different," she told Mat Snow in *Q.* "We've been through such a lot and never had a break, like a divorced couple that want to be apart, though when we split up as a couple, we knew we still wanted to be in a group.

Wanting to make music was what kept us together. But now we need space if we're not to destroy the goodwill that exists between us." The future of Eurythmics is unclear, and their last album, according to a *Stereo Review* contributor, "doesn't represent any bold new developments." Instead, "it reaffirms the talent and ability of one of rock's most captivating duos."

Selected discography

In the Garden, RCA (United Kingdom), 1982.
Sweet Dreams (Are Made of This) (includes "Sweet Dreams [Are Made of This]" and "Love Is a Stranger"), RCA, 1983.
Touch (includes "Here Comes the Rain Again," "Right by Your Side," and "Who's That Girl"), RCA, 1984.
Be Yourself Tonight (includes "Would I Lie to You?" and "Sisters Are Doin' It for Themselves"), RCA, 1985.
Revenge (includes "Missionary Man"), RCA, 1986.
Savage (includes "I Need a Man"), RCA, 1988.
We Too Are One (includes "Revival" and "Angel"), Arista, 1989.
Greatest Hits, RCA, 1991.

Other

Eurythmics Live (video recording), Polygram, 1987.
(Lennox as contributor) *Red Hot & Blue*, Chrysalis, 1990.
Greatest Hits (video recording), BMG, 1991.

Sources

Books

Contemporary Newsmakers, 1985 cumulative edition, Gale, 1986.
Hill, Dave, *Designing Boys and Material Girls: Manufacturing the '80s Pop Dream,* Blandford Press, 1986.
Stambler, Irwin, *The Encyclopedia of Pop, Rock and Soul,* revised edition, St. Martin's, 1989.
White, Timothy, *Rock Stars*, Stewart, Tabori, and Chang, 1984.

Periodicals

Creem, July 1984; August 1985; September 1985; December 1986.
High Fidelity, May 1988.
Los Angeles Times, August 2, 1986.
Melody Maker, January 29, 1983; July 9, 1983; November 19, 1983; May 4, 1985; November 22, 1986.
Ms., February 1986.
Musician, November 1983; July 1985; November 1985; August 1986.
New Yorker, March 14, 1988.
New York Times, July 17, 1983; February 5, 1984; August 3, 1984; September 3, 1989; November 12, 1989.
People, December 19, 1983; May 20, 1985; November 27, 1989.
Q, May 1991.
Rolling Stone, September 29, 1983; June 20, 1985; October 24, 1985; September 11, 1986.
Stereo Review, January 1990.

—*Michael E. Mueller*

Michael Feinstein

Pianist, singer, archivist

Show music aficionado Michael Feinstein is acclaimed as one of today's brightest young cabaret artists. A popular pianist and singer at cabaret spots across the country, Feinstein, who has also had successful one-man Broadway shows and record albums, specializes in vintage songs of the 1920s, 1930s, and 1940s—works by artists such as George and Ira Gershwin, Cole Porter, Harry Warren, and Irving Berlin. Feinstein sings in a pleasant and clear baritone voice, interspersing his act with entertaining bits of song nostalgia gleaned from his many years as a disciple of old music. A musical "purist," Feinstein is noted for his interpretations of old material, performing both standards and not-so-familiar songs with deference to lyrics, mood, and music. "Some singers get in the way of the song," he told Gerald Clarke in *Time*. "I never want to be more important than what I'm singing. I'm simply the instrument through which that song is sung."

Collected Records, Met Ira Gershwin

As a young boy growing up in Columbus, Ohio, Feinstein preferred the music his parents—both amateur performers—listened to and became an avid collector of old recordings. A self-taught pianist, he heard his first recording of George Gershwin's *Rhapsody in Blue* when he was eleven, and as he told Debra Wise in *Gentleman's Quarterly,* "it created a connection that I'd never felt with music before." Feinstein became an avid Gershwin buff and after moving with his family to California in 1976, had the opportunity to meet Ira Gershwin, his idol's lyricist-brother. The aging Gershwin was immediately impressed with Feinstein's vast knowledge of Gershwin music and hired him as a musical archivist. For the next six years, Feinstein became Gershwin's assistant, cataloging the lyricist's enormous collection of recordings, sheet music, scores, and unpublished manuscripts, and the two forged a close relationship. "He used to call me 'my boy,'" Feinstein told Wise. "He had always wanted children but his wife hadn't, so I really became the son he never had."

Began Performing, Made First Album

Gershwin also encouraged Feinstein in his performing career and introduced him to other songwriters of the period, including Harry Warren, whom Feinstein later worked for as an assistant. Feinstein began performing his beloved old songs at swank Hollywood parties and became a favorite of many celebrities, including Liza Minnelli, who asked him to be her accompanist on an appearance on *The Tonight Show*. Feinstein soon received a seventh-month engagement at West Holly-

Born Michael Jay Feinstein, September 7, 1956, in Columbus, OH; son of Edward (a sales executive for a sausage company) and Florence "Mazie" (Cohen) Feinstein.

Singer and pianist, 1974—. Performed in restaurant bars in Columbus area, 1974-76; personal archivist to lyricist Ira Gershwin, Los Angeles, CA, 1977-83; assistant to composer Harry Warren, Los Angeles, 1979-81; accompanist to performers, including Liza Minnelli, Rosemary Clooney, and Rose Marie, 1980-84; singer and pianist, Le Mondrian Hotel, West Hollywood, CA, 1984-85 and 1987; York Hotel, San Francisco, CA, 1985-87; Algonquin Hotel, New York City, beginning in 1986; Ritz-Carlton Hotel, Washington, DC, 1987. Concert performer.

Has performed numerous concerts, including the Broadway production and tour of *Michael Feinstein in Concert: Isn't It Romantic,* 1988-89, and Broadway production of *Michael Feinstein in Concert: Piano and Voice,* 1990. Has made numerous television appearances and appeared in the film *Scenes from the Class Struggle in Beverly Hills,* Cinecom, 1989. Editor, *Ira Gershwin Songbook.* Contributor to the *Washington Post.*

Addresses: *Home*—Los Angeles, CA. *Office*—c/o Winston Simone Management, 1780 Broadway, Ste. 1201, New York, NY 10019.

wood's Le Mondrian Hotel, followed by an engagement at the Plush Room in San Francisco's York Hotel, and received acclaim as an accomplished interpreter of old material. Music reviewer Gerald Nachman of the *San Francisco Chronicle* wrote that Feinstein was "better than anyone I've heard in years" and noted that he "sings the songs straight, yet with enormous style, charm, energy, understanding—and humor." Feinstein went on to record his first album in 1985, *Pure Gershwin,* which sold over 40,000 copies on the independent label Parnassus Records.

In 1986 Feinstein made his New York City debut at the famed Oak Room of the Algonquin Hotel. *New York Times* critic Stephen Holden called Feinstein "a natural entertainer whose curatorial experience supplies his act with a wealth of show-business lore that he skillfully incorporates as running patter" and noted his "youthful passion that inspirits vintage show tunes . . . with a joyous personal immediacy." Feinstein's appearances drew large crowds at the Oak Room and launched his second recording, *Michael Feinstein Live at the Algonquin,* also on Parnassus, which Clarke described as an

"enchanting" album. Feinstein's popularity grew rapidly, and his admirers included President Ronald Reagan and Nancy Reagan, who invited Feinstein in 1986 for the first of what would be several White House appearances. He made numerous television appearances on music specials and in 1987 had a cameo appearance as a nightclub singer on the television movie *The Two Mrs. Grenvilles.* Also in 1987 he had other sold-out engagements at leading hotels, including the Washington, D.C., Ritz-Carlton, and performed with Minnelli on her fall European concert tour.

Style Emphasizes Music, Charm

In 1988 Feinstein adapted his cabaret act to the Broadway stage, opening at the Lyceum Theatre in a one-man show entitled *Michael Feinstein in Concert,* which showcased songs by the Gershwins, Irving Berlin, and Harry Warren. The first act of Feinstein's show featured a nightclub-type atmosphere, while in the second act he left his piano to explore various aspects of the historic theater as a backdrop to his music. Feinstein expressed to Holden that the most exciting aspect of playing on Broadway was "the fact that many of these songs were written for the musical stage and it puts me closer to them by being able to interpret them in that context." Mimi Kramer praised the show in the *New Yorker:* "That Feinstein's cabaret-style material makes the transition to theatre as gracefully as it does is a tribute to the modesty of his musicianship. . . . Where other crooners attempt to put their own stamp on a popular song, Feinstein lets the song speak for itself, never upstaging a selection or putting himself forward unless it is to heighten a mood or feeling." Kramer added that "Feinstein's knowledge of the genre is exhaustive" and "the program becomes a meeting place to the timeless and the charmingly dated."

Feinstein later embarked on a successful national tour of *Michael Feinstein in Concert,* which ran into 1989. In 1990 he returned to Broadway with a second one-man show, *Michael Feinstein in Concert: Piano and Voice,* which ran for a four-week engagement at the intimate Golden Theatre. Holden, noting that Feinstein's stage presence had improved since his national tour, found his new show especially appealing. Feinstein's "romantic fantasy world of old-time show business becomes an irresistible place to visit," Holden commented, adding that the show, highlighted by Richard Rodgers/Lorenz Hart waltzes and songs by Burton Lane, has "the feeling of a generous—almost devotional—act of love." Holden concluded: "Mr. Feinstein has found a confident, entertaining balance between the three sides of his musical personality. One side is a precocious youth showing off for the grown-ups. Another is his impersonation of a debonair male archetype from old-time Hollywood musicals who flashes glittering smiles while indulging in Liberace-like pianistic flourishes. The third, and most valuable, is an obsessive archivist dedicated to the preservation and perpetuation of a cherished tradition."

Selected discography

Pure Gershwin, Parnassus Records, 1985, Elektra, 1987.
Michael Feinstein: Live at the Algonquin, Parnassus Records, 1986.
Remember: Michael Feinstein Sings Irving Berlin, Elektra, 1987.
Isn't It Romantic?, Elektra, 1988.
Over There: Songs of War and Peace c. 1900-1920, EMI/Angel, 1989.
The M-G-M Album, Elektra, 1989.

Michael Feinstein Sings the Burton Lane Songbook Volume 1, Elektra, 1990.

Sources

Gentleman's Quarterly, November 1988.
New York, April 7, 1986; May 9, 1988; October 19, 1990.
New Yorker, May 9, 1988.
New York Times, January 11, 1986; April 17, 1988.
New York Times Magazine, June 29, 1986.
People, April 14, 1986; May 4, 1987.
San Francisco Chronicle, May 4, 1985.
Stereo Review, December 1988; August 1989.
Time, May 4, 1987.
Vogue, February 1987.
Washington Post, January 26, 1986.

—*Michael E. Mueller*

Arthur Fiedler

Conductor

Arthur Fiedler garnered many distinctions during his fifty consecutive seasons as conductor of the Boston Pops. He helped bring classical music to mass audiences; conversely, he also gave lighter genres such as pop a respectability they would not have had if he had not performed and recorded their works with his orchestra. Fiedler's albums with the Pops have sold over fifty million copies, and his rendition of Danish composer Jacob Gade's "Jalousie" became the first record by a symphony orchestra to sell over a million copies. In addition to being the toast of the city of Boston while he led the Pops, Fiedler and his orchestra toured extensively throughout the United States and the rest of the world. For his musical efforts, the conductor received many tributes, including the United States' highest civilian award, the Medal of Freedom, and France's Legion of Honor. When Fiedler died in 1979, he was eulogized in *Newsweek* by Hubert Saal as "neither elitist nor specialist" and "renowned" for his "resoundingly middlebrow musical taste that embraced high and low with equal respect and zest."

Fiedler was born in Boston on December 17, 1894, to a musical family. His father played violin for the Boston Symphony, and his mother played the piano, though not professionally. So many of his father's ancestors had been violinists in Austria that over the years their surname became Fiedler, the German word for "fiddler." Not surprisingly, Arthur Fiedler's father determined that his son should continue in the family tradition, and provided him with violin lessons in his childhood. Fiedler, however, told Stephen Rubin in the *New York Times* that he did not particularly enjoy either those or the piano lessons he also received. "It was just a chore, something I had to do, like brushing my teeth," he explained. When his family moved to Berlin, Germany in 1910, Fiedler briefly rebelled against his father's plans for him and became an apprentice at a publishing firm there. He quickly tired of the business, however, and returned to his musical efforts.

Supported Hiself on the Violin

While his family was in Europe, Fiedler was fortunate enough to be accepted at Berlin's Royal Academy of Music. Though he concentrated on studying the violin, he also took classes in conducting, which, even then, he liked better. Fiedler used his violin to support himself, however, by playing in small orchestras and in cafes. He continued in this type of musical job when his family returned to the United States to avoid the dangers of World War I. By 1915 he had won a spot as a second violinist in the Boston Symphony Orchestra, hired by then-conductor Karl Muck.

Born December 17, 1894, in Boston, MA; died of cardiac arrest July 10, 1979, in Brookline, MA; son of Emanuel (a violinist) and Johanna (Bernfeld) Fiedler; married Ellen M. Bottomley, January 8, 1942; children: Johanna, Deborah, Peter. *Education:* Attended the Royal Academy of Music in Berlin, Germany.

Worked as an apprentice with a publishing firm in Berlin c. 1910; played violin in various orchestras and cafes in Berlin c. 1914; second violinist with the Boston Symphony Orchestra, 1915-18, viola, piano, organ, and celesta player and percussion player, beginning 1918; conductor of Cecilia Society Chorus and the MacDowell Club Orchestra, 1920s; formed Boston Sinfonietta, 1924; initiated the free outdoor Esplanade concerts in Boston, 1929; conductor of the Boston Pops orchestra, 1930-79. Toured extensively throughout the United States and abroad. Appeared on PBS television in the musical series *Evening at Pops,* beginning c. 1971.

Awards: Medal of Freedom, presented by President Gerald R. Ford, 1977; awarded the French Legion of Honor.

After a brief period in the U.S. Army—from which he was discharged for having flat feet—Fiedler returned to the Boston Symphony in 1918. For some time he played the viola for the orchestra, and also served as a substitute on many other instruments, including the piano, organ, celesta, and, of course, the violin. He longed to conduct, however, and though he remained with the Boston Symphony, he began conducting smaller musical groups such as the MacDowell Club Orchestra and the Cecilia Society Chorus. With some of his fellow Boston Symphony musicians, Fiedler formed the Boston Sinfonietta, a small chamber orchestra that specialized in performing unusual and little-heard classical compositions. As Richard Freed reported in *Stereo Review,* the Sinfonietta was "perhaps the only permanently constituted chamber orchestra in the country in the 1930s"; Freed went on to laud its achievements on disc thus: "The Sinfonietta made the premiere recording of Hindemith's viola concerto *Der Schwanendreher,* with the composer as soloist. With organist E. Power Biggs there were works of Handel, Corelli, and Mozart. There were the big Mozart Divertimento in B-flat Major, K. 287, and the Wind Serenade in C Minor, K. 388, Telemann's *Don Quichotte* suite, and such rarities as the marvelous little *Christmas* Symphony of Gaetano Maria Schiassi and a suite by Esajas Reusner (the latter with the first U.S. recording of the Pachelbel Canon as filler)."

Initiated Free Outdoor Concert

Not content with his many musical activities, Fiedler in 1927 began an effort to gain support for free outdoor concerts. He later told *Newsweek:* "I believed people should have an opportunity to enjoy fine music without always having to dip into their pockets." By 1929 Fiedler had his way, and he conducted selected members of the Boston Symphony in the first of what became known as the Esplanade Concerts, on the banks of Boston's Charles River.

The following year, Fiedler became permanent conductor of the Boston Pops, an orchestra drawn from the Boston Symphony for the purpose of performing lighter classical music. At its helm, Fiedler led the group to heights of popularity that had hitherto escaped it. By the end of his first season as the Pops' conductor, he had achieved great personal fame in and around the Boston area. He began recording with the Pops in 1935, and their popularity began to spread to the rest of the United States—and to the rest of the world.

Embraced the Beatles and Beegees

Throughout his lengthy tenure with the Pops, Fiedler was unafraid of innovation. In addition to serving up renditions of lighter classics such as Strauss waltzes, he would often add to his programs versions of Broadway tunes or popular hits of the day. With the Pops, Fiedler made recordings of the songs of George and Ira Gershwin, and was one of the first "serious" musicians to recognize the worth of the Beatles' efforts, successfully featuring some of their songs—including "She Loves You"—in Pops concerts. Shortly before his death from cardiac arrest on July 10, 1979, Fiedler and the Pops made an album of songs from the disco-celebrating film *Saturday Night Fever,* aptly titled *Saturday Night Fiedler.* Saal quoted Fiedler about his approach to music selection: "I think the snobs are missing something. There's no boundary line in music, I agree with Rossini: 'All music is good except the boring kind.'" Similarly, a *Time* reporter recorded more of the conductor's words: "My aim has been to give audiences a good time. I'd have trained seals if people wanted them."

Though towards the end of his time as leader of the Boston Pops Fiedler's health was poor and he needed the help of assistant conductor Harry Ellis Dickson, he remained active with the group practically up to his death. As *Time* reported: "Toward the end, the proud old man would shuffle unsteadily to the podium. But then, invigorated by the music, he seemed to shed 20 years."

Selected discography

With the Boston Pops

Fiedler's Favorite Overtures (includes "An Outdoor Overture," "Festive Overture," and "Overture di Ballo"), Deutsche Grammophon, 1971.

I Got Rhythm—Fiedler Conducts Gershwin (includes "Girl Crazy," "Suite," "Oh, Kay!" "Funny Face," "Let 'Em Eat Cake," "Of Thee I Sing," "Wintergreen for President," "Three Preludes," and "Second Rhapsody"), London, c. 1979.

Saturday Night Fiedler (includes "Saturday Night Fever Medley" and "Bachamania"), Midsong International, 1979.

Also recorded the albums *Tchaikovsky: The Nutcracker, Offenbach: Gaite Parisienne, Greatest Hits of the '20s,* and *Greatest Hits of the '70s,* in addition to many others.

Sources

Books

Dickson, Harry Ellis, *Arthur Fiedler and the Boston Pops: An Irreverent Memoir,* Houghton, 1981.

Moore, Robin, *Fiedler, the Colorful Mr. Pops: The Man and His Music,* DaCapo Press, 1980.

Periodicals

High Fidelity, February 1988.
Ladies' Home Journal, November 1977.
Newsweek, July 12, 1948; July 23, 1979.
New York Times, April 2, 1972.
Saturday Evening Post, September 1976.
Stereo Review, November 1979.
Time, July 23, 1979.

—*Elizabeth Wenning*

Judy Garland

Singer, actress

For more than three decades singer-actress Judy Garland claimed the hearts of audiences worldwide. She was the leading star of Hollywood musicals during their heyday in the late thirties and forties, playing wholesome, small-town girls loaded with big-time musical talent. Her rich, powerful voice and dynamic delivery celebrated mainstream American pop at a time when musicals still reflected either the eccentricities of vaudeville, or the conventions of opera and legitimate theater; she made American pop music acceptable, leading it to swing and later, to the mellow harmonies that dominated after World War II. When her movie career waned in the 1950s, Garland became a premier concert performer, renowned for her rapport with an audience. The love of music and desire to please so evident in her screen portrayals became almost palpable on stage, and she inspired a devotion at home and abroad that occasionally assumed the dimensions of a cult.

Garland's failed marriages, her suicide attempts, and her battles with her weight, alcohol, and pills only enhanced her vulnerability and appeal; *The Best of the Music Makers* cited performer Jerry Lewis as commenting that Garland "communicates for the audience. All the things people can't say for themselves. All the stout women identify with her, the losers in love identify . . . the insomniacs, the alcoholics and pill takers." Writing in the *New Yorker,* Ethan Mordden observed that Garland's "extraordinary singing style [was] so individual yet so uneccentric," allowing her to perform cabaret jazz, show tunes, or love ballads with equal mastery. "She made each song hers without taking anything away from the song," he decided. "Garland is . . . strangely familiar, permanently contemporary."

Garland was born Frances Gumm, the third daughter of vaudeville actors. At the age of two she toddled on to the stage of the Minnesota theater her father owned to sing "Jingle Bells," and was so taken with performing that she had to be forcibly removed. Following relocation to Los Angeles, Frances and her sisters formed a singing-dancing trio, The Gumm Sisters, with their mother accompanying them on the piano. The girls became the principal support of their family as their father's health declined, performing in vaudeville theaters around the country. After being mistakenly billed as "The Glumm Sisters" at one stop, they changed their name to "The Three Garlands" (and Frances became Judy); the youngest Garland emerged as the star of the act—"the little girl with the great big voice." When a Metro-Goldwyn-Mayer (MGM) agent heard Judy sing he signed her to a seven-year contract on the spot, recognizing in the untrained thirteen-year-old a wealth of natural talent.

For the Record...

Born Frances Ethel Gumm, June 10, 1922, in Grand Rapids, MN; died January 22, 1969, in London, England; daughter of Frank Avent (a vaudeville performer and movie theater owner) and Ethel Marian (a vaudeville performer and act manager; maiden name, Milne) Gumm; married David Rose (a composer), July 8, 1941 (divorced c. 1942); married Vincent Minelli (a film director), June 15, 1945 (divorced, 1951); married M. S. (Sid) Luft (a film producer), June, 1952 (divorced, 1963); married fifth husband, Mickey Deans; children: (second marriage) Liza Minelli; (third marriage) Lorna Luft, Joseph Luft. *Education:* Attended Lawler's Professional School in Los Angeles, CA, and Metro-Goldwyn-Mayer (MGM) studio school.

Made singing debut at father's Grand Rapids, MN, theater, 1925; family moved to Los Angeles, 1927; toured U.S. as member of singing-dancing act The Gumm Sisters (later became The Three Garlands), 1927-35; film performer, 1935-63, beginning with MGM, 1935-50; radio performer, beginning in 1936; recording artist, beginning in late 1930s; international concert performer, 1951-69; television performer, beginning in mid-1950s, including weekly television series *The Judy Garland Show*, 1963-64.

Motion picture performances include *Every Sunday Afternoon*, 1935, *Broadway Melody*, 1938, *Love Finds Andy Hardy*, 1938, *The Wizard of Oz*, 1939, *For Me and My Gal*, 1942, *Meet Me in St. Louis*, 1944, *Ziegfeld Follies*, 1944, *The Harvey Girls*, 1946, *Easter Parade*, 1948, *A Star Is Born*, 1954, and *I Could Go on Singing*, 1963.

Awards: Special Academy Award, 1940, for *The Wizard of Oz*.

Launched Career Over the Rainbow

By her fourth film for MGM Garland had emerged as a juvenile singing star, drawing notice with her memorable rendition of "Dear Mr. Gable" in the 1938 *Broadway Melody*. The following year she landed the plum role of Dorothy in the musical fantasy *The Wizard of Oz*—through which she became a virtual American pop-culture icon—singing "Over the Rainbow," her remarkable performance earning her a special Academy Award. For the next decade she made more than twenty films, including the "Andy Hardy" and "Babes" series with Mickey Rooney and musical classics like *Meet Me in St. Louis, The Harvey Girls,* and *Easter Parade,* also introducing such popular standards as "The Trolley Song" and "The Atchison, Topeka and the Sante Fe." Her

fresh appeal and musical energy made her an audience favorite, belying the troubling tenor of her life offscreen. In a studio system that perceived her as property, Garland was always told what to do, who to see, and how to look; from the beginning she was fed amphetamines to combat her natural chubbiness and barbiturates to bring rest. Hooked on pills and alcohol, exhausted by her unrelenting work schedule, and tormented by insecurity and fears, Garland began to crack by the late 1940s.

New Beginning As Concert Performer

In 1948 Garland delayed the production schedules of several films, showing up late, unprepared, and unwilling; she eventually suffered a nervous breakdown. By 1950, MGM had released her two years early from her $5,000-a-week contract—the dismissal prompting one of the star's numerous suicide attempts. Still, by the next year, Garland was staging a comeback in a different venue (the first of many such comebacks during her late career), and her four-week live engagement at the London Palladium proved an enormous success. Her subsequent show at the Palace Theater in New York City broke box-office records, and she came to realize that performing in concert was what she liked best— "To retire the [onscreen] character that never was," suggested Mordden, "and simply to make the music." From her Hollywood days, working with some of the best composers and arrangers, Garland came away with keen musical judgment and a repertory full of popular favorites; she learned "the architecture of a song," according to Mordden, "the weight, the build, the climax, the embellishments." This mastery of performance, along with her musical gifts, made Garland America's most popular female singer during the 1950s and 1960s.

Emotional Ties With Audience

Garland returned to the screen occasionally, most notably in the 1954 motion picture *A Star Is Born.* Unlike her earlier films, this movie suggested that show business stardom is not without price; Mordden noted that songs like "The Man That Got Away" and "It's a World" "sound different from the tunes Garland sang for L. B. Mayer—less golden and content." *People* critic Ralph Novak similarly observed that a "penetrating sense of tragedy and world-weariness began taking over Garland's voice" as her personal life deteriorated; her flawless diction became slurred at times, and her moving signature vibrato occasionally wavered out of control. Suffering from chronic hepatitis (due, in part, to her substance abuse) and failing with a weekly television series, Garland began to decline steadily after 1963. Her final concerts were fraught with drama and uncertainty: would she show? fall onstage? remember lyrics? retreat in terror? The suspense only reinforced the emotional ties she forged with her audiences; the entertainer once admitted that emotion *was* her business. "Garland's life demolishes that essential show-biz myth of her era—that to go out there a youngster and come back a star is heaven on earth," concluded Mordden. "The legend is sorrow, but the music remains vital. . . . She left behind . . . her extraordinary ability to communicate through a song."

Selected discography

Garland's first recordings, in the late l930s, were single releases for Decca records. She began recording albums in the mid-l940s for such labels as MGM and RCA Victor, and later, for Columbia and Capitol. The many reissues and compilations of her recordings include:

Live at the London Palladium, MFSL, 1982.
From the Decca Vaults, MCA, 1985.
(With Victor Young) *The Wizard of Oz/Pinocchio,* MCA.
The Best of Judy Garland from MGM Classic Films (1938-1950), MCA, 1988.
The Best of Judy Garland, MCA.
Judy Garland Collector's Items (1936-45), MCA.
The Hits of Judy Garland, Capitol.
Judy, Capitol, 1989.

Judy at Carnegie Hall, Capitol.
Judy! That's Entertainment, Capitol.
Judy Garland Live, Capitol, 1989.
Alone, Capitol, 1989.
Miss Show Business, Capitol, 1989.
Palace Two-a-Day: Judy Live at the Palace, February 1952, CITM.
Judy Garland, Volume 1: *Born in a Trunk, 1935-40,* Volume 2: *1940-45,* Volume 3: *Superstar, 1945-50,* AEI.
The Best of the Decca Years, Volume 1, MCA, 1990.

Sources

Books

Coleman, Emily R., *The Complete Judy Garland: The Ultimate Guide to Her Career in Films, Records, Concerts, Radio and Television, 1935-1969,* Harper, 1990.
The New Grove Dictionary of American Music, Macmillan, 1986.
Simon, George T., and others, *The Best of the Music Makers,* Doubleday, 1979.

Periodicals

New Yorker, October 22, 1990.
People, March 11, 1985.
Stereo Review, August, 1982.

—Nancy Pear

Dizzy Gillespie

Trumpeter, composer, bandleader

In 1989, the year he became 72 years of age, Dizzy Gillespie received a Lifetime Achievement Award at the National Association of Recording Arts and Sciences' Grammy Award ceremonies. The honor—one of many bestowed on the trumpet virtuoso—recognized nearly 50 years of pioneering jazz performances. That same year he received the National Medal of Arts from President George Bush "for his trail-blazing work as a musician who helped elevate jazz to an art form of the first rank, and for sharing his gift with listeners around the world."

Not letting age slow him down, Gillespie in 1989 gave 300 performances in 27 countries, appeared in 100 U.S. cities in 31 states and the District of Columbia, headlined three television specials, performed with two symphonies, and recorded four albums. He was also crowned a traditional chief in Nigeria, received the Commandre d'Ordre des Artes et Lettres—France's most prestigious cultural award—was named regent professor by the University of California, and received his fourteenth honorary doctoral degree, this one from the Berklee College of Music. The next year, at the Kennedy Center for the Performing Arts ceremonies celebrating the centennial of American jazz, Gillespie received the American Society of Composers, Authors, and Publishers' Duke Award for 50 years of achievement as a composer, performer, and bandleader. Fifty years after helping found a new style of progressive jazz that came to be known as bebop, Dizzy Gillespie is still contributing all he can to the development of modern jazz. His band is a virtual training ground for younger musicians. In 1990 he led and wrote the arrangements for a group that included bassist John Lee, guitarist Ed Cherry, drummer Ignacio Berroa, conga drummer Paul Hawkins, and saxophonist Ron Holloway. More than 40 years earlier Gillespie was the first bandleader to use a conga player. Employing Latin rhythms and forging an Afro-Cuban style of polyrhythmic music was one of Gillespie's many contributions to the development of modern jazz.

Influenced by Roy Eldridge and Louis Armstrong

As a trumpet virtuoso Gillespie stands firmly as a major influence in the development of the jazz trumpet. Before Gillespie there was New Orleans musician Buddy Bolden—the earliest known jazz cornetist—who was followed by King Oliver, Louis Armstrong, and Roy Eldridge. In his memoir, *To Be Or Not To Bop,* Gillespie described the influence of Armstrong and Eldridge on his trumpet playing: "Roy Eldridge was a French-style trumpet player. Eldridge was in a direct line from Louis Armstrong, and he was the voice of that era, the thirties. I hardly ever listened to Louis, but was always aware of

Born John Birks Gillespie, October 21, 1917; son of James (a bricklayer and musician) and Lottie Gillespie; youngest of nine children; raised in Cheraw, SC; married Lorraine Willis (a dancer), 1940. *Education:* Attended Laurinburg Institute.

Moved to New York City in 1937 and began playing trumpet in jam sessions with various musicians; played with the Teddy Hill Orchestra, beginning in 1937, and the Cab Calloway Orchestra, 1939-41; made first recording in 1939 with Lionel Hampton; joined Earl "Fatha" Hines band, 1942; with Sarah Vaughan, Charlie Parker, and others, formed new group headed by Billy Eckstein, 1943; also played for other bands, including the Duke Ellington Orchestra, c. 1943; formed quintet, 1944; has played in, led, and composed for numerous big bands, orchestras, and small groups throughout the world.

Awards: New Star Award from *Esquire* magazine, 1944; Lifetime Achievement Award from the National Association of Recording Arts and Sciences, 1989; National Medal of Arts from President George Bush, 1989; Commadre d'Ordre des Artes et Lettres (France), 1989; Duke Award from the American Society of Composers, Authors, and Publishers, 1989; and numerous other awards and honors, including several honorary degrees.

Addresses: *Home*—Camden, NJ.

where Roy's inspiration came from. So I was looking at Louis Armstrong, you see, because they are one and the same. My inspiration came through Roy Eldridge, from Louis Armstrong and King Oliver and Buddy Bolden. That's the way it happened." Gillespie played with bands in Philadelphia from 1935 to 1937 before moving to New York. In Philadelphia, where his family had moved from Cheraw, South Carolina, Gillespie learned Eldridge's trumpet solos from fellow trumpeter Charlie Shavers. It was then that Gillespie earned his nickname for his erratic and mischievous behavior. When Gillespie was in the Frankie Fairfax band in Philadelphia he carried his new trumpet in a paper bag; that inspired fellow musicians like Bill Doggett to call him "Dizzy." While Gillespie himself acknowledges the paper bag incident, he says the nickname didn't stick until later.

Gillespie's basic style of solo trumpet playing at that time involved "running them changes"—improvising on chord changes in a song and introducing new chord changes based on the song's melody. He had taught himself piano and used the instrument to experiment with new melodies and chord changes. When he went to New York in 1937 he did not have a specific job, but was introduced to other musicians by Shavers. Gillespie joined in jam sessions, sometimes after hours at clubs in Harlem like Monroe's Uptown House and Dicky Wells's. He would also sit in with bands; while jamming one night with Chick Webb's band at the Savoy Ballroom, Gillespie met Mario Bauza, a Cuban trumpeter who introduced him to Latin rhythms.

Already a Musical Force at 19

Within a year Gillespie was hired by the Teddy Hill Orchestra for a European tour when the regular trumpet player didn't want to go. Hill probably liked Gillespie's style, which was similar at that time to Roy Eldridge's; Eldridge had left Hill's band to join Fletcher Henderson. By 1937—when he was only 19—Gillespie had already made a name for himself among New York musicians, who couldn't help but notice his radically fresh take on solo trumpet playing: he utilized the upper register of notes above high C, played with great speed, and used new rhythms and chord changes. Gillespie made his first recordings with the Teddy Hill Orchestra just prior to leaving on a European tour with a revue that featured talent from Harlem's famed Cotton Club.

Gillespie joined the Cab Calloway Orchestra in 1939 and stayed until 1941. Gillespie wrote in his memoir, "It was the best job that you could possibly have, high class." Calloway played the Cotton Club and toured extensively. During this period Gillespie continued to play all-night jam sessions at Minton's and Monroe's Uptown House to develop his musical knowledge and style. In 1939 the most in-demand trumpet players for recording dates in New York were Eldridge, Shavers, and Buck Clayton. Gillespie was fourth on the list, but somehow managed to land a recording date with Lionel Hampton, which resulted in the famed "Hot Mallets" session. In this session Gillespie became the first musician to record in the modern jazz style with a small group. Lionel Hampton said of the session, as quoted in Gillespie's book, "[Gillespie] came out with a new style, came out with a bebop style. He came out with a different style than we'd ever heard before. A lot of people don't know that was the creation of bebop, the beginning of bebop." Of course, it wasn't called bebop just yet.

Gillespie left Calloway in 1941 following a misunderstanding. During a performance someone from the vicinity of the trumpet section was having fun aiming spitballs at the bandleader, who was singing in front of the band at the time. Naturally Calloway assumed Gillespie was responsible. By most accounts, however,

Gillespie was completely innocent and had been set up. Words led to action; Gillespie pulled a knife on Calloway and actually cut him a few times. While the two later reconciled and remained friends, Gillespie was forced to leave the band. This well-known incident illustrates the flip side of Gillespie's jovial personality; he often found himself in situations where he might need to defend himself, and was fully prepared to do so.

Inspired, and Inspired by, Charlie Parker

Gillespie joined the Earl "Fatha" Hines band in 1942, about the same time Charlie Parker did. Although Parker became famous as an alto saxophonist, he was playing tenor sax at that time. Gillespie first met Parker in Kansas City in 1940 when he was on tour with Cab Calloway. The two of them jammed together at the Booker T. Washington Hotel for several hours. Gillespie ventured in *To Be or Not to Bebop,* "I guess Charlie Parker and I had a meeting of the minds, because both of us inspired each other." They spent a lot of time together during their stint with the Hines band.

By the time he joined Hines, Gillespie had composed "A Night in Tunisia," one of his most famous songs. He was also writing arrangements for other bandleaders, including Hill, Calloway, Jimmy Dorsey, and Woody Herman. He wrote bebop arrangements, as most bandleaders at that time were interested in having one or two bebop numbers in their repertoires. Several musicians have commented that even if Gillespie had not been able to play the trumpet, he could have made a name for himself on the basis of his original compositions and arrangements. Other jazz standards credited in whole or in part to Gillespie include "Groovin' High," "Manteca," "Woody 'n You," "Con Alma," and "Salt Peanuts."

Bebop Born on 52nd Street

A large part of the Earl Hines band departed in 1943 to form a new group headed by Billy Eckstine. Former Hines members who joined Eckstine included Sarah Vaughan, Gillespie, Parker, and others. The band also featured saxophonists Gene Ammons and Dexter Gordon. Gillespie became musical director for Eckstine, whose backers got him a job on 52nd Street. Gillespie stayed with Eckstine for about seven months, touring and playing on 52nd Street. "The Street," as it was described by critic Pete Migdol in Gillespie's memoir, "was the hippest block with regard to its short distance and that amount of music. . . . This was the top talent street, and it was, of course, discoverer of a lot of the new people for that era."

After leaving Eckstine, Gillespie substituted in the Duke Ellington Orchestra for about four weeks, then formed his own group to play at the newly opened Onyx Club on 52nd Street. Gillespie had been playing bebop whenever he could since 1940, the year he married Lorraine Willis. Now he was able to play it full time. 52nd Street became the proving ground for a new jazz style that had previously been played primarily at late night jam sessions.

"The opening of the Onyx Club represented the birth of the bebop era," Gillespie recalled in his book. "In our long sojourn on 52nd Street we spread our message to a much wider audience." His first quintet at the Onyx Club in 1944 included Oscar Pettiford on bass, Max

> *The most important thing about our music was, of course, the style, how you got from one note to another, how it was played. . . . We had a special way of phrasing. Not only did we change harmonic structure, but we also changed rhythmic structure.*

Roach on drums, George Wallington on piano, and Don Byas on tenor sax. Gillespie had tried to get Parker to join, but he had temporarily returned to Kansas City.

Quintet Revolutionized Jazz

That year Gillespie received the New Star Award from *Esquire* magazine, the first of many awards he would receive in his career. Describing the new style his quintet played, Gillespie wrote, "We'd take the chord structures of various standard and pop tunes and create new chords, melodies, and songs from them." For example, Tadd Dameron's composition "Hothouse" was based on "What Is This Thing Called Love," and Parker's "Ornithology" came out of "How High the Moon." Gillespie also noted, "Our music had developed more into a type of music for listeners." There would be little dancing to bebop. Rhythm and phrasing, however, were also important to the new jazz style. "The most important thing about our music was, of course, the style, how you got from one note to another, how it was played. . . . We had a special way of phrasing. Not only did we change harmonic structure, but we also changed rhythmic structure."

Gillespie's quintet also played other clubs, including the Downbeat and the Three Deuces, where the group included Charlie Parker—by then on alto sax—and Bud Powell on piano. Gillespie also played for two months in Hollywood with Parker, vibraphonist Milt Jackson, bassist Ray Brown, pianist Al Haig, and drummer Stan Levy. This was the West Coast debut of bebop and it was very well received. In fact, it was around this time that the term "bebop" came into use. Gillespie recalled, "People, when they'd wanna ask for one of those numbers and didn't know the name, would ask for bebop. And the press picked it up and started calling it bebop. The first time the term bebop appeared in print was while we played at the Onyx Club."

1953 Triumph in Toronto

Gillespie's quintet and the presentation of modern jazz in that format reached its apex in 1953—with a concert at Massey Hall in Toronto that featured Gillespie, Parker, Powell, Roach, and legendary jazz bassist Charles Mingus. As Roach recalled in Gillespie's memoir, "The five people that Dizzy had originally thought about in the group at the Onyx didn't really materialize until we did Jazz at Massey Hall, that album, in 1953." Billed by jazz critics as "the greatest jazz concert ever," it was recorded by Mingus—a last-minute substitute for Pettiford—and later released on Debut Records. From the big bands and orchestras that he first organized in the late 1940s, to the small combos of the early 1950s that served as incubators for young musicians like saxophone giant John Coltrane, Gillespie's influence consistently defined modern jazz. Though the enterprise was short-lived, Gillespie had his own record label, Dee Gee Records, from 1951-53. He appeared at the historic first Newport Jazz Festival in 1954. And he later played the role of unofficial ambassador of jazz, beginning with a 1956 world tour sponsored by the U.S. State Department. These are just a few of the many accomplishments highlighting the career of this remarkably accomplished titan of contemporary American music.

Selected writings

(With Al Fraser) *To Be or Not To Bop: Memoirs of Dizzy Gillespie*, Doubleday, 1979.

Selected discography

(With the Quintet) *Jazz at Massey Hall*, Fantasy/Debut, 1953.

Dizzier and Dizzier, RCA, 1954.
Groovin' High, Savoy, 1955.
The Champ, Savoy, 1956.
The Dizzy Gillespie Story, Savoy, 1957.
Concert in Paris, Roost, 1957.
Jazz from Paris, Verve, 1957. *Dizzy in Greece*, Verve, 1957.
The Trumpet Kings, Verve, 1957.
For Musicians Only, Verve, 1958.
Manteca, Verve, 1958.
Birk's Works, Verve, 1958.
Dizzy Gillespie at Newport, Verve, 1958.
Dizzy Gillespie Duets, Verve, 1958.
Have Trumpet Will Excite, Verve, 1959.
The Ebullient Dizzy Gillespie, Verve, 1959.
The Greatest Trumpet of Them All, Verve, 1960.
Gillespiana, Verve, 1961.
An Electrifying Evening, Verve, 1962.
Carnegie Hall Concert, Verve, 1962.
Dizzy on the French Riviera, Philips, 1962.
New Wave, Philips, 1963.
Something Old, Something New, Philips, 1963.
Cool World, Philips, 1964.
The Essential Dizzy Gillespie, Verve, 1964.
Jambo Caribe, Limelight, 1964.
The New Continent, Limelight, 1965.
Montreux '77, Pablo, 1977.
Dee Gee Days, Savoy, 1985.
New Faces, GRP, 1985.
Oo Pop A Da, Affinity, 1985.
Dizzy Gillespie and His Sextets, Musicraft, 1986.
Dizzy Gillespie and His Orchestra, Musicraft, 1986.
Dizziest, RCA Bluebird, 1987.
Enduring Magic, Black Hawk, 1987.
Dizzy Gillespie and His Orchestra, Giants of Jazz, 1988.
Small Combos, Giants of Jazz, 1988.
(With Max Roach) *Max and Dizzy: Paris 1989*, A&M, 1990.

Sources

Books

Feather, Leonard, *The Encyclopedia of Jazz in the Sixties*, Horizon, 1966.
Feather, *The Encyclopedia of Jazz in the Seventies*, Horizon, 1976.
Horricks, Raymond, *Dizzy Gillespie and the Bebop Revolution*, Hippocrene, 1984.
Koster, Piet, and Chris Sellers, *Dizzy Gillespie, Volume 1: 1937-1953*, Micrography, 1986.
McRae, Barry, *Dizzy Gillespie*, Universe Books, 1988.
The New Grove Dictionary of Jazz, Macmillan, 1988.

Periodicals

Down Beat, December 1985; January 1986; September 1989; August 1990.

IAJRC Journal, Winter 1991.

Maclean's, March 20, 1989.

New Yorker, September 17, 1990.

—*David Bianco*

Josef Gingold

Violinist

"**I** consider Josef Gingold the greatest violin teacher I have ever known," cellist Janos Starker divulged to David Blum in *The New Yorker*. "His background is almost unparalleled; he has done practically everything that a string player can do in music—even played in Broadway shows. He's the only teacher I know who is equally qualified to teach the instrument, solo repertoire, orchestral repertoire, and chamber music. He also happens to be one of the most genuine human beings I've ever met." The eminent and beloved professor Gingold bears a legacy of tonal beauty to his students that *Musical America* cites "among the last links with the violin tradition of the late nineteenth century."

Gingold, who has received seven honorary doctorates and the celebrated American String Association's Teacher of the Year Award, has routinely ignored his official yearly teaching load of eighteen students, choosing instead to instruct as many as forty pupils and give weekly master classes. Teaching at all levels rather than just the advanced, Josef Gingold confessed to Blum, "To use the beautiful Hebrew word, it's a *mitzvah*—a blessed service—to be a teacher."

War Interrupted Music Lessons

Gingold was born October 28, 1909, in Brest Litovsk, Russia, the last child of the second marriage for both his parents, Anna (Leiserowitz) and Meyer Gingold. When Josef was three years old, his father gave him his first violin. Gingold smashed the instrument looking for the little man inside whom his father had told him played the music. Two years later, after Gingold had become accomplished on the violin, the five-year-old was about to leave home to study at a conservatory in Warsaw, Poland when World War I interrupted his family's plan. After the German invasion of Russian border towns, the Gingold family was forced to spend months in refugee camps. At one of the sites, Josef asked a soldier if he could play his violin. That night he was taken from his terrified mother by German soldiers who insisted he play at a party they were giving. Afterward, he was returned to his mother by the soldiers with pay—several bags of food.

Family Fled Homeland

To escape the widespread anti-Semitism of their homeland after the war, the Gingold family broke up. One son went to Israel while a daughter stayed in Paris. In 1920 the Gingolds followed another son to New York, with eleven-year-old Josef and his other two sisters. Money was tight at their home on the lower East Side of

For the Record. . .

Born October 28, 1909, in Brest-Litovsk, Russia (now Brest, Belorussian S.S.R., U.S.S.R.); immigrated to United States, 1920; son of Meyer (a shoe factory owner and insurance salesman) and Anna (Leiserowitz) Gingold; married Gladys Anderson (a violinist and pianist), October 14, 1934 (deceased, 1978); children: George. *Education:* Studied with Melzar Chaffee, Vladimir Graffman, 1922-1927, and Eugene Ysaye, 1927-1930.

Violinist, artist, and teacher. Toured northern Europe, 1927-1930; first violinist in the NBC orchestra, 1937-1943; member of the Primrose String Quartet, 1939-1942; member of the NBC String Quartet, 1941-1943; concertmaster, Detroit Symphony, 1943-1946; concertmaster and soloist, Cleveland Symphony, 1947-1960. Teacher, Case Western Reserve University, 1950-1960; professor of chamber music, Meadowmount School of Music, 1955-1981; faculty, Indiana University 1960—, distinguished professor of music, 1965—; teacher at various institutions, including Paris Conservatory, 1970-1981, Toho School, Tokyo, 1970, Copenhagen, 1979, and Montreal, 1980. Mischa Elman Chair, Manhattan School of Music, New York City, 1980-1981. U.S. representative on numerous International Competition juries.

Awards: Honorary degrees from Indiana University, Kent State University, Baldwin-Wallace College, Cleveland Institute of Music, and New England Conservatory of Music; named the American String Association's Teacher of the Year, 1968.

Addresses: Home—Bloomington, IN. *Office*—Department of Music, Indiana University, Bloomington, IN 47401.

New York; however, Josef continued his violin instruction under Melzar Chaffee at the Music School Settlement. Chaffee, who recognized Gingold needed exceptional guidance, recommended him to Vladimir Graffman, assistant of the renowned Leopold Auer. Although Josef had no prior formal music education before he met Graffman, he played his new exercises with an intuitive, flawless, left-hand position. Eventually, Graffman introduced Gingold to Heiffetz, regarded as the greatest violinist of the century, who was impressed with his youthful talent. As an adolescent, Gingold sought performances wherever he could, listening to Heiffetz, Casals, Szigeti, Hubermann, and Thibaud. Once, he stood outside Carnegie Hall, rushing in to hear Fritz Kreisler's encore when he had no money for a ticket. Through family friends, Graffman helped Gingold study in Belgium with Eugene Ysaye. When asked if Ysaye would accept Gingold, Ysaye replied, according to Blum, "But naturally. He is a born violinist." In 1928, at the age of eighteen, Gingold gave his first public performance in Brussels. He concertized northern Europe for the next three years.

In the next years, Gingold held various jobs, including working as a member of a walking fiddle corporation, playing a stint at the Ritz-Carlton Hotel, and performing at the Chicago World's Fair. His first steady job was as an assistant concertmaster for a Jerome Kern production on Broadway in October of 1931. He continued as a concertmaster for Kern on two more shows, and then one by Cole Porter. In 1937 he auditioned for the newly-formed NBC orchestra under Toscanini, where he reigned as first violinist from 1937 to 1943. Simultaneously, Gingold's reputation grew with his membership in two outstanding chamber groups, the Primrose Quartet and the NBC String Quartet. In 1944 he left Toscanini to become concertmaster of the Detroit Symphony under Karl Krueger. By 1947 he had caught the eye of George Szell, a major European conductor who came to the U.S. in 1939. Gingold became concertmaster under Szell with the Cleveland Orchestra and together, from 1947 to 1959, they built the group into "one of the most polished ensembles in the country," according to *Great Masters of the Violin*. The *New Yorker* declared that the pairing made Cleveland "one of the great orchestras of the world."

Teaching Reputation Soared

During the Cleveland years Gingold's reputation as an instructor grew. He taught at Case Western Reserve University, the Cleveland Music School Settlement, and served as the head of chamber music under Ivan Galamian at Meadowmount. He counted thirteen-year-old Itzhak Perlman, fourteen-year-old Pinchas Zukerman, and twelve-year-old Jaime Laredo among his students, but did not attempt teaching full-time until he became professor of violin at Indiana University in 1960. Contributing to the university's sterling reputation, Gingold has instructed prestigious, prize-winning soloists and concertmasters of eight major orchestras, including Miriam Fried, Nai Yuan Hu, Joshua Bell, Ulf Hoelscher, Dylana Jenson, Leonidas Kavakos, and William Preucil. He has taught master classes in Paris, Tokyo, Copenhagen, and Montreal, and held the eminent Mischa Elman Chair at the Manhattan School of Music. He has also served as the representative of the United States at international juried competitions, including the Queen Elisabeth in Brussels, the Wieniawski in Poland, and the Tchaikovsky in Moscow. Gingold was also a founder, first chairman and president of the jury of the International Violin Competition of Indianapolis in 1982.

Gingold was married to violinist and pianist Gladys Anderson on October 14, 1934. Since her death in 1978, Gingold has donated all his private teaching fees to a scholarship for gifted violin students set up in his wife's memory. Though having already celebrated his eightieth birthday at a gala concert given by his former students, Gingold continues to work in his teaching studio. Assessing the artist-teacher Josef Gingold, Pinchas Zuckerman declared to Blum, "I can honestly say he is the kind of man who comes along once in a century."

Selected discography

Josef Gingold at 75, 1975.
Faure: Violin Sonata in A, 1989.
Kreisler: Shorter Works and Transcriptions, 1989.

Duos: For Violin and Cello, 1990.

Sources

Books

Applebaum, Samuel and Sada Applebaum, *The Way They Play*, Paganiniana, 1972.
Schwarz, Boris, *Great Masters of the Violin*, Simon & Schuster, 1983.

Periodicals

American Record Guide, September-October 1989.
High Fidelity/Musical America, March 1985.
New Yorker, February 4, 1991.

—Marjorie Burgess

Berry Gordy, Jr.

Recording industry executive, entrepreneur

On the night of January 20, 1988, Berry Gordy, Jr., was inducted into the Rock and Roll Hall of Fame. His peers that evening were the Supremes, Bob Dylan, the Beatles, the Beach Boys, the Drifters, folk singer Woody Guthrie, blues and folk singer Leadbelly, and jazz guitarist Les Paul. Gordy was honored in the non-performing category for founding and developing Motown Industries. He originally formed the company in 1959 as the Motown Record Corporation. During the 1960s and early 1970s it grew from a Detroit-based record label specializing in rhythm and blues hits to a full-fledged entertainment corporation based in Los Angeles, active in television and motion pictures as well as records. In 1973 the magazine *Black Enterprise* recognized Motown Industries as the number one black owned or managed business. In 1988 Gordy sold Motown Records to entertainment giant MCA Inc. for $61 million. The sale did not include Motown's publishing division (Jobete Music Co. and Stone Mountain Music), nor its film and television divisions. Gordy would continue to run these operations as the Gordy Company.

Although Berry Gordy, Jr., the seventh of eight children of Berry, Sr., and Bertha Gordy, began the Motown Record Corporation in 1959, the entire Gordy family was called on to make their own special contributions. Indeed, Gordy did his best to foster a family feeling at Motown in the early days. Many of the performers were in their teens or early twenties; Gordy himself was barely 30. As performers were signed to the company they became new members of the "Motown family," and as in most families, there were incidents of conflict along the way. Gordy was forced to make some unpopular decisions, but throughout the years he kept the enterprise together and firmly on course, soon coming to be known as "Mr. Chairman."

Motown a Family Effort

Despite the fact that none of the Gordys made their names as entertainers, the family was very much a musical one. Its musicality made itself known not in performance, but in the continuing enterprise that has provided the world with numerous performers and countless popular songs. The following excerpt from a speech by the Honorable John Conyers, Jr., of Michigan, to the U.S. House of Representatives on April 19, 1971, ably reflects the familial nature of the Motown enterprise, as well as Gordy's sense of social responsibility.

"Mr. Speaker, 10 years ago a Detroit assemblyline worker, who had formerly been a prizefighter, saved $800 and started his own business. Like so many before him, he had ideas of what he could do and

For the Record. . .

Born November 28, 1929, in Detroit, MI; son of Berry, Sr. (owner of a plastering and carpentry service, a general store, and a printing business), and Bertha Gordy; married Thelma Coleman, 1953 (divorced, 1959); married Raynoma Liles (divorced, 1962); children: (first marriage) Hazel Joy, Berry IV, Terry; (second marriage) Kerry (son); Kennedy (son; with Margaret Norton).

Worked on an automobile assembly line and as a prizefighter c. early 1950s. Owned record store c. 1955. Cowrote songs, 1957—, including "Reet Petite," 1957, "To Be Loved" and "Lonely Teardrops," both 1958, "That's Why" and "I'll Be Satisfied," both 1959, "Money (That's What I Want)," 1960, "I Want You Back," "ABC," and "The Love You Save"; independent producer, 1958, and music publisher, 1958—. Founded Motown Record Corporation (later Motown Industries) in 1959; resigned as president of Motown Record Corporation, founded and assumed leadership of Motown Industries, 1973; sold Motown Records to MCA Inc. for $61 million, 1988; director of the Gordy Company (comprised of the Motown Industries publishing division—Jobete Music Co. and Stone Mountain Music—and film and television divisions), 1988—. Producer and coeditor of feature films, including *Lady Sings the Blues*, 1972. Director of feature films, including *Mahogany*, 1975, and *The Last Dragon*, 1985. *Military service:* U.S. Army c. 1951-1953.

Awards: Inducted into the Rock and Roll Hall of Fame, 1988.

Addresses: *Office*—The Gordy Company, 6255 Sunset Blvd., 18th Floor, Los Angeles, CA 90028.

wanted to try them in a business of his own. His name was Berry Gordy, Jr., and the company he created was the Motown Record Corp. Starting from their own home, the Gordy family has built Motown into the largest independent record firm in the world, and the only major black company in the entertainment business. Berry Gordy realizes that even in America factory workers cannot all become successful businessmen. Therefore, he believes that it is essential that each and every young person receive the maximum education possible. He knows that education is the passport to the future and that tomorrow belongs to the people who prepare for it today. One of the many ways Gordy puts his belief to work is through the Sterling Ball, a benefit which directly provides assistance in the form of scholarships to inner city high school graduates who wish to continue their education but are financially unable to do so. This annual charitable event has, to date, helped scores of young men and women, black and white,

reach an otherwise impossible goal—a college education. The benefit was originally conceived by Mr. Gordy and his sister, Mrs. Esther Edwards, vice president in the corporation, as a continuing and meaningful memorial to their late sister, Mrs. Loucye Gordy Wakefield, who had been the first vice president of Motown and a personal inspiration to all who knew her."

Women in High Places

Gordy's family supported his efforts to establish his own business from the start, with a 1959 loan of $800. Once the company was launched various family members played key roles in its continuing operations. While Gordy's brothers—Fuller, Robert, and George—participated in the Motown enterprise, it was his sisters who provided most of the help in the company's operations. Gordy believed in women as executives. His second wife, Raynoma, was an early vice-president, as was Janie Bradford, with whom Gordy cowrote the 1960 hit "Money (That's What I Want)." Later, Motown Productions—the film, television, and video arms of the corporation—would be skillfully guided by Suzanne De Passe. As Smokey Robinson wrote in his autobiography, "Berry was big on letting people prove themselves, based on skill, not sex or color."

In 1951 Gordy was drafted into the army, where he received his high school equivalency diploma. In 1953, no longer in the service, he married Thelma Coleman; a daughter, Hazel Joy, was born the following year. The couple would have two more children, Berry IV and Terry, before divorcing in 1959. While working on an auto assembly line, Gordy started a jazz-oriented record store—the 3-D Record Mart—around 1955, but it soon folded. Like Motown, it was financed largely by his family. At the time, Gordy was writing songs constantly, submitting them to magazines and contests. His big break came in 1957, when future soul star Jackie Wilson recorded "Reet Petite," which was written by Gordy, his sister Gwen, and Tyran Carlo. Jackie Wilson had just signed with the Brunswick label in 1956 and "Reet Petite" turned out to be his first hit. Gordy's team wrote four more hits for Wilson over the next two years: "To Be Loved" and "Lonely Teardrops" in 1958, and "That's Why" and "I'll Be Satisfied" in 1959.

Smokey Robinson a Key "Discovery"

In 1957 Gordy "discovered" Smokey Robinson, who would later become a rhythm and blues superstar. Gordy had just written "Lonely Teardrops" when Robinson and his group—then the Matadors—auditioned for Jackie Wilson's representatives. Present at the audition were Nat Tarnapol, owner of Brunswick Records and Wilson's manager, and Alonzo Tucker, generally described as "Jackie's music man." Gordy was also present, though he made it clear to Robinson that he did not work for Jackie Wilson. According to Robinson's oft-repeated account, Tucker rejected the Matadors for being too much like the Platters, another popular group of the time. Gordy, however, appeared very interested in the group, apparently because of their original material. He introduced himself as a songwriter, and Robinson noted in his book *Smokey: Inside My Life* that Gordy looked young for his age: "This boyish face hid the fact that he was 11 years older than me." Robinson also credited Gordy with having more songwriting savvy at that time than he did. He went on to report that Gordy expressed his views on songwriting after complimenting him on his rhymes, saying, "Songs are more than rhymes. Songs need a beginning, middle, and end. Like a story." It was the beginning of a long and beautiful friendship. Gordy is often credited with a discerning eye for talent, of which his discovery of Smokey Robinson is a prime example.

By 1958 Gordy was active as an independent producer, forming the nucleus of what would become Motown Records. He recorded, and leased recordings of, the Miracles, Marv Johnson, and Eddie Holland for the nationally distributed labels Chess, United Artists, and End. The same year he established Jobete to publish his songs. Jobete was named for Gordy's first three children, Hazel Joy, Berry IV, and Terry.

Moving toward becoming a full-fledged entrepreneur, Gordy was motivated by a number of factors. Certainly, his family background contributed to and supported his ambition. By then his friend, Robinson urged him to take control of his operations, especially in light of the pitifully small royalty checks he was receiving from the national labels. As a songwriter Gordy had to split his royalties with the music publisher; his way around this was to form his own publishing company, which was valued at nearly $100 million 30 years later. Finally, it was widely known that Gordy did not particularly like the way his songs were being produced at Brunswick. To move forward, he needed to take control and form his own corporation.

Company's Beginnings Were Modest

According to Robinson, Motown began with six employees who had been operating in 1958 out of an apartment on Gladstone in Detroit. In addition to Gordy and Robinson, they included Liles—not yet Gordy's wife at the time—Bradford, Robert Bateman, and Brian Holland. Holland and Bateman were a songwriting-

production duo that evolved a few years later into the famed Holland-Dozier-Holland team, when Brian's brother Eddie returned to Motown after his contract with United Artists expired.

In 1959 Motown released its first single on the newly formed Tamla label. The name "Tamla" is a variation on "Tammy," a popular song of the period sung by Debbie Reynolds. The Motown label was activated in 1960, and the company's third major label, Gordy, debuted in April of 1962. While the Motown sound had its roots in urban rhythm and blues, it was Gordy's plan to appeal to young people of all races with a kind of music that would retain some of its origins while adding other ingredients. Motown's early advertising slogan, "The Sound of Young America," reflected Gordy's desire for

> *Berry was my teacher and a great one. He told me exactly what he wanted and how he wanted me to help him get it. Berry insisted on perfection and attention to detail. I'll never forget his persistence. This was his genius.—Michael Jackson*

Motown's music to achieve widespread popularity. The company landed its first number one pop hit in 1961 with the Marvelettes' "Please Mr. Postman."

Crossover Dreams Realized

As late as 1962 Motown's releases were still appealing primarily to black audiences, as evidenced by their success on the rhythm and blues charts. That year the company placed 11 singles on the R & B Top 10. The company's strategy, as mapped out by Gordy, was to "cross over" to the white record-buying public. In fact, four singles managed to reach the Top 10 on the pop charts in 1962. The next year Motown placed six more singles on the pop Top 10, with Stevie Wonder's "Fingertips, Part 2" becoming its second number one pop hit.

1964 proved a watershed year for Motown. Four of the company's five top-10 pop hits went to Number One:

"My Guy," "Where Did Our Love Go," "Baby Love," and "Come See about Me." The other song, "Dancing in the Street," went to Number Two. Most importantly, Motown had hit on a winning combination with the Supremes singing songs written and produced by Holland-Dozier-Holland. The next year, five Motown releases reached Number One. Reflecting the company's success, Gordy purchased the Gordy Manor in Detroit.

Gordy's strategy for producing hits was paying off. While Gordy himself was a talented songwriter and hands-on producer, these strengths alone were not enough to make Motown a success. Rather, it was Gordy's ability to surround himself with talented people that made Motown a force in the music business. Motown's greatest songwriters and producers—Smokey Robinson, Eddie Holland, Lamont Dozier, Brian Holland—were complemented by a stable of other gifted writers and producers, all competing within the Motown system to produce hits. Often likened to an assembly line, Motown was indeed a music factory that was able to churn out hit after hit.

Gordy Looked Beyond Records

As Motown's popularity in the mid-1960s insured the company's success, Gordy began to move the company forward by pursuing other entertainment opportunities. As early as 1966 Motown established a West Coast office for expansion into movie production, to secure film roles for Motown stars, and to encourage the use of Motown songs in film soundtracks. Motown also announced its interest in becoming a "Broadway angel," a financial backer for Broadway plays. By 1968 Gordy had purchased a home in Los Angeles and moved there. During the next few years Motown established additional offices on the West Coast; the move from Detroit was finalized in 1972. For some within the company the move was an unpopular decision; for others, it opened up new opportunities. By that time Gordy had purchased comic Red Skelton's Bel Air estate and was living there.

The end of the 1960s brought a talented new group to Motown—the Jackson 5. Discovered by Bobby Taylor of Bobby Taylor and the Vancouvers and introduced to the public by former Supreme Diana Ross, the Jackson 5 hailed from Gary, Indiana. The group, and especially youngest member Michael, enjoyed close ties to Gordy, who often let the entire family stay at his home in California. Gordy headed a songwriting and production team within Motown—called the Corporation—that wrote and produced several chart-topping hits for the Jackson 5, including "I Want You Back," "ABC," and "The Love You Save." Michael Jackson was quoted in

The Motown Album as saying, "Berry was my teacher and a great one. He told me exactly what he wanted and how he wanted me to help him get it. Berry insisted on perfection and attention to detail. I'll never forget his persistence. This was his genius."

Diana Ross Helped Launch Motown Industries

In 1973 Gordy resigned as president of Motown Records to assume leadership of the new Motown entertainment conglomerate, Motown Industries, which included record, motion picture, television, and publishing divisions. His primary star was Diana Ross, whom Gordy began grooming for television and motion pictures as early as 1968, when she was featured with the Supremes and the Temptations on Motown's first television special, "T.C.B.: Taking Care of Business." A second special with the Supremes and Temptations followed in 1969. Ross starred in her first solo television special, "Diana," in 1971. It was widely rumored that Gordy and Ross enjoyed a special personal relationship prior to Ross's 1971 marriage to Robert Silberstein.

Gordy was involved as more than producer in Ross's first film role: singer Billie Holiday in the 1972 Paramount release, *Lady Sings the Blues*. Motown invested heavily in the film and by most accounts Gordy spent a great deal of time personally editing it. It was a promising start for Motown's film ventures; Ross received an Academy Award nomination for her performance. Her second film, 1975's *Mahogany*, marked Gordy's debut as a film director. It was followed by *The Wiz*, a 1978 Universal/Motown musical version of *The Wizard of Oz* that garnered largely negative reviews and did poorly at the box office. Motown would not enter the motion picture business again until Gordy's 1985 effort, *The Last Dragon*, an entertaining kung-fu musical that fared respectably well at the box office.

"Motown 25" Broke New Ground

Motown scored well in television with the NBC-TV special "Motown 25—Yesterday, Today, and Forever," which aired in 1983. Edited to a two-hour television special from a four-hour live performance, the show was a tribute to the genius of Berry Gordy. Among the highlights were reunions of the Jackson 5, the Miracles, and the Supremes, and solo performances by Michael Jackson and Marvin Gaye. The show garnered nine Emmy nominations for Motown; but perhaps more significantly, it was the most-watched variety special in the history of television.

Motown followed its anniversary special with the 1985

broadcast "Motown Returns to the Apollo." The show coincided with the reopening of the newly restored Apollo Theater in Harlem, marking its fiftieth anniversary. The special won an Emmy for best variety, music, or comedy program. Following the formula for success that Gordy implemented as far back as 1960—to reach as wide an audience as possible—Motown has made a number of its productions available for the home video market, including specials featuring Marvin Gaye and the Temptations.

Many books have been written by and about Motown's stars—Marvin Gaye, Smokey Robinson, the Temptations, the Supremes, Diana Ross, Mary Wilson—telling the story of Motown from several perspectives. Perhaps the final word will come from Mr. Chairman himself as Berry Gordy prepares his own autobiography for imminent publication. Through records, movies, videos, and now books, the heritage of Motown—and of the visionary behind it—will be preserved for and appreciated by future generations intrigued by the house that Gordy built.

Sources

Books

Benjaminson, Peter, *The Story of Motown,* Grove, 1979.
Bianco, David, *Heat Wave: The Motown Fact Book,* Pierian, 1988.
Fong-Torres, Ben, *The Motown Album,* St. Martin's, 1990.
Hirshey, Gerri, *Nowhere to Run,* Times Books, 1984.
Robinson, Smokey, with David Ritz, *Smokey: Inside My Life,* McGraw, 1989.
Singleton, Raynoma Gordy, with Bryan Brown and Mim Eichler, *Berry, Me, and Motown: The Untold Story,* Contemporary Books, 1990.
Taraborrelli, J. Randy, *Motown: Hot Wax, City Cool & Solid Gold,* Doubleday, 1986.
Waller, Don, *The Motown Story,* Scribner, 1985.

Periodicals

Detroit Free Press, May 15, 1983.
Rolling Stone, August 23, 1990.

—*David Bianco*

Arlo Guthrie

Singer, songwriter, guitarist

In November of 1965, Arlo Guthrie and a group of friends, after finding that the local trash facility in Stockbridge, Massachusetts, was closed, were arrested for dumping garbage onto private property. Two years later, Guthrie, son of legendary American folk singer Woody Guthrie, described the incident in "Alice's Restaurant," a rambling eighteen-minute "talking blues" song which related his arrest, conviction, and later denial by the U.S. draft board for military service. The song, which began as a underground hit and eventually sold over $1 million worth of records, catapulted the 20-year-old singer to instant fame and launched his own career as a folk artist.

"Symbolic of the clash between traditional values and the rebellious hippie culture," according to Janet Enright in *Maclean's,* the song became an anthem for the protest movements of the 1960s, and was the basis for the 1969 hit movie, *Alice's Restaurant,* which also starred Guthrie. Based on 95 percent fact, according to Guthrie, the song "Alice's Restaurant" drew a connection between his littering misdemeanor and his later being turned down for service in the U.S. Army. "Guthrie's musical conclusion," as Enright explains: "Was he not moral enough to join the army, burn women, kids, houses and villages after bein' a litterbug?" A contributor to the *New Yorker* described the song as "funny, personal, deft, surprising, and wild."

That Arlo Guthrie would become a folk artist was no surprise. The Guthrie house was always full of music, and Arlo grew up among the musical influence of not only his famous father, but frequent music guests such as Cisco Houston, Bob Dylan, and Leadbelly. He was playing harmonica by the age of three, and by six had learned the fundamentals of the guitar. He naturally turned to music as a career. As he told Kristin Baggelaar and Donald Milton in *Folk Music: More Than A Song,* after graduating from high school he realized he "really couldn't do anything else" and "decided to continue playing music for the fun of it." Arlo did attend college briefly, but dropped out to perform in small coffeehouses and clubs around the country, particularly along the East Coast.

"Alice's Restaurant" first became popular on New York City radio station WBAI, where Guthrie performed it in the spring of 1967. The radio station was swamped with listener-requests for the song, and it soon caught on with other disc jockeys. The summer of the same year, Guthrie performed the song at the Newport Folk Festival, and in the fall his hit album, *Arlo Guthrie,* was released. Guthrie commented to Baggelaar and Milton on the effect of the recording on his exposure as a folk artist: "I didn't change my style very much, but it sure made it possible to work a lot! It also made it possible to

Born Arlo Davy Guthrie, July 10, 1947, in New York, NY; son of Woody (a folksinger) and Marjorie Mazia (a dancer; maiden name, Greenblatt) Guthrie; married Jacklyn Hyde, October 9, 1969; children: Abraham, Cathyalicia, Annie Hays, Sarah Lee. *Education:* Attended Rocky Mountain College, Billings, MT. *Religion:* Converted to Roman Catholicism, 1977.

Singer, songwriter, early 1960s—. Appeared in film *Alice's Restaurant*, United Artists, 1969; formed band Shenandoah, late 1970s. founder of Rising Sun Records; publishes quarterly newsletter, *Rolling Blunder Review*. Coestablished Committee to Combat Huntington's Disease.

Addresses: *Home*—Washington, MA. *Agent*—c/o Harold Leventhal Management Co., 250 West 57th St., Ste. 1304, New York, NY 10019.

entertain a whole new audience, normally middle-of-the-road or country & western. . . . We started to generate interest among a broader range of folks."

Over the next decade Guthrie matured as an artist, displaying what Debra Rae Cohen in *Rolling Stone* described as a "distinctive folksy mixture of conscience, comedy, and virtuoso story telling." A contributor to *The Encyclopedia of Folk, Country, and Western Music* wrote that "Guthrie closed out the 1960s and came into the 1970s commanding growing respect as both an interpreter of new and old songs (mostly folk, but with forays into country and rock on occasion) and a writer of new ones, usually with a strong strain of humor." Among his more popular songs were "The Motorcycle Song" and "Pause for Mr. Clause"; in 1969, he secured his reputation as a performing artist when he was featured at the now-legendary Woodstock music concert. Throughout the 1970s, Guthrie "maintained his momentum, building up a following that cut across generation and stylistic lines," wrote *The Encyclopedia of Folk, Country and Western Music* contributor. And in 1972, he had a hit recording with his version of the Steve Goldman song, "City of New Orleans."

Guthrie's career reached a peak with the success of "Alice's Restaurant," yet he still maintains a loyal following as a folk artist, composing and recording new folk sagas in addition to old standards. From the late 1970s onward, he has performed concerts and recorded with his band Shenandoah, and has frequently toured with Pete Seeger and his group, The Weavers. Baggelaar and Milton noted that "traditional and contemporary folk interpretation" find common ground in Guthrie.

"Despite the transformation of folk music with the advent of electric instrumentation, some artists have maintained an authentic and personalized style of musical expression. Arlo Guthrie successfully bridges the gap between this era and the days that belonged to his folk-poet father Woody Guthrie."

Present throughout Guthrie's career has been the threat of Huntington's Disease, the hereditary nerve disorder to which his father succumbed and of which Arlo has a 50 percent chance of developing. With his mother, Arlo helped to establish the Committee to Combat Huntington's Disease, and he remains determined not to let the possibility of contracting the disease interfere with his music. As he told Enright: "The way that I deal with it is to live my life so it doesn't matter."

Selected Discography

Alice's Restaurant, Reprise, 1967.
Arlo, Reprise, 1968.
Running Down the Road, Reprise, 1969.
Washington Country, Reprise, 1970.
Hobo's Lullaby (includes "City of New Orleans"), Reprise, 1972.
Last of the Brooklyn Cowboys, Reprise, 1973.
Arlo Guthrie, Reprise, 1974.
(With Pete Seeger) *Pete Seeger/Arlo Guthrie Together in Concert*, Reprise, 1975.
Amigo, Reprise, 1976.
The Best of Arlo Guthrie, 1977.
Arlo Guthrie with Shenandoah, Warner Brothers, 1978.
Outlasting the Blues, Warner Brothers, 1979.
(With Seeger) *Arlo Guthrie and Pete Seeger: "Precious Friend,"* 1981.
Power of Love, Warner Brothers, 1981.

Sources

Books

Baggelaar, Kristin, and Donald Milton, *Folk Music: More Than a Song*, Crowell, 1976.
Cronkite, Kathy, *On the Edge of the Spotlight*, Morrow, 1981.
The Encyclopedia of Folk, Country, and Western Music, 2nd edition, St. Martin's, 1983.
Miller, Edwin, *Seventeen Interviews*, Macmillan, 1970.
Okun, Milton, *Something to Sing About*, Macmillan, 1968.

Periodicals

Maclean's, March 17, 1986.
New Yorker, January 6, 1968.

People, September 7, 1987.

Rolling Stone, September 6, 1979; February 11, 1988, August 24, 1989.

—Michael E. Mueller

Bill Haley

Singer, songwriter

Bill Haley is known the world over as the Father of Rock 'n' Roll. Haley was the first white artist to combine elements of rhythm & blues, western swing, and hillbilly music to produce the upbeat, danceable, and infectious sound known today as rock 'n' roll. With his band, the Comets, Haley released rock's first certifiable million-seller, "Rock Around the Clock," in 1954. According to Charles T. Brown in *Music U.S.A.: America's Country and Western Tradition,* Haley "was not original, although he felt that he had invented rock and roll. He simply put together available elements at the right time and had the good sense to get them before the public. But he was the catalyst necessary for rock and roll's success."

Brown's judgment might be unduly harsh. Haley was more than a mere catalyst: he was a clever performer with many years' experience who was able to create a package of rhythm & blues acceptable to white teenagers. Prior to Haley, early examples of rock 'n' roll had reached very few listeners, and some of the most exciting r & b work featured frankly sexual lyrics that rendered the form taboo among much of the white listening public. Haley incorporated the beat but left the erotic lyrics behind; the young post-war generation found a music it could dance to, a signature sound different from all the dance music of the past.

William John Clifton Haley was born July 6, 1925, in the Detroit suburb of Highland Park. While he was still young his parents moved the family east to Chester, Pennsylvania, a small town near Philadelphia. There Haley's father worked as a farmer and his mother played organ in church. Haley himself was interested in music from his earliest years, especially country and western music. Like many aspiring singers, he idolized Hank Williams, an artist whose up-tempo numbers hinted at the rock era to come.

Apprenticeship in Western Swing

In 1945 Haley left home for a long apprenticeship in country and western swing bands. His travels led him far and wide across the eastern half of the country; gradually he became an able guitar player and an affable showman. He returned to the Chester area in 1948 and formed his own ensemble, the Four Aces of Western Swing. This group could be heard weekly over WPWA in Chester, where Haley also worked as a disc jockey.

Haley's performances on WPWA brought him to the attention of a Philadelphia-area record producer, Jack Howard. Howard thought he might be able to make Haley a hillbilly music star, and at his suggestion Haley re-named his group Bill Haley and His Saddlemen. Under Howard's direction Haley cut three singles, none of which sold outside the Philadelphia area. That exposure was enough, however, to attract the attention of Dave Miller, owner of a slightly larger pop label in Philadelphia. It was Miller who suggested that Haley record "Rocket 88," an r & b hit. That tune sold some 10,000 copies—not a phenomenal success, but encouraging.

In 1951 Haley took a regular gig at a dance bar in New Jersey. While there he began performing an upbeat number called "Rock the Joint" that proved very popular with the young crowd. Like "Rocket 88," "Rock the Joint" was originally a black hit. Haley recorded it early in 1952 and it eventually sold 150,000 copies. By then Haley was signed to the larger Essex label and his band had been re-named the Comets. Haley and his group left behind their country garb, donned tuxedos, and added a tenor saxophonist and drummer to their ranks. From there, Bill Haley and the Comets took off.

"Rock Around the Clock" Burned Slowly

In 1953 they recorded a number Haley wrote himself, "Crazy Man, Crazy." The song—Haley's first Top Ten hit—proved especially popular in dance halls. At the time, Haley was sitting on another number, "Rock Around the Clock," but Miller discouraged him from recording it. Finally Haley left the Essex label, signed with Decca, and brought "Rock Around the Clock" to the recording studio. The song was released on May 10, 1954. Initially, "Rock Around the Clock" did not sell well, but a Haley follow-up, "Shake, Rattle, and Roll," made the Top Ten. In the wake of that success, Decca decided to re-release "Rock Around the Clock." The tune was featured prominently in the film "The Blackboard Jungle," one of the first movies geared toward the rebellious teens of the 1950s.

"Rock Around the Clock" spent seven weeks at Number One on the pop charts in 1955 and has subsequently sold more than 20 million copies. The song brought Haley into the limelight he had sought for more than ten years and made him a veritable superstar. He and the Comets turned out three more hits in 1955, "Dim Dim the Lights," "Birth of the Boogie," and "Razzle Dazzle," and then embarked on a dizzying round of concert appearances in the United States and England.

Backed by the spirited saxophone playing of Rudy Pompelli and fine side work of a variety of other musicians, Bill Haley and the Comets caused a sensation wherever they performed. Unfortunately for Haley, however, other singers were quick to incorporate the new sound and almost immediately edged him out of the record market. The aging, homely Haley could hardly compete with the likes of Elvis Presley, Jerry Lee Lewis, and the outrageous Little Richard; after 1955 he had only one hit, "Skinny Minnie."

Second Career Abroad

American fans might have shrugged Haley off, but British and Mexican fans were more respectful. Haley and his Comets staged fabulously successful tours of England in the mid-1960s and again in the mid-1970s, on both occasions upstaging more modern acts. Throughout the 1960s Haley recorded music in Mexico and sold the majority of his singles there. He also toured the United States, but his performances there were confined to smaller stages.

Bitter over the indifference he faced in his native country, Haley became a recluse as the 1970s progressed. In one of his last interviews he said: "I wrote 'Rock-a-

Beatin' Boogie,' which was the song that gave rock 'n' roll its name. Remember how it started out? 'Rock, rock, rock everybody! Roll, roll, roll everybody!' Well, that started it. The story has got pretty crowded as to who was the father of rock. These days, you'd think everybody did it. But we were the first. I haven't done much in life except that. And I'd like to get credit for it." Indeed, Haley's was no small accomplishment. His music was a breakthrough combination of styles that had previously been split along racial lines, conjured at a time when a young audience with increasing record-buying power was craving novelty.

Bill Haley died in his sleep on February 9, 1981, in the small town of Harlingen, Texas. Stuart Colman offered a tribute to Haley in the book *They Kept On Rockin'*: "Leaders in the music world are always predestined, and Bill had every right to be a star. . . . Whatever . . . [the] criticisms of the Haley style of music, the fact remains that the slick three chord pop songs at which

> *The story has got pretty crowded as to who was the father of rock. These days, you'd think everybody did it. But we were the first. I haven't done much in life except that. And I'd like to get credit for it.*

he so excelled, have always been the hardest to write successfully." Colman concluded, "Rest assured, any future songwriter would give his eye teeth to unlock the secret of some of the all-time greats created by Bill Haley and the Comets!" Fittingly, Bill Haley was inducted into the Rock 'n' Roll Hall of Fame in 1986 as one of its first members.

Selected discography

Singles; with the Saddlemen

"Rocket 88," Holiday, 1951.
"Green Tree Boogie," Holiday, 1951.
"Jukebox Cannonball," Holiday, 1951.

Singles; with the Comets

"Rock the Joint," Essex, 1952.
"Crazy Man Crazy," Essex, 1953.
"Sundown Boogie," Essex, 1954.
"Rock Around the Clock," Decca, 1954.
"Shake, Rattle, and Roll," Decca, 1954.
"Dim Dim the Lights," Decca, 1954.
"Mambo Rock," Decca, 1955.
"Razzle Dazzle," Decca, 1955.
"Rock a Beatin' Boogie," Decca, 1955.
"See You Later, Alligator," Decca, 1955.
"Rockin' Through the Rye," Decca, 1956.
"Rockin' Rollin' Rover," Decca, 1957.
"Skinny Minnie," Decca, 1958.
"Tamiami," Warner Bros., 1960.
"Chick Safari," Warner Bros., 1960.
"Tenor Man," Newtown, 1963.
"Dance Around the Clock," Newtown, 1963.
"Burn That Candle," Apt, 1965.
"Haley a-Go Go," Apt, 1965.
"A Little Piece at a Time," Janus, 1972.
"Kohoutek," MGM, 1974.
"Within This Broken Heart of Mine," Arzee, 1977.

Albums; with the Comets

Bill Haley and the Comets, Essex.
Rock Around the Clock, Decca.
Rock 'n' Roll Stage Show, Decca.
Rockin' the Oldies, Decca.
Rockin' Around the World, Decca.
Rockin' the Joint, Decca.
Shake, Rattle and Roll, Decca.
Bill Haley's Chicks, Decca.
Haley's Juke Box, Warner Bros.
Bill Haley's Scrapbook, Kama Sutra.
Bill Haley & His Comets, Warner Bros.
Golden Hits of Bill Haley & the Comets, MCA.
Greatest Hits of Bill Haley & the Comets, MCA.
Rock and Roll Is Here to Stay, Gusto.
Rock and Roll, Crescendo.
Rock Around the Country, Crescendo.
Bill Haley & the Comets From the Original Master Tapes, MCA.

Sources

Books

Brown, Charles T., *Music U.S.A.: America's Country & Western Tradition*, Prentice-Hall, 1986.
Colman, Stuart, *They Kept on Rockin'*, Blandford Press, 1982.
Given, Dave, *The Dave Given Rock 'n' Roll Stars Handbook*, Exposition Press, 1980.
Lillian Roxon's Rock Encyclopedia, Grosset, 1978.

The Marshall Cavendish Illustrated History of Popular Music,
    Volume 1, Marshall Cavendish, 1989.
The Rolling Stone Record Guide, Rolling Stone Press, 1979.
Stambler, Irwin, *Encyclopedia of Pop, Rock, and Soul,* St. Mar-
    tin's, 1974, revised edition, 1989.
Swenson, John, *Bill Haley, The Daddy of Rock and Roll,* Stein &
    Day, 1983.

Periodicals

New York Times, February 10, 1981.
Rolling Stone, March 19, 1981.

—Anne Janette Johnson

Hall
&
Oates

Pop duo

Hailed as "exponents of blue-eyed soul" by critic Ron Givens in *Stereo Review,* Daryl Hall and John Oates have been performing as a duo since the late 1960s, but first gained widespread attention with their 1975 RCA debut album. The record, *Daryl Hall and John Oates,* included the hit single "Sara, Smile," which proved so popular that it renewed interest in their previous efforts, especially the 1973 Atlantic album, *Abandoned Luncheonette.* Many albums and hits have followed; among the latter are "Rich Girl," "Private Eyes," and "Say It Isn't So."

Both halves of the duo loved music from their early years. Hall, born in or near Philadelphia on October 11, 1948, was the son of two classically trained musicians. Though they gave him voice and piano lessons in the hope that he too would follow the classical path, Hall was enchanted by the sounds of rock and roll. By the time Hall was in junior high, he was catching rides to Philadelphia to become involved in the city's vibrant rhythm and blues scene. He hung out on corners with black vocal groups who were impressed enough by his

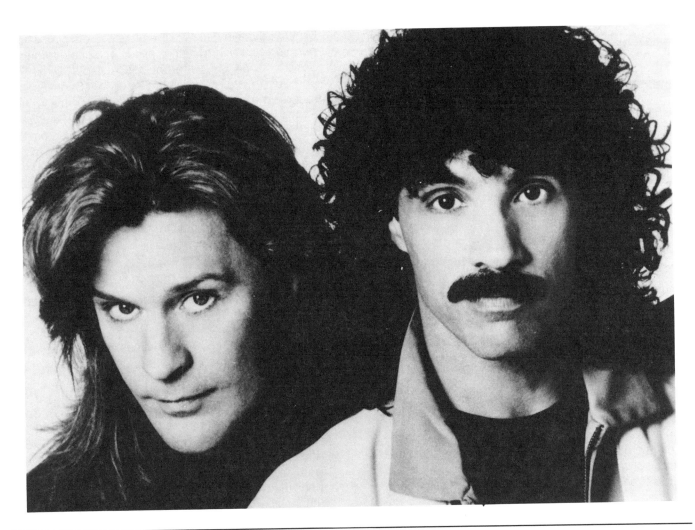

devotion to let him sing with them. Meanwhile, unwilling to disappoint his parents, he continued his education in classical music. Hall began to experience success in both genres simultaneously: He would sing with the Philadelphia Orchestra in the afternoon and at night sing backup for performers like Motown great Smokey Robinson in small city clubs.

Singing Backup Provided a Springboard

John Oates, on the other hand, was born in New York City on April 7, 1949, to parents who liked rock and roll and encouraged his interest in it. His mother even took him to concerts by pioneer rock artists like Bill Haley and the Comets. Oates started guitar lessons when he was eight years old and eventually perfected a routine in which he imitated the style of Elvis Presley. Like Hall, after Oates's family moved to the Philadelphia area, he often went to the city as a teenager to see soul acts like Sam and Dave or Gary U.S. Bonds. Oates also spent a lot of time dancing at local record hops, in addition to practicing with various bands he formed with his friends. He too eventually became a studio backup singer and musician.

Hall and Oates met in 1967, around the time both attended Temple University. They quickly became friends because of their shared interest in soul and rhythm and blues. Oates also began playing occasional sessions with Hall's rock band, Gulliver. By 1969 they had left Gulliver to perform as a pair. At that time both Hall and Oates were also interested in folk music; their first album on Atlantic, *Whole Oates,* released in 1972, had a predominantly folk sound. Though this effort was generally ignored by critics and fans alike, the two musicians were undaunted. Their next release, *Abandoned Luncheonette,* had more of the "blue-eyed soul" feel that would ultimately became their trademark; it fared better, garnering good reviews and scoring a minor hit with "She's Gone."

"Sara, Smile" Started Something

Ever experimental, Hall & Oates's third release, *War Babies,* had a harsher, more metallic rock tone, which largely alienated their burgeoning audience. Recalling concert performances of the same period, Hall told Michael Ryan in *People:* "We played a few gigs where people actually threw things at us." The duo returned to a mellow, soul sound for their RCA debut, *Daryl Hall and John Oates.* The album's single, "Sara, Smile," raced up the charts in Europe as well as the United States and Hall & Oates launched a successful world tour. Meanwhile, both critics and fans harkened back to *Abandoned Luncheonette* to get more of the pair's talent, and "She's Gone" belatedly became a much bigger hit than it had been originally. Hall & Oates kept their new found popularity going with the 1976 release of *Bigger Than Both of Us,* scoring another smash with the catchy single, "Rich Girl."

Their next three albums, however, did not go over as well. One, *Along the Red Ledge,* was more rock-oriented than their previous successes; another, *X-Static,* was influenced by disco. But with the 1980 release of *Voices,* Hall & Oates were back on track, collecting a series of platinum albums. *Voices* included a hit remake of the Righteous Brothers classic "You've Lost That Lovin' Feelin'," along with the chart-climbing "Kiss on My List." The following year's *Private Eyes* fared just as well, scoring hits with the upbeat title cut and "I Can't Go For That." Next came *H2O,* which featured "Did It in a Minute," "Maneater," the slow ballad "One on One," and "Family Man." Not content when they released a greatest hits collection, *Rock 'n' Soul Part One,* to rest upon their laurels, Hall & Oates included new hits on the album as well: "Say It Isn't So," and "Adult Education."

Duo Split Temporarily

Despite their success, after 1984's *Big Bam Boom,* which yielded the hits "Out of Touch" and "Method of Modern Love," and the popular live album *Live at the Apollo,* the long-time team split to pursue individual projects. Oates helped produce albums for other musical groups, while Hall recorded his second solo effort, *Three Hearts in the Happy Ending Machine. Hearts,* like Hall's previous solo album, *Sacred Songs,* drew respectful remarks from critics, but Hall & Oates fans were disappointed; neither disc sold well.

Nonetheless, as Hall predicted in a 1986 interview with Steve Dougherty in *People,* the duo did re-team to record again. In 1988 they released *Ooh Yeah!* on Arista and had the satisfaction of watching two singles, "Everything Your Heart Desires" and "Missed Opportunity," become popular with Top Forty audiences. Not only fans, but critics too welcomed Hall & Oates's reunion effort; Hank Bordowitz in *High Fidelity,* for instance, proclaimed gleefully that *"Ooh Yeah!* attacks the brain and breeds there, causing you to hum incessantly." Hall & Oates's follow-up album, 1990's *Change of Season* also produced a hit with "So Close."

Selected discography

Whole Oates, Atlantic, 1972.
Abandoned Luncheonette (includes "She's Gone"), Atlantic, 1973.
War Babies, Atlantic, 1974.
Daryl Hall and John Oates (includes "Sara, Smile"), RCA, 1975.
Bigger Than Both of Us (includes "Rich Girl"), RCA, 1976.
Beauty on a Back Street, RCA, 1977.
Livetime, RCA, 1978.
Along the Red Ledge (includes "It's a Laugh" and "I Don't Want to Lose You"), RCA, 1978.
X-Static, RCA, 1979.
Voices (includes "How Does It Feel to Be Back," "You've Lost That Lovin' Feeling," "You Make My Dreams Come True," and "Kiss on My List"), RCA, 1980.
Private Eyes (includes "Private Eyes" and "I Can't Go for That"), RCA, 1981.
H2O (includes "Did It in a Minute," "Maneater," "One on One," and "Family Man"), RCA, 1982.
Rock 'n' Soul Part One (includes "Say It Isn't So" and "Adult Education"), RCA, 1983.
Big Bam Boom (includes "Out of Touch" and "Method of Modern Love"), RCA, 1984.
Live at the Apollo, RCA, 1985.
Ooh Yeah! (includes "Everything Your Heart Desires," "Missed Opportunity," "Downtown Life," "I'm in Pieces," "Talking All Night," "Rockability," "Rocket to God," "Soul Love," and "Realove: Keep on Pushin' Love"), Arista, 1988.
Change of Season (includes "So Close"), Arista, 1990.

Solo LPs by Daryl Hall

Sacred Songs, RCA, 1980.
Three Hearts in the Happy Ending Machine (includes "Dreamtime"), RCA, 1986.

Sources

High Fidelity, July 1988; November 1988.
Mademoiselle, September 1981.
Newsweek, February 20, 1984.
People, May 25, 1981; April 15, 1985; December 15, 1986.
Rolling Stone, March 22, 1979; January 17, 1985; May 5, 1988.
Stereo Review, April 1978; September 1988.

—Elizabeth Wenning

John Hammond

Jewelry promoter, record industry
executive, music writer

**Jazz promoter, record industry
executive, music writer**

With his uncanny ability to recognize musical talent, record industry executive John Hammond shaped the musical taste of American listeners for more than five decades, discovering the performers and tapping the trends that would define each musical generation. Instrumental in the careers of Billie Holiday, Benny Goodman, Count Basie, Aretha Franklin, Bob Dylan, Bruce Springsteen, and many others, Hammond had no financial stake in the artists he promoted. Instead, he was driven by his sheer love of music and by his enthusiasm for unique and exceptional talent.

Especially devoted to jazz and its practitioners, Hammond was enraged—during the 1930s—that the best jazz players were kept from a decent living and the recognition they deserved simply because they were black; a civil rights activist throughout his lifetime, Hammond worked tirelessly to erase the music industry's color barrier, promoting black artists on major recording labels and integration within bands. Late in that decade his "From Spirituals to Swing" concerts at Carnegie Hall brought legitimacy to American black music and appreciation for jazz around the world. "Hammond had an eye for buried treasure. He unearthed it, collected it, brought it to light as a self-appointed missionary, the phonograph record was his instrument," wrote Leslie George Katz in the *New York Times Book Review*. "By bridging worlds he opened gates. Others were doing it, but he went to inspired lengths." Writing in *Down Beat,* John McDonough concurred: "One has to look beyond music to understand the forces that governed his deepest passions. . . . Music wasn't just an artistic pursuit in his view, it was a social force—both an agent and an expression of broad social and political meaning. This is what gave substance to Hammond's instinct for new musical voices."

Early Life of Privilege and Music

Hammond was born into a life of great wealth and privilege: his father was a prominent lawyer and corporate executive and his mother, a Vanderbilt daughter. Home was a six-story mansion in New York City, where John Jr. fell in love with music—early classical pieces on the family phonograph and jazz and blues heard in the servants' quarters. Here, too, he first became privy to the discrimination against race and class that he would later fight so hard to eradicate. An avid record collector by the age of twelve, Hammond recalled that "the simple honesty and convincing lyrics of the early blues singers, the rhythm and creative ingenuity of the jazz players, excited me the most." His forays into the city often ended at Harlem's Alhambra Theatre or Roseland Ballroom where black artists like Bessie Smith

Born John Henry Hammond, Jr., December 15, 1910, in New York, NY; died July 10, 1987, in New York, NY; son of John Henry (an attorney and corporate executive) and Emily Vanderbilt (Sloane) Hammond; married Jemison McBride, March 13, 1941 (divorced, 1948); married Esme O'Brien Sarnoff, September 8, 1949 (deceased, 1986); children: (first marriage) John Paul, Douglas (deceased), Jason; (second marriage) Rosita Sarnoff (stepdaughter). *Education:* Attended Yale University, 1929-31; studied music at the Juilliard School.

Apprentice reporter for Portland, ME, *Evening News,* 1929-30; free-lance record producer for Victor, Vocalion-Brunswick, and other labels; disc jockey, announcer, and producer of live jazz shows for New York City radio station WEVD, 1932; American recording director for English Columbia and Parlaphone Co., 1933-36; associate recording director for Columbia Records, 1939-42 and 1946; president of Keynote Records, 1946-47; recording director of Majestic Records, 1947; vice-president of Mercury Records, 1947-52; producer for Vanguard Records, 1953-58; producer, director of talent acquisition, and vice-president of Columbia Records, 1958-76; independent record producer and consultant, 1976-87; chairman of the board of Hammond Music Enterprises, 1982-87.

Producer of plays and concerts, including *From Spirituals to Swing* series, 1938-39 and 1967. Lecturer at New York University, 1953-56.

Awards: Special Grammy Award, 1971, for his work in Columbia Records' reissue of the Bessie Smith library.

and Fletcher Henderson performed. Entering Yale University in 1929, Hammond worked as a summer apprentice for the *Portland Evening News,* an eye-opening post that taught him about the civil rights movement, labor unions, and politics. It also awakened in him a new passion—writing—which would soon come to serve his musical and social agendas.

Wrote for *Gramophone, Melody Maker*

Hammond entered the music business in the early thirties as a jazz writer for British publications *Gramophone* and *Melody Maker.* At the same time he used his income from family trust funds to subsidize and promote the recordings of black artists; for a while he produced jazz programs for a New York radio station and staged jazz concerts at the Manhattan theatre he

bought expressly for the purpose, using racially mixed bands. Becoming the American recording representative for the English branch of Columbia Records in 1933, Hammond soon befriended an unknown clarinetist, Benny Goodman, and persuaded him to recruit musicians from Harlem for a recording session backing legendary blues singer Bessie Smith. In 1934 the promoter also supervised the first recordings of a recent discovery, Billie Holiday, who he decided was "the best jazz singer I had ever heard."

With Hammond's help, Goodman gathered jazz talent for a permanent band, including black pianist Teddy Wilson and, later, vibraphonist Lionel Hampton. The integrated band was one of the country's first to perform live, and with hit after hit the band ushered in the swing era. Count Basie was also a Hammond discovery, heard on a Chicago experimental radio station in the mid-thirties. The promoter convinced Basie and his black nine-member band to come to New York City and record, and their great success propelled black music further into the mainstream. Hammond also brought boogiewoogie piano to white audiences for the first time when he resurrected the career of Meade Lux Lewis, as well as bringing to prominence Charlie Christian, the brilliant jazz musician who pioneered the electric guitar. Continuing to write about his musical discoveries and enthusiasms, Hammond also engaged in civil rights activities: aiding striking Kentucky coal miners, reporting on the Scottsboro case for *Nation* and *New Republic,* challenging worker conditions in the record-manufacturing industry, and serving on the executive board of the NAACP.

Bob Dylan: "Hammond's Folly"

Hammond worked as assistant recording director for Columbia Records from 1939 until the outbreak of World War II. Following the war he worked for a number of labels in a variety of capacities; with Mercury Records, for instance, he focused on classical music recordings, and at Vanguard he helped produce the first high fidelity jazz recordings, some featuring artists he had worked with years before.

Rejoining Columbia in 1958, Hammond was involved in talent acquisition and record producing until his mandatory retirement seventeen years later. Focusing on folk music and rhythm and blues as well as jazz, he was responsible for signing such talents as blacklisted folk singer Pete Seeger, Canadian poet and vocalist Leonard Cohen, and the unknown Bob Dylan, whose ragged voice and undistinguished musicianship prompted other Columbia executives to refer to him as "Hammond's folly." When Columbia wanted to drop Dylan after his first album fell flat, Hammond insisted that "this superlative artist with an acuity of vision of American life" be given a second chance—a judgment vindicated by Dylan's subsequent legendary status. Other Hammond discoveries in later years included Aretha Franklin, George Benson, Bruce Springsteen, and Stevie Ray Vaughan; rediscoveries included Eubie Blake and Alberta Hunter.

The retired executive continued as a consultant and independent record producer until suffering a stroke in the mid-eighties, his passion for music and zest for discovery still unabated. In his autobiography, *John Hammond on Record,* he explained the fuel that fired him. "I still expect to hear, if not today then tomorrow, a voice or a sound I have never heard before, with something to say which has never been said before."

Selected writings

(With Irving Townsend) *John Hammond on Record,* Ridge Press/ Summit Books, 1977.

American correspondent for *Gramophone,* 1931-33, *Melody Maker,* 1933-37, and *Rhythm,* 1937-39; music critic for *Brooklyn Eagle,* 1933-35; columnist for *Down Beat,* 1934-41. Associate editor of *Melody News,* 1934-35; coeditor of *Music and Rhythm,* 1942-43; music editor of *Gentry,* 1956-57. Contributor of articles on music and social issues to periodicals, including *Metronome, New York Times,* and *Saturday Review.*

Sources

Books

Contemporary Authors, Gale, Volume 106, 1982, Volume 123, 1988.
Newsmakers, Gale, 1988.
Hammond, John, with Irving Townsend, *John Hammond on Record,* Ridge Press/Summit Books, 1977.

Periodicals

Down Beat, October, 1987.
New York Times Book Review, November 20, 1977.
Rolling Stone, August 27, 1987.

—*Nancy Pear*

Lionel Hampton

Bandleader, percussionist, singer

For more than 50 years jazz musician and bandleader Lionel Hampton has captivated world audiences with his rhythmic drive and exuberant showmanship. A pioneering jazz vibraphonist with the Les Hite and Benny Goodman orchestras in the 1930s, Hampton went on to form his own big band, one of the most popular and enduring large jazz ensembles of all time. Specializing in stirring his musicians and fans into a rhythmic frenzy, the bandleader is notorious for letting numbers go on and on until every soloist has improvised into exhaustion; once, in Harlem's Apollo theater, his audience's enthusiastic stomping and jumping cracked the balcony and forced an evacuation.

The temporary base of jazz greats Quincy Jones, Charlie Parker, Fats Novarro, and Dinah Washington over the years, the Hampton band has played an important part in the history of jazz. It was one of the first jazz ensembles to use the electric bass guitar and organ. Yet, for all Hampton's significant contributions to music, the performer wants—according to George T. Simon in *The Best of the Music Makers*—"to be remembered most for spreading happiness and good will." "Hampton cavorts about the stage like a neophyte trouper trying to impress his first paying customers," wrote Arnold Jay Smith in *Down Beat,* describing the showman in his fiftieth year of performing, at age sixty-nine. "He is always smiling, enjoying his playing and that of others, expressing that pleasure by 'yeah-ing' whenever the spirit moves him."

Hampton displayed his musical leanings as a child, forever thumping on the rungs of chairs or on his grandmother's pots and pans. Christmas gifts were usually a set of children's drums, which seldom survived his enthusiasm for very long. Wanting to play real drums, Hampton got a job during high school as a newsboy for the *Chicago Defender,* and within a week realized his wish in the newsboys' jazz band. After graduating from high school in 1928 he headed for Los Angeles to play in the orchestra of family friend Les Hite and remained there for the next four years, developing his skills and acquiring local celebrity as a jazz drummer.

Once, when jazz great Louis Armstrong fronted for Hite's band in a recording session, Hampton discovered an unused vibraphone in the studio and mastered it within the hour; Armstrong's 1930 recording, "Memories of You," features Hampton in the first jazz vibraphone solo ever recorded. The young musician was absolutely smitten with the versatility of his new percussion instrument—its ability to be both animated and lyrical. Other jazz performers had used the vibraphone before, but none had approached Hampton's invention and rhythmic mastery on an instrument used—until

Born Lionel Leo Hampton, April 20, 1909 (some sources say April 12, 1908, or 1913, or 1914), in Birmingham, AL, raised in Chicago, IL; son of Charles (a pianist and singer) and Gertrude (Whitfield) Hampton; married Gladys Riddle (a seamstress who became his business manager), November 11, 1936 (deceased, 1971). *Education:* Attended the University of Southern California, 1934. *Politics:* Republican. *Religion:* Christian Scientist.

Drummer in *Chicago Defender* newsboys jazz band during high school; drummer and vibraphonist in Les Hite's band, Los Angeles, 1928-32; performed in own jazz group, Los Angeles, 1933-35; vibraphonist with the Benny Goodman Quartet and occasional performer in Goodman's full band, 1936-40; bandleader, vibraphonist, drummer, pianist, and singer for the Lionel Hampton Orchestra, 1940-65; leader and performer in jazz combo The Inner Circle, 1965—. Has appeared in motion pictures, including *The Benny Goodman Story*, 1955; has appeared on radio and television; musical director of television station WOOK, Washington, D.C., 1962; founder of recording labels Glad-Hamp and Who's Who in Jazz, 1978.

Professor of music at Howard University, Washington, D.C., 1981—. Has made numerous international goodwill tours; human rights commissioner of New York City, 1984-86; creator of Lionel Hampton Jazz Endowment Fund, 1984; United Nations ambassador of music, 1985.

Addresses: *Record company*—Glad-Hamp, 1995 Broadway, New York, NY 10023.

that time—decoratively, like chimes. "That watery deposit-bottle sound, redolent of vaudeville, somehow makes his rhythmic force more impressive," judged Kevin Whitehead, discussing Hampton's "Hot Mallets" recordings in *Down Beat.*

In 1936 "the King of Swing," clarinetist Benny Goodman, heard Hampton performing on vibes and persuaded the percussionist to tour with him, pianist Teddy Wilson, and drummer Gene Krupa as the Benny Goodman Quartet. Much admired, the group became enormously successful with hits like "Dinah" and "Moonglow." Hampton occasionally played drums and sang in Goodman's full band as well. Also recording with pick-up bands of celebrated sidemen from other jazz ensembles—the Victor recordings are now coveted collectors' items—Hampton became one of the swing era's premiere figures, prompting him to form his own big band in 1940. Initially comprised of young, un-

known, promising musicians from around the country, the Hampton orchestra reflected its leader's ebullient nature, with an emphasis on showmanship, energy, and excitement. Conducting, singing, and playing the vibes and the drums, Hampton also took to entertaining audiences on the piano with his unique "trigger-finger" style: forefingers only, like vibraphone mallets, ripping through single-note passages.

Starting with the 1941 hit "Flying Home," Hampton and his orchestra dominated the big band field for the next two decades. When it became evident—during the early sixties—that the days of the big bands were over, he pared down to The Inner Circle, a jazz combo of eight or so musicians, still assembling the big band for reunions and special occasions. Engaging in a number of goodwill tours since the 1950s, Hampton has brought the excitement of jazz to people around the globe; at home, he has worked hard to have America's black musical heritage taught at colleges and universities, and for other social and political concerns.

While observers have noted a tendency in Hampton's groups to emphasize audience-pleasing and past achievements over invention and musicianship, most share the sentiments of *Down Beat* contributor John McDonough. "He presides over an outstanding all-star band which is never called upon to do much more than huff and puff familiar riffs," allowed McDonough, reviewing a recording of the entertainer's fiftieth anniversary concert at Carnegie Hall. "But that's all Hampton's bands have ever had to do." And that, apparently, has been more than enough.

Selected writings

(With James Haskins) *Hamp: An Autobiography,* Warner Books, 1989.

Selected discography

Singles

"Drum Stomp," RCA Victor, 1937.
"Down Home Jump," Victor, 1938.
"Hot Mallets," Victor, 1939.
"Central Avenue Breakdown"/"Jack the Bellboy," Victor, 1940.
"Flying Home," Decca, 1942.
"Hamp's Boogie Woogie," Decca, 1944.
"Hey Ba-ba-rebop," Decca, 1945.
"Air Mail Special," Decca, 1946.
"Midnight Sun," Decca, 1947.
"Real Crazy"/"I Only Have Eyes for You," Vogue, 1953.

Albums

Play Love Songs, Verve.
Travelin' Band, Verve.
Gene Krupa-Lionel Hampton-Teddy Wilson with Red Callender, Verve.
The Hampton-Tatum-Rich Trio, Verve.
King of the Vibes, Verve.
Airmail Special, Verve.
Flying Home, Verve.
Swinging With Hamp, Verve.
Hamp, Verve.
Hamp's Big Four, Verve.
Hamp and Getz, Verve.
Lionel Hampton and His Giants, Verve.
Here Come the Swingin' Bands, Verve.
The Genius of Lionel Hampton, Verve.
Lionel Hampton '58, Verve.
Halleluja Hamp, Verve.
The High and the Mighty, Verve.
All-American Award Concert, Decca.
Crazy Rhythm, EmArcy.
Golden Vibes, Columbia.
Wailin' at the Trianon, Columbia.
Lionel Hampton Swings in Paris, Contemporary.
Hamp in Paris, EmArcy.
Lional Hampton Swings, Perfect.
Open House, Camden.
Moonglow, Decca.
Jazz Flamenco, Victor.
Just Jazz All Stars, GNP.
Just Jazz, Decca.
Jivin' the Vibes, Camden.
Jam Session in Paris, EmArcy/Harmony.

Apollo Hall Concert, 1954, Epic.
Newport Uproar, RCA.
At Newport '78, Timeless.
Ambassador at Large, Glad-Hamp.
Big Band Live, Glad-Hamp.
Chameleon, Glad-Hamp.
Made in Japan, Glad-Hamp.
Outrageous, Glad-Hamp.
Rarities, Glad-Hamp.
Sweatin' with Hamp, MCA.
Midnight Blues, Glad-Hamp.

Composed *King David Suite* (a four-part jazz composition for symphony), 1953.

Sources

Books

Feather, Leonard, *The New Edition of the Encyclopedia of Jazz*, Horizon Press, 1960.
The New Grove Dictionary of Jazz, edited by Barry Kernfeld, Macmillan, 1988.
Simon, George T., and others, *The Best of the Music Makers*, Doubleday, 1979.

Periodicals

Down Beat, August l0, 1978; April 1982; July 1985; April 1988; May 1990.
New York Times Book Review, December 3, 1989.

—*Nancy Pear*

John Wesley Harding

Singer, songwriter

With the release of his first major-label LP, *Here Comes the Groom,* in 1990, John Wesley Harding quickly became a favorite singer-songwriter among music critics. He also gained a substantial following with his solo acoustic performances and popular video. Harding's second album, *The Name Above the Title,* released in 1991, demonstrated that his initial success was no accident and convinced many of his admirers that his evolution as a writer and vocalist would be even more impressive than they had imagined.

Harding was born Wesley Harding Stace in Hastings, England, on October 10, 1965, the son of two school-teachers. "My mother was a mezzo-soprano opera singer," he said in an interview with *Contemporary Musicians,* but she gave up singing for teaching; his father plays jazz piano in addition to teaching. Harding himself would later go in the opposite direction. Though he grew up listening to and loving pop music, playing folk songs in local pubs by age seventeen, his career at first looked to be an academic one. He studied English literature at Cambridge University, earned a first—the highest undergraduate grade—and began work toward a Ph.D there in political and social theory. Soon, however, he put aside his graduate work to play music. "I started getting money for doing concerts," he explained to *CM.* "Also, I think I did my Ph.D, although I enjoyed it very much, because I didn't know what else I was going to do."

"Discovered" at Early Gig

Taking his stage name from an album by the most famous of all folk-rock artists, Bob Dylan, Harding performed a set of original songs at a performance in London in the summer of 1988; fortunately for his career, several music industry people attended the show and approached him. Soon afterward he went on tour with the group Hothouse Flowers in the United Kingdom and singer-songwriter John Hiatt in the U.S. Later that year, he released a live album recorded for less than one thousand pounds, during one performance, aptly titled *It Happened One Night.* The title of the record, released by the British label Demon, comes from the 1934 film by acclaimed director Frank Capra, who also made the film *It's a Wonderful Life.* Harding's admiration for Capra can be seen in the titles of his subsequent LP's, the first of which he named for another Capra film, and the second for the director's autobiography.

Harding then put together a band that included the bassist and drummer from British singer-songwriter Elvis Costello's group the Attractions, and recorded a demo that impressed Seymour Stein, president of Sire

For the Record. . .

Born Wesley Harding Stace, October 22, 1965, in Hastings, England; son of Christopher (a schoolteacher) and Molly (a former opera singer, and schoolteacher; maiden name, Townsend) Stace. *Education:* Jesus College, Cambridge University, B.A. in English, graduate study in political and social theory. *Politics:* "Imaginative." *Religion:* Born Methodist, but "All the gods are in Hollywood."

Singer, songwriter. Worked as an usher in an art cinema, played folk music in pubs while pursuing graduate studies; discovered by music industry representatives, toured as opening act in the United Kingdom and U.S., and recorded "live" album *It Happened One Night*, all 1988.

Awards: Received a first (highest possible grade) from Cambridge University; various poetry prizes.

Addresses: *Home*—P.O. Box 1429, London, England W6 OQJ. *Record company*—Sire Records, 75 Rockefeller Plaza, 20th Floor, New York City, NY 10019. *Manager*—Glen Colson (London). *Publicist*—Deb Bernadini (New York).

Records. Harding met with Stein and, as he told Andy Craft in *Bomb*, "played Seymour three songs in his office and he said, 'Okay, you've got it. You're signed.'" Stein assigned producer Andy Paley, who had just produced an album with former Beach Boys leader Brian Wilson, to work with Harding. The songwriter's first release for Sire was *God Made Me Do It: The Christmas EP*, which included the title song from Harding's later LP, *Here Comes the Groom*, two other original songs, a solo acoustic rendition of Madonna's hit "Like a Prayer," and a lengthy interview with British comic Viv Stanshall called "A Cosy Promotional Chat."

Impressed Critics With *Groom*

Recorded quickly with The Good Liars—a band that included Pete Thomas and Bruce Thomas from the Attractions, guitarist Steve Donelly, and keyboardist Kenny Craddock—*Here Comes the Groom* appeared in 1990 and received exceptional reviews. Robert Hilburn of the *Los Angeles Times* called it "the first great album of the 90's," comparing Harding's lyrics to those of Dylan and Costello. *Rolling Stone* referred to *Groom* as an "impressive major-label debut." Most critics noted in some way the similarities between Harding's singing and writing style and those of Costello, but Harding made no attempt to conceal his influences. In fact, in the last song on the CD and cassette of *Groom*, "Bas-

tard Son," he sings "Bob Dylan is my father, Joan Baez is my mother," and goes on to list a number of his other favorite songwriters in the lyrics. Folk singer John Prine—a Harding favorite and one of the many artists named in "Bastard Son"—called *Groom* one of the best albums of the year. The LP also contains "Things Snowball," a duet sung and composed with Los Angeles songwriter Peter Case. The single from the album, "The Devil in Me," spawned a video that aired extensively on MTV. Harding immediately went on the road for the 1990 Lafftour, along with rock bands The Ocean Blue and The Mighty Lemon Drops. Performing solo with an acoustic guitar, Harding captured the attention of fans across the U.S. with his witty songs and hilarious between-song patter. He toured a few months later with fellow singer-songwriter Michelle Shocked. Harding also appeared on two 1990 Sire/Reprise compilation albums, *Just Say Da*, to which he contributed a live version of his satirical "When the Beatles Hit America", and *Where The Pyramid Meets The Eye*, a tribute to psychedelic rock pioneer Roky Erickson. To the latter Harding contributed a high-energy version of Erickson's "If You Have Ghosts." In 1991 he collaborated with singer-songwriter Steve Wynn on a song called "Warning: Parental Advisory" for yet another Sire anthology, *Just Say Anything*, released in response to controversy over warning stickers on albums.

First Album No Fluke

Harding's second Sire LP, *The Name Above the Title*, garnered additional positive reviews. "I wanted the people who liked the first album to know that it wasn't a fluke," he told Erin Culley in *Hits*. He seemed to have made his point. *People's* Craig Tomashoff, while noting the still-strong resemblance of Harding's work to that of Dylan and Costello, observed that the music "burrows right into your pleasure center." Jock Baird wrote in *Musician* that the record "unpacks an engaging rogue's gallery of characters and story lines, all placed in solid rock settings." Harding's preoccupation with the movies is especially clear on this LP: Featuring a song called "The Movie of Your Life," the record is structured like a film, with a short instrumental theme at the beginning and a lively band introduction serving as closing "credits." *The Name Above the Title*—which again made excellent use of the Good Liars—was recorded in a month and contains 14 original songs and one cover, a lush reworking of Tommy James and the Shondells' 1960s classic "Crystal Blue Persuasion." Other songs on *Name* include "The Person You Are," for which Harding himself conceived the video, "Bridegroom Blues," a rocker with a hip-hop beat that Harding claims was recorded in about an hour and which he intended as a sequel to "Here Comes the Groom," and two soul-influenced ballads, "Driving in the Rain" and "Save a Little Room for Me."

In 1991, true to his literary leanings, Harding published a small book of his lyrics, *Collected Stories: 1990-1991*, as a publicity gesture. The lyrics appear in slightly altered form, frequently with parenthetical remarks in prose by Harding. The book seemed to answer a growing demand: Many admiring reviewers had wondered why Harding never included lyric sheets with his albums.

By mid-1991 fans and critics alike seemed to see past Harding's obvious influences to a new and original talent. As Tomashoff ventured in *People,* "In the end, Harding may remind you of a lot of people, but the true testimonial to his abilities will come a few years from now. Some smart singer-songwriter will happen along, and the first thing you'll say is, 'Doesn't he sound a lot like John Wesley Harding?'"

Selected discography

It Happened One Night, Demon Records, 1988.
God Made Me Do It: The Christmas EP (includes "Here Comes the Groom," "Like a Prayer," and "A Cosy Promotional Chat"), Sire/Reprise, 1989.
Here Comes the Groom (includes "Bastard Son," "Things Snowball," and "The Devil in Me"), Sire/Reprise, 1990.
Just Say Da (compilation; includes "When the Beatles Hit America"), Sire/Reprise, 1990.
Where the Pyramid Meets the Eye (compilation; includes "If You Have Ghosts"), Sire/Reprise, 1990.

Just Say Anything (compilation; includes "Warning: Parental Advisory"), Sire, 1991.
The Name Above the Title (includes "Bridegroom Blues," "The Person You Are," "Driving in the Rain," "Save a Little Room for Me," and "Crystal Blue Persuasion"), Sire/Reprise, 1990.

Selected writings

Collected Stories: 1990-1991 (lyrics), Warner Bros., 1991.

Sources

Books

Harding, John Wesley, *Collected Stories: 1990-91,* Warner Bros., 1991.

Periodicals

Bomb, Summer 1991.
Hits, March 25, 1991.
Los Angeles Times, February 17, 1990.
Musician, July 1991.
People, March 18, 1991.
Rolling Stone, March 22, 1990.

Other source material was gathered from an interview with John Wesley Harding conducted on July 15, 1991.

—*Simon Glickman*

Billie
Holiday

Singer

Billie Holiday is considered by many to be the greatest of all jazz singers. In a tragically abbreviated singing career that lasted less than three decades, her evocative phrasing and poignant delivery profoundly influenced vocalists who followed her. Although her warm, feathery voice inhabited a limited range, she used it like an accomplished jazz instrumentalist, stretching and condensing phrases in an ever-shifting dialogue with accompanying musicians. Famous for delivering lyrics a bit behind the beat, she alternately endowed them with sadness, sensuality, languor, and irony. Rarely singing blues, Holiday performed mostly popular material, communicating deep emotion by stripping down rather than dressing up words and lines. "If you find a tune that's got something to do with you, you just feel it, and when you sing it, other people feel it, too," Holiday once explained. According to the *Penguin Encyclopedia of Popular Music*, "She was the first and is perhaps still the greatest of jazz singers, if the essence of jazz singing is to make the familiar sound fresh, and to make any lyric come alive with personal meaning for the listener."

Holiday's life was a study in hardship. Her parents married when she was three, but her musician father was seldom present and the couple soon divorced. Receiving little schooling as a child, Holiday scrubbed floors and ran errands for a nearby brothel so she could listen to idols Louis Armstrong and Bessie Smith on the Victrola in its parlor. Brutally raped at ten, she was sent to a reformatory for "seducing" her adult attacker; at fourteen she was jailed for prostitution. Determined to find work as a dancer or singer in Harlem, Holiday moved to New York City in 1928 and landed her first job at Jerry Preston's Log Cabin, where her vocals moved customers to tears. Discovered in another Harlem club by jazz record producer John Hammond in 1932, she made her first recording a year later with Benny Goodman's orchestra. She began to record regularly for Columbia, usually under the direction of Teddy Wilson, backed by small studio bands comprised of the day's best jazz sidemen. These included saxophonist and soulmate Lester Young, whose style approximated Holiday's own; it was he who gave the pretty, dignified young singer the nickname "Lady Day."

Segregation Made Touring Difficult

Intended largely for a black jukebox audience, the Wilson discs—mostly silly and second-rate love songs that white singers had declined to record—were quickly and cheaply made. But Holiday and company transformed them into jazz treasures, immediately appreciated by musicians, critics, and jazz afficianados, if not

Born Eleanora Fagan, April 7, 1915, in Baltimore, MD; died of cardiac arrest, July 17, 1959, in New York City; daughter of Clarence Holiday (a jazz guitarist) and Sadie Fagan (a domestic); married James Monroe (marriage ended); married Louis McKay (separated).

Jazz singer. Began career in Harlem clubs, 1930; made recording debut with Benny Goodman ensemble, 1933; performed and recorded with various jazz bands, including those of Teddy Wilson, 1935-39, Count Basie, 1937, and Artie Shaw, 1938; solo recording artist and performer in theaters and nightclubs, 1940s and 1950s. Appeared in short film *Rhapsody in Black*, 1935, feature film *New Orleans*, 1946, and on television program *Sound of Jazz*, 1957.

Awards: *Esquire* silver award, 1945 and 1946, gold award, 1944 and 1947; *Metronome* poll winner, 1945-46.

the public at large. These hundred-odd songs—delivered in a light, bouyant style—are today considered among Holiday's most significant work. Forgoing club engagements in 1937 to tour with Count Basie's orchestra, Holiday went on to become one of the first black vocalists to be featured with a white band when she fronted for Artie Shaw a year later. Life on the road proved bitter for the singer, though; racial segregation made simple things like eating, sleeping, and going to the bathroom logistically difficult. Fed up when she could not enter one hotel through the front door with the rest of the Shaw orchestra, Holiday abandoned touring, returning to New York clubs and cabarets as a solo artist.

With Columbia's permission Holiday recorded "Strange Fruit," a controversial song about southern lynchings, for Commodore in 1939. It became a favorite of the interracial crowd for whom she performed at the Cafe Society, a Greenwich Village haunt of intellectuals and the political left. Holiday began to attract a popular following and indulged her taste for slow, melancholy songs about love gone bad, which communicated the hunger and despair that were starting to pervade her own life. Introduced to opium and heroin in the early forties by first husband James Monroe, she began her lifelong struggle with narcotics and alcohol addiction— Monroe the first in a succession of men who would feed that addiction, squander her earnings, and physically abuse her. Jailed for a year on drug charges after a sensational trial in 1947, Holiday had her cabaret license revoked and was thus prohibited from performing in the clubs and nightspots that suited her best. Unable to stay drug-free as long as she remained involved with the music scene, she would face other arrests.

Artistry Prevailed Over Inferior Production

Holiday recorded for Decca from 1944 to 1950. Because the company sought to make her over into a popular singer, much of her material for that label was overarranged, dominated by strings, and largely ordinary. Still, Holiday's artistry prevailed in songs like "Ain't Nobody's Business If I Do" and "Lover Man." Recording for Verve from 1952 to 1957, the singer frequently returned to the small group format that best fit her glimmering voice, but by then her instrument had begun to falter from years of abuse. Her desire and range dwindling, her voice scratchy and tired, Holiday still retained her unique timing and phrasing and— when she wanted—her ability to move listeners. Recording many American standards for Verve by Cole Porter, George Gershwin, and Rodgers and Hart, her personal interpretations made them seem new again. While deemed too painful to listen to by some critics, Holiday's later recordings are esteemed by others, who find the singer's ability to communicate at its peak. In *High Fidelity* Steve Putterman, for instance, judged her Verve recordings "devastating," because "tonal beauty and emotional expressiveness worked inversely for Holiday: The more her pipes gave out, the more penetrating and affecting her delivery became."

Although industry insiders in the late 1950s—Frank Sinatra for one—acknowledged her as "unquestionably the most important influence on American popular singing in the last twenty years," when the singer succumbed in 1959 to cirrhosis of the liver, kidney trouble, and cardiac arrest at the age of forty-four, her passing was noted by the general public as much for her lurid personal life as for her musical contributions. Time has since diminished the glare of Holiday's frailties and her musical gifts shine brighter than ever. Describing Holiday in a *Down Beat* review of one Verve collection as "the woman who taught the world that the interaction and feeling of jazz musicians was the ultimate key to interpreting the great American song lyric," Will Friedwald remarked: "I guess you can't inject so much real passion into a song without scaring the pants off some people. . . . *Billie Holiday on Verve, 1946-59* is essential music by the most haunting and hypnotic voice—indeed, sound—in all of recorded music."

Selected writings

(With William Duffy) *Lady Sings the Blues* (autobiography), Doubleday, 1956.

Selected compositions

Wrote and co-wrote songs, including "Fine and Mellow," "God Bless the Child," and "Don't Explain."

Selected discography

Holiday's recordings can be divided into four segments: From 1933 to 1942 she largely recorded for Columbia (with some discs for Okeh, Vocalion, and Brunswick); from 1944 to 1950 she was on the Decca (now MCA) label; and from 1952 to 1957 she recorded for Verve. She also recorded two important sessions with Commodore in 1939 and 1944.

Singles

"Did I Remember?"/"No Regrets," Vocalion/Okeh, 1936.
"Billie's Blues," Vocalion/Okeh, 1936.
"Strange Fruit"/"Fine and Mellow," Commodore, 1939.
"Loveless Love," Okeh, 1941.
"God Bless the Child," Okeh, 1941.
"Gloomy Sunday," Okeh, 1941.
"Lover Man," Decca, 1944.

Reissues and compilations

Billie Holiday: The Golden Years (includes "Riffin' the Scotch," "These Foolish Things," "Pennies Prom Heaven," "I Can't Give You Anything But Love," and "When You're Smiling"), Columbia.
Lady Day, Columbia.
Billie's Blues, Columbia.
Billie Holiday's Greatest Hits, Columbia.
Lady in Satin, Columbia.
The Original Recordings, Columbia.
The Quintessential Billie Holiday, five volumes, Columbia.
The Billie Story, volume 1 (includes "Don't Explain," "Ain't Nobody's Business If I Do," "Lover Man," and "Solitude"), MCA, volumes 2 and 3, Columbia.
From the Original Decca Masters, RCA.

Lady's Decca Days, MCA.
The Best of Billie Holiday (includes "Travelin' Light," "I Thought of You," and "Willow Weep for Me"), Verve.
All or Nothing at All, Verve.
The Billie Holiday Songbook, Verve.
Body and Soul, Verve.
The Complete Billie Holiday on Verve, 1946-1959, Verve.
The Essential Billie Holiday, Verve.
The First Verve Sessions, Verve.
Jazz at the Philharmonic, Verve.
Lady Sings the Blues, Verve.
The Last Recordings, Verve.
Songs for Distingue Lovers, Verve.
Stormy Blues, Verve.
Fine and Mellow/I'll Be Seeing You (includes "Lover Come Back to Me," "Embraceable You," and "My Old Flame"), Commodore.

Sources

Books

Chilton, John, *Billie's Blues*, Stein & Day, 1975.
Feather, Leonard, *The New Edition of the Encyclopedia of Jazz*, Horizon Press, 1960.
The New Grove Dictionary of Jazz, edited by Barry Kernfeld, Macmillan, 1988.
Penquin Encyclopedia of Popular Music, edited by Donald Clarke, Viking, 1989.
Simon, George T., and others, *The Best of the Music Makers*, Doubleday, 1979.
Tudor, Dean, *Popular Music: An Annotated Guide to Recordings*, Libraries Unlimited, 1983.

Periodicals

Down Beat, February 1986; July 1989.
Esquire, October 1989.
High Fidelity, January 1986; May 1987.
New York Herald Tribune Book Review, August 5, 1956.
People, June 1, 1987.
Stereo Review, March 1981.

—Nancy Pear

Cissy Houston

Singer

When Whitney Houston skyrocketed to superstardom, many wondered what had made her an overnight sensation. Those on the musical scene, however, knew that Whitney's role model was her very talented mother, Cissy. The elder Houston has had a lengthy musical career as a gospel, pop, and blues singer. In fact, one reviewer for the *Los Angeles Times* commented that mother Cissy's performance at an AIDS benefit put "daughter Whitney to shame."

Cissy Houston started singing at the age of five with the family gospel group, the Drinkard Singers, in Newark, New Jersey. After years of singing gospel, she crossed over into the pop world and formed the group Sweet Inspirations with Sylvia Sherwell, Myrna Smith, and Estelle Brown. Before they recorded on their own, they were to perform on literally hundreds of songs for other artists. Labels they worked under included Atlantic Records in Memphis, Muscle Shoals, and New York.

Then in 1968 the experienced group decided to perform on their own. In that year they released their only two albums: *Sweet Inspirations* and *What the World Needs Now is Love*. They made the Top 20 that year with the hit single "Sweet Inspiration." Soon after, however, Cissy left to pursue a solo career and the rest of the group did back up work for many artists.

Cissy then went on to use her musical talents in a variety of ways. She was the first person to record "Midnight Train to Georgia," which later became a big hit for Gladys Knight and the Pips. She has done backup work for a numerous artists, including Elvis Presley, Aretha Franklin, and her niece, Dionne Warwick, and recorded with Wilson Pickett, Connie Francis, and Nina Simone. She also scored successes as a solo artist by recording "Tomorrow" and "Think it Over," from the musical *Annie*.

Nightclub performing is one of Cissy's strong points. In this venue she best showcases her talents as a crossover artist, combining pop, gospel, and blues. *Variety* reported on a nightclub act that Houston performed, concluding: "Houston has carved out a niche that defies easy categorization." She turned the country song "You Are Always on My Mind" into a rythym and blues number and sang "Just the Two of Us" in a rock and roll tempo.

Although she has always maintained a busy schedule, the success of daughter Whitney has helped Cissy's career. "All of a sudden, I'm being discovered," Houston commented in *Jet*. "People are now realizing that she's my daughter and that I taught her and she worked with me in clubs and concerts. Now people are saying 'Oh, that's who that is.'" And this notoriety has translated into more bookings and more work for the elder

Born Emily Drinkard; married John Houston (a Newark, NJ, city administrator); children: Whitney, Gary.

Sang with gospel group the Drinkards; formed group Sweet Inspirations c. 1968; sang backup vocals with the Sweet Inspirations for Atlantic, Muscle Shoals, and New York records; backup singer for Elvis Presley, Aretha Franklin and Dionne Warwick; has recorded with Luther Vandross, David Bowie and daughter, Whitney Houston. Has appeared on *The David Letterman Show*; subject of PBS television program, *Sweet Inspiration*, 1988; has sung in AIDS benefit concerts; director of church choir at New Hope Baptist Church in Newark.

Addresses: *Home*—Newark, NJ.

Houston: "It has helped me a great deal," she told *Jet*. "More and more people call every day. I really wanted to slow down but I'm getting just as busy."

In 1988 a Public Broadcasting Service television program on Houston's life was made, titled *Cissy Houston: Sweet Inspiration*. The program chronicled Houston's long career and her impact on the music business. Houston's musical flexibility was showcased in her sessions with such diverse artists as David Bowie, Dionne Warwick, and Luther Vandross. Some artists shared anecdotes about Cissy's music teaching style. According to Vandross, she was a taskmaster who could "make the people around her want to sing their best." Houston responded: "God didn't give you talents to keep to yourself. He gave them to you to share and that's exactly what I try to do. I try to train people to sing out their feelings in their own way."

Houston was very flattered by this video tribute to her life. She remarked in *Billboard* that the program is "the kind of thing that usually only happens at graveside. So the whole thing is very special to me."

One of the program's topics looks at why so many gospel artists received criticism for moving into popular music in the 1950s and 1960s. As one who came under this kind of attack, Houston commented: "I am a person who believes in what I am doing, whether in church or in secular music. It's all about the love you feel inside. It's really ridiculous, the attacks some gospel singers endure. They just don't know you inside, within your heart, or they wouldn't say those things."

Houston is a very spiritual person, as the years of singing gospel music attest. It has been said that no matter where Houston is on any given Saturday night—in a recording session with Luther Vandross, David Bowie, or her daughter, or in a smoky nightclub belting out songs—by 8 a.m. the next morning she will be directing her Radio Choir at the New Hope Baptist Church. She commented in *McCalls*: "The voice is God-given. . . . What I have is only what God gave me, and I've just expanded on that." Throughout her lengthy career, she has kept her life in perspective, and relied on her spirituality. "I've been very fortunate in this business," she remarked in *Jet*. "I've never stopped working even without a current hit record. Somehow or another God has made it so that I could always keep going."

Selected discography

Sweet Inspirations, Atlantic, 1968.
What the World Needs Now is Love, Atlantic, 1968.

Sources

Billboard, March 5, 1988.
Jet, April 14, 1986.
McCalls, May 1989.
Teen, December 1986.
Variety, July 30, 1986.

—Nancy Rampson

Howlin' Wolf

Singer, guitarist, harmonica player

Howlin' Wolf, born Chester Arthur Burnett in West Point, Mississippi, was awarded an honorary doctor of arts degree from Chicago's Columbia College in June of 1972; it read: "Premiere man of American Music, you have sung and made songs of hard-time blues and mighty joys that cry to make the world fair." Howlin' Wolf—along with Muddy Waters—revolutionized urban blues in Chicago after World War II.

The raw, rasping, guttural power of Wolf's fierce voice, combined with his imposing physical presence and wild stage abandon, made him unforgettable. His influence stretched far beyond the realm of the blues; British rock performers Eric Clapton, The Rolling Stones, and The Yardbirds merged Wolf's blues with white rock and roll in songs like "Smokestack Lightning," "Ain't Superstitious," "Back Door Man" and "Little Red Rooster." Wolf was an experimental bluesman who formulated a wide range of moods and possibilities for his songs. He was also notably consistent: Throughout his career he retained the style, vigor, and flavor of the Mississippi Delta blues of his early years.

Grew Up with the Blues

Howlin' Wolf was born on June 10, 1910. He grew up one of six children on the Young and Myers cotton plantation, where both of his parents worked. The Delta farmlands were rife with the blues, which were part of most social gatherings. When Wolf was a child his grandfather would tell him stories of wolves in Mississippi. Once, something frightened the young Chester and he ran howling upstairs, which prompted his family to dub him the Howlin' Wolf. Wolf adopted this name for himself early on, and—at 6' 3" and 300 pounds—lived up to it as an adult.

Wolf's father presented him with his first guitar when the bluesman was 18. With the exception of the World War II years, during which he served in the Army—stationed in Seattle, Washington—Wolf spent most of his adult life, until the age of 38, farming in Arkansas and Mississippi. It wasn't until his father's death in 1949 that he devoted himself entirely to the blues.

Learned from the Greats

Throughout his young life Wolf had his pick of blues greats for mentors: Charlie Patton lived on a nearby plantation and taught Wolf much about showmanship. Sonny Boy Williamson married Wolf's stepsister Mary in the early thirties and showed Wolf the ins and outs of the harmonica during the courtship. Wolf himself was married briefly to Willie Brown's sister. Wolf's childhood idol was singer Jimmie Rodgers, who was noted for his "blues-yodel." Wolf tried to emulate the yodel, but found that his efforts sounded more like a growl or a howl. "I couldn't do no yodelin'," Barry Gifford quoted him as saying in *Rolling Stone,* "so I turned to howlin'. And it's done me just fine." Wolf met legendary Delta blues singer Robert Johnson in Robinsonville, Mississippi, and they played together briefly. Shortly thereafter Johnson was poisoned—by a jealous girlfriend or husband. "This is all part of the blues," Wolf reportedly remarked on hearing the news of his colleague's demise.

In 1948 Wolf formed his first band in Memphis, Tennessee. "That's where I got my break," he recounted in the *New York Times.* "Back in the country the people weren't able to pay you too much. Sometimes you'd work all night for a fish sandwich, glad to get it, too." At first Wolf played gigs by himself, often earning only $50 working from 7:00 p.m. to 7:00 a.m. He decided that it would be better to have some other musicians help take the load off of him. His first band featured Willie Steele on drums, Willie Johnson and M. T. Murphy on guitars, Junior Parker on harmonica, and Destruction on piano. Wolf would alternate between harmonica and guitar— he had taken up electric when he was in the Army—but usually concentrated on singing.

Radio Exposure Brought Record Contract

Wolf sold advertising spots at this time for the thirty-minute planter's broadcast he had secured for himself on station KWEM in West Memphis. The radio show was what eventually earned him a recording contract, as he had gone as far as he could by word-of-mouth reputation. Wolf grabbed the attention of Ike Turner, then a young Artists & Repertoire man for West Coast-based RPM Records. Turner produced the first Howlin' Wolf sides for that label, which in turn were used to secure a contract with Sam Phillips's Sun Records. Wolf's first hits were "How Many More Years" and "Moanin' at Midnight." The masters cut for Sun were then sold to Chicago's Chess Records; Wolf went to Chicago in 1952, leaving his band behind in Memphis. He opened a small club there on 13th and Ashland to showcase local blues talent, his own included.

Wolf's animated stage presence was a departure for bluesmen at that time. He writhed, moaned, climbed up draperies, pounded on posts, rolled on the floor, and was gruff and blustery in order to hammer his songs home. His vocals were menacing and sounded unnatural at times, as though a primal force propelled them from his throat. He was tremendous in presence and voice and quickly became familiar on the Chicago blues scene. He did not merely *sing* words: He infused them with life and feeling, transcending the limitations of blues music through the sheer force of his voice and personality.

Love-Hate Relationship with Muddy Waters

A legendary rivalry between Howlin' Wolf and fellow Chicago blues giant Muddy Waters soon arose; much of it, however, has been blown out of proportion. Waters got Wolf his first job in Chicago. "I got in touch with him because I didn't know nobody here," Wolf reported to Peter Guralnick, as related in *Feel Like Going Home.* "He carried me around to the clubs and helped me get started." They shared a grudging admiration for each other. Waters led better bands, but it was Wolf who left a unique mark on everything he touched. Some obvious evidence of the rivalry does exist: Wolf did stall and stretch out his set at Michigan's Ann Arbor Blues Festival in 1969 in an attempt to prevent Waters from getting onstage. And when Waters's *Electric Mud* album came out in 1968, Wolf followed with his own "psychedelic" record—*The London Howlin' Wolf Sessions*—which never sat too well with Waters and was not perceived as great material. In fact Wolf himself viewed the release as disastrous, dismissed it as "birdshit," and denied having had anything to do with it. The record company maintained that it was initiated at Wolf's insistence after the success of Waters's *Electric Mud*. Despite the fracas it generated, Wolf's ill-fated excursion into psychedelics was brief. From then on he continued to evoke his traditional style: the rough vocal tone, the lyrical falsetto, and a slapdash feel. He would act out the drama of "Smokestack Lightning" by sighting the train, hopping on board, and then sadly "going down slow."

Wolf was a fiercely domestic man, a provider, a volunteer within the Chicago community, and an investor in property in his native Delta country. He was a jealous husband, but his diminutive wife Lillie didn't mind one bit: She knew what Wolf was like and it suited her just fine. They had two daughters, Barbara and Betty Jean, and lived simply but comfortably in a house on Chicago's south side. Wolf was a peaceful, pensive, near-sighted man with a pipe when at home; Lillie saw little of the onstage Wolf. He had a true lust for life and his pragmatic, insightful views frequently were at odds with those trying to make a living off his talent. As a result, Wolf earned a reputation for an unpredictable and sometimes difficult temperament. He was suspicious of everyone—particularly managers—and usually for good reason. Not surprisingly, he was known to howl with rage if a situation warranted it. Wolf's forceful, stubborn personality and solid values garnered quite a lot of respect from the people at Chess Records and from other musicians as well.

Delta Instincts Guided Him to the End

Wolf never read music. He would sit on a metal chair in the studio, wearing big horn-rimmed glasses, shirt open, cradling a beat-up guitar, playing according to what sounded right to him. According to Guralnick, Wolf would say to his longtime backup guitarist Humbert Sumlin and the studio man playing lead, "I want you playing against each other, the two parts playing against each other." This usually addled the studio man—almost always a reading musician. Typically Wolf had to demonstrate what he wanted and run through it until his back-up players understood through sheer instinct.

After nearly a quarter century of remarkable performances throughout the U.S. and abroad—not to mention his famed Chicago act—Howling Wolf died peacefully, of complications arising from kidney disease, on January 10, 1976, in a Chicago hospital; he was 65. He had sang the blues almost until the time of his death, despite his illness; his last public appearance was with renown blues guitarist B. B. King at the Chicago Amphitheater in November of 1975. While undergoing kidney treatment in the hospital he frequently had fans smug-

gle forbidden foods to him. He once escaped to enjoy a full meal of meat and potatoes; no one could find him. Hours later, sated, he arrived back at the hospital licking his lips. Wolf can be heard howling his own

---

I couldn't do no yodelin', so I turned to howlin'. And it's done me just fine.

---

fitting epitaph on "Smokestack Lightning"—one of the most beautiful blues songs ever written: "Fare you well, never see me here no more, oh, don't you hear me."

Selected discography

Big City Blues, United, 1966.
The Real Folk Blues (recorded c. 1956-65), Chess, 1966.
(With Hubert Sumlin, Otis Spann, Willie Dixon, and others) *More Real Folk Blues* (recorded c. 1953-57), Chess, 1967.
The London Howlin' Wolf Sessions (featuring Eric Clapton, Steve Winwood, and The Rolling Stones), Chess, 1971.
Message to the Young, Chess, 1971.
The Back Door Wolf, Chess, 1973.
Change My Way, Chess, 1977.
Moanin' in the Moonlight (recorded 1951-59), Chess, reissue, 1987.
Cadillac Daddy: Memphis Recordings, 1952, Rounder, 1989.
Chicago: 26 Golden Years, Chess.
His Greatest Sides, Vol. 1, Chess.
Howlin' Wolf: Moanin' in the Moonlight, Chess.
Live and Cookin' at Alice's Restaurant, Chess.
Evil, Chess.
Howlin' Wolf: Chess Blues Masters, Chess.
The Legendary Sun Performers: Howlin' Wolf (British import), Charly.
I'm the Wolf, Vogue.
This Is Howlin' Wolf's New Album (British import), Cadet C.
From Early til Late, Blue Night.
Going Back Home (British import), Syndicate Chapter.
Heart Like Railroad Steel: Rare and Unreleased Recordings, Vol. 1, Blues Ball.
Can't Put Me Out: Rare and Unreleased Recordings, Vol. 2, Blues Ball.
Ridin' in the Moonlight, Ace.
(With Funny Papa Smith) *Howlin' Wolf & Funny Papa Smith,* Yazoo.

Sources

Books

The Blues Line: A Collection of Blues Lyrics from Leadbelly to Muddy Waters, compiled by Eric Sackheim, Schirmer, 1969.

Christgau, Robert, *Christgau's Record Guide,* Ticknor & Fields, 1981.

Guralnick, Peter, *Feel Like Going Home,* Outerbridge & Dienstfrey, 1971.

The New Rolling Stone Record Guide, edited by Dave Marsh and John Swenson, Random House/Rolling Stone, 1979.

Oliver, Paul, *Conversation with the Blues,* Horizon Press, 1965.

Periodicals

Creem, November 1972.

New York Times, January 12, 1976.

Rolling Stone, August 24, 1968; February 12, 1976.

—*B. Kimberly Taylor*

Chris Isaak

Singer, songwriter, instrumentalist

Chris Isaak's moody, anachronistic music is an unlikely addition to the pop charts, but after years of near-obscurity the handsome Californian is on the brink of major stardom. Virtually since his debut album appeared in 1985 Isaak has had a cult following—and the raves of critics—but he broke through to the public's attention in 1991 with the top ten hit "Wicked Game." Since then Isaak has been quite happy to bring his jazz- and rockabilly-influenced sound to large theaters and concert halls. "I'm doing the same thing, but more people are watching," he told the *Boston Globe.* "It's real strange to me that it's happened so quick. We've been doing this for years, but it just seems like all of a sudden people are showing up and paying attention. But you know, we're diggin' it."

Success has been slow in coming to Isaak because he places artistic merit before marketability. A number of his early albums failed to sell because his fifties-style rockers and ballads sounded so *different* from standard pop fare. Isaak told the *Washington Post:* "I heard all those other records that didn't use any guitars and I heard all those guys who couldn't sing at all, and they didn't stick in my mind at all. . . . I mean, do you think Wynton Marsalis wakes up every morning and says, 'Jazz is never going to sell as much as pop, so I'm going to change what I'm doing?' No, you have to do what you're going to do. I'm always going to make records where the emphasis is on a good song with the voice out front."

Forged His Own Identity

Unlikely as it seems, a singer-songwriter who plays the accordion and calls up images of Roy Orbison has succeeded on his own terms. At one time Isaak and his band Silvertone were fixtures on the West Coast rock scene and were favorites of such Hollywood notables as actor-turned-director Sean Penn and director David Lynch. In fact, Lynch's inclusion of Isaak's music in the soundtracks of *Blue Velvet* and *Wild at Heart* helped launch the rocker on a national level. Critics have always praised Isaak's music, however, even though his debut album sold only 14,000 copies on release. "No one else has so successfully drawn from the past, with an artist's eye, reassembling the disparate images, sounds, styles and artifacts of pop-culture history into one persona," wrote Michael Goldberg in *Rolling Stone.* "Of course, Isaak would be just another two-bit Elvis clone if he didn't manage to transcend all the stagy photos, contrived outfits and retro minutiae. Sure, that stuff is fun; it has its charm. But what matters is his music, which is the genuine article."

Isaak grew up with a healthy distrust of fads and trends.

For the Record. . .

Born in 1956 in Stockton, CA; son of a forklift operator. *Education:* University of the Pacific, B.A., 1980.

Singer, songwriter, guitarist, 1980—. With James Calvin Wilsey (guitar), Kenney Dale Johnson (drums), and Rowland Salley (bass), formed band Silvertone, 1981; signed with Warner Bros. Records c. 1985, and released first album, *Silvertone,* 1985. Had first Top Ten hit, "Wicked Game," 1991. Songs have been featured in the film soundtracks of *Blue Velvet,* De Laurentis, 1986, and *Wild at Heart,* 1990. Amateur boxer c. 1976-80.

Addresses: *Record company*—Reprise (Warner Bros.), 3300 Warner Blvd, Burbank, CA 91510.

He was raised in Stockton, California, a blue-collar town some sixty-five miles east of San Francisco. Isaak was a radio buff who wired his whole back yard in order to pull in esoteric stations from all over America and Canada. "I listened to tons of stuff as a kid," he told the *Boston Globe.* "I'd listen to the radio very late at night, laying in bed. All through high school, people probably thought I was the world's sleepiest guy or just a dummy. During the first three classes each day, I would just sleep because I'd been up until 4:30 or 5 listening."

Despite his interest in music, Isaak never considered pursuing a singing career. Still, he had an instinct for the offbeat style and a stubborn pride in his individuality. After high school he enrolled at the University of the Pacific, where he studied filmmaking, English, and journalism. He also boxed, mostly as an amateur, and had his nose broken seven times. "I was definitely on the outside," Isaak told the *Chicago Tribune* of his college years. "I'd drive across town over to the old Santa Fe Depot on the south side of Stockton and box all day, and it was all blacks and Mexicans and a couple of white trash guys like myself, and then I'd go across town to this university and it was all these upper-crusty guys with that Poupon kind of mustard. I didn't really fit in with either side."

Isaak cultivated an artistic look by dressing in bizarre thrift shop clothing from other eras. He became devoted to music in 1979, when he was spending a semester in Japan. "There was this Elvis song that really knocked me out called 'I'll Never Let You Go,'" Isaak said in the *Washington Post.* "I liked the song so much that I sang it and sang it. One day, the Japanese lady that lived downstairs from me started singing it too. She couldn't speak English. She had learned it phonetically from hearing me. That's when I decided to give singing a try."

After graduating from college, Isaak moved to San Francisco. "When I came down from Stockton, I was pathetic," he told the *Washington Post.* "I had this bright lime green suit with black velvet buttons. I thought that was how musicians dressed; I didn't really know. I kept going down to this nightclub and standing outside the door until they eventually said, 'Do you want to come in for free?' Then I'd go in and look for people who looked like someone who might want to be in my band."

Played Nightclubs

By 1981 Isaak had formed a small band called Silvertone. The group played in the San Francisco nightclubs and bars, alternating fifties hits with more and more of Isaak's original material. They literally began at the bottom but soon became favorites in the Bay area. Producer Erik Jacobsen became a big Silvertone fan and eventually helped to secure a recording contract with Warner Brothers Records. The debut album, *Silvertone,* was released in 1985.

The nation's pop music critics simply loved *Silvertone.* *Washington Post* contributor Joe Sasfy wrote: "Chris Isaak's 'Silvertone' is not only one of the most striking debut albums of the year, it is also one of the few albums of the '80s offering a thoroughly contemporary rock sound fashioned from America's musical roots." Goldberg called the work "terrific," praising its "sparse, Sun Sessions-like production, . . . twanging Duane Eddy-ish guitar playing and Isaak's romantic, larger-than-life voice."

The accolades notwithstanding, Isaak's first album—and his second, *Chris Isaak*—sold very few copies at first and received almost no radio air time. Some influential people did notice Isaak, however—Lynch, for one, and rocker John Fogerty, who called Isaak "a skyscraper against the landscape." Even Roy Orbison befriended Isaak and began writing a few songs with him before Orbison's fatal heart attack.

Inevitably Isaak was compared to Orbison, and to Presley, due to his falsetto vocals and moody tunes about love gone sour. Isaak is frankly uncomfortable with the comparison. For one thing, his music has a distinctive contemporary edge, even though its style harks back to earlier years. Furthermore, Isaak is simply unwilling to try to fill someone else's shoes. "When you compare somebody to Roy Orbison or Elvis, it's like parking a speedboat next to the Queen Mary," he told the *Boston Globe.* "What I do is nice, but I'm not trying to compare to those guys, because it makes my work look tiny. I have hopes that if I keep working hard, some day I'll have a couple of songs that'll add something to music. But I'd drive myself crazy if I thought I had to be like Elvis or Orbison, because I just don't think it's possible. Those guys are once in a generation."

"Wicked Game" Led to National Fame

Isaak's third album, *Heart Shaped World,* seemed destined to follow its two predecessors into obscurity. Fortunately for Isaak, a disk jockey in Atlanta heard the instrumental version of the rocker's "Wicked Game" in the soundtrack of Lynch's *Wild at Heart* and decided to track down the original song. The DJ then added "Wicked Game" to his station's playlist, and before long requests for the tune were pouring in. A single was released, and it slowly climbed into the Billboard top ten, pulling the album along after it. Two years after its release, *Heart Shaped World* emerged as Isaak's first gold album, and "Wicked Game" became his first hit.

Isaak has since moved from nightclubs to large theaters and the realms of MTV. "After years of playing to avid fans and very few others, Isaak is pleased as punch," wrote Sam Wood in the *Philadelphia Inquirer.* "He's finally found his audience. Several different audiences, actually." Those audiences are responding warmly to Isaak's wild rockers and his heart-rending ballads. Isaak has had his share of broken romances, and he explores his own personal pain in his lyrics. "A lot of times it's just stuff that I can't say to anybody," he told the *Chicago Tribune* of his songs. "Those ideas get stuck in my head and the only way I can say 'em is in music. The way I write, I sit down with a guitar, and usually it's in the dark, and I just start singing like I'm talking to myself. It all comes out at one time, the melody and the words."

Now that stardom has found him, Isaak is besieged with film and television offers, some of them quite tempting. He told the *Philadelphia Inquirer,* however, that he is not at all interested in changing careers. "I'd never give up music, because I like to sing more than anything," he said. "More than *anything.* People always ask me, 'What do you do on your time off?' I tell 'em I sing, 'cause that's what I like to do. Call me a one-dimensional shallow person, but if I got time off, I grab my guitar and play some more."

Selected discography

Silvertone, Warner Bros., 1985.
Chris Isaak, Warner Bros., 1987.
Heart Shaped World, Reprise, 1989.

Sources

Periodicals

Boston Globe, July 6, 1989; March 3, 1991; May 10, 1991.
Chicago Tribune, April 28, 1991; May 19, 1991.
Philadelphia Inquirer, May 17, 1991; May 20, 1991.
Rolling Stone, June 20, 1985; May 21, 1987.
Washington Post, August 15, 1985; May 12, 1987; May 17, 1991.

—*Anne Janette Johnson*

Etta James

Singer

Etta James is one of the most woefully overlooked figures in the history of blues and rock. She was never granted due credit for influencing tremendously popular acts like The Rolling Stones, Rod Stewart, Diana Ross, Janis Joplin, and an entire generation of musicians who have lauded her as a bridge between rhythm and blues and rock and roll. Recording some of the first ever rock and roll records as a teenager in the 1950s, James had a unique bird's-eye view of rock's origins. Not limiting herself to rock, however, she went on to make potent soul records in the sixties and seventies, adding further polish to a career that has spanned nearly four decades.

James has performed for black audiences in the South, blues fans in the North, rock fans on both coasts and even opened tours for The Rolling Stones. Her booming mid-range and throaty lower register—both powerful enough to shake you out of your seat—are her trademarks. Born in 1938 in Los Angeles, she was raised singing gospel hymns in her local church choir. James was a child prodigy, performing on Los Angeles gospel radio broadcasts by the age of five.

In the 1950s, when James was still a teenager, she formed a singing group called The Creolettes with two other girls. West Coast rhythm and blues titan Johnny Otis discovered James in 1954. "We were up in San Francisco," Otis recalled in *Rolling Stone*, "for a date at the Fillmore. That was when it was black. . . . I was asleep in my hotel room when . . . my manager phoned. He was in a restaurant and a little girl was bugging him: she wanted to sing for me. I told him to have her come around to the Fillmore that night. But she grabbed the phone from him and shouted that she wanted to sing for me NOW. I told her that I was in bed—and she said she was coming over anyway. Well, she showed up with two other little girls. And when I heard her, I jumped out of bed and began getting dressed. We went looking for her mother since she was a minor. I brought her to L.A., where she lived in my home like a daughter." Despite her determination to audition for Otis in his hotel room, James remarked later in *Rolling Stone*, "I was so bashful, I wouldn't come out of the bathroom."

"Roll with Me, Henry" Took Off

Otis took the Creolettes on the road with him in 1954, paid them each $10 a night, and changed their name to The Peaches. The trio first recorded with Modern Records, producing a track called "Roll with Me, Henry"—later changed to the less sexually suggestive "The Wallflower"—that was considered a reply to Hank Ballard's leering hit "Work with Me Annie." In 1955 James made "Good Rocking Daddy," which became a

117

For the Record. . .

Born in 1938, in Los Angeles, CA; father was Italian; married to Artis Mills; children: Donto and Sametto (sons).

Singer, 1943—; recording artist and concert performer, 1954—. "Discovered" by Johnny Otis in San Francisco, 1954; toured with Otis, 1954; recorded first record, "Roll with Me, Henry," with The Peaches for Modern Records; toured with Little Richard; sang backup for Marvin Gaye, Minnie Riperton, Harvey Fuqua, and Chuck Berry; began recording with Chess Records, c. late 1950s.

Awards: N.A.A.C.P. Image Award, 1990; inductee of the (San Franciso) Bay Area Blues Society Hall of Fame.

Addresses: Manager—DeLeon Artists, 1931 Panama Court, Piedmont, CA 94611.

ten chart-making hits from 1960 through 1963. In 1960 two of her songs made rhythm and blues charts. In 1961 four ascended to the charts, including the slow and soulful number-two hit "At Last." In 1962 three of James's songs landed on the chart, including "Something's Got a Hold on Me," which went to Number Four. 1963 saw another chart-topper and in 1966, James recorded the blues masterpiece "Call My Name." The following year she moved to Fame Studios in Muscle Shoals, Alabama. It was there that she scored the biggest hits of her career: the self-penned, beautiful, aching "I'd Rather Go Blind" and the raw, rollicking "Tell Mamma." In spite of her popularity, however, James was never able to break out of the black market in the 1960s; ironically, her singing style of purring, pointing, and little-girl pouting, was copied by Supreme Diana Ross, who *was* able to score hits in the white music market.

Influenced Janis Joplin

In 1969, during a closed recording session, James spied a young woman in the corner of the studio in wrinkled clothes, with a velvet purse and a bottle of whiskey. "What's she doing here?," James asked, as the story was reported in the *New York Post*. "Shhhh. That's Janis Joplin," someone said, "She's a big star." James stared at her for a few moments, and then remembered Joplin from years earlier, when the sixties rock and roll star was only 13 years old. James had been playing in Tulsa, Oklahoma, and Joplin walked right up the back stairs of the black club, and into James's dressing room. James let the girl visit for a while, and they talked about music. Throughout her career it was apparent that Joplin had been influenced by James's brassiness, rawness, and deep-voiced angst.

After a hiatus of several years, James returned to the public eye in 1973, back with Chess Records. Her style had changed somewhat: she no longer pouted; instead, she cried, pleaded, and shouted as she had as a child in the choir of Los Angeles's St. Paul Baptist Church. A portion of the proceeds from her 1973 album went to the maintenance of Los Angeles and New York City methadone programs, which aid heroin addicts trying to get off the drug. For 15 years, James was addicted to heroin; in March of 1974 she kicked the habit after checking in to the Tarzana Psychiatric Hospital in California. That year she recorded "Come a Little Closer." The song displays a curious tension: James moans and scats through a series of rich changes, tossing in heart-stopping descending arpeggios in what is widely considered *the* apex of secular spirit-singing.

hit. Then, Georgia Gibbs recorded a cover of "Roll with Me, Henry," calling it "Dance with Me, Henry"; it became a pop smash. James, Otis, and Ballard split the royalties three ways. "That's one time when we were not unhappy with a white cover [of a song originally recorded by a black performer]," Otis told *Rolling Stone*.

After this success James went on tour with fifties rock and roll sensation Little Richard. "I was so naive in those days," James admitted in the same *Rolling Stone* piece. "Richard and the band were always having those parties. I'd knock on the door and they'd shout 'Don't open it! She's a minor!' Then one day I climbed up on a transom, and the things I saaaaaw. . . ." After her stint with Richard, James sang backup on records by soul greats Marvin Gaye, Minnie Riperton, and Harvey Fuqua; she also lent her voice to many 1950s hits of early rock legend Chuck Berry, an association that would lead to a longstanding friendship. With her ripe, whiskey-cured, brawling belts, James was well on her way to becoming queen of the blues.

Early Sixties Proved Ripe

James began an association with Chicago's Chess Record company in the late l950s, recording several numbers on Chess's subsidiary label, Argo. In those early days, James, Gaye, Curtis Mayfield, and many other fledgling greats lived in Chicago's low-budget Sutherland Hotel. "We were hungry, starving musicians," James revealed in *Rolling Stone*. This changed abruptly, however, when James hit the mother lode with

In 1988 James made *The Seven Year Itch* for Island Records; aptly titled, it marked her first record contract in seven years. James sought to regain her raw, Southern sound for this album, and she had another goal: "I wanted to make an album that was saying a woman is no different than a man," she stated in the *New York Times*. "A woman can sing just as strong songs. She can be just as raunchy and just as weak. And I like the whole challenge of a woman standing up there and telling a man where to get off."

Etta James's mother once hounded her to forget rock and roll—"devil's music" to her—in favor of jazz. James has explored both. Later in life she became more experimental with rock. "People don't know how to slot me," she continued in the *Times*. "That's been a problem all my life. I bump, I grind, I howl—but what am I—Soul? Blues? Rock? Jazz? I like it all," she said.

Selected discography

At Last, Cadet, 1961.
Etta James Sings for Lovers, Argo, 1962.
Etta James, Argo, 1962.
Rocks the House, Chess, 1963.
Top Ten, Cadet, 1963.
Queen of Soul, Argo, 1964.
Etta James Sings Funk, Chess, 1965.
Call My Name, Cadet, 1966.

Tell Mama, Cadet, 1967.
Losers Weepers, Cadet, 1970.
Etta James, Chess, 1973.
Come A Little Closer, Chess, 1974.
Peaches, Chess, 1974.
Deep in the Night, Warner Bros., 1978.
Changes, MCA, 1981.
(With Eddie "Cleanhead" Vinson) *Blues in the Night*, Fantasy, 1986.
(With Vinson) *The Late Show*, Fantasy, 1987.
The Seven Year Itch, Island, 1988.
The Sweetest Peaches, Part I: 1960-66, Part II: 1967-75, Chess, 1989.
Sticking to My Guns, Island, 1990.

Sources

Boston Globe, November 6, 1986.
New York Daily News, November 3, 1988.
New York Post, June 18, 1974; February 13, 1981.
New York Times, June 28, 1974; November 19, 1982; November 20, 1988.
People, August 12, 1974.
Rolling Stone, June 15, 1974; August 10, 1978.
Time, July 17, 1978.

—*B. Kimberly Taylor*

Jane's Addiction

Rock band

Perhaps best known by the public at large for their outrageousness—lewd stage antics, songs challenging conventional morality, outspoken views on drugs, censored album covers—Jane's Addiction is also acclaimed for making accomplished, progressive rock music. Centered around the gritty, unfiltered, vaguely insect-like lyrics of lead vocalist and songwriter Perry Farrell, the Los Angeles foursome offers, in the words of *Rolling Stone* contributor Michael Feingold, "a strange but addictive brew of image and sound as intense as a horrific nightmare, beautiful as a heavenly dream, calculated to both endear and offend."

Musically, Jane's Addiction scores high marks with what David Handelman called in *Rolling Stone* its "wondrous fusion of funk, metal, punk and pretty acoustics"; the band is largely noted, however, for its distinct shock value. According to Erik Davis in *Rolling Stone,* Jane's much-touted 1988 album, *Nothing's Shocking,* managed "to be distinctively perverse in a [heavy-metal] world already saturated with bad taste and bacchanalia." Likewise, listening to *Ritual de lo Habitual,* the group's

For the Record. . .

Group formed in Los Angeles, 1986, disbanded, 1991; members included **Perry Farrell** (lead vocals and songwriter), born Perry Bernstein c. 1960, in Queens, NY, son of a jeweler, married Casey Niccoli (a filmmaker) c. 1991; **Eric Avery** (bass), born c. 1966, stepson of Brian Avery (an actor); **David Navarro** (guitar), born c. 1968, father was in advertising; and **Steve Perkins** (drums), born c. 1968, son of a plastics salesman and hair-salon manager.

Farrell was formerly with the band Psicom, 1981-85; Avery and Perkins were formerly with the band Disaster. Farrell has also directed, with Niccoli, the home video *Gift*, Warner Bros., c. 1991.

Awards: Voted best underground band and best hard rock/metal band by the *L.A. Weekly*, c. 1987; gold record for *Ritual de lo Habitual*.

Addresses: *Record company*—Warner Bros., 3300 Warner Blvd., Burbank, CA 91510.

survived four years—long enough to release an independent album that became a success on some college radio stations. Around 1985, however, Farrell set out to start a new band which, as Handelman noted, "wouldn't fit," and would openly confront issues like censorship and sexuality. He named the group Jane's Addiction after a drug-addicted prostitute who supported the band in its early days.

Joined first by bassist Eric Avery, and then by guitarist David Navarro and drummer Steve Perkins, Farrell and Jane's Addiction soon became a hit on the Los Angeles underground music scene. Playing at the Scream, the Pyramid, and the Roxy, the group featured the brash numbers "Pigs in Zen" and "Whores," in addition to slower, wrenching songs like "I Would for You" and the melodic, almost tender, "Jane Says." Farrell, as Handelman noted, moved across the stage "like a witch doctor, letting fly with his electronically processed, howling vocals." Outlandishly frocked, he sported a day-glow girdle—later opting for a black vinyl bodysuit—nosering, ghoulish mascara, and neon dreadlocks, the latter favored by other band members as well.

subsequent album, "is not a passive experience, as the band's version of life's ugly-beautiful is designed to provoke reaction," allowed *Stereo Review*. "The horror and grandeur of sex, art, garbage, crime, pain and pleasure . . . are held up for all to see with a naked honesty."

"Look, Don't Look Away"

Jane's Addiction is the brain-child of multi-media artist Farrell, whose compositions—"Whores," "Had a Dad," and "Idiots Rule"—amply display the philosophy of "*look,* don't look away," he described to Handelman. Born Perry Bernstein in New York City, Farrell attended college in California, but dropped out his freshman year after a nervous breakdown. "I like things that are esoteric and strange," he told Handelman, "and school is not full of esoteric and strange things." He worked a number of odd jobs, including a stint as an exotic dancer in a Los Angeles club, before deciding to become a singer.

With no musical training, Farrell began working in his basement apartment, recording songs into a tape recorder. He took the name of his brother, Farrell, as his surname, in an attempt to create a pun on the word *peripheral.* His first band, Psicom, formed in 1981,

Comparisons to Led Zeppelin

Jane's Addiction was soon hailed by local critics as a successor to seminal heavy-metal rockers Led Zeppelin—a comparison that would crop up again and again. In 1987 the group released a concert album on Triple X Records. By that time, intense competition was churning among major record companies wanting to sign Jane's Addiction on the strength of their reputation and the acoustic "Jane Says." Insisting on creative autonomy, Farrell and Jane's Addiction finally agreed on Warner Bros., which in 1988 released the much-lauded *Nothing's Shocking.*

Nothing's Shocking was praised by Steve Pond in *Rolling Stone* as "music that scrapes against the smooth surfaces of commercial pop." Pond noted that the group was at its "disturbing best" with "hard-boiled riff rockers, unsettling, lyrically incisive and musically excessive." One of the best cuts, according to Pond, was "Jane Says," which he described as an "acid-etched portrait of an addict, . . . [and] worthy Left Coast successor to [New York City denizen Lou Reed's] 'Walk on the Wild Side.'" By Pond's reckoning the band's many comparisons to Led Zeppelin resulted from their ability to create music that was "simultaneously forbidding and weighty, delicate and ethereal."

Ritual Cemented Stature

With 1990's *Ritual de lo Habitual*, Jane's Addiction proved that *Nothing's Shocking* was no fluke. *Stereo Review* described the effort as consisting of "exorcisms . . . of punk-funk guitar," "Farrell's sluicing, androgynous vocals," and "art-rock tone poems . . . emanating from a fertile erotic subconscious." While a *Guitar Player* reviewer felt that *Ritual de lo Habitual* didn't quite match the quality of *Nothing's Shocking*, he nonetheless called it "a ferocious set of art-metal," saying it "reeks of the funky danger that's been missing from most mainstream rock for 20 years."

Despite limited commercial airplay, *Ritual de lo Habitual* managed to break *Billboard's* Top Twenty and earned Jane's Addiction a gold record. Sales were undoubtedly helped by the furor over the record's cover—a Farrell creation featuring a primitivist sculpture of three naked women and icons of the sinister-seeming Mexican spiritual movement Santeria—that ensued when some record-store chains charged the band with obscenity and declined to carry the record. (In response, the album was distributed to several stores and record clubs in a generic white cover printed with the First Amendment.) *Nothing's Shocking* had faced a similar, if not so well-publicized, predicament two years earlier. Sales of *Ritual* were also helped when MTV viewers caught an eyeful of Jane's Addiction in the unsettling, but high-spirited video for "Been Caught Stealing," one of the record's most infectious cuts.

Lollapalooza

Jane's Addiction loomed large in the music press during the summer of 1991 when they launched the Lollapalooza Tour, which *Spin* contributor Dean Kuipers succinctly termed "an enormous traveling music and alternative-living festival." Envisioning an annual event, Farrell expressed his inspiration to Kuipers thus: "As my main experiment, I want to see what happens with a major exchange of information. I don't like the idea of the world being controlled by the news media. We need to exchange ideas somewhere else, another forum. The cafes aren't being used anymore, so let's try it at a festival. Everybody's all of a sudden aware at a different level." Headled by Jane's Addiction, the tour—featuring rap master and street-culture spokesman Ice-T, post-punk emissaries The Butthole Surfers, The Rollins Band, Siouxie and the Banshees, Nine Inch Nails, and the cutting-edge rock 'n' roll outfit Living Colour—

visited 21 cities, was attended by nearly 500,000 people, and sold out across the country.

Throughout its relatively short career, Jane's Addiction has insisted on doing things its own way—usually Farrell's. Aside from his scandal-provoking cover offerings, Farrell has also directed many of the videos for the group's songs, some that have been refused airplay on MTV because of nudity. Adding to their notoriety, various members of the band have at times spoken out about their love-hate relationship with drugs. Making an oblique reference to his own use of heroin, Farrell pointedly told Handelman that he doesn't "think it's anybody's business if I want to sit there and bang myself on the head with a board." Outspoken onstage, offstage, and on their recordings, Jane's Addiction is unlikely to acquiesce—even at the prospect of further commercial success—to what mainstream consumers of popular music deem acceptable. "Our music is an escape, a journey," drummer Perkins commented to Handelman. "And it represents drug-ridden, f—ed-up people—whether we are or not. I like when people are *inspired* by the music, not just going to see some industry band out to sell records. We might make choices that are harmful to us moneywise, but I don't want to see a bunch of bored old fellas playing just like the record." In September of 1991 *Rolling Stone* reported that Jane's Addiction—true to their convention-defying mandate—would break up after a limited series of post-Lollapalooza dates in Australia and Hawaii.

Selected discography

Jane's Addiction, Triple X, 1987.
Nothing's Shocking, Warner Bros., 1988.
Ritual de lo Habitual, Warner Bros., 1990.

Also recorded "Ripple" for *Deadicated: A Tribute to the Grateful Dead*, Arista, 1991.

Sources

Creem, October 1987.
Guitar Player, December 1988; January 1991; March 1991.
Musician, August 1988.
New York Post, November 1, 1988.
Q, May 1991; July 1991.

Rolling Stone, October 22, 1987; October 20, 1988; February 9, 1989; October 18, 1990; February 7, 1991; September 9, 1991.

Spin, June 1991.

Stereo Review, December 1990.

—*Michael E. Mueller*

Robert Johnson

Robert Johnson, the legendary Mississippi Delta blues singer, was a real person; that much is known. The mystery that is his life and art occurred between such well-defined events as his birth in 1911, the revelation of his remarkable musical skills around 1931, two recording sessions in 1936 and 1937, and his death in 1938. When the first album of his recordings was released in 1961 very little was known about Robert Johnson. By the time Columbia Records released *Robert Johnson: The Complete Recordings* in 1990 more was known, but the mystery remained.

Like other early Delta blues singers, Robert Johnson was part and parcel of an oral tradition that began with a mixture of field hollers, chants, fiddle tunes, and religious music and ended up as the blues. The Mississippi Delta, 200 miles of fertile lowlands stretching from Memphis, Tennessee, in the north to Vicksburg, Mississippi, in the south, was one of the primary locales in which the blues originated and developed. Johnson is critically recognized as the culmination of the Delta blues tradition, as exemplified by Delta blues artists Charley Patton, Son House, Skip James, and others. Characteristically, Delta blues are sung by a single artist playing an acoustic guitar, often using a bottleneck or similar instrument on the frets to achieve a distinctive sound. The next generation of musicians—and those who outlived Johnson—may have grown up in the Delta, but most left it to go north and sing the city blues of Chicago. Muddy Waters and Howlin' Wolf are two prominent Chicago bluesmen, both originally from the Delta, who knew Robert Johnson and were heavily influenced by him.

Waters, born McKinley Morganfield, grew up in the Delta, and though he never actually met Robert Johnson, his single encounter with him has been widely quoted. As Waters described the meeting in *American Visions,* among other sources, "It was in Friar's Point, and this guy had a lot of people standin' around him. He coulda been Robert, they said it was Robert. I stopped and peeked over, and then I left. He was a dangerous man." Knowledge of Johnson, like that of his music, has come largely through recollections of musicians and others who knew him. Two of the best sources of information have been legendary Delta singer Son House, himself Johnson's elder, and Johnny Shines, a contemporary who met Johnson in 1935 and traveled with him for a while. Additional information has been uncovered by researchers, who have helped to establish Johnson's birth date as May 8, 1911. Some of the circumstances of Johnson's death particularly remain unclear; there is even a dispute over the true site of his grave.

Born May 8, 1911, near Hazlehurst, MS; son of Julia Major Dodds and Noah Johnson (a plantation worker); died of probable poisoning August 16, 1938, near Greenwood, MS; believed buried in an unmarked grave at Mt. Zion Church, near Morgan City, MS, new evidence indicates burial site as Payne Chapel Memorial Baptist Church, near Quito, MS. Married twice.

Itinerant blues singer and guitarist, recording artist, composer. Traveled throughout the South and as far north as Detroit and Chicago, playing in small clubs—juke joints—and at informal gatherings. Disappeared in 1930, returned with a guitar and uncanny musical prowess. Recorded 16 songs, including "Kind Hearted Woman," "I Believe I'll Dust My Broom," "Sweet Home Chicago," and "Terraplane Blues," for the American Record Company (ARC), November, 1936; recorded 13 songs for ARC, June, 1937.

Columbia Compilation Renewed Interest

Fortunately, the recordings remain and the issuance of *Robert Johnson: The Complete Recordings* has refocused attention on the life and artistry of this legendary bluesman. Throughout his career and posthumous fame, recordings have played an important role in Johnson's art and its influence on younger musicians. Johnson himself was probably influenced by early blues artists like Skip James, who was recorded in 1931, the year that Johnson amazed his elders with his mastery of the guitar. James's eerie, peculiarly unique style appears throughout Johnson's recordings, most notably in "32-20 Blues," which he adapted from James's "22-20 Blues."

Johnson first came to the attention of modern musicians, notably the rock generation of the 1960s, with the release of *King of the Delta Blues Singers* in 1961. Due to the country blues revival of the time, older musicians who had sung as young men in the 1930s began to enjoy a second career and renewed popularity among hip, new audiences. Johnson's album contained selections from his 1936 and 1937 recording sessions, some of them previously unreleased. The album revealed a tremendous talent on vocals and guitar as well as an amazing ability in the lyrics of Johnson's self-composed blues. The album challenged younger rock musicians and showed them what the blues were all about. Johnson's first album was so popular that it was reissued in 1969; a second followed in 1970. Bob Dylan has written that Johnson was one of two musicians—the

other being Woodie Guthrie—who most influenced him. Among the Robert Johnson songs covered by rock musicians in the 1960s and later were "Love in Vain" and "Stop Breakin' Down"—recorded by the Rolling Stones—and "Crossroad Blues"—recorded by Eric Clapton with Cream.

Compositions Became Blues Standards

Many of Johnson's compositions had also become blues standards by the 1960s, thanks to Chicago blues artists Waters and Elmore James. In 1951 Elmore James recorded Johnson's "Dust My Broom," making it a national hit. "Sweet Home Chicago," another Johnson composition, has been played and recorded by countless Chicago bluesmen. As a traveling musician who had crisscrossed the Delta region many times and gone as far north as Detroit and Chicago in the previous six years, Johnson had ample opportunity to refine his lyrics, judging their popularity and impact by his audiences' reactions. A traveling musician like Johnson would have played to a variety of gatherings, from Saturday night juke joint crowds to friendly groups gathered for outdoor picnics. As Johnny Shines recalled, Robert Johnson was a rambling man who was ready to hop a freight at the drop of a hat. "He was a natural rambler," Shines told Pete Welding, as recorded in the *Down Beat Music Yearbook*. "His home was where his hat was, and even then lots of times he didn't know where that was. We used to travel all over . . . used to catch freights everywhere. Played for dances, in taverns, on sidewalks."

While these types of playing conditions provided Johnson with a means of refining his songs, it was the discipline of the three-minute 78 rpm record that drove him to hone them into a more commercial form. He crafted his songs with a self-conscious artistry; he sang of women, drinking, traveling, and the devil. His lyrics contain haunting metaphors and vivid personifications. Rather than joining interchangeable "floating verses," as many other Delta bluesmen did, Johnson made each song a statement, with intentionally developed themes. As Greil Marcus noted in the *New York Times,* Johnson's songs have "an immediacy which is unmatched in the blues, and an impulse toward drama."

Johnson recorded 29 songs for the American Record Company, which eventually became part of the Columbia Broadcasting System. His complete recorded canon includes 29 masters, plus 12 surviving alternate takes, all recorded at two ARC sessions held in San Antonio and Dallas. Johnson got started recording the way many other Delta musicians did—by auditioning. H. C.

Speir was a white ARC talent scout who ran a music store in Jackson, Mississippi. He had been acting as a talent scout for seven years and was responsible for getting blues artists Patton, House, Skip James, Tommy Johnson, and others into the recording studio. Speir passed Robert Johnson on to Ernie Oertle, another ARC talent scout and salesman in the mid-South, who offered to take him to San Antonio to record in November of 1936.

Rudimentary Recordings Captured Magic

Johnson's first session in San Antonio lasted three days. Sixteen songs were recorded in the Gunter Hotel, where ARC had set up equipment to record a number of musical acts, ranging from the Chuck Wagon Gang to groups of Mexican musicians. "Kind Hearted Woman" was the first song recorded. Also captured in San Antonio were "I Believe I'll Dust My Broom" and "Sweet Home Chicago," both of which became post-war blues standards. "Terraplane Blues," known for its metaphoric lyrics, became a regional hit and Johnson's signature song. Most of the selections were released on Vocalion 78s, but three songs and several interesting alternate takes remained unissued until they appeared on the Columbia albums. Six months later, in June of 1937, Johnson was called back to record. The two-day session took place in a Dallas warehouse where, once again, ARC had set up its recording equipment to capture many different acts. This time 13 songs were recorded and 10 were released during the following year.

While Johnson's professional recording career can be measured in months, his musical legacy has survived more than 50 years and is likely to become timeless. Critics have written a great deal about his genius, his unusual vocal style, his innovative guitar work, and the sensibility of his lyrics. As Peter Guralnick wrote in *Searching for Robert Johnson*, "There is no end of quoting and no end of reading into the lyrics, but unlike other equally eloquent blues, this is not random folk art, hit or miss, but rather carefully selected and honed detail, carefully considered and achieved effect."

Mysteries of His Life Have Made Johnson a Legend

Like many of his songs, which help reveal the kind of life he led, Robert Johnson's life itself has had a "considered and achieved effect," not only on his contemporaries, but also on subsequent generations of musicians. During his life, tales were circulated about him, explaining the unknown aspects of his life; and when he was murdered in 1938, at least three versions were given credibility—that he was stabbed to death by a jealous husband, stabbed by a woman, or poisoned by parties unknown. Subsequent research, based on eyewitness accounts, indicates that he was poisoned by a jealous husband. In August of 1938 Johnson and Honeyboy Edwards were playing at a house party in Three Forks, near Greenwood, Mississippi. Johnson became too familiar with the companion of the man who had hired him to play, and he drank some poisoned whiskey and died three days later. Welding, quoting Shines's account in the *Down Beat Music Yearbook*, related that by the time the story reached Shines, who had left Johnson to live with his own family in Memphis, Johnson had been "poisoned by one of those women who really didn't care for him at all. And Robert was almost always surrounded by that kind . . . seems like they just sought him out. . . . And I heard that it was something to do with the black arts. Before he died, it was said, Robert was crawling along the ground on all

> *Johnson was poisoned. . . . And I heard that it was something to do with the black arts. Before he died, Robert was crawling along the ground on all fours, barking and snapping like a mad beast. That's what the poison done to him.—Johnny Shines*

fours, barking and snapping like a mad beast. That's what the poison done to him."

Sold Soul to the Devil in Crossroads Bargain

Shines's reference to "the black arts" evokes another myth about Johnson: namely, that he sold his soul to the devil in order to achieve mastery over the guitar. The myth grew in response to an absence of information about how Johnson had learned to play the guitar so well. As a teenager he had had a reputation among older musicians, like House and Willie Brown, for being a pest who would grab their instruments and try to play them. House had to tell him, "You shouldn't do that, Robert. You're worrying the people. . . . You can't play, and you're just keeping up a lot of noise with it." As House recalled for Welding in the *Down Beat Music Yearbook*, Johnson ran away from home for about six months—though some sources say his absence spanned nearly two years— when his stepfather wanted him to work in the fields with him. More reliable sources attribute Johnson's 1930 departure and extended absence from Northern Mississippi to the death of his first wife and subsequent remarriage. When Johnson returned he had his own guitar. Robert Jr. Lockwood and a subsequently discovered photograph confirm that Johnson's guitar of choice was a Gibson Kalamazoo. Johnson demonstrated such a great ability upon his return home—most likely the fruits of bluesman Ike Zinnerman's tutelage—that House believed he had "sold his soul to the devil in exchange for learning to play like that."

Although Johnson never confirmed the story, another Delta blues musician, Tommy Johnson, once told his brother the same tale about going down to the crossroads to meet the devil at midnight. Folk researchers draw a parallel between the devil in the story and the African Yoruba god, Legba, the trickster, whose favorite haunt was a crossroads. It seems Johnson knew the life he sang about quite well, and his songs are rife with devil imagery. As if hiding some secret talent, he would often turn his back when he felt the eyes of another musician were watching him too closely. All of which adds to the myth, but takes nothing away from the music of the shadowy blues artist who came to be known as the "King of the Delta Blues Singers."

Selected discography

King of the Delta Blues Singers, Columbia, 1961.
King of the Delta Blues Singers: Volume 2, Columbia, 1970.
Robert Johnson: The Complete Recordings, Columbia, 1990.

Sources

Books

Charters, Samuel, *The Bluesmen*, Oak Publications, 1967.
Guralnick, Peter, *Searching for Robert Johnson*, Dutton, 1989.
Marcus, Greil, *Mystery Train*, Dutton, 1975.
Palmer, Robert, *Deep Blues*, Viking, 1981.

Periodicals

American Visions, June 1988.
Chicago Tribune, January 5, 1990.
Down Beat Music Yearbook, 1966.
Esquire, October 1990.
Living Blues, No. 94, 1990.
Musician, January 1991.
Nation, October 8, 1990.
New York Times, November 22, 1970.
Record Research, No. 43, May 1963.
Rolling Stone, October 18, 1990.
Wilson Library Bulletin, November 1975.

Additional information provided by Robert Johnson historian Stephen C. LaVere.

—David Bianco

Carole King

An introspective, stage-frightened woman with a wispy though resonant voice, Carole King seemed an unlikely bet in the early 1970s to become one of the top-selling recording artists of all time. But she moved quickly into that elite class with just one album, 1971's *Tapestry,* which by itself has sold more than 14 million copies worldwide and was the best-selling LP of all time until the Bee Gees surpassed it at the height of the disco craze with their *Saturday Night Fever* soundtrack. While *Tapestry* made King a household name as a singer, her previous career as a songwriter had already firmly established her reputation in recording industry circles. As Jon Pareles and Patricia Romanowski reported in the *Rolling Stone Encyclopedia of Rock,* "King has had two outstanding careers. Throughout the Sixties, she was one of pop's most prolific songwriters, writing the music to songs like 'Will You Love Me Tomorrow' and 'Up on the Roof,' with most lyrics by her first husband, Gerry Goffin. Then in 1971, with her multimillion-selling *Tapestry,* she helped inaugurate the Seventies' singer/songwriter style."

King seemed to arrive at the peak of her talents just in time to take advantage of a post-psychedelic generation that yearned for songs with a more personal, acoustic sound and lyrics that reflected simpler values. Actually, King's arrival at the superstar level was due more to a long fermentation in the shadows of the music industry.

First Hit Before Age 20

Born Carole Klein on February 9, 1942, in Brooklyn, New York, King took an early interest in music and had formed her first band, the Co-sines, while still in high school. While attending Queens College, King met Goffin; the two began what would become a long personal and professional relationship. Along with notable songwriters Neil Sedaka—a childhood friend of King's—Cynthia Weil, and Barry Mann, King and Goffin joined Al Nevins and Don Kirshner's Aldon Music company and composed hundreds of songs in the Brill Building's cubicles, famous for incubating hit songs for decades. In 1961, King—who was not yet 20—and Goffin had their first hit when "Will You Love Me Tomorrow" became a Number One single for the Shirelles.

In the early 1960s there was a strong push among music publishers for songs written exclusively for black artists; King's longtime interest in rhythm and blues stylings gave her a head start on the competition, as evidenced by the Drifters's Top Ten hit with the King-Goffin composition "Up on the Roof." Soon, Goffin and King were the hottest songwriters in the business. They

For the Record. . .

Born Carole Klein, February 9, 1942, in Brooklyn, NY; married Gerry Goffin (a lyricist; divorced); married Charles Larkey (a musician; divorced); married Rick Evers (a musician; deceased, 1978); children: (first marriage) Sherry, Louise; (second marriage) Molly, Levi. *Education:* Attended Queens College.

Formed group the Co-sines while in high school; began collaborating on compositions with lyricist Gerry Goffin, 1959; hired by Aldon Music song publishers, 1959; had first hit single, cowritten with Goffin, performed by the Shirelles, "Will You Love Me Tomorrow," 1961; formed group The City, 1968; solo singer-songwriter, 1970—; has appeared on numerous television specials and in off-Broadway stage productions.

Awards: Grammy Awards for album of the year, for *Tapestry,* record of the year, for "It's Too Late," song of the year, for "You've Got a Friend," and for best pop female vocalist, all 1971.

Addresses: *Home*—Idaho. *Record company*—Capitol Records, Inc., 1750 North Vine St., Hollywood, CA 90028.

and Danny Kortchmar, a former member of the New York City club band Flying Machine, who introduced King to that group's vocalist, James Taylor. Because of King's stage fright, The City never toured; their only LP was an unsuccessful effort for Lou Adler's Ode label called *Now That Everything's Been Said.*

At this point it was Taylor who provided the encouragement King needed to take the next logical step in her career. Taylor had been much impressed by many of King's compositions for The City, particularly "You've Got a Friend," which he later turned into a hit himself. Taylor urged King to continue to write and record her own songs; the result was the 1970 album *Writer,* which displayed flashes of a new maturity in King's writing along with her richly textured piano chords. *Writer* enjoyed just enough success to merit another solo effort, *Tapestry,* which featured the hits "I Feel the Earth Move," "So Far Away," "It's Too Late," and King's own version of "You've Got a Friend," which Taylor had already taken to Number One on U.S. charts. *Tapestry* made it to Number One on the album charts, scored four Top Ten hit singles, and remained on the charts for 302 straight weeks—until 1977.

Tapestry Hard to Top

Understandably, King could never quite duplicate the incredible success of *Tapestry,* but for a period of years after its release she continued to produce quality work on LPs like *Music, Rhymes and Reason, Fantasy,* and *Wrap Around Joy.* King switched to Capitol Records in 1975 and immediately produced the gold record *Simple Things,* but it seemed clear by this time that her most productive period had passed. She continued recording into the 1980s, but sporadically and never with as much success as in earlier years. By that time she had become something of a recluse, preferring to live quietly in her Idaho home and make only a few concert appearances. King did, however, break new ground in her career in 1988 by appearing in an off-Broadway play called *A Minor Incident.*

followed their chart-topping success with the hits "Hi-De-Ho" for Blood, Sweat, and Tears, "One Fine Day" for the Chiffons, "Natural Woman" for Aretha Franklin, "Oh, No, Not My Baby" for Maxine Brown, and "Locomotion," the Number One hit the Goffins wrote for their seventeen-year-old baby-sitter, Little Eva. As Jon Landau wrote in *Rolling Stone:* "The songs of Goffin and King are superb examples of the songwriting craft of the Sixties. Finely honed to meet the demands of the clients who commissioned them, and written with the requirements of AM radio always firmly in mind, they still managed to express themselves in a rich and personal way. Like Hollywood directors who learned how to make the limitations of the system work for them and in the process created something of their own pop vision."

Met James Taylor

A mid-1960s attempt by Goffin, King, and Al Aronowitz to launch their own Tomorrow label failed, as did the Goffin marriage, which ended in divorce and King's move to Los Angeles with their two daughters. King was relatively inactive during this period, although she did continue to write both music and lyrics. In 1968 she formed a group called The City with bassist Charles Larkey—who would become her second husband—

Selected discography

Writer, Ode, 1970.
Tapestry, Ode, 1971.
Music, Ode, 1971.
Rhymes and Reasons, Ode, 1972.
Fantasy, Ode, 1973.
Wrap Around Joy, Ode, 1974.
Thoroughbred, Ode, 1976.
Simple Things, Capitol, 1977.

Welcome Home, Capitol, 1978.
Greatest Hits, Ode, 1978.
Touch The Sky, Capitol, 1979.
Pearls: Songs of Goffin & King, Capitol, 1980.
One to One, Atlantic, 1982.
Speeding Time, Atlantic, 1983.
City Lights, Capitol, 1989.

Sources

Books

Bane, Michael, *Who's Who in Rock,* Facts on File, 1981.

Clifford, Mike, *The Harmony Illustrated Encyclopedia of Rock,* Harmony Books, 1986.
Hardy, Phil, and Dave Laing, *Encyclopedia of Rock,* Schirmer, 1988.
Pareles, Jon, and Patricia Romanowski, *The Rolling Stone Encyclopedia of Rock,* Rolling Stone Press, 1983.
Stambler, Irwin, *Encyclopedia of Pop, Rock, and Soul,* St. Martin's, 1974.

Periodicals

People, August 20, 1979.
New York Times, April 5, 1989.

—David Collins

Rahsaan Roland Kirk

Instrumentalist

When Rahsaan Roland Kirk stood before an audience in the 1960s and seventies he resembled a fantastic, surreal, one-man band. A stritch—an instrument resembling a dented blunderbuss—hung well below his knees and a quasi saxophone called a manzello was usually wrapped around his neck at the ready. A tenor saxophone with a flute conveniently placed in the bell added to the picture. Also hanging from Kirk's neck was an arsenal of homemade instruments: a foot-long siren whistle held together with globs of tape, a song flute shortened so that it appeared to be a fat, black cigar—which he played with his nose—and a rectangular humming cube dubbed The Evil Box. Kirk played all three horns simultaneously, looking very much like a kid trying to eat three bananas at once. Making this weird spectacle all the more impressive was that Kirk was also blind.

Though he seemed gimmicky to some club owners, Kirk transcended his status as a freakish attraction and played with a virtuosity and searing emotionalism reminiscent of jazz greats John Coltrane and Sidney Bechet. When he put all three horns in his mouth, blowing like a whale, what spouted forth sometimes sounded like a bagpiper's band skirling in a Fourth of July parade. In 1963 *Time* magazine reported that "Roland Kirk . . . meshes a thrumming beat, a fertile imagination and an impish humor to achieve an exciting union of the pagan and the modern spirit—as if Pan were suddenly found piping merrily in a rush-hour subway." Anyone who can pop a child's plastic song flute into his right nostril during a flute solo and trill out a brief duet can't be all bad. In fact, this is an impossible feat for most musicians.

Spectacle Did Not Mask Talent

Kirk was a self-taught musician and a self-described "progressive jazz musician and a humorist." When he laid aside the stritch—forerunner of the alto saxophone—and manzello—forerunner of the soprano saxophone—the whistle, and The Evil Box, his tenor solos were smooth, flowing and wild. When he played siren whistle solos—by placing the whistle's bell directly on the microphone and simultaneously blowing and humming—he produced an effect not unlike a room full of mumbling sleepers.

Blind from the age of two, Kirk reported in *Ebony,* "I think a nurse put too much medicine in my eyes, and my mother didn't find out about it until too late." By age five he wanted to be a bugle boy at a camp where his parents were counselors. Kirk's uncle played piano and Kirk would accompany him by tooting along on a water hose. By the time he was ten he had progressed

For the Record. . .

Born Roland Kirk in 1936; died in 1977; married wife, Edith; children: Rory Stritch Kirk. *Education:* Attended the Ohio State School for the Blind.

Jazz instrumentalist. Joined Boyd Moore Band at age 15, Columbus, OH; played briefly with a rhythm and blues band in Texas; began recording in Chicago, c. 1960-62; played with Charles Mingus, New York City, c. 1962; played at Newport Jazz Festival, 1969. Invented the *rokon* whistle.

Awards: *Down Beat* awards from international jazz critics, 1961 and 1963.

to trumpet. Kirk's doctor noticed how distended his cheeks were when he played, so he worried about Kirk's eyes, and discouraged the youth from playing for two years. Kirk attended the Ohio State School for the Blind in Columbus. At 12 he took up the saxophone and clarinet. At 15 he was playing with Boyd Moore's band—a well-known combo in the Columbus area. Kirk played rhythm and blues and was billed as The Walking Blind Man. About that time he had a prophetic dream in which he was playing two instruments simultaneously. There followed a three year "search for the sound." He told a music store proprietor in Columbus about the dream and the man took him to the store's basement, where he kept a few antique instruments. Kirk found a manzello there and began playing it, along with his tenor, in Boyd Moore's band. "The search," he said, "was over." Later, at the same place, he found his stritch.

Approval From Charlie Parker

Moore quickly perceived Kirk as "getting too modern and too far out," so Kirk and a drummer friend headed to Los Angeles. They were going to pedal there from Ohio on a tandem bicycle, but a nervous Mrs. Kirk persuaded them to take a bus. Kirk did not have much luck in Los Angeles, however, so he moved to Texas with a rhythm and blues band. When that band dissolved he headed back to Columbus via St. Louis. He went to hear sax legend Charlie Parker in St. Louis and sat way in the corner, playing along with Parker's "Half Nelson" on his plastic song flute. According to *Sun Magazine* contributor James D. Dilts, Parker heard him, and after finishing his set, approached Kirk and said, "I can tell by the way you play on this little thing that you've got something, so keep it up."

In 1960 Kirk lit out for Chicago. There he made some records and found success, but he cut an odd figure in the studio. *Down Beat* magazine's Don DeMicheal was on hand. When someone asked Kirk in the studio why he played the siren whistle, Kirk explained, "I hear sirens in my head." DeMicheal later commented, "I expected him at any moment to take out a bag of goofer dust and cast hexes on us all."

Crossed Over at Newport

In 1962 Kirk landed in New York City. It wasn't long before he came to the attention of leading jazz bassist Charlie Mingus; within a few weeks word was out that there was a new talent in town. After a stint with Mingus, Kirk went out on his own. At the Newport Jazz Festival during the summer of 1969 he broke through to the vast young white audience, while achieving major prominence within the black realm. Between songs he offered wry comments concerning LSD, making love, racism, politics and television. He was particularly vocal about the dearth of black musicians featured on U.S. television, and about the pilfering of black music by white culture—without the establishment of proper credit.

Kirk invented a whistle called the rokon and had 45 instruments in his home. He added Rahsaan to his name because it occurred to him in a dream. "I have no religion that you get out of books," Kirk told Dilts. "I am not a Muslim. My whole religion has been in this dream religion. My life has been motivated by dreams." Kirk's stylistic province comprised nearly every jazz idiom and genre from blues shouting to free form, though his roots seem thickest in the swing era. In 1974 he traveled with a huge gong, foghorn, and a whistle, which he used to silence an inattentive crowd. "I want respect even if I'm playing in a snake pit," he asserted to Don Delliquanti in *People.* Kirk's loyal fans sensed his need to communicate from a sphere more noisy, but paradoxically, more ordered and lovely than their own.

Selected discography

Rip, Rig and Panic, Limelight, 1967.
Here Comes the Whistleman, Atlantic, 1967.
Left and Right, Atlantic, 1969.
Natural Black Inventions, Root Strata, Atlantic, 1971.
Blackness, Atlantic, 1972.
Bright Moments (live), 1973.
(With Jack McDuff, Joe Benjamin, and Arthur Taylor) *Kirk's Work* (recorded 1961), Mercury, 1977.

(With Richard Wyands, Hank Jones, Art Davis, Wendell Marshall, and Charlie Persip) *We Free Kings* (recorded 1961), Mercury, reissued, 1986.

(With Ira Sullivan) *Introducing Roland Kirk* (recorded 1960), Chess, 1990.

1990 Rahsaan: The Complete Mercury Recordings of Roland Kirk (recorded 1961-65).

The Man Who Cried Fire, Night, 1991.

The EmArcy Jazz Series (reissue), Polygram.

Case of the 3-Sided Dream in Color, Atlantic.

The Inflated Tear, Atlantic.

Sources

Down Beat, May 23, 1963.

Ebony, May 1966.

New York Herald, May 27, 1962.

New York Times, April 3, 1971; May 30, 1971; July 7, 1973; December 16, 1990.

People, July 15, 1974.

Reporter, June 5, 1967.

Sun Magazine (Balitmore), April 30, 1967.

Time, August 9, 1963.

Village Voice, September 3, 1970; December 25, 1990.

Washington Post, April 29, 1970.

—*B. Kimberly Taylor*

Evgeny Kissin

Evgeny Kissin has been a musical prodigy since the age of two, when he began to play the piano. His mother, a piano teacher, never taught him, but instead sent him to Moscow's Gnessen School for musically gifted children, where he was enrolled through 1991. Kissin has had only one piano teacher, Anna Pavlovna Kantor, and has never entered the competitive recital circuit. Kissin's advanced interpretations and specialized skills have grown with intensive tutelage, yet his personality and individualism have remained intact. Kissin explained his personal philosophy of music to *Time:* "True art gives birth to good as opposed to evil. Right now we are going through a very turbulent time. The goal of musicians is to make our art, which is humane, kind and international, prevail over all the other things that are evil."

By the age of ten, Kissin was already becoming an international legend, without the benefit of an American debut. Harold C. Schoenberg, a music critic for the *New York Times,* was invited by conductor and violinist Vladimir Spivakov to hear Kissin play. Schoenberg recalled that "the boy had everything—fingers, tone, and an uncanny ability to know exactly when to modify a tempo, how to accent an inner voice, how to highlight a phrase in the subtlest and most musical of ways. All this at 12." In 1988 Herbert von Karajan, a conductor and talent scout, summoned Kissin to play the Tchaikovsky concerto with the Berlin Philharmonic. This attention earned Kissin offers from recording companies. Schoenberg described Kissin as a "Romantic pianist in the old Russian tradition." Some critics have suggested that Kissin's style is unspoiled because he avoids traditional performance competitions. Peter G. Davis, a music critic for *New York,* remarked that Kissin was outstanding because he "never had to [compete]." Generally, the competition school of piano demands a hard, even, and uniform technique in all of its students. Kissin's style stands out from his regulated peers. An emotional style of play, Romanticism, according to Schoenberg, "looks back to a period when a controlled sonority, a singing line, power without banging, tempo modification and poetry were what the great Slavic Romantic pianists represented."

Kissin made his long-awaited United States debut on September 20 of 1990, at the Avery Fisher Hall with the New York Philharmonic and received a standing ovation from the sellout crowd. A few days later he played a recital at Carnegie Hall. Donal Henahan of the *New York Times* attended Kissin's debut, and reported, "It is not often that a young pianist with the technical tools of a Mr. Kissin resists the urge to whip up visceral excitement purely by playing fast and loud. . . . At times he took an embroidered run so softly that the piano seemed to be murmuring Chopin's thoughts to itself, reminding a listener that, according to contemporary reports, that is exactly how the composer himself played his music." Remarks about the controlled power of Kissin's playing dominated reviews of these concerts. *New York*'s Peter G. Davis marveled that Kissin could "project the combative force of Prokofiev's warlike Sonata No. 6 quite this powerfully and yet temper the onslaught with so much expressive urgency."

Critic Michael Walsh wrote in *Time* of Kissin's performance of Schumann's *Symphonic Etudes* at the Carnegie Hall recital that the Russian played "the series of challenging variations as if he were inventing the piece as he went along." Attesting to the maturity of Kissin's interpretations in an *Entertainment Weekly* review of the album *Yevgeny Kissin in Tokyo* that included works by Rachmaninoff, Prokofiev, Liszt, Chopin, and Scriabin, Walsh concluded, "the point is simply that . . . Kissin plays with the passion of a young man and the taste of an old one."

Kissin relaxes in the time allotted after more than thirty concerts a year by playing Scott Joplin rags and reading the works of Russian authors Pushkin and Tolstoy. Often described as quiet and nervous, Kissin projects a modest character. He downplayed his musical abilities by expressing his tentativeness to approach the works of German composer Ludwig van Beethoven. In an interview with Abigail Kuflik of *Newsweek,* Kissin remarked that "maybe it was easier for me as a young person to play romantic music, to play music with the heart. Beethoven it's nicer to play also with the mind. Maybe that's why I had to become old." It seems probable that the young Russian, armed with a durable talent based on sturdy philosophy, will survive prodigy intact and proceed to adult genius.

Selected discography

Carnegie Hall Debut Concert, RCA (Red Seal), 1990.
Evgeny Kissin: A Musical Portrait, RCA (Red Seal), 1990.
Yevgeny Kissin in Tokyo, Sony Classical, 1990.
Two Inventions for Piano, RCA.

Sources

Entertainment Weekly, October 26, 1990.
New York, September 2, 1990; October 22, 1990.
New York Times, September 22, 1990; October 7, 1990.
Newsweek, October 22, 1990.

—*Christine Ferran*

Christine Lavin

Singer, songwriter

B efore Roger Deitz interviewed Christine Lavin for *Sing Out!* magazine, he watched her finish a lesson with instructor Mike Moore. Moore was not teaching Lavin voice or guitar technique; a Georgia and Florida state champion, he was helping her through a particularly complicated baton twirling routine. This may seem a strange pastime for a musician. But for Lavin—who in concert twirls while her tape recorded "deepest thoughts" wonder "What if I drop it" and "Did I leave my iron on?"—it is an integral part of her show. It also comes in handy when she loses her voice, as she did at the 1988 Ann Arbor Folk Festival. Lavin, whose music is sometimes labeled pop, more often folk, and occasionally even stand-up comedy, is, as Vin Scelsa described in *Penthouse,* "a driving force and enthusiastic cheerleader of the eighties Folk Revival."

Lavin has built a reputation as one of *the* observers and chroniclers of modern urban life, with recordings like "Prisoners of Their Hairdos," "Sensitive New Age Guys," "Good Thing He Can't Read My Mind," and "Mysterious Woman," a brilliant parody of folk-pop singer Suzanne Vega. Although she has received little attention on mainstream radio stations, Lavin has built a wide following among critics, folk music fans, and public radio listeners. In his *Penthouse* article on Lavin, Scelsa called her "one of the country's best songwriters. Period. Regardless of genre or backup instrumentation. For her literacy, humor, and compassion, her keen, observant eye and ability to translate the most mundane moments into magic, I can only compare her to the likes of, say, a [songwriting giant like] Paul Simon." Concurring in the *Utne Reader,* Jay Walljasper wrote, "Her lilting, elegant voice and sweet, soft melodies belie a tart wit that is somewhat similar to [cartoonist and writer] Lynda Barry's. . . . At times hilarious, at times absurd, at time touching, and sometimes all three at once, Lavin is not going to be mistaken for one of those warbling songbirds who give folk music a bad name. She's definitely got an '80s edge."

Learned Guitar From Public Television

Lavin grew up one of nine siblings in Peekskill, New York, where her father was an administrator at a military academy. As she explained in *Frets Magazine,* her mother felt that each of her children needed something that made them individual, because she was afraid they would get lost in such a big family; Lavin got the role of family guitarist. She couldn't afford lessons, so she learned how to play by watching New York City's public television station, which broadcast guitar lessons twice a week. "So if you contributed to public

For the Record. . .

Born c. 1952; raised in Peekskill, NY; daughter of a military academy administrator. *Education:* Attended Rockport State.

Singer, songwriter, concert performer, recording artist. Worked as a waitress, baker, and occasional performer, Cafe Lena, Saratoga Springs, NY, 1975-1976; worked as a wandering minstrel in a Mexican restaurant, and at Bellevue Hospital, New York City. Became involved with the Speakeasy (a cooperatively run folk club), New York City, and its music publication, *Fast Folk Music Magazine.* Recorded *Another Woman's Man;* and *Future Fossils,* 1984, on her own label, Palindrome (later picked up for national distribution by Philo/ Rounder Records). Appeared frequently at national folk festivals c. late 1980s.

Addresses: *Home*—New York City. *Agent*—Katherine Moran & Associates, P.O. Box 60, Weare, NH 03281. *Record Company*—The Rounder Records Group, 1 Camp St., Cambridge, MA 02140.

lasted until the fall, earning enough money to buy a better guitar.

Fast Folk Broadened Her Horizons

In the early 1980s a New York club called the Speakeasy asked Lavin to perform. Her then-manager told her not to take the job because, she said, "It's just a bunch of *folk* musicians hanging around at this club behind a *falafel* stand! You don't want to be involved with *these* people," Lavin told *Frets.* Shortly thereafter she realized this manager was "sort of a maniac" and in checking out the club found it exactly the place she wanted to be. At the Speakeasy she became involved with the house writers cooperative that had created *Fast Folk Music Magazine.* A non-profit production, *Fast Folk* is published every six weeks; a subscription includes a twelve-cut record as well as a magazine containing essays, reviews, bios, and a guide to folk music events. Since joining the *Fast Folk* team, Lavin has written for, produced, and edited several issues of the magazine. She has also worked on publicity and has emceed performances at the Speakeasy club.

During the early years of her involvement with *Fast Folk,* Lavin also worked full-time at New York's Bellevue Hospital. She told *Sing Out!* that those were her "giving-up years." She took some guitar lessons and performed occasionally, but felt it was time to try something else. She did not give up on her music completely, however, and managed to record her first album, *Another Woman's Man,* during this period. In 1984, after giving up the "giving up period," she recorded *Future Fossils,* which she produced herself. At that point Lavin was becoming a fixture on the New York folk scene. With the release of *Beau Woes and Other Problems of Modern Life* in 1986, critics began to pay attention. A review in *Spin* noted that the album "presents a clever lyricist equally adept with humorous tales and sensitive ballads." By this time Lavin was developing a wide following in clubs and festivals across the country.

television, you played a part in my musical development," she told Deitz in *Sing Out!* In the same interview, she said that her musical influences also came from mass media, as she couldn't afford records either. Lavin listened to New York's WNEW-FM, and the musicians she heard there—Bob Dylan, Judy Collins, Pete Seeger, Phil Ochs, Joni Mitchell—shaped her musical taste. Lavin attended Rockport State and in 1975, after a sojourn in Florida, moved to the Cafe Lena in Saratoga Springs, New York. In *Sing Out!* she explained that she had a goal of someday opening a club, so she took a waitress and bread-baking job at the cafe to see what running a club was like. The time she spent there was a "tremendous education," as it afforded her the opportunity to hear some of the greats of folk music. In February of 1976 folk-pop singer Don McLean's manager heard Lavin perform at the cafe; he told her that if she learned to play the guitar better and moved to New York City, she might have a career in music. As fate would have it, singer-songwriter Dave Van Ronk visited the club the same evening and reiterated the manager's suggestion that she move to New York. Van Ronk also offered to really teach her how to play the guitar; by March she had moved. Two months later Lavin found herself working as a wandering minstrel in a Mexican restaurant on Columbus Avenue. The job was less than ideal; in fact, she told *Sing Out!,* she hated it. Yet in spite of such incidents as being ordered to sing while a knifing occurred in the restaurant, she

Shed Reliance on One-liners

The 1988 release of *Good Thing He Can't Read My Mind* marked an important change in Lavin's style: While the earlier albums were distinguished by the singer's very witty and ironic comments on American culture, this one included only two outright comic songs. In David Hinckley's *New York Daily News* review of the album, he suggested that Lavin may have wondered if her wit and charm were overshadowing her songs, and reported that in *Good Thing* she had created "her most 'produced' work and the [one] least reliant on one-liners." Scelsa agreed: "There is less immediate silliness than on past efforts; her humor has grown more subtle." Lavin told *Sing Out!* that it had actually taken time to become comfortable performing the more serious songs. The humor worked as a shield; it was easier to be funny under pressure. She had also felt that the often too-serious folk music needed some lightening up. Critics took the change as a sign of Lavin's maturing style and burgeoning talent.

Lavin's career took a worrisome turn in 1989 when she began having trouble with a tendon in her hand, a grave problem for someone who makes a living playing the guitar. According to Lavin, the difficulty stemmed from holding her instrument wrong, and also from carrying too many heavy things. Fortunately, she caught the disorder early enough to avoid surgery, but her recovery included treatment at the Miller Health Institute for the Performing Arts, physical therapy, and lessons with members of the Metropolitan Opera orchestra on how to properly hold her guitar.

Attainable Love Marked Artistic Maturity

Lavin's continuing maturation as a songwriter was particularly evident in her 1990, self-produced album, *Attainable Love*. According to Rounder Records, it found its way onto many critics' ten-best lists. *Billboard* magazine called it "delectable," and described one track, "The Kind of Love Your Never Recover From," as "gut-wrenching storytelling of the first order." "Sensitive New Age Guys"—penned with John Gorka and featuring a choral group comprised of all the sensitive guys she could find in New York—became a favorite on alternative radio stations. *Attainable Love* often focuses on the darker side of relationships; as the *New York Daily News* wrote, it "takes a wider psychological perspective," than do her previous albums.

After *Attainable Love* Lavin directed her attention to what was possibly folk's first all-female supergroup. In 1990 Lavin joined up with folk singers Patty Larkin, Megon McDonough, and Sally Fingerett; calling themselves "The Four Bitchin' Babes," they set out on tour. According to Rounder Records, one publication raved, "If one great woman folk singer on stage is a sheer delight, then this group's quadruple bill is the height of bliss." In 1991 Rounder released a live recording of the show titled *"Buy Me Bring Me Take Me: Don't Mess My Hair. . .": Life According to Four Bitchin' Babes*, complete with the "feminist fight song" made famous by Nancy Sinatra, "These Boots Are Made For Walking."

Placing Lavin in a genre slot became no easier as her popularity grew and her writing matured. She doesn't mind her usual "folk" label, and as she told *Sing Out!*, her roots are definitely in folk music. But she sees herself moving in a more "multi-dimensional," more "theatrical direction." "Eventually," she mused, "I think I will be viewed as doing a one-woman show—or 'An evening with Christine Lavin.'" The best role for Lavin may be as social commentator. "It's as semidetached observer that Lavin is most striking," *People* concluded. "If we could get her and Loudon Wainwright III named our national folk music laureates, we'd have most of the country's problems accurately described, if not solved, in no time."

Selected discography

Another Woman's Man, Philo, 1987 (recorded before 1985).
Future Fossils, Philo, 1985.
Beau Woes and Other Problems of Modern Life, Philo, 1987.
Good Thing He Can't Read My Mind (includes "Mysterious Woman"), Philo, 1988.
Attainable Love (includes "Sensitive New Age Guys" and "The Kind of Love You Never Recover From"), Philo, 1990.
(With Patty Larkin, Megon McDonough, and Sally Fingerett) *Buy Me Bring Me Take Me: Don't Mess My Hair. . .": Life According to Four Bitchin' Babes* (includes "Prisoners of Their Hairdos"), Philo, 1991.
Compass, Philo, 1991.

Also recorded for *Fast Folk Music Magazine* and contributed to *On A Winter's Night*, North Star Records.

Sources

Frets Magazine, March 1987.
Mother Jones, October 1989.
Ms., April 1986.
New York Daily News, March 29, 1988; February 11, 1990.
New York Times, February 23, 1990.
Penthouse, June 1988.
People, March 12, 1990.
Sing Out!, Summer 1989.
Spin, March 1986.
Washington Post, January 18, 1988; June 24, 1988.

Wilson Library Bulletin, June 1989.
Utne Reader, January/February 1989.

Other sources include album liner notes and Rounder Records album profiles.

—*Megan Rubiner*

Leadbelly

Singer, songwriter, guitarist

The legendary "King of the Twelve-String Guitar," Huddie Ledbetter—known as "Leadbelly"—was one of the most famous and influential American folk artists of the twentieth-century. Many of his songs—including such classics as "Good Night, Irene," "The Midnight Special," "Rock Island Line," "Old Cottonfields at Home," "Gray Goose," and "Take This Hammer"—are standards of American folk music that have been performed and recorded by countless artists. A talented musician with a commanding stage presence and voice, Leadbelly captivated audiences in the 1930s and 1940s with his powerful songs, many of them rooted in his brutal experiences as a black man in the Deep South. Folk archivist Alan Lomax, who together with his father John introduced Leadbelly in the 1930s, was quoted by Ray M. Lawless in *Folksingers and Folksongs in America* as saying, "[Leadbelly's] steel voice, his steel arm on the twelve strings and his high-voltage personality captured audiences everywhere. More than any other singer, he demonstrated to a streamlined, city-oriented world that America had living folkmusic—swamp, primitive, angry, freighted with great sorrow and great joy."

The achievement of Leadbelly is remarkable, considering the turbulence of his personal life. He is perhaps as famous for his often violent temperament, over-indulgences in alcohol, numerous liaisons with women, bouts with the law, and prison terms, as he is for his music. A contributor to *Rolling Stone* wrote, "The legend of Leadbelly is by now inextricable from the man's life." He was born in the Deep South, and it was there that his musical talent was shaped. From his family he learned spirituals, work songs, and lullabies, and by the time he was ten, he could play an accordion given to him by an uncle. His father gave him his first guitar, and when he was sixteen, Leadbelly left his native Louisiana for a life of roaming, music, and working at various jobs. For the next few years he was exposed to various types of music and amassed a variety of songs—blues, jazz, cowboy songs, work songs—all the while frequenting brothels, getting in violent and bloody scrapes, and landing himself in prison. Leadbelly was, as Lawless comments, "a strange, enigmatic personality," and his life was also a testament to the conditions of the turn-of-the-century American South, where oppression and hostile treatment of blacks remained little changed from the days of the Civil War.

The experience of prison fed into Leadbelly's music, and his music twice helped him out of prison. In 1925, the governor of Texas commuted a thirty-year murder sentence for Leadbelly, after Leadbelly improvised a song on his own behalf for the governor. The lyrics, as George T. Simon reported in *Best of the Music Makers,* went: "I'se your servant compose this song. / Please

Born Huddie Ledbetter, January 21, 1885 (some sources say 1888), in the Caddo Lake district near Mooringsport, LA; died of amyotrophic lateral sclerosis (Lou Gehrig's Disease), December 6, 1949, in New York, NY; father was a farmer; married Martha Promise, January 21, 1935.

Traveling musician in Louisiana, Arkansas, and Texas, early 1910s; chauffeur and bodyguard with folklorists John and Alan Lomax, throughout the South, late 1934; concert performer, New York City, 1935-49; toured Europe, 1949; appeared on CBS-Radio show, *Back Where I Come From*.

A film, *Leadbelly*, loosely based on Ledbetter's life, was released by Paramount Pictures in 1976.

Gov'nor Neff lemme go back home. / Please Honorable Gov'nor be good an' kind, / If you don' get a pardon, will you cut my time?'' In 1930 Leadbelly was again sentenced to prison, this time in Louisiana for attempted murder. His music had, however, come to the attention of folklore archivist John Lomax, who obtained permission to record Leadbelly's songs for the Library of Congress Archives. Leadbelly's second term was commuted after he served three years, and he worked as chauffeur and bodyguard to John and Alan Lomax as they toured the South in search of folk material.

Leadbelly arrived with the Lomaxes in New York City in late 1934, and they arranged a series of concert appearances at northeastern colleges. Leadbelly was a hit with audiences and critics alike, and during the 1930s and 1940s, played to acclaim in New York City and throughout the rest of the United States. Frequently he performed with other folk giants of the day, including Woody Guthrie, Pete Seeger, Sonny Terry, and Big Bill Broonzy. Lawless described Leadbelly's spell with audiences: "Leadbelly was . . . a vigorous and compelling personality. Furthermore, he was a superb storyteller. It was his habit to introduce a song with a preliminary spoken story, so that the listener was in the mood when the song came. Thus, as the Lomaxes have pointed out, he was a true folk artist, transmuting the materials he found into something different, often something strange and beautiful, into a new song."

Leadbelly received praise in Europe also, and in the fall of 1949, he traveled there for a series of concerts. While on tour, he came down with symptoms of Lou Gehrig's Disease—the muscle-atrophying disease that would eventually kill him—and had to return to New York City.

He died there on December 6, 1949, at the height of his musical career. Ironically, Pete Seeger and his group The Weavers had a huge hit with Leadbelly's "Good Night, Irene" shortly after his death. Seeger commented in *Rolling Stone* on the spirit of Leadbelly: "Some black people bad-mouthed him: 'Only white folks like us to sing like that.' But his power was such that if he ever got a chance, he changed their minds, because he sang some of the greatest protest songs of all time. He had the heart of a champion. I mean, when he went out onstage, he wanted to conquer that audience. And he did."

Selected discography

During his lifetime, Leadbelly made numerous recordings, including those for the Library of Congress, 1934, American Record Corp., New York City, 1935, RCA Victor, June, 1940, and Capitol Records.

Leadbelly Sings, Folkways, 1962.
Ledbetter's Best, Capitol, 1963.
Midnight Special, RCA Victrola, 1964.
Good Night Irene, Allegro, 1964.
Play-Party Songs, Stinson.
Memorial, Stinson.
Leadbelly Legacy, Folkways.
Last Session, Folkways.
Take This Hammer, Verve/Folkways, 1965.
Leadbelly, Archive of Folk Song, 1966.
Hands Off Her, Verve/Folkways, 1966.
From the Last Sessions, Verve/Folkways, 1967.
Legend, Tradition, 1970.
Leadbelly, Columbia, 1970.
Shout On, Folkways.

Sources

Books

Baggelaar, Kristin, and Donald Mitton, *Folk Music: More Than a Song*, Thomas J. Crowell, 1976.
The Encyclopedia of Folk, Country and Western Music, St. Martin's, 1983.
Lawless, Ray M., *Folksingers and Folksongs in America*, 2nd edition, Duell, Sloan, and Pearce, 1965.
Lomax, John A., and Alan Lomax, editors, *Negro Folk Songs as Sung by Leadbelly* (includes commentary by Leadbelly), Macmillan, 1936.
Simon, George T., *Best of the Music Makers*, Doubleday, 1979.

Periodicals

New York Times, December 7, 1949.

Rolling Stone, February 11, 1988.
Time, December 19, 1949.

—Michael E. Mueller

Andrew Lloyd Webber

Composer, producer

British composer Andrew Lloyd Webber "has spun a worldwide empire unmatched in the history of musical theater," wrote Michael Walsh in *Time.* The first composer, in 1983, to have three musicals play simultaneously on Broadway and London's West End—a feat he duplicated in 1988—Lloyd Webber has amassed a string of hits and awards in his twenty-year career with such shows as *Jesus Christ Superstar, Evita, Cats,* and *The Phantom of the Opera.* Known for their elaborate productions and lush scores, Lloyd Webber musicals have enjoyed lengthy stage runs—in 1991 *Cats* was playing in its ninth year on Broadway—while touring professional productions have played in more than fifteen countries across North America, Europe, South America, Asia, and Australia. Also a noted theatrical producer and entrepreneur, Lloyd Webber is the founder of the sprawling Really Useful Group, which comprises a production company, a music-publishing and record division, a video company, and the refurbished Palace Theatre of London. His personal fortune has been estimated to exceed $200 million.

Lloyd Webber's success can be attributed to his particular blend of showmanship and craft, which have made him a favorite of theatergoers. Productions of his musicals are often lavish, while his musical scores—which display such varied influences as rock 'n roll, country, blues, and opera—demonstrate his often-praised gift for melody. Critics differ wildly, however, on Lloyd Webber's contributions to musical theater. To some, as John Rockwell commented in the *New York Times Magazine,* "he is the savior and regenerator of the very genre of the musical," "a composer of melodic genius and telling theatrical savvy," and "as a producer,... regarded as a resource for the revitalization of the musical on both sides of the Atlantic." On the other hand, others regard Lloyd Webber as "a cheap panderer to the lowest common denominator, derivative and faceless" or "the instigator of the current penchant for glitzy spectacle on Broadway." Rockwell points out, however, that "one thing about Andrew Lloyd Webber on which all squabbling observers must agree,... is that he is hugely, even astonishingly successful."

First Composition at Age 9

Lloyd Webber grew up among an accomplished musical family. His late father William was director of the London College of Music, his mother Jean is a piano instructor, and his brother Julian, for whom Andrew composed *Variations,* is a noted concert cellist. As a young boy, Lloyd Webber played the piano, violin, and French horn, and his first composition, six short pieces titled *The Toy Theatre Suite,* was published when he was nine years old. He was exposed to many types of music in his household; as he told Robert Palmer in the *New York Times,* he was "brought up to believe that music was just music, that the only division within it was between good music and bad." Particularly fond of American musicals, Lloyd Webber staged productions in a toy theater he set up in his family's home. His musical idol was composer Richard Rodgers, composer of such stage classics as *Oklahoma, The King and I,* and *South Pacific,* the latter Lloyd Webber's personal favorite.

Breakthrough With *Superstar*

When Lloyd Webber was in college, he was introduced to Tim Rice, a record producer and aspiring lyricist, who shared Lloyd Webber's tastes in rock 'n roll. Their first collaboration was a musical—as yet unproduced—based on the life of a Victorian philanthropist named Dr.

Barnardo, entitled *The Likes of Us.* They achieved recognition for their second collaboration, *Joseph and the Amazing Technicolor Dreamcoat,* an innovative adaptation of the biblical tale of Joseph and his twelve brothers. Mixing various musical styles, including opera, rock, country-western, and calypso, *Joseph* was first performed by the boys' choir of London's St. Paul's School, and received a favorable notice from a *Sunday Times* music critic. It was later expanded into a two-act musical and demonstrated the songwriters' gift for parody, featuring the Pharaoh of Egypt as an Elvis Presley-type performer. Lyricist Rice commented to Walsh: "Without realizing it . . . we were breaking new ground by forgetting about Rodgers and Hammerstein."

Lloyd Webber and Rice returned to a biblical theme in their next venture, the hugely successful rock opera *Jesus Christ Superstar.* A rendering of the last seven days in Jesus's life, the musical—initially unable to find a producer—was released as an album and sold nearly three million copies in the United States. On the strength of the album, the 1971 Broadway production generated unprecedented advance ticket sales of over $1 million and went on to run for 720 performances, despite protests from religious groups who took offense at the parodic portrayals of biblical figures and the questions raised about Jesus's life as a man. Many critics, conceding that the show was provocative, praised its innovations for the musical theater. Although *Superstar* was not the first rock musical ever produced, as Rockwell noted, it "pretty much established the use of rock within the context of the musical. . . . What Lloyd Webber achieved was the expansion of the musical-theater composer's resources to include rock, at a time when most American writers for the musical theater continued to resist it."

Evita Earned 7 Tonys

Lloyd Webber and Rice's next collaboration, *Evita,* turned out to be an even greater success. Based on the life of Eva Peron, wife of Argentine dictator Juan Peron, *Evita* employed an elaborate stage production by Hal Prince, including murals, parades, and banners, and a lushly orchestrated score by Lloyd Webber. As with *Superstar, Evita* was first released as an album, which, coupled with the success of its London stage premiere, created much excitement for its 1979 Broadway opening. *Evita* went on to run for nearly four years on Broadway, and received a total of seven Tony Awards, including Best Musical of the Year. Despite its commercial success, Lloyd Webber and Rice were criticized, as Walsh reports "for glorifying the right-wing Eva and Juan Peron, even though they intended the show as an allegory of the deteriorating political situation in Eng-land in the mid-1970s." However, Frank Rich of the *New York Times*, a perennial Lloyd Webber critic, stat-ed in the documentary *The Andrew Lloyd Webber Story*, that "while Evita may in some ways be a naive and simplistic historical view of the Perons, as show business lyric writing Rice's work is very clever, and I think Lloyd Webber responded with a more interesting score and a more varied score than usual."

Articulated "New English Musical"

Rice and Lloyd Webber parted ways after *Evita,* and in his next stage offering, Lloyd Webber set upon what seemed an unlikely subject: a musical rendering of a group of obscure T. S. Eliot poems entitled *Old Possum's Book of Practical Cats*. Working with director Trevor Nunn, Lloyd Webber assembled the spectacle *Cats*, which featured a band of seven synthesizers, full orchestra, special effects, a large cast of singers and dancers in cat costumes, and a specially designed set resembling a larger-than-life junkyard. *Cats* won sev-eral Tony Awards, including the Best Musical of 1983, and featured the hit song, "Memory," which was rec-orded by several artists, including Barbra Streisand and Judy Collins. Although lacking in plot—a criticism raised against many of Lloyd Webber's musicals—*Cats,* according to Stephen Holden in the *New York Times,* "comes closer to solving the problems of the bookless musical than any of Mr. Lloyd Webber's previ-ous scores," adding that "because it is a suite of songs rather than a dramatically structured musical pageant, it isn't weighed down with tedious passages of connec-tive recitative." Rockwell cites *Cats* as "the key musical in [Lloyd Webber's] career, the show that defined him on his own, [and] established the very idea of a new English musical."

Song & Dance combines two separate Lloyd Webber works, *Tell Me on a Sunday,* originally a mini-opera for television, and *Variations,* a choreographed selection of music Lloyd Webber adapted from Italian composer Niccolo Paganini's *A-minor Caprice No. 24. Song & Dance* ran for two years in London, and was a hit on Broadway with Bernadette Peters in the starring role of Emma. Lloyd Webber's next musical, the fantasy *Star-light Express,* featured a cast of more than twenty people on roller skates and depicted a competition between various types of trains. Originally conceived as a collection of genre songs—rock, rap, blues, and gospel—*Starlight* was scorned, as Walsh noted, for being "an overblown extravaganza." Lloyd Webber himself was disappointed with the final outcome. "It was a mistake to have put it anywhere near where it could be considered a Broadway musical," he told

Walsh. True to Lloyd Webber's track record, however, the musical was a commercial success on both the West End and Broadway.

Broke Records With *Phantom*

Lloyd Webber's *Phantom of the Opera,* first produced in London in 1986, was one of the most awaited musi-cals of the 1988 Broadway season, amassing an un-precedented $16 million in advance ticket sales. Based on the 1911 Gaston Leroux novel about a disfigured genius who falls in love with a beautiful Swedish singer at the Paris opera, *The Phantom of the Opera* is consid-ered to be among Lloyd Webber's most accomplished musicals. Marilyn Stasio noted in *Life* that Lloyd Web-ber fans praise "its operative sweep, effusively melodic themes, irresistibly bigger-than-life characters, and above all, the achingly romantic quality of its love story." Rockwell called *Phantom* "Lloyd Webber's most undisguisedly operatic work yet. . . . Its Victorian, melo-dramatic scenario suits his grandiose rock-symphonic predilections, as well as the ingenious panache of [production designer Hal] Prince's staging and Lloyd Webber's knack for even more stirring tunes than usu-al." Another production marvel, *Phantom* features a boat sailing along a subterranean waterway and a huge chandelier that appears to crash to the floor.

Critical Reviews: "Of No Interest"

Lloyd Webber's 1989 musical, *Aspects of Love,* debuted on the West End and premiered on Broadway the following year. With a complex and twisted plot, *As-pects of Love* is based on the novel by British writer David Garnett, a member of the famous Bloomsbury literary group. The musical revolves around the inter-twining lives and loves of a circle of friends, and nearly the entire show is sung, with little dialogue between characters. The show received many negative reviews—one London critic called it "a second-rate musical, based on a third-rate novel"—yet Lloyd Webber considers it one of his more enduring efforts. He told the *New York Times* that *Aspects of Love* would "outlive and outlaugh all my other shows, because 100 percent of the world loves love." Regarding negative criticism of his work, he added: "The reviews from the critics are of no interest to me."

Walsh wrote: "It has been fashionable to dismiss Lloyd Webber as a panderer to the basest melodic cravings of the mass audience, hammering home a few repeti-tive themes amid overblown orchestral climaxes and distracting technological gimmickry. His scores have been derided as derivative and too dependent on pastiche—meretricious parrotings of his Broadway betters (Rodgers) and his operatic antecedents (Puccini).'' Lloyd Webber scoffs at such views of his work, telling Walsh: "People talk about commercialism, but in actual fact, I really fight it an awful lot. I don't think that way. I put an awful lot into these scores. It is not just a matter of two or three songs repeated and repeated. If people think it is, they are crazy. The reason why the public responds is that the pieces are very rich.''

Selected discography

Joseph and the Amazing Technicolor Dreamcoat, [London], 1969, new issue, MCA, 1974, Broadway cast recording, Chrysalis, 1982.

Jesus Christ Superstar: A Rock Opera, Decca, 1970, *Jesus Christ Superstar: The Original Motion Picture Soundtrack Album,* MCA, 1973.

Evita, London cast recording, MCA, 1976, *Evita: Premiere American Recording,* MCA, 1979.

Variations, MCA, 1977.

Tell Me on a Sunday, Polydor, 1980.

Cats (includes "Memory"), London cast recording, Geffen, 1981, Broadway cast recording, Geffen, 1983.

Song & Dance, London cast recording, Polydor, 1982, Broadway cast recording, RCA Red Seal, 1985.

Starlight Express, London cast recording, Polydor, 1984, Broadway cast recording, MCA, 1987.

Requiem, Angel, 1985.

The Phantom of the Opera, London cast recording, Polydor, 1987.

Aspects of Love, London cast recording, 1989.

Sources

Books

Newsmakers, Gale, 1989.

McKnight, Gerald, *Andrew Lloyd Webber,* St. Martin's, 1984.

Walsh, Michael, *Andrew Lloyd Webber, His Life and Works: A Critical Biography,* Abrams, 1989.

Periodicals

Business Week, April 23, 1990.

Christian Century, March 18-25, 1987.

Life, February, 1988.

Maclean's, June 8, 1987; February 8, 1988.

New York, September 20, 1982.

New York Times, February 10, 1982; September 1, 1982; July 3, 1983; June 8, 1986; December 20, 1987; June 26, 1990; January 23, 1991.

New York Times Magazine, December 20, 1987.

People, December 27, 1982; January 3, 1983; March 3, 1986; March 7, 1988.

Time, January 18, 1988.

U.S. News & World Report, February 1, 1988.

Other

The Andrew Lloyd Webber Story (documentary), PBS, 1988.

—*Michael E. Mueller*

Nick Lowe

Singer, songwriter, guitarist, producer

Multi-faceted Nick Lowe—the English singer, songwriter, guitarist, and record producer—"has usually made more of a mark on pop history than pop charts," a contributor to *Creem* once wrote. As a producer, Lowe is considered one of the main forces behind the English New Wave movement of the 1970s, producing records by New Wave progenitors Elvis Costello, Graham Parker, and the Pretenders. As a songwriter, his songs have been recorded by many artists, especially on the British label Stiff Records, which showcased New Wave talent in the 1970s. Lowe began his own solo performing career around 1978 and caused a flurry with two acclaimed albums that launched a short-lived music phase called "power pop." Irwin Stambler in *The Encyclopedia of Pop, Rock and Soul* wrote that Lowe's diverse talents perhaps stood in the way of his making more of an impact as a performer. "It's possible that had Nick Lowe not demonstrated abilities in so many areas of pop music, from record production to performing, that he might have made his mark as a superstar during the 1970s. As it was, he set a hectic pace for himself that crammed more into each year than many people in the field achieve in a career."

Lowe started playing guitar in bands while a teenager, and around 1965 formed a group called Kippington Lodge with his school chum, guitarist Brinsley Schwarz. The group reorganized and took the name Brinsley Schwarz in 1969, and became a central band among what was a burgeoning pub circuit in Great Britain during the early 1970s. A cult favorite, Brinsley Schwarz bore heavy influences of American country-rock music, such as that performed by Neil Young. Lowe's contributions to the group were many; aside from revealing his versatility as a musician—Lowe played base as well as guitar—Brinsley Schwarz's 1970 debut album notes listed Lowe as the writer or cowriter of all the songs. On their follow-up album, Lowe wrote all but one of the cuts. While with Brinsley Schwarz, Lowe also began working with guitarist-singer Dave Edmunds, who produced the group's 1974 album, *The New Favorites of Brinsley Schwarz,* and who collaborated with the group—under the name The Electricians—on the soundtrack to the 1974 David Bowie film, *Ziggy Stardust.*

The Force Behind Stiff

Brinsley Schwarz split up in 1975; Lowe began working as a singer, songwriter, recording engineer, and producer for Stiff Records, the pioneering British New the American group Blondie, and displayed Lowe's and Edmunds's masterful range of rock and roll influences. Lowe also launched his solo career in 1978 with an album entitled *Jesus of Cool* in England, released in the United States as *Pure Pop for Now People*. The album, backed by Rockpile, was heralded as an accomplished amalgamation of various rock influences, and many critics placed Lowe at the helm of an influential movement called "power-pop" that combined the classic rock and roll of the late 1950s with melodious modern pop strains. According to Perry Meisel in the *Village Voice,* Lowe's *Pure Pop for Now People* demonstrated a "command of more styles of rocking than any honest artiste is supposed to have." Coupled with his similarly acclaimed 1979 album *Labour of Lust,* Lowe gained the nickname "The Basher," in reference to his open invasion of rock styles of the past; Lowe's studio motto, as James Henke reported in *Rolling Stone,* was to "bash it now; tart it up later." Lowe explained his "bashing" to Palmer: "I hear things, and sometimes I consciously steal them. But I make a distinction: I tend to copy a feeling or a style rather than a certain record of some bloke who happens to be popular."

Wave label of the 1970s. Stiff signed a number of promising New Wave acts, and as Stambler noted, drew on Lowe's "experience to help develop showcase recordings for many of them." The label released various sampler records, which featured Lowe productions and original compositions. Included among the stable of Stiff artists was Elvis Costello, perhaps the most influential of New Wave artists, whose first three albums were produced by Lowe. Lowe also produced Graham Parker's debut album, the debut single of the Pretenders, and what is widely considered the first British punk album, *Damned Damned Damned* by The Damned. Robert Palmer wrote in the *New York Times* that Lowe was "important as a producer and molder of raw talent" at Stiff. "His somewhat unorthodox methods involved putting off-beat but distinctive artists together with solid bands (often including some of his former associates), helping them work out concise arrangements that held most of their songs to under three minutes, and recording them very intensively, often knocking out an album in a week or two."

Nervy Songwriting

Lowe's solo career made it possible to showcase not only his performing abilities, but his songwriting talents, which had been obscured over the years. Among his trademark songs are "Cruel To Be Kind"—Lowe's only American Top Forty single—"So It Goes," "Marie Provost," "I Knew the Bride," and "(What's So Funny 'Bout) Peace, Love and Understanding"—one of Costello's signature songs—all featuring Lowe's characteristic nervy and eccentric lyrics. In a review of Lowe's 1982 first New York City performance since the break-up of Rockpile, Palmer noted in the *New York Times* that the concert was "a chance to appreciate the batch of witty, ingeniously constructed, exceptionally tuneful songs he has written since he began making singles for Stiff Records in the mid-1970s." Palmer added that Lowe's newer songs weren't as "cutting or as demented as some of his earlier material, but they are as finely crafted as anything he has done."

Solo Career Followed Rockpile

In 1978 Lowe formed the short-lived group Rockpile with Edmunds, which also included guitarist Billy Bremner and drummer Terry Williams. Rockpile, with Lowe on base, became a popular touring band in Great Britain and the United States, opening for Elvis Costello and

Throughout the 1980s Lowe continued to release albums, though 1982's *Nick the Knife* and the following year's *The Abominable Showman* were generally panned as lacking many of the qualities of his first solo albums. Regarding *The Abominable Showman,* Mitchell Cohen complained in *Creem* that "the nastiness and gleeful perversity" of Lowe's earlier work was absent, and that he'd "pretty much stripped his pop of the impurities that brought *Pure Pop for Now People* to life." Lowe himself was disappointed with the records. "I was bored doing my own stuff," he told Jim Farber in the *Daily News.* "With the sort of music I do, it's very hard to bluff that you're having a good time. An important ingredient in my music is that spark of enthusiasm, which you can't buy in shops. So the last two records sounded kind of labored." Lowe successfully rebounded, however, with 1984's *Nick Lowe and His Cowboy Outfit,* which showed a "rejuvenated rock & roll sensibility," said Kurt Loder in *Rolling Stone,* and demonstrated "rock & roll composed and performed with real commitment to form, not a semi-sarcastic contempt for it."

Entered '90s with a Bang

Lowe continues to record and produce music his own way and has not acquiesced to popular tastes. His 1990 album, *Party of One,* is, in the opinion of *Musician* contributor Charles M. Young, "undoubtedly [his] finest album—hilarious, full of hooks, wonderfully quirky." Lowe once told Farber his working credo: "I dig the stuff I do. There's no one who does similar music, and so I shall continue to do it." Lowe has also expressed contempt for much of today's popular music. "There seems to be a sound which all records have got to have nowadays in order to get on the radio," he told Karen Schlosberg in *Creem.* "The best records, I think, have a sort of spontaneity and a little element of the human being at work; I'm not interested in getting it all right, all correct. I listen to the radio nowadays and I keep on dying to hear a record with a mistake on it."

Selected discography

With Brinsley Schwarz

Brinsley Schwarz, 1970.
Despite It All, 1971.
Silver Pistol, 1972.
Nervous on the Road, 1972.
Please Don't Ever Change, United Artists, 1973.
The New Favorites of Brinsley Schwarz, United Artists, 1974.
(With Dave Edmunds) *Ziggy Stardust* (film soundtrack), 1974.
Brinsley Schwarz (contains *Brinsley Schwarz* and *Despite It All*), Capitol, 1978.

Fifteen Thoughts of Brinsley Schwarz, United Artists, 1978.

With Rockpile

Seconds of Pleasure, c. 1979.

Solo albums

Bowi (EP; a response to David Bowie's LP, *Low*), Stiff Records, c. 1977.
Pure Pop for Now People (released in England as *Jesus of Cool;* includes "So It Goes" and "Marie Provost"), Columbia, 1978.
Labour of Lust (includes "Cruel To Be Kind"), Columbia, 1979.
Nick the Knife, Columbia, 1982.
The Abominable Showman, Columbia, 1983.
Nick Lowe and His Cowboy Outfit, Columbia, 1984.
16 All-Time Lowes, Demon, 1985.
The Rose of England (includes "I Knew the Bride"), Columbia, 1985.
Pinker and Prouder Than Previous, Columbia, 1988.
Party of One, Warner Brothers, 1990.

Contributed to *Bunch of Stiffs, Stiff Live Stiffs,* and *Hits Greatest Stiffs,* all Stiff Records, all 1977. Also recorded *Americathon: Music From the Original Motion Picture Soundtrack,* Lorimar Records, 1979.

Sources

Books

The Rock 'n' Roll Years, Crescent Books, 1990.
The Rolling Stone Encyclopedia of Rock & Roll, edited by Jon Pareles and Patricia Romanowski, Rolling Stone Press, 1983.
Stambler, Irwin, *The Encyclopedia of Pop, Rock, and Soul,* revised edition, St. Martin's, 1987.

Periodicals

Creem, June 1983; March 1986.
Daily News, August 14, 1984.
Down Beat, November 1979; May 1990.
Musician, October 1985; June 1990.
New York Times, July 22, 1979; March 26, 1982; March 29, 1982; August 8, 1984.
People, June 20, 1988; April 16, 1990.

Rolling Stone, June 29, 1978; September 20, 1979; May 27, 1982; July 5, 1984; September 12, 1985.
Stereo Review, June 1988.
Village Voice, July 23, 1979; April 3, 1990.

—*Michael E. Mueller*

Wynton Marsalis

Trumpet player

Wynton Marsalis is "potentially the greatest trumpet player of all time," proclaimed Maurice Andre, the famed classical trumpet virtuoso. Given Marsalis's technical prowess—"from astonishing scales to clean, quick-tongued repeated notes to gossamer phrasing to impeccable arpeggios," as Leslie Rubenstein described in *Stagebill*—it is understandable why he has received such an accolade and why he is often hailed as the savior of modern jazz. But there are disbelievers, critics who consider him too conservative, technical, studied, elite. Marsalis's detractors think he lives up to the *Rolling Stone* title "the hottest lips in America" even when he is not blowing his horn. Passionate—some would say obstinate—about his desire to return jazz to its purest form, Marsalis is not afraid to preach his beliefs over the heads of legends. They are not amused. *Rolling Stone*'s Steve Bloom quoted the late Miles Davis: "Sometimes people speak as though someone asked them a question. Well, nobody asked him a question." But Marsalis is purposeful, undaunted. He told Bloom: "I love the music, above everything else. That's all I answer to."

Marsalis's impeccable background is well documented: Born in the jazz cradle of New Orleans, he received his first trumpet at age six from the great Dixieland trumpeter Al Hirt, in whose band Marsalis's father, Ellis, was the pianist. He did not begin playing in earnest, however, until he was twelve, when he heard a recording of jazz trumpeter Clifford Brown. Marsalis then began studies with John Longo, who exposed the young student to the classical repertoire of the instrument. At fourteen he was a featured soloist with the New Orleans Philharmonic Orchestra. At seventeen he was invited to a summer session at the famed Berkshire Music Center at Tanglewood, Massachusetts, which waived its normal eighteen-year-old age requirement. After graduation from high school (3.98 grade point average, National Merit Scholarship finalist), Marsalis accepted a scholarship to the elite Juilliard School of Music in New York City. In addition to full-time studies there, he played with various orchestras, including the Brooklyn Philharmonic. In 1980, during his summer vacation, Marsalis began touring with Art Blakey, the famous jazz drummer. After his second year at Juilliard

he walked away to tour with jazz pianist Herbie Hancock's V.S.O.P. quartet. That same year Marsalis received a recording contract from Columbia Records to record both jazz and classical music, and subsequently formed his own jazz group. He was twenty years old.

Classically Trained Jazz Musician

From this prodigious beginning Marsalis has evolved into a musician who easily traverses the space between a blues lament and a baroque exaltation, between a small, smoky New York jazz club and Washington's prestigious Lincoln Center. His movements between the two styles, however, are not with equal steps. He is classically trained, but considers himself foremost a jazz musician. Jane O'Hara pointed out in *Maclean's* that "Marsalis's classical training may have offered a temporary refuge from the black ghetto, but there is no question about the prodigal son's real musical home: 'I have studied Bartok and Stravinsky and I love them,. . . but jazz is in the present tense.'" Marsalis further defined this idea to Howard Mandel of *Down Beat:* "Jazz is the most precise art form of this century [because of] the time. . . . What the musicians have figured out is how to conceive, construct, refine, and deliver ideas as they come up, and present them in a logical fashion. What you're doing is creating, editing, and all this as the music is going on. This is the first time this has ever happened in western art. Painting is paint*ed*. Symphonies are writ*ten*. Beethoven improvised, but by himself, over a score. When five men get together to make up something, it's a big difference." Early in his career, Marsalis said this to *People's* Barbara Rowes: "Beethoven did things with rhythms that are really hip, but there's no way that can be compared with modern jazz." Five years later, in his discussion with Rubenstein, Marsalis offered a more comprehensive understanding of the relationship between classical and jazz: "What the two styles do share . . . is a spirituality, and the ability to elevate the audience. That's what music is, elevation and improvement. Just as Beethoven improved folk melodies, Charlie Parker improved 'I'll Remember April.'"

Technique Drew Criticism

Such views and outspokenness have helped Marsalis delineate his *raison d'etre,* but they have also drawn the sharp pens of critics. Marsalis has always maintained that it is easier for a young musician to master classical music than jazz. Critics of his early jazz work agreed. In the *New Yorker,* Whitney Balliett remarked, "Technique, rather than melodic logic, still governs his improvising, and the emotional content of his playing remains skittish." *Down Beat,* quoted by Bloom, opined, "[Marsalis] seems to be detached from his prodigious maturity by not having experienced abandon. . . . Musicians, like artists, must live if they are going to make significant contributions."

Since these quotes Marsalis has "lived," and as Thomas Sancton noted in *Time,* even Marsalis "admits that the shoot-from-the-lip style of his early years went too far at times: 'I was like 19 or something, man—you know, wild. I didn't care.'" He has since become, Sancton deemed, "a less strident and more articulate advocate for the cause. Says pianist and composer Billy Taylor: 'Wynton is the most important young spokesman for the music today. His opinions are well founded. Some people earlier took umbrage at what he said, but the important thing is that he could back it up with his horn.'"

Jazz a Metaphor for Democracy

Marsalis's passionate advocacy for the proper understanding of and respect for jazz since his early years rests on the belief, as Sancton emphasized, that "jazz is not just another style of popular music but a major American cultural achievement and a heritage that must not be lost." In the same article, Marsalis asserted that jazz is such a part of our heritage it is a metaphor for democracy: "It shows you how the individual can negotiate the greatest amount of personal freedom and put it humbly at the service of a group conception."

Fortified by such a philosophical and spiritual belief, Marsalis strives to educate the next generation of possible jazz players on the contributions of past generations of jazz masters. Cognizant of his own lack of jazz education in his early years—critic Stanley Crouch, quoted by Sancton, explained that the young Marsalis "didn't know anything about Ornette Coleman, Duke Ellington, or Thelonius Monk. His dad had tried to make him listen to Louis Armstrong, but he had this naive idea that Louis was an Uncle Tom"—Marsalis now visits schools when touring to inform and perhaps reform the musical and cultural attitudes of aspiring musicians. In 1987, he helped launch a three-year jazz education program in the Chicago school system. But his commitment isn't fulfilled by singular visits to schools. Sancton noted that Marsalis "stays in touch with many of the students he meets, offering them pointers over the phone, inviting them to sit in on his gigs and sometimes even giving them instruments."

Lauded by Critics

From this devotion to the cause have come recordings that show an increase in depth and maturity. Although, as mentioned, Marsalis's early work was faulted by critics for lacking emotion, later recordings were lauded (Marsalis has since won eight Grammy Awards and is the only person in history to have won back-to-back classical and jazz Grammys in two consecutive years). Fred Bouchard in *Down Beat* said 1986's *J Mood* offered "an intimate revelling in sensuous sounds, the sense of quirky unpredictability in the original melodies and the solo lines (no cliches here), an unexpected quietude and austerity on many tracks." A *Rolling Stone* reviewer felt *Marsalis Standard Time, Vol. 1* "tugging at the beat with willful elasticity and venturing out with confident improvisations heightened by the clarity of his technique." And Michael Azerrad, writing for *Rolling Stone,* found *Majesty of the Blues* to be "an artistic quantum leap forward." If "whorehouses still played jazz in the front room," he wrote, "this is what it would sound like."

The technical virtuosity evident on these recordings is brought to the fore on Marsalis's classical ventures. Balliett labeled the *Haydn/Hummel/Mozart Concertos* "a beautiful record, full of the silver and bells and sunlight of perfectly played brass," while Bouchard noted that Marsalis "has a natural flair for the witty exuberance, jazzy metrics, and peripatetic lines" of the concertos on the *Jolivet/Tomasi* recording.

A "Shepherd" of the Music

The recordings, the educational programs, the concerts, and the interviews have all shown parts of the intellectual and artistic Wynton Marsalis. From these sources critics have gleaned their definitions. On Marsalis's uniqueness, James Haskins noted in his book *Black Music in America: A History Through Its People* that "because of his versatility, Wynton Marsalis brought a highly technical sense to his jazz playing and a vividness and immediacy to his classical playing that no one else had ever been able to do." But Sancton observed that Marsalis's effect seems to extend beyond any individual ability or achievement: "It is the fact that, largely under his influence, a jazz renaissance is flowering on what was once barren soil." Perhaps, however, the simplest understanding of Marsalis's effect, his message, and his ability belongs to a member of his group, saxophonist Wes Anderson. Sancton quoted him: "Wynton is someone who can guide us. He's one of the shepherds of this music."

Selected discography

Fathers and Sons, Columbia, 1982.

Wynton Marsalis, Columbia, 1982.

Think of One, Columbia, 1983.

Wynton Marsalis: Haydn/Hummel/Mozart Trumpet Concertos, CBS Masterworks, 1983.

Hot House Flowers, Columbia, 1984.

Wynton Marsalis/Edita Gruberova: Baroque Trumpet Music, CBS Masterworks, 1984.

Black Codes (From the Underground), Columbia, 1985.

J Mood, Columbia, 1986.

Jolivet/Tomasi: Trumpet Concertos, CBS Masterworks, 1986.

Carnaval, Columbia, 1986.

Marsalis Standard Time, Vol. 1, Columbia, 1987.

Live at the Blues Alley, Columbia, 1988.

Wynton Marsalis: Baroque Music for Trumpets, CBS Masterworks, 1988.

A Portrait of Wynton Marsalis, CBS Masterworks, 1988.

Majesty of the Blues, Columbia, 1989.

A Crescent City Christmas Card, Columbia, 1989.

The Resolution of Romance, Columbia, 1990.

Sources

Books

Haskins, James, *Black Music in America: A History Through Its People,* Crowell, 1987.

Periodicals

Atlantic, April 1988.

Down Beat, July 1984; December 1986; January 1987; November 1987; January 1988; October 1988.

Maclean's, March 26, 1984.

New Yorker, June 20, 1983.

People, February 20, 1984; November 24, 1986; September 18, 1989.

Rolling Stone, November 8, 1984; December 17, 1987; July 13, 1989.

Stagebill, Fall 1989.

Time, November 7, 1983; October 22, 1990.

—*Rob Nagel*

George Martin

Record producer

industry, Martin works out of his two AIR studios, located in London and on the Caribbean island of Montserrat.

Strong Musical Background

Martin became a record producer by way of his own background in music. After serving during the Second World War with the British Fleet Air Arm, he attended London's Guildhall School of Music for three years, during which time he studied music composition and classical music orchestration in addition to his studying the piano and oboe. In 1950, he was hired as the assistant to Oscar Preuss, then head of Parlophone Records, and was charged with overseeing the label's classical record repertoire.

Because Parlophone was such a small company, Martin was able to quickly gather much experience and responsibility. He eventually began working with the label's established jazz artists, and produced several bestselling records by Scottish dance bands. Considered something of a maverick, Martin sought out new and untapped markets for the label and produced a string of hit comedy records by such artists as Peter Ustinov, Peter Sellers, and Bernard Cribbins. In 1955, at the age of 29, he was named head of Parlophone, and became one of the youngest persons ever to be put in charge of a record label.

Signed the Beatles to a Recording Contract

As head of Parlophone, Martin continued to maintain the label as a producer of humorous records, but he also wanted to acquire successful pop artists. When he was approached by Beatles' manager Brian Epstein in 1962, the group had been turned down by every major record label. Convinced, however, that the Beatles had all the right pop elements—infectious songs, winning personalities, and good group voices—Martin signed them to a contract and set out to record them in EMI's Abbey Road studios. That same year, the Beatles' first single, "Love Me Do," backed on the flip side by "P.S. I Love You," reached number seventeen on the British charts, and was followed with "Please Please Me," which went all the way to Number 1.

The craze for the Beatles—dubbed Beatlemania by the press—began in England and in little more than a year the "Fab Four" would similarly overtake the United States with the single "I Want to Hold Your Hand." As Martin recalled in his 1979 autobiography, *All You Need Is Ears,* "suddenly the whole thing snowballed and mushroomed and any other mixed metaphor you care

British record producer George Martin is sometimes referred to as the "Fifth Beatle," a mark of the important contributions he made to the phenomenal music career of the rock group Beatles. As head of EMI's Parlophone Records in London, Martin signed the Beatles to their first-ever recording contract in 1962 and went on to produce all their records—both with Parlophone and, later, at his own AIR (Associated Independent Recording) studios—throughout the band's seven years together. Martin's recording savvy, along with his abilities as an arranger and scorer, helped shape the Beatles' music in a way that highlighted their immense songwriting and performing talents.

At the same time, Martin produced other successful Parlophone pop artists, including Gerry and the Pacemakers, Cilla Black, and Billy J. Kramer, transforming small Parlophone into a pop-hit machine during the 1960s. In Martin's biggest year—1963—records he produced were number one on British pop charts for a record 37 weeks of the entire year. Today, still respected as one of the foremost producers in the recording

Born January 3, 1926, in London, England; married Sheena Chisholm, January 3, 1948 (divorced); married Judy Lockhart-Smith, June 24, 1966; children: (first marriage) Alexis, Gregory; (second marriage) Lucy, Giles. *Education:* Attended Guildhall School of Music, London, 1947-50.

Parlophone Record label, EMI Records, London, England, assistant to head of label, 1950-55, head of label, 1955-65; founding head of AIR (Associated Independent Recording) Studios, London, 1965—, and Montserrat, 1979—. Producer of records by the Beatles.

Composed original film scores for *Take Me Over, Crooks Anonymous,* and *Calculated Risk;* contributor of musical scores to film *Yellow Submarine, Pulp,* and *Live and Let Die;* musical director for film *A Hard Day's Night;* musical scorer for film *Sgt. Pepper's Lonely Hearts Club Band. Military service:* Served in British Fleet Air Arm, 1943-47.

Awards: Recipient of four Grammys; numerous gold, silver, and platinum records; Academy Award nomination for best musical direction, 1965, for *A Hard Day's Night;* Rocky Award, 1976, for "Producer of the Year"; Ivor Novello Award (England); honorary doctorate, Berklee College of Music, 1982; inducted into TEC Hall of Fame, 1989.

to think of. From that moment, we simply never stood still." The Beatles's first album, *Please Please Me,* was recorded in the span of one day and, like virtually every Beatles recording which followed, soared to Number 1 on the charts.

Martin's primary role as producer of the Beatles' early records was to direct recording sessions and oversee the group's pop sound. Under his guidance, for example, "Please Please Me" became an upbeat number instead of the ballad originally intended by the Beatles, while "Can't Buy Me Love," began distinctively on the chorus segment of the lyric. His producer role diversified with the Beatles' song "Yesterday," as orchestration by Martin was used for the first time, and—drawing upon his music training—he became both the arranger and scorer of the Beatles' music. Martin's classical influence can be heard in the string quartet of "Yesterday," in addition to the orchestral segments supporting "Strawberry Fields" and "Eleanor Rigby." Martin's scoring and composition capabilities would eventually lead to his work as scoring films for a handful of movies in the 1960s and 1970s, including the Beatles' *Yellow Submarine.* In 1965 Martin's musical direction of the Beatles'

A Hard Day's Night earned him an Academy Award nomination for best musical direction in a film.

Pioneered Recording as an Art Form

As the Beatles' music became more sophisticated, and as technological developments such as stereo allowed for wider-ranging production opportunities, Martin became an important link between the Beatles' musical concepts and their actual recordings. The crowning achievement of their association came in 1967 with the lavishly-produced *Sgt. Pepper's Lonely Hearts Club Band,* which is considered by many to be the hallmark of the "concept album" in pop music. In *All You Need Is Ears,* Martin described *Sgt. Pepper* as "the watershed which changed the recording art from something that merely made amusing sounds into something which will stand the test of time as a valid art from." Regarding the Beatles' successful career as a whole, Martin notes the contributions of each member, and his own, as essential—but he singles out songwriters John Lennon and Paul McCartney as the leading talents. In his autobiography, Martin calls Lennon and McCartney "two tunesmiths of genius. . . . [who] simply couldn't understand the need for complication."

From 1965 until the Beatles' breakup, Martin produced the group from his AIR studios in London, which he and several other EMI record executives formed after leaving the company over wage and royalty disputes. In 1979, Martin opened an additional AIR studio in the British protectorate of Montserrat in the Caribbean. Situated on a thirty-acre site atop a 500-foot ridge, AIR Montserrat is considered one of the state-of-the-art recording studios in the industry. Martin has produced several artists there, including ex-Beatle Paul McCartney and his *Tug of War* album. Among the other prominent artists that Martin has produced at AIR are Jeff Beck, Kenny Rogers, Ella Fitzgerald, Neil Sedaka, and the group America.

Philosophy as a Record Producer

While technological advancements in the 1980s such as digital recording and multi-track machines have made it easier for producers to make records, it hasn't necessarily resulted in better recordings, according to Martin. He told Susan Borley in a 1987 *Audio* profile that "better music's got to come from the heart, it's got to come from creativity. I don't think it's necessary to have the extremes of technology. It's like sitting in a comfortable chair, you know, instead of sitting in a hard-back. It doesn't make you sit any fitter, probably less."

Asked whether he would rather go back to the older days with less sophisticated equipment, as in the Beatles' early recordings, he told Borley: "The only thing I yearn for is recordings that are more spontaneous. Today everything is so clinically controlled, and everything is so meticulously accurate. . . . This worries me because I think the heart is going, and I'd like to get back to humanity and mistakes."

Sources

Books

Clarke, Donald, editor, *The Penguin Encyclopedia of Popular Music*, Viking, 1989.

Martin, George, with Jeremy Hornsby, *All You Need Is Ears*, St. Martin's, 1979.
Martin, George, editor, *Making Music: The Guide to Writing, Performing and Recording*, Morrow, 1984.

Periodicals

Audio, May 1978; June 1987.
Billboard, May 19, 1979; March 7, 1987; October 7, 1989.
Musician, July 1987.
Rolling Stone, June 18, 1987.

—*Michael E. Mueller*

Glenn Miller

Trombonist, bandleader

With his orchestra, bandleader Glenn Miller "synthesized all the elements of 'big band' jazz and gave a generation of young people the apotheosis of dance music: smooth, sophisticated, and with a patina of sentimentality," declared critic Ralph De Toledano in *National Review*. Miller's popularity as a music maker began in 1939, and, with standards such as "Moonlight Serenade," "In the Mood," and "Tuxedo Junction," lasted until he broke up his orchestra to join the U.S. Army Air Corps in 1942.

Miller was born on March 1, probably in the year 1909, in Clarinda, Iowa. His family moved around a great deal during his youth, to places including North Platte, Nebraska, and Grant City, Oklahoma. In the latter town, at the age of thirteen, Miller milked cows to earn money to buy a trombone. He did not, apparently, count on music to be his career, because he finished high school and attended classes at the University of Colorado for two years. During his time in college, though, he continued playing the trombone, and worked briefly with Boyd Senter's band in Denver. After that, however, the lure of music proved too strong, and Miller left the University to try his luck on the west coast of the United States.

The budding trombonist played with a few small bands there until 1927, when he joined Ben Pollack's orchestra. Shortly afterwards, Pollack and his musicians moved to New York, and Miller found so many opportunities there that he left Pollack's band. In addition to playing the trombone, he did arrangements for the likes of Victor Young, Freddy Rich, and others. Miller felt optimistic enough about his burgeoning career in 1928 to marry Helen Burger, a woman he had met at the University of Colorado.

During the 1930s, Miller helped Ray Noble start an orchestra, played for other bandleaders, and put together a swing band for Columbia Records. But he was already planning to have a big band of his own, and turned down a lucrative job with the Metro-Goldwyn-Mayer film company to work on the project. In 1937, Miller's dream became a reality when he put together musicians such as Charlie Spivak, Toots Mondello, and Maurice Purtill to form the Glenn Miller Orchestra. Though Purtill soon left to play with Tommy Dorsey—who at that time was better known than Miller—the orchestra carried on for the rest of the year, playing one-night stands in various cities.

In 1938, however, Miller temporarily suspended the band. Purtill's absence brought about problems with the orchestra's rhythm section that continued to plague its leader, and Miller felt the need to reorganize from the ground up. He did so, using only a few of the band's original members. Later that year the Glenn Miller Orchestra added singer Marion Hutton to its roster, and

Born March 1, c. 1909, in Clarinda, IA; disappeared over the English Channel while on an airplane flight from England to Paris, December 1944; son of Lewis Elmer and Mattie Lou (maiden name, Cavender) Miller; married Helen Burger, October 6, 1928. *Education:* Attended the University of Colorado, 1924-26.

Trombone player, bandleader, arranger, and composer. Played briefly with Boyd Senter's band in Denver, Colorado, during the mid-1920s; played with other small bands c. 1926; played with Ben Pollack's orchestra, beginning 1927; helped Ray Noble organize his American orchestra during the early 1930s; formed and led Glenn Miller Orchestra, 1937-42; captain in U.S. Army Air Corps, beginning 1942. Appeared in films, including *Sun Valley Serenade,* Twentieth Century-Fox, 1941, and *Orchestra Wives,* Twentieth Century-Fox. Composer of popular songs, including ''Moonlight Serenade.''

---

by 1939, the band had made it big, playing to standing-room-only crowds in New York City.

Miller's orchestra was famous for its well-blended, balanced sound. Critics have noted that it was not a vehicle for star soloists, but rather that emphasis was placed on the output of the entire band. Miller was known to discourage musicians who stood out from the rest of the orchestra, and praise those who combined well with their fellows. The Glenn Miller Orchestra was acclaimed by a large variety of fans because it played many different types of big band music—everything from hot jazz to popular ballads. During the late 1930s and early 1940s, Miller and his band gifted audiences with classic hits such as ''Chattanooga Choo Choo,'' ''Pennsylvania 6-5000,'' and ''A String of Pearls.''

In 1942, while it was still extremely successful, Glenn Miller decided to break up his orchestra in order to accept the rank of captain in the U.S. Army Air Corps. He was on a routine flight over the English Channel when his plane disappeared. Like that of other orchestra leaders of the big band era, Glenn Miller's music has enjoyed a resurgence in popularity in recent years, and his orchestra is considered by critics to have been one of the best of its time.

Selected discography

Singles; on RCA

''Moonlight Serenade,'' 1939.
''Falling Leaves,'' 1940.
''Johnson Rag,'' 1940.
''In the Mood,'' 1940.
''Pennsylvania 6-5000,'' 1940.
''Tuxedo Junction,'' 1940.
''The Booglie Wooglie Piggy,'' 1941.
''Chattanooga Choo Choo,'' 1941.
''Elmer's Tune,'' 1941.
''Moonlight Cocktail,'' 1941.
''I've Got a Gal in Kalamazoo,'' 1942.
''A String of Pearls,'' 1942.
''Little Brown Jug.''

LPs

Glenn Miller: The Popular Recordings, 1938-42 (three compact discs), RCA, 1990.

Sources

Down Beat, September 1989; June 1990.
Look, August 13, 1940.
National Review, March 5, 1990.
Newsweek, January 15, 1940.
People, March 13, 1989.

—Elizabeth Wenning

Thelonious Monk

Pianist, composer, bandleader

When Thelonious Monk began performing his music in the early 1940s, only a small circle of New York's brightest jazz musicians could appreciate its uniqueness. His melodies were angular, his harmonies full of jarring clusters, and he used both notes and the absence of notes in unexpected ways. He flattened his fingers when he played the piano and used his elbows from time to time to get the sound he wanted. Critics and peers took these as signs of incompetency, treating his music with "puzzled dismissal as deliberately eccentric," *Jazz Journal* noted. "To them, Monk apparently had ideas, but it took fleshier players like pianist Bud Powell to execute them properly." The debate over his talent and skill continued as the years passed, but Monk eventually earned a strong following. By the time of his death in 1982, he was widely acknowledged as a founding father of modern jazz.

The *New York Post* once called Monk "one of jazz's great eccentrics." During concerts and recording sessions he would rise from his bench every so often and lunge into a dance, emphasizing the rhythm he wanted from his band members with his 200-pound frame. With his strange hats, bamboo-framed sunglasses, and goatee, he became an obvious subject for Sunday supplement caricatures. There was also the way he talked: He and his peers were known for popularizing such expressions as "groovy," "you dig, man," and "cool, baby." Most Americans, however, first heard of Monk in the early 1950s when he was arrested for allegedly possessing drugs—for Monk, one of several instances of legal harassment that would create severe obstacles to his work.

Piano Prodigy

Thelonious Sphere Monk was born on October 10, 1917, in Rocky Mount, North Carolina. The first music he heard was from a player piano that his family owned. At the age of five or six he began picking out melodies on the piano and taught himself to read music by looking over his sister's shoulder as she took lessons. About a year later the family moved to New York City. Monk's father became ill soon afterward and returned to the South, leaving the boy's mother to raise him and his brother and sister by herself. She actively encouraged her young son's interest in music. Though the family budget was tight, Monk's mother managed to buy a baby grand Steinway; when Monk turned 11 she began paying for weekly lessons. Even at that age it was clear that the instrument was part of his destiny. "If anybody sat down and played the piano," Monk recalled in *Crescendo International,* "I would just stand there and watch 'em all the time."

Born Thelonious Sphere Monk, Jr., October 10, 1917, in Rocky Mount, NC; died of a stroke, February 17, 1982, in Weehawken, NJ; son of Thelonious and Barbara Monk; wife's name, Nellie; children: Thelonious, Jr., and a daughter, nicknamed Boo.

Began playing piano at age 11; toured with traveling evangelist's show during the 1930's; became house pianist at Minton's Club in New York City, c. 1940; played with various bands in New York until 1944; led small groups until 1959; formed big band, 1959; led quartet, 1960s; toured internationally, 1971-72; made last appearance at Carnegie Hall, March, 1976.

Awards: *Down Beat* critics poll 1958 and 1959; honored with special tribute at President Jimmy Carter's 1978 White House jazz party.

As a boy Monk received rigorous gospel training, accompanying the Baptist choir in which his mother sang and playing piano and organ during church services. At the same time, he was becoming initiated into the world of jazz; near his home were several jazz clubs as well as the home of the great Harlem stride pianist James P. Johnson, from whom Monk learned a great deal. By age 13 he was playing in a local bar and grill with a trio. A year later he began playing at "rent" parties—thrown to raise money for rent—which meant holding his own among pianists who would each perform marathon displays of virtuosity. Monk gained further distinction at the Apollo Theater's famous weekly amateur contests, which he won so often that he was banned from the event. At 16 he left school to travel with an evangelical faith healer and preacher for a year-long tour that indoctrinated him into the subtleties of rhythm and blues accompaniment.

Upon returning to New York, Monk began playing non-union jobs. In 1939 he put his first group together. An important gig came in the early 1940s, when Monk was hired as house pianist at a club called Minton's. It was a time of dramatic innovation in jazz. Swing, the music of older jazzmen, had become inadequate for postwar society. In its place, a faster, more complex style was developing. The practitioners of this new music, called bebop, created it virtually on the spot, "in jam sessions and discussions that stretched past the far side of midnight," *Keyboard* explained. "According to jazz folklore, this activity centered on Minton's, and as the house pianist there, Monk was at the eye of what would become the bebop hurricane."

Yet while Monk was pivotal in inspiring bebop, his own music had few ties to any particular movement. Monk was an undisputed and independent original, and the proof was in his compositions. "More than anyone else in the Minton's crowd, Monk showed a knack for writing," *Keyboard* remarked. "Years before his piano work would be taken seriously, he would be known for his composing. In fact, most of the classic Monk tunes, such as 'Blue Monk,' 'Epistrophy,' and "Round Midnight,' were written during his gig at Minton's or before 1951."

Charged With Narcotics Possession

As the 1940s progressed and bebop became more and more the rage, Monk's career declined. In 1951 he was arrested with Bud Powell on a questionable charge of narcotics possession. Not only was he confined for 60 days in prison, but the New York State Liquor Authority rescinded his cabaret card, without which he could not play local club dates. For several years he survived only with the help of his good friend and patron the Baroness Nica de Koenigswarter.

By the mid-1950s, though, Monk's fortune took a turn for the better. In 1954 he gave a series of concerts in Paris and cut his first solo album, *Pure Monk* (now out of print). A year later he began recording for the Riverside label. His following grew, and as *Keyboard* reported, his mystique grew as well. "Program notes for the Berkshire Music Barn Jazz Concert in 1955 read, 'Monk is the Greto Garbo of jazz, and his appearance at any piano is regarded as a major event by serious followers of jazz.'" In 1957 Monk opened an engagement at New York's Five Spot, leading a powerful quartet with then-jazz newcomer John Coltrane on saxophone. The eight-month gig was pivotal for Monk, who "found himself at the center of a cult," according to *Keyboard*. "Audiences lined up to see his unpredictable performances, his quirky, quietly ecstatic dances during horn solos, his wanderings through the room." Several masterful discs he recorded for Riverside in the late 1950s—*Brilliant Corners, Thelonious Himself,* and *Monk with Coltrane*—increased his notoriety, rendering him "the most acclaimed and controversial jazz improviser of the late 1950s almost overnight." It didn't either hurt that both Coltrane and saxophonist Sonny Rollins were acknowledging him as their guru.

Erratic Behavior

The strange behavior that Monk displayed in public sometimes got him into trouble. A *New York Times* review of the 1989 Monk documentary *Straight, No*

Chaser commented on his temperament, revealing that the great pianist was "acutely sensitive and moody and perhaps a manic-depressive. . . . Illness eventually made it impossible for him to perform." In 1958 he was arrested for disturbing the peace and his cabaret license was revoked a second time. Forced to take out-of-town gigs, he was separated from his two main sources of stability—New York City and his wife Nellie—and his eccentricities thus intensified. During one episode in 1959 in Boston, state police picked him up and took him to the Grafton State Hospital, where he was held for a week. Around 1960 his cabaret club card was restored and he returned to playing New York clubs. Now when he played a gig his wife accompanied him.

Toward the end of the 1950s Monk began to receive the prestige he had long deserved. His late fifties recordings on Riverside fared so well that in 1962 he was offered a contract from Columbia. As a performer he was equally successful, commanding $2,000 for week-

> He would rise from his bench every so often and lunge into a dance, emphasizing the rhythm he wanted from his band members with his 200-pound frame.

long engagements with his band and $1,000 for single performances. In 1964 Monk appeared on the cover of *Time* magazine—an extremely rare honor for a jazz artist.

Withdrew from the Limelight

In the early 1970s, Monk made some solo and trio recordings for Black Lion in London and played a few concerts. But, beginning in the mid-1970s he isolated himself from his friends and colleagues, spending his final years at the home of the Baroness de Koenigswarter in Weehawken, New Jersey. After playing a concert at Carnegie Hall in March of 1976, Monk was too weak physically to make further appearances. He died on February 17, 1982, after suffering a massive stroke.

There was "a Monk fever in the jazz world" for at least two years before the pianist's death, observed *Village Voice* contributor Stanley Crouch. But, as record producer Orrin Keepnews observed in *Keyboard,* per-

forming Monk's music is no easy feat. His "material can be basically divided into two categories: difficult and impossible." Monk's eccentric piano technique also raised eyebrows among music critics. Concerning those who criticized his technique, Monk told *Crescendo International,* "I guess these people are surprised when they hear certain things that I've done on records. They must feel awful silly about saying I don't have no technique. Because I know you've heard me make some fast runs. You can dig how stupid the statement is."

Looking back on his career, Monk told *Crescendo International,* "As for the hard times I've had—I've never been jealous of any musician, or anything. Musicians and other people have told lies on me, sure, and it has kept me from jobs for awhile. . . . But it didn't bother me. I kept on making it—recording and doing what I'm doing, and thinking. While they were talking I was thinking music and still trying to play."

Selected discography

(With Sonny Rollins, Frank Foster, Ray Copeland, Julius Watkins, Percy Heath, Curly Russell, Willie Jones, and Art Blakey) *Monk* (recorded 1953-54), Prestige.

The Riverside Trios (recorded 1955-56), Milestone.

The Complete Riverside Recordings: 1955-61, Riverside, 1987.

(With Rollins, Ernie Henry, Oscar Pettiford, and Max Roach) *Brilliant Corners,* (recorded 1956), Riverside.

(With Pettiford and Blakey) *The Unique Thelonious Monk* (recorded 1956), Riverside.

Thelonious Himself (recorded 1957), Riverside, reissued 1987, Fantasy.

Monk With Coltrane (recorded 1957), Jazzland.

European Tour (recorded late 1950s), Denon.

(With Johnny Griffin, Ahmed Abdul Malik, and Roy Haynes) *Misterioso* (recorded 1958), Riverside, reissued 1985.

Alone in San Francisco (recorded 1959), Riverside, reissued 1987, Fantasy.

At Town Hall (recorded 1959), Riverside.

Evidence (recorded 1959 and 1960), Milestone.

In Person (recorded 1959 and 1960), Milestone.

(With Joe Gordon, Charlie Rouse, Harold Land, and others) *At the Blackhawk* (recorded 1960), Riverside, reissued 1988, Fantasy.

Thelonious Monk and the Jazz Giants, Riverside.

Monk in Italy (recorded 1961), Riverside, reissued 1991, Fantasy.

April in Paris/Live, Milestone, 1961.

(With Rouse, Frankie Dunlop, and John Ore) *Monk's Dream* (recorded 1962), reissued 1987, Columbia.

The Composer (recorded 1962-64 and 1968), Columbia, 1988.

Live at the Village Gate (recorded 1963), Xanadu, 1985.

Solo Monk, Columbia, 1965.

(With Blakey, Copeland, Gigi Gryce, Coleman Hawkins, John Coltrane, and Wilbur Ware) *Monk's Music* (recorded mid-1960s), Riverside.

Straight, No Chaser, Columbia, 1966.

The London Collection, three volumes, Black Lion, (Volume 3 recorded 1971; reissued 1990).

The Best of Thelonious Monk: The Blue Note Years, Blue Note, 1991.

Sources

Books

Chilton, John, *Who's Who of Jazz: Storyville to Swing Street,* Chilton, 1972.

Giddons, Gary, *Rhythm-A-Ning: Jazz Tradition and Innovation in the 80s,* 1986.

Hentoff, Nat, *The Jazz Life,* Da Capo, 1975.

Periodicals

Crescendo International, June 1984.
Daily News, February 18, 1982.
Jazz Journal, August 1964.
Jazz Review, November 1958.
Keyboard, July 1982.
New York Post, February 18, 1982; September 30, 1989.
New York Times, September 30, 1989.
Time, February 28, 1964.
Village Voice, March 9, 1982.

—*Kyle Kevorkian*

Milton Nascimento

Singer, songwriter

Multi-talented Milton Nascimento is frequently acclaimed as Brazil's greatest musician. His haunting voice is often described in terms of something from heaven, "an agonizingly pure tenor that often slips into an ethereal falsetto," Larry Rohter wrote in the *New York Times*. As a songwriter and harmonist, he weaves a startling blend of musical influences, including Brazilian and African folk strains, European classical music, the Brazilian bossa nova, even the rock sound of the Beatles, creating melodies which Jon Pareles in the *New York Times* noted can "seem as simple as nursery chants or as serpentine as jazz tunes." His Portuguese lyrics range from themes of universal love and the spiritual unification of the child and adult, to expressions of the struggle of oppressed people in Latin America and throughout the world. He has collaborated with and inspired numerous Latin American musicians, and has won the admiration of diverse American artists, including jazzmen Wayne Shorter, Herbie Hancock, and Pat Metheny, and rock stars Paul Simon and Sting. In the opinion of Pareles, Nascimento reigns as "one of the greatest musicians alive."

Nascimento has been a major star in Brazil and Latin America for over twenty years. One concert in Belo Horizonte, Brazil, in 1984, drew upwards of over 150,000 fans, and in recent years Nascimento has also commanded sold-out performances in major U.S. cities. Outside of Brazil, Nascimento is often categorized as a jazz artist, yet as Robert Palmer observed in the *New York Times,* "many of the songs he writes and performs are complicated and tricky enough to tax the interpretive abilities of the best jazz improvisers." Nascimento is uncomfortable having his music described as jazz. "It's not that I don't like jazz," he told Rohter. "It's that I don't like labels. Here in Brazil, we listen to everything, and in my little town in the interior of Minas Gerais we never worried about it. We just sang whatever appealed to us."

Mountains Encouraged Inventive Harmonies

Nascimento was raised by adoptive white parents in the small town of Tres Pontas, in the Brazilian state of Minas Gerais. To this day, he considers the countryside of Minas Gerais his center. "Minas is my *alimentacao,* my nourishment," he told Pamela Bloom in *Musician.* "Everything I am, mentally, physically, spiritually resides in Minas." It was in his isolated village that Nascimento developed what Rohter called his "sophisticated harmonic sense." He and his boyhood musical friends, which included his keyboardist Wagner Tiso, would listen to radio broadcasts from Rio de Janeiro and Sao Paulo, and the transmissions were partially interrupted by the surrounding mountains. "They'd play a song we like, and we'd copy the lyrics and the melody, but we had to invent the harmonies out of our own heads," he told Rohter. "Months later, we'd get to a big city to play the song and see that our harmonies were completely different from the original."

Nascimento travelled to Sao Paulo in 1965, and as an unknown bass player struggled to find work in a saturated club scene. His compositions began to gain recognition, however, and the famous Brazilian singer Elis Regina, who recorded several of his songs, secured him a performance on the national television music program, *Fino da Bossa*. His big break came in 1967, however, when three of his songs were showcased at the prestigious First International Pop Song Festival in Rio de Janeiro. Unknown to Nascimento, who was wary of competitions and the egoism involved, a singer-friend entered the songs for him. After his impressive showing in the song festival, he became highly sought-after by recording companies in Rio. Nascimento's first two albums, *Travessia* (1967) and *Milton Nascimento* (1969) established him as a major new talent in Brazil, and with his 1969 A & M album *Courage,* he was touted to American musical audiences as the successor to bossa nova stars such as Joao Gilberto and Antonio Carlos Jobim.

Preferred Brazilian Recording Business

Nascimento felt uncomfortable, however, with the recording business in North America, preferring the more intimate, collaborative nature of the music scene in Brazil. "I'm used to being the friend of my songwriting partners," he explained to Rohter. "So I would get there to the United States, and first you had to talk with the agent, then the publishing company, then the lawyer. The last thing would be the person himself, and by then I'd generally be tired and discouraged." He also found American producers interested in steering him away from the originality of his conceptions and ideas, so for many years Nascimento concentrated on recording in Brazil. Not until the 1980s, with his stature as an international star secure, was Nascimento able to work with the American recording industry on his own terms.

Nascimento has continually exerted his musical independence, despite barriers in his own country. In 1985, a civilian government was restored in Brazil after twenty-one years of military rule, and throughout much of his career, Nascimento has had to work within censorship guidelines, often at personal risk. His 1973 album, *Milagre dos Peixes,* was produced under the severest of restrictions, and many Brazilian musicians at the time had opted to work outside of the country. "We'd write something, the censors would send it back, stamped *No Way,*" he told Bloom. "We'd have to write the same thing in a way that the censors wouldn't notice but the people would understand." Nascimento's solution, as Bloom related, was "'to transform my voice into an instrument' that could register all his defiance, anger and sadness that lay behind his censored lyrics." Many of Nascimento's songs, including "San Vicente" and "Maria, Maria," have become anthems in not only Brazil, but throughout the Spanish-speaking countries of Latin America. His song "Coracao de Estudante" became a rallying cry for many Brazilians who in 1984 took to the streets demanding free elections in Brazil and an end to military rule.

An Exchange Across Barriers

Collaboration and musical sharing is essential to Nascimento, who works with several lyricists, but predominantly Fernando Brant. Nascimento views music as an exchange across barriers, and a way to reach many. "I can sing in Portuguese and still communicate with people who don't know the language," he told Palmer. "You can get your own feelings and images from the music, and when people do that, it makes me very happy. Every time I sing a song, it will have a different feeling for *me,* because the music changes as I change in my life, I work from the heart, and the heart speaks for itself." Palmer described such an exchange in his review of a 1984 Nascimento concert at Carnegie Hall. "Perched atop a stool with his guitar in hand, he communicated with sunny smiles, casual gestures, and richly textured singing that seemed to sketch exceptionally fine shadings of emotional nuance. . . . The intent of most of Mr. Nascimento's songs—longing, desire, evocations of childhood, hopes for a Latin America freed from racial, social and economic inequality—came through strongly."

Musicians throughout Latin America have travelled to Brazil to work with Nascimento, as have many from the United States. Jazz saxophonist Wayne Shorter met Nascimento in 1974 and the following year their collaborative *Native Dancer* was released, an album that many consider to be one of the most influential jazz recordings of the 1970s. Nascimento treasures the bond with other musicians, and lists among his influences American jazz artists Miles Davis, Pat Metheny, Hubert Laws, and Shorter. "There's something very beautiful that happens with music," he told Bloom. "It's as if you are walking down the street looking at many different faces, and suddenly you feel strongly they have something in common with you."

Nascimento's vast array of influences are showcased throughout his over twenty-five albums. *Clube da Esquina* (1972), "The Club on the Corner," was a landmark collaboration re-creating the street music scene he was a part of in Minas Gerais. *Minas* (1975), noted Bloom, "surveys a stark interior landscape of contrapuntal voices (notably chanting children) that intersect Milton's at odd angles," and, according to Palmer, is "a dream-like album of drifting, luminous moonscapes that is perhaps Mr. Nascimento's best single disk." *Geraes* (1976), added Bloom, "charts a regional folktrail, while songs like 'Girou, Girou,' with its sudden wordless vocal flight, suggest a bruised sensuality struggling for release." The above three albums display vintage Nascimento, according to Palmer: "Deft musical transitions and snatches of sound from the countryside or from city streets are used subtly to give each album its particular flux of moods and to impart a song-by-song narrative flow of almost cinematic clarity." Several of Nascimento's albums of the 1980s have become easily available to American record buyers, and amply showcase his harmonic and songwriting talents, including *Anima* (1982), *Encontros e Despedidas* (1985), *Yauarete* (1987), and *Miltons* (1989).

Messages Behind the Music

Nascimento's 1982 *Missa dos Quilombos* is a mass-oratorio dedicated to the story of blacks in Brazil from slavery to current times. In working on the ambitious project, Nascimento discovered that many slavery documents had been destroyed over the years by government officials, "to eliminate the black spot on Brazil's history," as he told Stephen Holden in the *New York Times,* and he had to travel around the country to interview people. Since the restoration of civilian rule in Brazil in 1985, Nascimento has had the opportunity to be more forthright with the messages in his music. In recent years he has especially spoken out on the preservation of the Amazon river region. His 1991 album, *Txai,* focuses on the plight of indigenous peoples of the Amazon basin and the destruction of the rain forest, and incorporates the haunting folk music of several jungle tribes. "Those of us who hold microphones become the voice of those who do not have microphones," he was quoted as saying by Geri Smith in *Americas.* "We have to alert others to what is happening in this world. We have to talk about preserving our planet, the earth, green things, animals, human beings—talk about how people treat each other."

Nascimento's popularity continues to expand outside of Brazil. Steve Heilio wrote in *Beat:* "Milton appears before huge audiences in his home country, and his select smaller performances overseas at such events and places as the Montreux Jazz Festival and Carnegie Hall are both celebrations of pride and joy for expatriate Brazilians and eye-openers for open-minded music lovers of all nationalities. A quarter-century after his career began, Milton is an international music treasure whose melodies and messages know no borders."

Selected discography

Travessia, Sigla, 1967.
Milton Nascimento, EMI/Odeon, 1969.
Courage, A&M, 1969.
Clube da Esquina, EMI/Odeon, 1972.
Milagre dos Peixes, EMI/Odeon, 1973,
Milagre dos Peixes ao Vivo, EMI/Odeon, 1974.
Minas, EMI/Odeon, 1975.
(With Wayne Shorter) *Native Dancer,* Columbia, 1975.
Milton, A&M, 1976.
Geraes, EMI/Odeon, 1976.
Clube da Esquina 2, EMI/Odeon, 1978.
Journey to Dawn, A&M, 1979.
Sentinela, Ariola, 1980.
(With George Duke) *A Brazilian Love Affair,* Epic, 1980.
Cacador de Mim, Ariola, 1981.
Missa dos Quilombos, Ariola, 1982.
Paixao e Fe, EMI/Odeon.
Anima, Ariola, 1982, reissued, Verve, 1990.
Milton Nascimento ao Vivo, Barclay, 1983.
Encontros e Despedidas, Polydor, 1985.
A Barca dos Amantes, Polygram, 1987.
(With Sarah Vaughan) *Brazil Romance,* [New York City], 1987.
Yauarete, CBS, 1987.
Miltons, CBS, 1989.
Txai, CBS, 1991.

Sources

Americas, July/August 1988.

Beat, Volume 10, Number 2, 1991.

Cash Box, December 2, 1989.

Down Beat, September 1984; November 1989.

Jazz Times, August 1986.

Musician, September 1986; September 1987; October 1988.

New York Times, June 1, 1984; June 4, 1984; May 4, 1986; June 25, 1986; June 28, 1986; July 27, 1988; July 30, 1988; November 16, 1989; April 4, 1991.

Village Voice, June 12, 1984; July 1, 1986.

—*Michael E. Mueller*

Youssou N'Dour

Singer, composer, drummer

Youssou N'Dour is an international star in a field of popular music that has come to be known as "Afro-pop" or "world beat." He is a singer, composer, and drummer whose style has been given the name "mbalax." N'Dour's own particular brand of mbalax has become so popular and widespread that he is often credited with inventing the genre. Ronnie Graham has explained in *The Da Capo Guide to Contemporary African Music* that mbalax is a generic Senegalese music characterized by a percussion base and featuring an improvised solo on the sabar drum. It has also been described as modern Senegalese rock.

Graham described Senegalese pop music of the late 1980s as "a sophisticated blend of the old and the new," with the old being primarily Cuban-influenced melodies and rhythms that dominated Senegalese music prior to the 1970s. The development of local styles was seriously hindered by the French philosophy of exporting its own culture to its colonies; local idioms, instruments, and traditions did not begin to appear in urban contemporary music until the 1970s, after Senegal had achieved independence. The tama, a small talking drum, was introduced in the 1970s and became a popular lead instrument.

N'Dour's take on mbalax features a rhythmic dance band consisting of as many as 14 members, including multiple percussionists, guitarists, saxophonists, and backing vocalists. As N'Dour achieved greater recognition and acceptance among Western audiences in Europe and the United States during the late 1980s, he was relieved of some of the pressure to incorporate Western rock styles into his own music. Although he is fluent in French, Arabic, and his native Wolof, N'Dour's English is not very good. Thus, he is at his best when able to present an appealing and authentic brand of African pop, with its own unique rhythms and vocalizations sung in Wolof, one of Senegal's major native languages.

N'Dour was born in 1959 in Dakar, the capital of Senegal, on the west coast of Africa. He grew up in a traditional African community within the Medina section of the city. "Living on the street was like being in a family," the musician was quoted as saying in the *Detroit News*. "Everybody knows one another, there's a great feeling of togetherness." N'Dour's father was a mechanic who discouraged him from a musical career. His mother, however, was a griot in the community. A griot is a West African musician-entertainer whose performances include tribal histories and genealogies; N'Dour's mother was a respected elder who kept the oral tradition of the community's history alive through traditional songs and moral teachings.

With his mother's encouragement, N'Dour would sing

at kassak, a party to celebrate circumcision. As N'Dour described his work then to the *Detroit Metro Times,* "Sometimes on one street there would be four or five kassaks going on at the same time. They would start in the evening and I would go to one and sing two numbers, then on to the next. . . . Sometimes I used to sing at 10 kassaks a night. Gradually, my friends and others encouraged me and gave me confidence, because they liked my singing."

By the age of 14, N'Dour was performing in front of large audiences and had earned the nickname, "Le Petit Prince de Dakar," or "The Little Prince of Dakar." As a teenager he joined the Star Band, the best-known Senegalese pop band of the time, recording with them and performing in clubs in Dakar. By the time he was 20, he had left the Star Band to form his own group, Etoile de Dakar (Star of Dakar). They recorded three albums in Dakar and had a hit with their first single, "Xalis (Money)." Then they relocated to Paris and reformed as the Super Etoile de Dakar (Superstar of Dakar).

Toured Europe and the United States

The European milieu provided N'Dour with a range of new musical influences. Looking back in 1990, he stated in the *Detroit News:* "When I started to play music, I was playing traditional music. But when I came to Europe to listen to the sounds around me, by 1984 I had a new attitude. I'm a new person now, opening fast. I like to change. I'm African, yes, but I like to play music for everybody. But my identity is African. That will never change." From his base in Paris, N'Dour and the Super Etoile began to win over Western audiences to the sound of mbalax. The Super Etoile consisted of 14 members, probably the largest aggregation with which N'Dour would ever perform. The group used traditional Wolof and African rhythms behind N'Dour's unique tenor. N'Dour continues to sing in Wolof, his vocal style often compared to the Islamic chanting heard in mosques and temples.

By the mid-1980s, the group was ready for a major international breakthrough; in addition to playing at N'Dour's nightclub in Dakar, the Thiosanne, they had toured the United States, Great Britain, and Holland. Remembering his audiences in Dakar and his friends from the Medina, N'Dour made it a point to return there. A song he wrote, "Medina," celebrates his old neighborhood and his old friends, who he told the *Detroit News* "are still my friends today and are the people I have around me."

In 1985 N'Dour and Super Etoile released *Immigres,* which became a classic in the Afro-pop field. It was issued in the United States three years later. N'Dour increased his exposure to Western audiences in 1986 by appearing as a drummer on Paul Simon's *Graceland* album. He recorded the *Nelson Mandela* album in Paris that year and toured the United States twice with Super Etoile, once on their own and once opening for Peter Gabriel. N'Dour sang backing vocals on Gabriel's *So* album; in fact, Gabriel is the Western musician most responsible for bringing Youssou N'Dour to America and other Western nations.

N'Dour continued to tour with Peter Gabriel in 1988, reducing the size of his band to six pieces and a dancer. In the summer of that year, N'Dour played New York's first International Festival of the Arts at the Beacon Theatre. The influence of American music on N'Dour was revealed in his half-set of American pop and soul, during which singer Nona Hendryx joined him for a song in English and Wolof. *New York Times* writer Jon Parelis wrote of N'Dour, "What makes Mr. N'Dour an international sensation, along with the dance rhythms of mbalax, is his unforgettable voice, a pure, pealing tenor that melds pop sincerity with the nuances of Islamic singing." Noting that mbalax has always combined international influences with Senegalese traditions, Parelis expressed his concern that American pop was diluting the effect of N'Dour's singing and the band's rhythms. N'Dour would later echo this concern in *Rolling Stone,* saying "It's a very difficult balance to keep the roots and bring in a bit of the Western world."

In the fall of 1988, N'Dour gained even greater international exposure as part of Amnesty International's "Human Rights Now!" world tour. At London's Wembley Stadium, N'Dour joined pop stars Bruce Springsteen, Sting, Gabriel, and Tracy Chapman to sing Bob Marley's classic reggae song, "Get Up, Stand Up." It was the start of a 44-day tour of five continents, including such nations as Hungary, India, Zimbabwe, Argentina, and Brazil. Only two U.S. dates were included, Los Angeles and Philadelphia.

Diverse Lyrical Content

N'Dour's original songs feature political and social commentary. He also writes and performs songs with a personal lyric content—about his old neighborhood and childhood pals, the youth of his country, and about roaming the countryside with a friend. In 1989 Virgin Records released an N'Dour album, *The Lion (Gaiende).* It was recorded in Paris and Dakar and was produced by George Acogny and David Sancious, who have combined backgrounds in jazz, pop, and rock. The Super Etoile, then an eight-piece band, was joined by some Western musicians, including pop-jazz saxophonist David Sanborn. Gabriel and N'Dour sing a duet on one of the album's tracks, "Shaking The Tree." N'Dour sings in Wolof on the album, but English translations of the lyrics are provided. In a review of *The Lion, New York Times* commentator Parelis again expressed his concern that too much Western influence was creeping into N'Dour's music and writing, "Despite an undercurrent of Senegalese drums, the rippling vocal lines and dizzying polyrhythms that made Western listeners notice him are usually truncated."

By the fall of 1989, Super Etoile was back to full strength with 12 pieces for N'Dour's club dates in the United States. The extra percussion and instrumentation helped restore the driving rhythm of N'Dour's music. Reviewing a performance at New York's the Ritz, Parelis described the "two percussionists whose doubletime and tripletime rhythms restored mbalax's sense of swift, sprinting momentum." He noted that the intricate cross-rhythms combined ably with a firm downbeat to provide a mix of Western and Senegalese styles. The show ended with a song—about toxic waste—intended as a single from N'Dour's Virgin album, *Set.*

Set deals with personal emotions, social problems, and political issues. N'Dour remarked on the record in the *Detroit News:* "Most of the songs I heard in my youth were either love songs or traditional songs recounting the history of the people that I come from—praise songs, historical songs. The lyrics of my own works today I consider to be about the society in which I live, the world in which I live. I want my words to have an educational function."

Selected discography

Singles

"Toxiques," Virgin, 1990.

Albums

Nelson Mandela, Polydor, 1986.
Immigres, Virgin, 1988.
The Lion (Gaiende), Virgin, 1989.
Set, Virgin, 1990.

Sources

Books

Graham, Ronnie, *The Da Capo Guide to Contemporary African Music,* Da Capo, 1988.

Periodicals

Detroit Free Press, October 5, 1990.
Detroit Metro Times, October 3, 1990.
Detroit News, October 5, 1990.
Down Beat, May 1987.
New York Times, July 2, 1988; July 2, 1989; November 8, 1989.
Newsweek, September 12, 1988.
People, October 10, 1988.
Rolling Stone, July 13, 1989.

—*David Bianco*

The Nitty Gritty Dirt Band

Country group

In addition to producing the pop hits "Mr. Bojangles" and "Make a Little Magic," the Nitty Gritty Dirt Band "changed the way rock fans listened to country music" with their 1972 triple album *Will the Circle Be Unbroken,* attested critic Jimmy Guterman in *Rolling Stone.* Seventeen years later, band members Jimmy Ibbotson, Bob Carpenter, Jeff Hanna, and Jimmie Fadden got together not only with past group members Levon Helm, John McEuen, and Bernie Leadon, but with many stars of acoustic country music to record and release *Will the Circle Be Unbroken: Volume II.* This follow-up was hailed by Bob Allen of *Country Music* as "the sort of record you'll find yourself listening to again and again and enjoying more with each and every spin."

The Nitty Gritty Dirt Band released their first album—aptly titled *The Nitty Gritty Dirt Band*—on Liberty Records in 1967. The record included their first smash, the now-classic "Mr. Bojangles," Jerry Jeff Walker's bittersweet song about a jailed dancer-turned-vagrant. The group was also the first to record singer-songwriter Kenny Loggins's "House at Pooh Corners." But after

For the Record. . .

Band members have included **Ralph Barr** (born in Boston; guitar and vocals), **Jackson Browne** (born October 9, 1948, in Heidelberg, Germany; guitar and vocals), **Bob Carpenter, Jimmie Fadden** (born March 9, 1948, in Long Beach, CA; guitar, harmonica, and vocals), **Jeff Hanna** (born July 11, 1947, in Detroit; guitar and vocals), **Levon Helm** (born May 26, 1942, in Marvell, AR; drums, mandolin, and vocals), **Jimmy Ibbotson, Bruce Kunkel** (born c. 1948, in Long Beach; guitar, violin, and vocals), **Bernie Leadon, John McEuen** (born December 19, 1945, in Long Beach; guitar, violin, and vocals), and **Les Thompson** (born in Long Beach; base, guitar, and vocals).

Recording and concert act, 1967—. Group formed in Long Beach, CA, 1966; released first album, *The Nitty Gritty Dirt Band,* on Liberty, 1967.

Addresses: *Record company*—MCA Records, Inc. (UNI Distribution Corp.), 70 Universal City Plaza, Universal City, CA 91608.

the Nitty Gritty Dirt Band's initial success, they were not much in the public eye until they decided to record *Will the Circle Be Unbroken.* The group members, always interested in country music and adding folk-country flavor to their pop material, got together with country music pioneers Roy Acuff, Maybelle Carter, and Earl Scruggs to make an album of traditional country favorites. In the words of Bob Millard, reporting in *Country Music,* the resulting effort "brought together titans of traditional country music with fireballs of a younger generation, mixing traditional bluegrass and folk with [the Nitty Gritty Dirt Band's] own brand of early country-rock."

The band had conceived of *Will the Circle Be Unbroken* in order to pursue their personal interests and were surprised at the response it received; the record sold a million copies and according to Millard, continues to sell roughly 30,000 copies yearly. As Allen pointed out, the album, "played a significant role in initiating a younger, hipper audience into the pleasures of traditional country music." *Will the Circle Be Unbroken* influenced later artists as well. Band member Hanna told Millard that "a lot of people like Ricky Skaggs, Jerry Douglas, Mark O'Connor or the guys in Newgrass Revival have told us that [the album] inspired them. For younger guys, not only was it some really great versions of a lot of those tunes, but it was also [saying] 'here's these young, hip guys playing country music' and it

made 'em stop and think." *Will the Circle Be Unbroken* increased the prestige and popularity not only of the Nitty Gritty Dirt Band but of the older country stars performing on it.

During the late 1970s and early 1980s the group shortened its name to The Dirt Band and had a couple of pop hits—1979's "An American Dream" and 1980's "Make a Little Magic," from albums of the same titles. As the 1980s continued, however, they returned to the original version of their name and began concentrating on country music anew. In 1987 the Nitty Gritty Dirt Band released the country-flavored *Hold On,* which music writer Alanna Nash predicted "could end up on several of the music charts and not cheat buyers of any persuasion." But by 1989 the Nitty Gritty Dirt Band had decided that it was time for a sequel to their distinctive shared effort; thus, *Will the Circle Be Unbroken: Volume II* was born.

In the years between the two *Circle* albums, the Nitty Gritty Dirt Band had its share of personnel changes, and so, in addition to rounding up both classic country artists and some of the late 1980s' most distinguished acoustic country performers, they also invited many of their own former band members to help on *Volume II.* Veterans of the first *Circle* like Acuff, Scruggs, and Vassar Clements returned; the late Maybelle Carter was represented by her daughter and son-in-law, June Carter and Johnny Cash, and also by granddaughter Roseanne Cash. Country artists Emmylou Harris, Ricky Skaggs, and Highway 101's Paulette Carlson were also included on *Volume II.* While Allen cited Nitty Gritty Dirt Band member Carpenter's "lovely duet" with Harris on "Riding Alone," he also praised the fact that the Band "willingly fades into the shadows to lend able background vocals and instrumental support to their talented guests." Other noteworthy tracks from *Volume II* include "Don't You Hear Jerusalem Moan," "One Step over the Line," and "Life's Railway to Heaven." In 1990 the Nitty Gritty Dirt Band released *The Rest of the Dream,* of which critic Ralph Novak of *People* assured readers: "They get by quite nicely this time, *without* a little help from their friends."

Selected discography

The Nitty Gritty Dirt Band (includes "Mr. Bojangles"), Liberty, 1967.
Ricochet, Liberty, 1967.
Rare Junk, Liberty, 1968.
Alive, Liberty, 1969.
Uncle Charlie and His Dog Teddy, Liberty, 1970.
All the Good Times, United Artists, 1972.
Will the Circle Be Unbroken (compilation), United Artists, 1972.

Stars and Stripes Forever, United Artists, 1974.

Dream, United Artists, 1975.

Dirt, Silver, and Gold, United Artists, 1976.

The Dirt Band, United Artists, 1978.

An American Dream (includes "An American Dream"), United Artists, 1979.

Make a Little Magic (includes "Make a Little Magic"), United Artists, 1980.

Jealousy, Liberty, 1981.

Hold On (includes "Fishin' in the Dark," "Joe Knows How to Live," "Blue Ridge Mountain Girl," "Baby's Got a Hold on Me," "Oleanna," "Dancing to the Beat of a Broken Heart," "Tennessee," and "Angelyne"), Warner Bros., 1987.

Workin' Band, 1988.

Will the Circle Be Unbroken: Volume II (compilation; includes "Riding Alone," "Don't You Hear Jerusalem Moan," "One Step over the Line," "Grandpa Was a Carpenter," and "Life's Railway to Heaven") Universal, 1989.

The Rest of the Dream (includes "Just Enough Ashland City," "The Rest of the Dream," "From Small Things," "Waitin' on a Dark-Eyed Gal," and "Blow Out the Stars, Turn Off the Moon"), MCA, 1990.

Greatest Hits, Curb/CEMA, 1990.

Live Two Five, Capitol, 1991.

Sources

Country Music, September/October 1987; July/August 1989; September/October 1989.

People, August 20, 1990.

Rolling Stone, May 18, 1989.

Stereo Review, August 1987.

—*Elizabeth Wenning*

N.W.A.

Rap group

The rappers in N.W.A. see themselves as reporters, and the stories they cover are not pretty. Having grown up amidst drug deals and gang violence in the Compton section of Los Angeles, the members of N.W.A. rap about urban America's ugliest realities and offer no apologies for the brutality and cynicism in their lyrics. *Orlando Sentinel* correspondent Robert Hilburn wrote: "Pushing the imagery much further than anyone before, N.W.A. features sirens and gunshots as back-drops to its . . . tales of drug dealing and police con-frontations. . . . The defiant N.W.A. refuses to pass judgment or offer itself as a role model. The group's name echoes its bold, incendiary nature: Niggers With Attitude."

N.W.A. formed in Los Angeles in the late 1980s, when an admitted former drug dealer decided to invest his earnings in a record company. The leader of the group, Eazy-E founded Ruthless Records "with money gained illegally on the streets," according to *Rolling Stone*. He then recruited some of his friends to form a rap act, most notably Ice Cube, who wrote many of the raps on

the group's debut album. Other N.W.A. members include producers Dr. Dre and Yella and mixer M.C. Ren.

In 1989 N.W.A. released their debut album, *Straight Outta Compton,* a vivid evocation of the bitter and dangerous world from which the group's members had emerged. The work was decidedly controversial—one song, "F— tha Police," derided police, making claims of brutality. *Richmond Times-Dispatch* contributor Mark Holmberg described the album as "a preacher-provoking, mother-maddening, reality-stinks" diatribe that "wallows in gangs, doping, drive-by shootings, brutal sexism, cop slamming and racism." However, a reviewer for *Newsweek* acknowledged that *Straight Outta Compton* "introduced some of the most grotesquely exciting music ever made."

A *Newsweek* reviewer added, "Hinting at gang roots, and selling themselves on those hints, they project a gangster mystique that pays no attention where criminality begins and marketing lets off." Defending the group's stance, original N.W.A. member Ice Cube told *Rolling Stone:* "Peace is a fictional word to me." "Violence is reality. . . . You're supposed to picture life as a bowl of cherries, but it's not. So we don't do nothin' fake."

Work Incited Controversy

Because of its controversial lyrics, little air time was granted to *Straight Outta Compton*—even by rap radio stations—and MTV refused to show the group's debut video, claiming it "glorified violence." Despite this lack of mainstream exposure the album sold a million copies, making stars of its five Compton natives. Criticism rained down on the group—the F.B.I. officially condemned "F— the Police" for encouraging violence

against law-enforcement officers, and the group members were allegedly harassed by police officers during a concert at Detroit's Joe Louis Arena. Ice Cube told the *Richmond Times-Dispatch* that the group's negative image among authority figures didn't bother N.W.A. "We don't want the key to any cities," he announced. "We like to be real . . . wake up and smell the coffee, this is the way it is."

Their defiant attitude firmly established, N.W.A.'s members became premier performers of "gangster" rap, an arm of rap music that chronicles often violent and squalid urban conditions without preaching. As M.C. Ren explained in *Rolling Stone,* "We don't go around telling people, 'Don't do drugs,' or preaching safe sex, cause everybody's gonna do what they want regardless."

Violence and Profanity Condemned

The group's subject matter and its lyrics, rife with four-letter words and sexual suggestion, have aroused heated controversy among critics. Some reviewers feel that N.W.A. glamorizes gang violence. In the *Washington Post,* David Mills wrote: "The hard-core street rappers defend their violent lyrics as a reflection of 'reality.' But for all the gunshots they mix into their music, rappers rarely try to dramatize that reality—a young man flat on the ground, a knot of lead in his chest, pleading as death slowly takes him in. It's easier for them to imagine themselves pulling the trigger." On the other hand, *Wichita Eagle-Beacon* correspondent Bud Norman noted that while N.W.A.'s members refuse to condemn the violence they describe, "they don't make it sound like much fun. . . . They describe it with the same non-judgmental resignation that a Kansan might use about a tornado."

Ice Cube answered the charges against N.W.A.'s lyrics. "We're not trying to make a buck off of violence," he told the *Richmond Times-Dispatch.* "We're not on the good side or the bad side of anything. We're in the middle, like a reporter would do. We tell [listeners] what's going on. If you want to go bad, you got to deal with the consequences." He added: "If you don't like it, if you don't understand it, don't buy the records. Don't come to the concert."

Second Album Topped Charts

After *Straight Outta Compton* Ice Cube left the group to pursue a solo career—allegedly, according to *Rolling Stone,* because of a financial dispute. Because Ice Cube had written many lyrics, the group's 1991 album,

Efil4zaggin, marked a new direction for N.W.A. Nonetheless, the new release occupied the number one spot on the charts without a hit single or play on radio stations and MTV. Once again, the group caused controversy. The title of the album, read backwards is *Niggaz4life.* Although the group's members refer to themselves with this word, many find it offensive. In addition, N.W.A.'s references to women—most often as bitches—caused an uproar. As Alan Light in *Rolling Stone* remarked, "the second half of the album . . . stands as a graphic, violent suite of misogyny unparalleled in rap." Former member Ice Cube was also the target of N.W.A.'s insults with one song, "B.A."—for traitor Benedict Arnold—aimed at him.

The unbridled success of *Efil4zaggin* among both black and white listeners startled and dismayed critics. The group earned substantial media attention as "experts" tried to explain N.W.A.'s appeal. Some suggested that the bad attitude and raunchy lyrics of what a reviewer for *Time* called a "rap mural of ghetto life, spray-painted with blood," appealed to listeners. Helping to launch sales of the album was a new group of customers—white middle-class teenagers—who latched on to the hard-core sound of N.W.A. As M.C. Ren explained, "White kids have been seeing so many nega-tive images of blacks in the media for most of their lives. Now they have a chance to see something real. White kids got hip."

Selected discography

Straight Outta Compton, Ruthless Records, 1989.
100 Miles and Runnin' (EP), Ruthless Records, 1990.
Efil4zaggin, Ruthless/Priority, 1991.

Sources

Houston Post, June 18, 1989.
Newsweek, March 19, 1990; July 1, 1991.
Orlando Sentinel, October 26, 1990.
Richmond Times-Dispatch, June 30, 1989.
Rolling Stone, June 29, 1989; August 8, 1991.
Time, July 1, 1991.
Washington Post, September 2, 1990; March 19, 1991.
Wichita Eagle-Beacon, August 3, 1989.

—*Anne Janette Johnson*

The Nylons

A cappella group

The Canadian vocal quartet the Nylons—for more than a decade one of the most popular a cappella groups on the contemporary music scene—began attracting attention in Canada in 1979, performing 1950s and 1960s classics such as "The Lion Sleeps Tonight" and "Duke of Earl" in addition to their own compositions. The Nylons quickly landed a recording contract with Attic Records for Canada; shortly afterwards, Open Air Records—a division of Windham Hill—began releasing their albums in the United States. Their fifth effort, aptly titled *Rockapella,* was lauded as an "impressive musical statement" by critic Robin Tolleson in *Down Beat.*

The Nylons made their professional debut in a Toronto, Ontario, restaurant early in 1979. At that time the group was composed of three former musical theater performers—Marc Connors, Paul Cooper, and Claude Morrison—along with bass singer Ralph Cole. They sang a cappella, which, as David Livingstone noted in *Maclean's,* is "the art of singing with no instrumental accompaniment." Fans appreciated the skill with which

For the Record. . .

Group formed in 1979; made professional debut in Ontario, Canada. Members include **Marc Connors, Paul Cooper, Claude Morrison,** and **Ralph Cole; Arnold Robinson** replaced Cole in 1981; **Claude Desjardins** replaced Morrison.

Recording and performing act since, early 1980s—. Recorded first U.S. release, *One Size Fits All,* on Open Air, 1982.

Addresses: *Record company*—Windham Hill, P.O. Box 9388, Stanford, CA 94305.

the Nylons managed this difficult feat, and by 1980 the group became one of the favored "cabaret acts" of Toronto, in Livingstone's words. That year the group also took their act on the road, appearing with great success in western Canadian cities such as Vancouver.

At about this time, the Nylons were signed by Attic Records. Their self-titled debut album featured spirited remakes of "Love Potion Number Nine," "The Lion Sleeps Tonight," "Duke of Earl," and "Up on the Roof," as well as original numbers such as "Me and the Boys," "A Million Ways," and the risque "Something About You." But despite the great number of older songs on the Nylons' albums, group member Marc Connors assured Livingstone: "We want to be on the cutting edge of things. If we take some of our repertoire from the '50s and '60s, it's because that music was based on vocals."

By 1982 the Nylons, after replacing Cole with former Platters member Arnold Robinson, had released their first album in the United States, *One Size Fits All,* on Open Air Records. It featured interesting originals such as "That Kind of Man" and "Prince of Darkness," and remakes of "Silhouettes," "Up the Ladder to the Roof," and "Town Without Pity." Livingstone had high praise for the Nylons' performance on the last song: "With one soaring voice rising above a bed of ornate harmonies, 'Town Without Pity' becomes not a corny rival of a Gene Pitney hit but a stirring comment about the intolerance afoot on a 'grey and granite planet' that seems closer than ever to falling apart."

During the years of their early releases, the Nylons' live concerts were apparently something to see. According to Livingstone, the singers' microphones were covered in "glittery" pantyhose, but, of course, it was their music that captivated audiences. "By the end of the evening everyone was standing, clapping and smiling," Livingstone reported, and he summed up by saying that "the group embodies the kind of snappy, polished showmanship that keeps audiences coming back for more."

The Nylons quickly added fans on U.S. college campuses to their growing legions of Canadian devotees. *Seamless,* the Nylons' second U.S. release, featured some favorites from their first Attic Records effort, along with standards such as "This Boy," and "Remember (Walking in the Sand)." Eventually, the group added percussion instruments to their recording, and in 1987 the title track of their album *Happy Together* received airplay on many U.S. radio stations, as did their remake of "Kiss Him Goodbye." In 1989, the Nylons released *Rockapella* on the Windham Hill label. Reviewer Robin Tolleson of *Down Beat* had praise for the original "No Stone Unturned" as well as for the group's a cappella versions of "Poison Ivy" and "Drift Away." He concluded that "the Nylons can breathe within their songs, really let loose and feel it, and that makes all the difference in the world."

Selected discography

The Nylons (includes "The Lion Sleeps Tonight," "Love Potion Number Nine/Spooky," "A Million Ways," "Something About You," "Duke of Earl," "Rock and Roll Lullaby," "Find the One I Love," "Some People," "Up on the Roof," and "Me and the Boys"), Attic Records, c. 1981.

One Size Fits All (includes "That Kind of Man," "Silhouettes," "Town Without Pity," "Prince of Darkness," "Romance," "Up the Ladder to the Roof," "Heavenly Bodies," "Bop 'Til You Drop," "Please," and "So Long"), Open Air Records, 1982.

Seamless (includes "The Lion Sleeps Tonight," "Up on the Roof," "This Boy," and "Remember"), Open Air Records, 1984.

Happy Together (includes "Happy Together," "Chain Gang," and "Kiss Him Goodbye"), Open Air Records, 1987.

Rockapella (includes "Love, This Is Love," "Drift Away," "Wildfire," "Another Night Like This," "No Stone Unturned," "Count My Blessings," "Dream," "Poison Ivy," "Busy Tonight," and "Rise Up"), Windham Hill, 1989.

Four on the Floor, Scotti Bros., 1991.

Sources

Down Beat, October 1989.
Maclean's, March 8, 1982.

—Elizabeth Wenning

The Pogues

Rock band

Traditional Irish folk music collides with punk-rock grit and shamelessness in The Pogues. Led by sparingly-toothed and grumbling singer-songwriter Shane MacGowan, the London-based octet specializes in highly-charged songs bespeaking tales of alcohol over-indulgence, illicit love, death, urban blight, and political protest, all set to music recalling the folk melodies of Irish ballads, jigs, drinking songs, and sailor chantys. Comprised of English and Irish musicians, The Pogues sport a largely acoustical sound, wielding an array of various folk and modern instruments. On the surface, their sound bears echoes of traditional Irish folk groups such as The Clancy Brothers or The Dubliners, yet, as Richard Grabel wrote in *Creem,* The Pogues are easily distinguished: "The Pogues . . . infuse . . . traditional music with punkish energy and abandon, an anarchic spirit, and a hard, aggressive, stomping instrumental approach. Then they hook it up with MacGowan's lyrics—tales of universal soldiers and wayward London boys and revolutionary dreams and ordinary people full of life and hope—

For the Record. . .

Band formed in 1982, in London, England, as Pogue Mahone; members include **Philip Chevron,** born c. 1958 (guitar); **James Fearnley,** born c. 1958 (accordian); **Jem Finer,** born c. 1958 (banjo); **Darryl Hunt,** born c. 1953 (replaced original base player **Cait O'Riordan,** 1986); **Shane MacGowan,** born December 25, c. 1958 (vocals and songwriting); **Andrew Ranken,** born c. 1958 (drums); **Peter "Spider" Stacey,** born c. 1958 (whistle); and **Terry Woods,** born c. 1946 (cittern).

Recording and performing group, 1982— . Released first single, "Dark Streets of London," on Pogue Mahone label, and signed with Stiff Records, 1984.

Addresses: *Record company*—Island Records, Warner Communications Company, 75 Rockefeller Plaza, New York, NY 10019.

extraordinary lyrics that turn these wild jigs into resonant epics."

The hard-drinking bard figure of Dublin, Ireland-born MacGowan has been the focal point of The Pogues since their formation in the early 1980s. His acclaimed lyrics, laced with "Joycean melancholy and a candid preoccupation with mortality," according to Steph Paynes in *Rolling Stone,* movingly evoke outcasts of London society. Raised in Dublin until he moved with his parents to London at the age of six, MacGowan was expelled from a prominent English school when he was fourteen, and drifted through a number of odd jobs before becoming a punk musician in the late 1970s. MacGowan has recounted in interviews of beginning to drink heavily and unabated from his early teens on, and the characters of his songs are similarly well-acquainted with alcohol. Mark Peel in *Stereo Review* commented that "the wastrels and drunkards, the profligates and rebels who populate MacGowan's songs are the victims of demons beyond their control—social, economic, political, and psychological demons along with the evil spirits that come tumbling out of a bottle. Yet even at their most profane they fight back with defiant dignity." MacGowan sings in a grumbling and gruff voice which is perfectly matched to his tales of woe. Elizabeth L. Bland wrote in *Time:* "MacGowan sing-snarls like a saloon rowdy. . . . There is nothing pretty about a MacGowan vocal; the beauty comes later, after he has given the ear a good boxing, and the lyrics settle—very gently, really—on the heart."

The Pogues rose out of the North London punk scene of the early 1980s when MacGowan, who had founded the punk-group Nipple Erectors (a.k.a. The Nips), joined English tin whistle player Spider Stacey to sing Irish folk songs in a popular London rock club. Disgruntled with a dying-out punk scene, the musicians began performing old standards at pubs in a highly-revved and furious fashion. They were soon joined in their musical venture by ex-Nips guitarist Jim Fearnley, and the group initially named itself Pogue Mahone (Gaelic for "kiss my ass"). Pogue Mahone began performing their energized folk alongside MacGowan originals throughout London, and three other musicians were recruited for a sextet, including drummer Andrew Ranken, banjo player Jem Finer, and female bass guitarist Cait O'Riordan. Acoustic instruments such as the accordion and fiddle were added, and as Stacey recalled to Lisa Russell in *People,* "we'd pick up instruments we couldn't play and do Irish folk songs at 140 miles an hour, playing them badly, but with spirit." Alcohol was a frequent accessory of the group, and Pogue Mahone soon became famous for drunken and boisterous stage performances, while steadily gaining recognition among the London music scene as innovative musicians. Paynes noted that "musically, Pogue Mahone concocted an ingenious new recipe of punk-infused Irish traditional music—ditties with a vengeance."

Signed to Stiff

The group came to the attention of the rock group The Clash, who hired them in 1984 as the opening act for a musical tour. The same year, The Pogues— featuring a shortened, less outrageous, name—were signed to a recording contract with Stiff Records, which in 1984 released the group's first album, *Red Roses for Me.* Their second album, *Rum, Sodomy and the Lash*— taken from an expression of Winston Churchill describing life in the Royal Navy—was produced by singer-songwriter Elvis Costello and brought them wider attention in both Britain and the United States. The album also spawned their first British hit single, "A Pair of Brown Eyes." Phil Chevron, formerly of the punk group Radiators from Space, joined The Pogues after their first album, and Terry Woods, a multi-instrumentalist, came on board after their second. O'Riordan married Costello and left the group in 1986, and was replaced by Darryl Hunt, who had been a roadie of The Pogues.

Appealed to Fans *and* Critics

Many critics consider The Pogues' million-selling 1988 album, *If I Should Fall from Grace with God,* to be their finest effort. Peel describes it as "a riotous, whirling, reeling brawl of tavern ribaldry, pock-marked love songs, boozy prayers, gutter balladry, Thatcher-bashing, and, above all, Joycean romanticism." Among the tracks is MacGowan's and Finer's "Fairytale of New York," a duet featuring singer Kirsty MacColl, which recounts a soured romance that began among the bliss of a previous Christmas season. "You scumbag, you mag-got/You cheap, lousy faggot," the lovers howl, "Happy Christmas, your ass/I pray God it's our last." Kurt Loder in *Rolling Stone* notes the song's "combination of sea-sonal buoyancy (conveyed by the arrangement's Gaelic pipes and lush strings) and personal disillusionment is unlike anything else in recent pop." Chevron's "Thou-sands Are Sailing" is a moving song of modern-day Irish immigration to the United States, while MacGowan's "Streets of Sorrow/Birmingham Six," one of The Pogues' more overt political songs, protests the imprisonment of six Irishmen for a bombing in England. The convicted men's only crime, the song goes, was "being Irish in the wrong place/and at the wrong time." Loder notes that "the anger here seems very real," while "the music puts it across like a punch in the face."

The Pogues' 1989 album, *Peace and Love,* was worked on more fully in the recording studio and as a result, features a more polished sound. Some reviewers, like *Down Beat*'s Frank Alkyer, felt the album suffered from an overproduction of MacGowan's vocals, yet accord-ing to Bland, *Peace and Love* is still "full of spunk and sass." The album features a broader sampling of writ-ing and vocal contributions by other group members, including Chevron's desperate and driving love song, "Lorelei," Finer and Ranken's jazz instrumental entitled "Gridlock," and Finer's solo, "Misty Morning, Albert Bridge," which deals with being separated from his family. Elizabeth Wurtzel noted in *People,* however, that the "best material still comes from MacGowan," con-cluding that "no one else mixes the usual Pogue style drinking jigs with shots of joy and anger the way he can." David Handelman in *Rolling Stone* found the ensemble effect of The Pogues particularly impressive in *Peace and Love,* commenting that "the playing, which encompasses such diverse instruments as the hurdy-gurdy, the cittern and the mandola, is faultless and stirring."

Music Celebrates Contradiction

The lyrics of The Pogues' songs, particularly MacGowan's contributions, express what Karen Schoemer in the *New York Times* called "desperation," yet they are "almost always pitted against the jubilant fast tempos and merry accordion whirl of Irish music, and that conflict between the insanely joyful and the intoxicatingly sad." MacGowan commented to Grabel that The Pogues' music reflects "the way life is. . . . One minute you're up, the next minute you're down" and similarly noted to Russell that he simply feels "there's lots of good in this world and lots of ugliness. Can't have one without the other." An additional dichotomy surrounding The Pogues is their reputation as drunken boozehounds versus their acclaimed accomplishments as musicians. They continually strive against the conception of themselves as a drunken group of hoodlum musicians. Some peo-ple think the band lives "in a lake full of Guinness," Finer complained to Russell, and while the band does not deny its fondness of alcohol, the image of drunks is, as Finer told Russell, "the Irish stereotype being put on this band because of the type of music we play." Chevron commented to Handelman that The Pogues "represent the people who don't get the breaks. Ne'er-do-wells with all sorts of quirks and foibles, the least likely pop stars. People can look at us and say, 'My God, if that bunch of tumbledown wrecks can do it, so can I.'"

Selected discography

Red Roses for Me, Stiff, 1984.
Rum, Sodomy and the Lash, Stiff, 1985.
Poguetry in Motion (EP), Stiff, 1986.
If I Should Fall from Grace with God, Island, 1988.
(Contributors) *Live for Ireland,* MCA, 1988.
Peace and Love, Island, 1989.
Yeah, Yeah, Yeah, Yeah, Yeah (EP), Island, 1990.
(Contributors) *Red, Hot & Blue,* Chrysalis, 1990.
Hell's Ditch, Island, 1991.

Group also contributed songs to the film *Sid & Nancy,* Samuel Goldwyn Co., 1986, and appeared in the film *Straight To Hell,* Island Pictures, 1987, and in the film *Completely Pogued,* 1988. Also appeared on television show *Saturday Night Live,* NBC-TV, 1990.

Sources

Books

MacGowan, Shane, *Poguetry: The Lyrics of Shane MacGowan,* Faber, 1989.
Scanlon, Ann, *The Pogues: The Lost Decade,* Omnibus, 1989.

Periodicals

Creem, September 1986.

Down Beat, February 1991.

Folk Roots, June 1989.

High Fidelity, May 1988.

Melody Maker, October 27, 1984; May 11, 1985; December 21-25, 1988; November 18, 1989; November 25, 1989.

Musician, May 1986.

New York Times, June 25, 1988; August 20, 1989; March 16, 1990.

People, August 8, 1988; October 16, 1989; January 28, 1991.

Rolling Stone, November 21, 1985; February 25, 1988; October 6, 1988; November 16, 1989.

Stereo Review, May 1988; November 1988.

Time, August 21, 1989.

—Michael E. Mueller

Leontyne Price

Opera singer

When Leontyne Price's angelic voice trailed off that night at New York's Lincoln Center in 1985, signaling the end of her final performance of the title role in Verdi's *Aida*—a role that has become synonymous with her name—the ensuing applause that embraced the great diva's farewell will forever echo, not only through the famed home of the Metropolitan Opera but through Price's heart as well. "That moment, I was a sponge, and I'll have all that moisture the rest of my life," Price told Robert Jacobson of *Opera News*. "I soaked that in. It's the most intense listening I've ever done in my life. For a change, *I* listened. I have every vibration of that applause in my entire being until I die. I just will *never* recover from it. I will never receive that much love as long as I live, and I would be terribly selfish to expect that much ever again."

Seldom has an artist received applause that was so genuine and so deserved. After all, Price was *57 years old* that evening, performing one of the most demanding roles in the repertoire, and yet her voice was as full as the day she first performed *Aida* in 1957 and literally set the standard for its perfection. But then Price's voice, her instrument, was so rare and special to her that she had taken great pains throughout her career to guard it from overuse, and to not destroy it performing roles that she thought she couldn't handle.

If the time was not right, or she didn't think she could handle a certain part, Price was known to reject the invitations of such great conductors as Herbert von Karajan, Rudolf Bing, or James Levine with the wave of a hand. For this, she became known in music circles as arrogant and "difficult," but for the fiercely independent Price it was a matter of survival to be selective. "The voice is so special," she told *Opera News*. "You have to guard it with care, to let nothing disturb it, so you don't lose the bloom, don't let it fade, don't let the petals drop."

First Black International Opera Star

Whether she was known as "the girl with the golden voice" or "the Stradivarius of singers," Price is, without question, one of the great operatic talents of all time. The fact that she was the first black singer to gain international stardom in opera, an art-form theretofore confined to the upper-class white society, signified a monumental stride not only for her own generation, but for those that came before and after her.

By the time her career was in full blossom, for example, it was no longer a shock to white audiences to see black singers performing roles traditionally thought of as "white." In opera, the singing and the music are tantamount, and thanks to Price, black singers could now be judged solely on their artistic merit. And as the most successful heir of the great African-American vocal tradition, Price's achievements in opera can be seen as a justification for her lesser known but equally great predecessors, such as Marian Anderson and Paul Robeson.

Indeed, it was during an Anderson concert in Jackson, Mississippi, in 1936 that Mary Violet Leontyne Price, then just nine years old, first decided that she would dedicate her life to singing. From that day forward, she was driven to recreating the power and beauty which Anderson had brought to the stage. And with her 1985 retirement, Price has just as enthusiastically passed the torch to a new generation of young singers. "You have no idea how wonderful it is to know you had a part in the exposure of some of the great, marvelous talent," she told Jacobson. "I feel like a mother, a mother hen."

"Collard Greens and Caviar"

Though endowed with a miraculous talent, Price points to her own mother as the source of her common sense, which in no small way helped her to channel and safeguard that talent for such a long and glorious career. "You need [common sense] as much as you need talent in the career, Robert," Price told Jacobson. "Common sense, which means your own vibes, and going with them. I'm just homespun. I am still home-

spun. It's sort of down home, very country. I think of myself as a strange mixture of collard greens and caviar."

Price was born in Laurel, Mississippi, on February 10, 1927. Her father, James Price, worked in a sawmill, and her mother, Kate, brought in extra income as a midwife. Both parents were amateur musicians, and encouraged their daughter to play the piano and sing in the church choir at St. Paul's Methodist Church in Laurel. Price graduated from Oak Park High School in 1944, then left home for the College of Education and Industrial Arts (now Central State College) in Wilberforce, Ohio. There, she studied music education with the idea of becoming a music teacher, but her hopes of becoming an opera singer had not faded. When the prestigious Juilliard School of Music in New York offered her a four-year, full-tuition scholarship, Price leapt at the chance and arrived in the big city in 1949.

"Midas Touch" at Juilliard

With living expenses so high in New York City, Price for a time feared that she would have to follow the path of some of her friends and take a job singing in blues clubs and bars, which would have been a little like Michelangelo working as a housepainter. But Elizabeth Chisholm, a longtime family friend from Laurel, came to Price's rescue with generous patronage, and the young singer was free to study full-time under vocal coach Florence Page Kimball. "It was simply the Midas touch from the instant I walked into Juilliard," Price told *Opera News.* "I learned things about stage presence, presentation of your gifts, how to make up, how to do research, German diction, et cetera." From Kimball, she went on to add, Price learned the steely control which would allow her to perform at top voice over so many performances, "to perform on your interest, not your capital. What she meant was, as in any walk of life, there should be something *more* to give."

Price thrived at Juilliard, and her role as Mistress Ford in a student production of Verdi's *Falstaff* caught the eye of composer Virgil Thomson, who cast her in a revival of his opera *Four Saints in Three Acts,* Price's first professional experience. This in turn led to a two-year stint (1952 to 1954) with a revival of Gershwin's *Porgy and Bess,* which toured the U.S. and Europe. During this time Price married her co-star in that opera, William C. Warfield. The marriage was a disappointment, however, and the two divorced in 1973 after years of separation.

Began Professional Career

In 1954 Price made her concert debut at New York's Town Hall, where she exhibited great skill with modern compositions; a magnetic performer, she enjoyed the concert format and continued to tour regularly throughout her career, much to the chagrin of opera purists. Fast becoming a darling of the New York critics, Price soon saw her career take off. In 1955 she appeared in Puccini's *Tosca* on NBC television, thus becoming the first black singer to perform opera on television. And she was so well received that she was invited back to appear on NBC telecasts of Mozart's *Magic Flute* (1956), Poulenc's *Dialogues of the Carmelites* (1957), and Mozart's *Don Giovanni* (1960).

One of the most fruitful associations of Price's career began in 1957, when she was invited by conductor Kurt Herbert Adler (he had seen her performance in *Tosca*) to make her American operatic debut as Madame Lidoine in *Dialogues of the Carmelites* with the San Francisco Opera. In later years, San Francisco seemed to be the place where Price returned to challenge herself with new roles, thus expanding her repertoire.

In fact, Price first performed *Aida* there—under quite unusual circumstances. "The first *Aida* I did, period, anywhere, was on that stage, by accident," Price said in *Opera News.* "I've always threatened to give two wonderful medals to two wonderful colleagues who happened to have two wonderful appendectomies and gave me two wonderful opportunities to sing *Aida.* They are Antonietta Stella in San Francisco in 1957 and Anita Cerquetti at Covent Garden in 1958. The year I did *Dialogues,* Stella had an emergency appendectomy. Adler walked into the room and asked if I knew *Aida.* I told him yes, and I was on. I went through the score with Maestro Molinari-Pradelli, and I knew every single, solitary note and nuance. I had it ready to travel. After that *Aida* was definitely part of my repertoire. That was being in the right place at the right time."

Expanded Repertoire Abroad

In the following years, Price expanded her repertoire significantly on American soil, with such distinguished companies as the Chicago Lyric Opera and the American Opera Theater as well as the San Francisco Opera. She credits the great conductor Herbert von Karajan with introducing her to European audiences. Price's debut on that continent came at Vienna's Staatsoper in 1958 as Pamina in *Zauberflöte,* not in *Aida* as has been commonly written. Her second European performance was in *Aida* at the same theater, and she quickly forged a reputation in Europe with a string of appearances on such venerable stages as London's Covent Garden, Verona's Arena, the Salzburg Festival, and Milan's historic La Scala, where her *Aida* won the hearts of Verdi's own countrymen.

Her international prominence now secure, Price returned home to make her debut at the mecca of American opera, New York's Metropolitan Opera, and thus began a long, often controversial, but always glorious

> *Price was, without question, one of the great operatic talents of all time.*

association with that revered institution. Her Leonora in *Il Trovatore* on January 27, 1961, brought a standing ovation of 42 minutes, the longest ever given at the Met. Over the next several years Price was a staple in Metropolitan productions. When the company moved its home to the impressive new Metropolitan Opera House at Lincoln Center, director Rudolf Bing extended Price the ultimate honor of opening the house in the world premier of Samuel Barber's *Antony and Cleopatra.*

Shone in *Antony and Cleopatra*

Although the opera itself was not well received, Price was magnificent, having dedicated herself to the role with total commitment. "*Antony and Cleopatra* was *the* event of the century, operatically speaking," Price told *Opera News.* "I was there! I lived the life of a hermit for a year and a half, so as not to have a common cold. From the moment I was asked to do this, I simply did everything I possibly could to have it be right. I accepted that responsibility with the greatest happiness. This was the greatest challenge of my life."

Clearly on top of the opera world, Price appeared in 118 Metropolitan productions between 1961 and 1969, when she drastically cut back her appearances not only in New York but elsewhere. It was here that she began to strike some opera insiders as ungrateful, vindictive, and arrogant, but Price insists that she was merely protecting herself from overexposure. "If I don't want to do something, I don't do it—nothing against anyone or the institution," she told Jacobson. "If you say yes to something that may not go, *you* are discarded—not the people who asked you to do it. They have something else to do. You are part of a unit, and they need your expertise to make the unit better. . . . The thing that's been misunderstood is that I don't give a lot of rhetoric before I say no. I just say no. It saves everybody time, and maybe because I don't give a reason, it's taken in a negative way.''

Later Focused on Recitals

In the 1970s Price drastically cut the number of opera appearances, preferring to focus instead on her first love—recitals—in which she enjoyed the challenge of creating several characters on stage in succession. Her career credits include countless recordings, many of them on the RCA label, which enjoyed an exclusive 20-year contract with the diva. She has won 13 Grammy Awards, the Presidential Medal of Freedom (the nation's highest civilian award) in 1965, the Kennedy Center Honors for lifetime achievement in the arts in 1980, and the First National Medal of Arts. She has appeared on the cover of *Time* magazine, and she

performed at the White House in 1978. Price has lived alone for years in a townhouse in New York City's Greenwich Village.

Sources

Books

Baker, Theodore, *Baker's Biographical Dictionary of Musicians,* Schirmer, 1984.
Hitchcock, H. Wiley, *The New Grove Dictionary of American Music,* MacMillan, 1986.
Souther, Eileen, *The Biographical Dictionary of Afro-American and African Musicians,* Greenwood Press, 1982.

Periodicals

Opera News, July 1985; August 1985.

—David Collins

Professor Longhair

Pianist

With a complicated piano style that integrated blues, rhumba, African, and Jamaican rhythms, Professor Longhair was one of a handful of musicians whose work inspired the growth of rock 'n' roll. Next to Fats Domino, Longhair is known as one of New Orleans' most influential musicians. Longhair, however, never knew fame and fortune—he was virtually out of work in the 1960s and he died a poor man. A resurgence of popularity in the 1970s helped to popularize Longhair with a younger generation. After his death in 1980, his music lived on in the legions of performers he influenced, including Dr. John, Fats Domino, Huey Smith, James Booker, and Allen Toussaint.

Born Henry Roeland Byrd in a small, Klan-infested town in Louisiana, Longhair moved to New Orleans with his family when he was a young boy. Longhair used to dance outside hotels, where he was exposed to the piano styles of such musicians as Kid Stormy Weather. After failing at guitar lessons, he taught himself to play a piano that he found abandoned in an alley. Modeling his playing on the artists he had heard, he also infused his own combination of boogie-woogie, calypso, jazz, samba, and dance rhythms. The effect was so unique his style was virtually impossible to copy.

Jerry Wexler, one of Longhair's producers, said that he had once played a Professor Longhair record to a world-famous jazz pianist. "Totally intrigued," Wexler recounted in *Rolling Stone*, "that man . . . tried to duplicate Fess' style. An hour and some busted knuckles later, he retired in confusion. 'I heard it,' he said, 'but it's impossible to play.'"

Longhair collected rhythms wherever he went. In the 1930s, as a member of the Civilian Conservation Corps, he worked with men from many different countries, including Spain, the West Indies, Puerto Rico, and Jamaica. "I just copied all their changes and beats," Longhair confessed, "and kept the ones I liked."

Also in the early 1930s he earned a living as a dancer, teamed up with Champion Jack Dupree and Redd Foxx. Foxx and Dupree were to quickly move on and split up the trio. Longhair stuck around New Orleans and got his big break in 1949, when he was asked to sit in for Dave Bartholomew's keyboardist at the Caldonia Inn. The club's manager, Mike Tessitore, promptly fired Bartholomew and hired Longhair, dubbing the long-locked musician "Professor."

The next year, Longhair made his most popular record, *Bald Head*. He worked for a while with a variety of backup bands, with names such as Professor Longhair and the Clippers and Roy Byrd and his Blues Jumpers. In 1954 he suffered a stroke that kept him hospitalized for nearly a year. He was plagued with varying illnesses

For the Record. . .

Born Henry Roeland Byrd, December 19, 1918, in Bogalusa, LA; died of a heart attack, January 30, 1980; son of James and Mae Byrd (both musicians); married Alice, c. 1940; seven children (one deceased).

Street dancer in New Orleans, c. 1929; served in the Civilian Conservation Corps in the 1930s; prizefighter; dancer in floor shows at nightclubs, including work with Redd Foxx and Champion Jack Dupree; war veteran; piano player in nightclubs, c. 1949; toured with various groups, including the Four Hairs Combo, Professor Longhair and His Shuffling Hungarians, Roy Byrd and His Blues Jumpers, and Professor Longhair and the Clippers, 1949-60; did solo work as Roy "Bald Head" Byrd and Roland Byrd; worked for One Stop Record store, c. 1968; toured the U.S. and Europe in the 1970s as Professor Longhair and the Blues Scholars; appeared at Montreux Jazz Festival, Newport Jazz Festival, and the Grande Parade du Jazz in Nice, France; toured Scandinavia.

for the rest of his life—pulmonary edema, bronchitis, and cirrhosis, to name a few. Records made between 1955-59 were not well received and Longhair was out of work for much of the 1960s. At one point, he worked sweeping out a record store owned by a man who helped him record his biggest hit single, "Go to the Mardi Gras." Although Longhair had written this song, he never received royalties for it. He was destitute for most of his life, living in badly-kept dwellings in New Orleans slums. Two separate fires devastated his rental homes. It wasn't until the last year of his life that he could finally afford to buy a small bungalow.

In the early 1970s his career turned around. At a Mardi Gras festival, he virtually brought the house down. A spectator recalled that "when he started playing that upright—it sounds like a cliche—but everything else stopped dead on the other stages. There were four acts playing, simultaneously, and the crowd just gathered and gaped. They had never heard anything like him. It was truly a magic moment."

In 1973 Atlantic released a compilation of Longhair's earlier hits, entitled *New Orleans Piano.* And Longhair continued to record in that decade, releasing three albums: *Rock and Roll Gumbo, Live on the Queen Mary,* and *Crawfish Fiesta.* Sales never reached dizzy-

ing heights, but Longhair traveled both in the U.S. and abroad, playing in clubs and in festivals that showed young fans what his music was all about.

However, his resurgence was not to last for long. On January 30, 1980, Longhair suffered a massive coronary and died in his sleep. Three days earlier, he had performed at the club Tipitina, named after one of Longhair's famous songs. His manager, Allison Kaslow, had remarked that the performance "was total perfection." Longhair had told her, "Tonight I finally got it together."

At his funeral, he was remembered with bountiful bouquets from many music greats, including the Neville Brothers, Fats Domino, Irma Thomas, Paul McCartney, and others. Allen Toussaint commented that "it would be difficult for anyone ever to play like Fess did, to get his energy and his sound, because it had so much to do with the way women would jump and wriggle when he played, and the feelings he brought to the music from the way he lived, the people he knew in the streets and alleyways of New Orleans."

Posthumous releases of Longhair, including *Mardi Gras in New Orleans* and *The London Concert,* continued to sell well into the early 1980s.

Selected discography

Bald Head, Mercury, 1950.
New Orleans Piano, Atlantic, 1972.
Rock 'n' Roll Gumbo, Barclay, 1975.
(Contributor) *New Orleans Jazz and Heritage Festival,* Island, 1976.
Live on the Queen Mary, Harvest, 1978.
Crawfish Fiesta, Alligator, 1980.
Mardi Gras in New Orleans, Krazy Kat, 1982.
The London Concert, JJP, 1984.

Sources

Down Beat, April 1980.
New York Times, July 31, 1980.
Rolling Stone, March 20, 1980.
Spin, May 1987.
Time, February 11, 1980.

—Nancy Rampson

Queen

Rock band

Following their debut in 1973, Queen, a completely different sort of band, was hailed as "a fresh, new breeze into the world of rock." The English group is perhaps best known for their flamboyant lead singer Freddie Mercury, whose dramatic vocal style and outrageous onstage antics have formed much of the band's reputation and personality—deservedly or not. Often overlooked are the band's considerable musical skill and their talent for songwriting—the four members of Queen have been responsible for an impressively imaginative and diverse body of work that includes such songs as the ingenious operatic experiment "Bohemian Rhapsody," the harmonic "Somebody to Love," the playful "Fat Bottom Girls," the cocky "We Will Rock You/ We Are the Champions," the rhythmic "Crazy Little Thing Called Love," and what became a popular football stadium anthem, "Another One Bites the Dust."

Formed in 1971, Queen's lineup includes guitarist Brian May and drummer Roger Taylor, both former members of the band Smile, vocalist/keyboardist Freddie Mercury, and bass player John Deacon. After a short time

For the Record. . .

Band formed in England in 1971; members include **Freddie Mercury** (born Frederick Bulsara, September 8, 1946, in Zanzibar), lead vocals and keyboards; **Brian May** (born July 19, 1947, in Hampton, Middlesex, England), lead guitar; **John Deacon** (born August 19, 1951, in Leicester, England), bass; and **Roger Meadows Taylor** (born July 26, 1949, in Kingslynn, Norfolk, England), drums. Taylor has children. All four members have attended universities: Mercury has a degree in graphic design and illustration; May has a degree in physics and has done graduate work in astronomy; Taylor has a degree in biology; and Deacon earned a degree in electronics with first-class honors.

Awards: *Rolling Stone* Reader's Poll citations for single of the year, 1976, for "Bohemian Rhapsody," and 1980, for "Another One Bites the Dust," and for artist of the year, 1980.

Addresses: *Record company*—Hollywood Records (Elektra), 75 Rockefeller Plaza, New York, NY 10019.

spent in rehearsal, the group began their search for a record company in 1973 and signed almost immediately with EMI. Their self-titled first album sold extremely well in both Britain and the United States, and their second album, *Queen II,* yielded the British top-ten single "Seven Seas of Rhye." Queen's big breakthrough in the United States came in 1975 with *Sheer Heart Attack*—a best-selling album containing the top-ten single "Killer Queen." Their successful tour season met with mixed criticism. One writer for the *New York Times* introduced them as "a British quartet still subscribing to the principles of blitzkrieg rock," referring to the group's lavish production values, and commented that though their music was "scarcely superoriginal," the band evidently "touched a responsive chord that should allow Queen to reign quite happily in this area."

Innovative Album Reached Number One

The following year the group hit number one in the United States with the remarkable *A Night at the Opera* album featuring Taylor's amusing "I'm in Love with My Car," Deacon's catchy "You're My Best Friend," and two of May's sensitive and often overlooked tunes, the time-travel-inspired ballad "'39" and more delightful fantasy fare of "The Prophet's Song." The album also spawned a major worldwide hit in "Bohemian Rhapsody"—an unprecedented six-minute cut that mingled "introspection with Gilbert and Sullivan operatics," as a

Time critic described it. The group followed their masterwork with another in the same vein. *A Day at the Races* contained Mercury's falsetto-laced "Somebody to Love," another catchy Deacon cut, "You and I," and still more gentle departures from the "blitzkrieg" rock they had been known for in May's lovely Japanese/English anthem "Teo Torriatte (Let Us Cling Together)."

Known for simply being themselves, Queen offered audiences a bravado sound coupled with a campy style that would likely have met with disdain a short decade before. As Brian May told *Time:* "We're not styled on anybody." And no one could successfully style themselves on Queen, who in the mid-1970s prided themselves on not using synthesizers but instead "complex overdubbings of electric guitar with varied amplifiers" which gave their albums a full orchestral sound, as the *Time* writer noted. Another unique feature was their use of dazzling *a cappella* interludes and flawless vocal harmony as in "The Prophet's Song" and "Somebody to Love." Such poetic and sensitive moments, however, were balanced by songs like "Death on Two Legs," which included such language as "You suck my blood like a leech . . . you're a sewer rat decaying in a cesspool of pride." The group's multifaceted style was echoed by Mercury's chameleon-like vocals; as Ralph Novak of *People* commented, "Not many vocalists can go from sweet to abrasive as rapidly as he can."

Versatility Captured New Audiences

The group's popularity increased with glowing reviews for the 1977 single release of "We Are the Champions" and the delightful rockabilly-style "Crazy Little Thing Called Love" from the 1980 album *The Game,* which was both a commercial success and well received by critics. "Another One Bites the Dust," a funky pseudo-rap cut, provided the group with a successful single, topping both the soul and pop charts in the United States. This departure from the heavily overdubbed and complex musical styles of earlier hits attracted a large black audience that had, for the most part, been ignoring Queen the previous decade.

Two years later, *Hot Space* continued the sound of "Another One Bites the Dust," devoting an entire side to funky, danceable tunes that appealed to a much broader audience than in the past. Still, the album met with mixed reviews and was their slowest seller since *Queen II.* A well-crafted record with an impressive compositional range and tight vocal harmonies "grafted seamlessly into [a] kinetic brew," the disk was nevertheless faulted because under the superb production the group was grinding out what Sam Sutherland in *High Fidelity* labeled a "noxious mix of sexual manipulation and mean spiritedness" in such cuts as "Back Chat" and "Body Language." The latter made little impact on the singles chart before vanishing entirely. Even the more melodic "Life Is Real (Song for Lennon)," a eulogy for John Lennon, was criticized by Sutherland as "cheapened by the precision with which Queen apes the vocal and keyboard timbres of 'Imagine.'"

Queen's 1984 album, *The Works,* fared much better than *Hot Space.* Layered vocals and multitracked guitars were cut out, leaving "a lean hard-rock sound, making *The Works* perhaps the first record to refute the maxim that the words Queen and listenable are, of necessity, mutually exclusive," as *Rolling Stone* contributor Parke Puterbaugh observed. The group offered such thundering tracks as "Tear It Up" and "Hammer to Fall," balanced against the more melodic "Keep Passing the Open Windows," the fifties-style "Man on The Prowl" and the harder to classify "Is This the World We Created. . .?," which Puterbaugh termed "an acoustic meditation on hunger and hate and generational responsibility." Despite such critical praise, the album failed to produce a top hit.

Became International Superstars

While Queen's American chart success was on the decline, the group was enjoying increasing popularity as an international stage act, rivalling the Rolling Stones and Bruce Springsteen in their drawing power. A 1981 concert in Brazil set records for the largest paying audience to see a single performance by one band, and the group's set at the 1985 Live Aid fund-raising concert was lauded by fans and critics. The band's stage performances have been balanced between new material and crowd pleasers—even numbers impossible to reproduce on stage, such as "Bohemian Rhapsody," whose complicated, layered, *a cappella* vocal section is filled in by tape as lights flicker crazily around the empty stage. Queen's notorious stage pyrotechnics have earned them a reputation as a can't-miss concert act. As May told Charles McCardell in *Musician,* "Somewhere in the course of the last couple of years, something clicked and we reached a new level. We weren't only a pop group anymore. We sort of got written in as one of the thing[s] people have to see."

The band had not played a live date in the United States since 1982, however, and by the late 1980s Queen was meeting with some scathing criticism from American critics. *A Kind of Magic,* released in 1986, won great regard in Britain and elsewhere, but U.S. fans were unimpressed, and the album sank back as a non-event "absolutely bankrupt of gauche imagination . . . domi-

nated by barren slabs of synthscape," as *Rolling Stone* contributor Mark Coleman commented. Taylor's "Radio Ga Ga," which placed high on the charts in nineteen countries, made it only to the sixteenth slot in the United States. Any power the group previously had demonstrated was absent on the album, replaced by what Coleman characterized as "a mechanical thud rather than a metalized threat."

The group's musical style was changing, and so were attitudes toward them. As Taylor commented, "We never tried to pander to what we feel people want. A lot of people want to hear rehashes . . . but that would be death for us. That's really unfair, because we have changed a lot." "We really start with a clean slate each time," May similarly told McCardell. "No matter the producer, no matter the song, it's still Queen. We don't have to reproduce any formulas. And we've never had an audience that hemmed us in." Nevertheless, the band has been looking to recapture their lost American popularity. As May continued: "America now for us is an island. We have every territory around it, but we don't have that big corner of the world."

We never tried to pander to what we feel people want. A lot of people want to hear rehashes, but that would be death for us.

With the 1991 release of *Innuendo,* Queen regained some of the critical respect and radio airplay they had lost in the States. Craig Tomashoff of *People,* for instance, noted that *Innuendo* "is so over-the-top it's enjoyable," and added that "it's nice to hear this reversion to the old exaggerated ways." "There's no getting around the new album's craft," Chuck Eddy stated in *Rolling Stone,* for "these old entertainers sound like they've decided to stop trying so hard, like they're finally satisfied with their lot in life." And that lot, the critic concluded, is a considerable one: "Queen is well aware that its forte has always been eclectic excess for its own sake. . . . These shameless all-time glam survivors would try anything once, and amid their messes they attained classical-kitsch pinnacles, helped invent rap music and . . . [have been] explicitly acknowledged as an important inspiration by arty hardcore ensembles and funk-metal and industrial-drone bands alike."

Selected discography

Queen, EMI, 1973.
Queen II (includes "Seven Seas of Rhye"), EMI, 1974.
Sheer Heart Attack (includes "Killer Queen"), EMI, 1974.
A Night at the Opera (includes "Bohemian Rhapsody," "You're My Best Friend," "'39," and "The Prophet's Song") EMI, 1975.
A Day at the Races (includes "Somebody to Love"), EMI, 1976.
News of the World (includes "We Will Rock You/We Are the Champions"), EMI, 1977.
Jazz (includes "Fat Bottom Girls"), EMI, 1978.
Live Killers, EMI, 1979.
The Game (includes "Crazy Little Thing Called Love" and "Another One Bites the Dust"), EMI, 1980.
Flash Gordon (film soundtrack), EMI, 1980.
Greatest Hits, EMI, 1981.
Hot Space, EMI, 1982.
The Works, EMI, 1984.
A Kind of Magic, Capitol, 1986.
The Miracle, Capitol, 1989.
Innuendo, Hollywood, 1991.

Sources

Books

Anderson, Christopher P., *The New Book of People,* Perigee, 1986.

Periodicals

Detroit Free Press, August 6, 1982.
High Fidelity, August 1982.
Musician, November 1986.
New York Times, May 9, 1974; February 18, 1975; February 7, 1976; February 7, 1977; December 3, 1977; November 18, 1978; January 1, 1982; July 21, 1982; July 30, 1982.
People, August 25, 1986; April 1, 1991.
Rock Express, Number 106, 1986.
Rolling Stone, January 25, 1979; April 12, 1984; October 9, 1986; March 7, 1991.
Time, February 9, 1976.

—Meg Mac Donald

Queen Latifah

Rap singer

Queen Latifah, whom Lisa Kennedy of *Mother Jones* called one of the hottest artists on the burgeoning Tommy Boy label, has worked hard for her success, but not by stepping on fellow rappers on her way to the top. Latifah is known for her refusal to participate in the well-publicized feuds among various factions of rap performers. "I might rebut if somebody challenged me, but I'd make it funny, not nasty," she said in *Rolling Stone.* Attesting to her feelings of solidarity with other rappers, she has stated that she would rather present a united artistic front than suggest a clique fractured by infighting and clashing ambitions.

Applauded for her social politics as well as her gift for rhyme, Latifah—from an Arabic word meaning "delicate" or "sensitive"—seems to pursue a well-rounded image, with social commentary in its place, but entertainment firmly in the foreground. "I'd rather throw in a line or two about drugs," she has said, "just to make you think. I can have fun and still show I'm on the ball." Her music, according to *Interview,* borrows freely "from hiphop, House, jazz, and reggae," all saturated by Latifah's sense of self and a pride seemingly untouched by vanity.

While some vocal artists are never quizzed about the message of their music, rappers are often asked to philosophize about fellow musicians and ideas in rap; Latifah holds her own, but will not be made into a spokesperson. Her strength is often misinterpreted as a feminist message. *Rolling Stone* contributor Alan Light testified that "Latifah bristles at the suggestion that she is part of a 'women's movement' sweeping rap. 'Me, M.C. Lyte, Roxanne Shante, we got record deals because we're good,' she said. 'We deserve them, not because we happen to be women.'"

Rejects Feminist Label

Like many young women, Latifah dislikes the label "feminist," believing it carries strident overtones. "I'm not a feminist. . . . I'm just a proud black woman. I don't need to be labeled," she said in *Interview.* According to Dominique DiPrima in *Mother Jones,* "'Ladies First,' [Latifah's] duet with British rapper Monie Love, touches female pride without preaching. Her whole style is a feminist statement—she is the Queen, never the victim." Not surprisingly, several of the cuts on Queen Latifah's LP *All Hail the Queen* begin with tongue-incheek references to her "royal" status, such as "All hail the queen," and "Dance for me."

Related to the debate over feminism in women's rap is the dominance of men in rap—and all music—production. In her *Mother Jones* article about women in rap,

DiPrima described the business and its relationship to gender: "The rap music business, like most other businesses, is controlled by men, making it risky to really speak out. In addition to the business end, many female groups rely on the artistic support of men to write, produce, and advise them." By way of example, Latifah co-mixed only two of the 15 tracks on her album.

Maintains Control in Male-Dominated Business

DiPrima also pointed out that "popular male rappers make guest appearances on women's records, feature women on theirs, and plug them on stage and on vinyl." This is true of *All Hail the Queen,* which features Daddy-O of Stetsasonic, KRS-One, and members of De La Soul. Latifah, however, seems to find her current level of artistic control sufficient; she firmly calls *All Hail the Queen* "hers" and discusses the album's concept as her own. Suggesting that in a live setting one can transcend gender roles, the Queen told Kennedy: "This is a business where you sell off your talent, and to me the proof is usually at the show. There's no double standard with your fans."

Queen Latifah, usually clad in what *Entertainment Weekly* described as "African-print pajama suits, skull caps, and big wooden bracelets and earrings," *is* critical of the sexist images of women presented by some male rappers. In a rare moment of universal criticism she stated: "Those women are pretty shallow. They look like skeezers, and that's the problem. A lot of those females don't have respect for themselves. Guys are exploiting them." Dimitri Ehrlich of *Interview* congratulated Latifah on her positive image: "I think it's great that the women you chose for your dancers have the kind of image that young people can look up to." Latifah sees materialism as one cause of the acceptance of male-dependent women, contending that "females don't respect themselves; they only think materialistically. They want mon-

ey, but they don't think, I'm gonna get this money on my own. They think, I'm gonna get money from this guy."

Latifah's larger commitment to unity in rap is apparent in her defense of male rappers; she told *Entertainment Weekly* that the most memorable entertainment-world moment in 1990 was "when the [censorship] controversy over 2 Live Crew pushed their album to double platinum status and when they were cleared of charges." Although her own lyrics are not considered sexually provocative—as were 2 Live Crew's—Latifah believes fervently in an artist's unfettered freedom to express him or herself. In this way she is among the mainstream of her colleagues; where her opinion varies is in her defense of male rappers against charges of hating women.

Outspoken Views on Sexism

She told *Interview:* "I wouldn't even say it's sexist. It's sexist in the sense that they're talking about a female, but that's usually exaggerated for the humor. Others speak the truth. They are not talking about women like me and you; they're rapping about women who wear dresses halfway up the behind—women who use their bodies, not their minds. I'd say the guys are wrong, because instead of educating women, they're exploiting them. But I can't say they're wrong for what they're saying. I've been on the road and seen girls who don't know a guy sleep with him in twenty minutes 'cause he's in a group. That's the kind of girl they're talking about. . . ."

DiPrima summed up the importance of Queen Latifah's success: "Women like Latifah provide role models—models of women in control, speaking their minds and getting their own, without being an accessory to some guy. These role models aren't just important to young girls but to young men as well who are getting accustomed to the independent women as a peer. Everywhere I go I hear guys listening to Latifah or Lyte, not as FEMALE RAPPERS but simply as def lyricists."

Selected discography

All Hail the Queen, Tommy Boy, 1989.
Nature of a Sista, Tommy Boy, 1991.

Sources

Entertainment Weekly, December 28, 1990.

Interview, May 1990.

Mother Jones September/October 1990.

Nation, April 16, 1990.

Rolling Stone, February 22, 1990.

Time, May 27, 1991.

—Christine Ferran

Jean-Pierre Rampal

Flutist, conductor

"**R**ampal plays with an abundance of ame (soul) and a tenderness that is potent at its core," wrote Eugenia Zukerman, describing a Jean-Pierre Rampal performance in *Esquire*. "With a profoundly expressive musicality, he is a poet-flutist nonpareil." Until Rampal began his international career in the 1950s, only the violin, cello, and piano were considered solo rank by classical instrumentalists. The first virtuoso to perform flute recitals solo, Rampal gives one hundred twenty concerts a year on four continents. Though his more than three hundred recordings make him a likely candidate for the most highly transcribed classical artist in history, Rampal confessed in his autobiography *Music, My Love* that he "stumbled into a musical career." "There are people whose careers are well planned, even predestined," he related in his introduction. "Mine was a mixture of chance and destiny."

Rampal was born January 7, 1922 in Marseilles, France, to Joseph and Andree (Roggero) Rampal. In spite of the fact that his father was a professor of flute at the Marseilles Conservatory, neither of his parents recommended Rampal make music his career. Since his mother preferred a steady income to the vagabond life of a musician, she encouraged the boy, who ranked at the top of his class, to become a doctor. Although his father did not influence Rampal to study medicine, he discouraged Rampal's interest in the flute. Refusing to give Rampal lessons until he was twelve years old, Rampal's father relented only when he needed students to fill up his flute class at the Conservatory. Rampal advanced quickly on the flute, winning first prize at the Conservatory after two years of study in 1937. In his early teens, he was second chair flutist (his father was first) in the Classical Concert Orchestra of Marseilles. His first professional recital prompted several encores at the Salle Mazenod in Marseilles when he was sixteen, but this did not turn him from his intentions for a medical career.

Occupation Spurred Musical Career

In 1943 the German occupation of France changed the course of Rampal's life. Since he was twenty-one, the third-year medical student faced service in the German military. He had kept up his playing along with his studies in urology and opted to join a German military orchestra. While a member of the orchestra, he received permission to audition at the Paris Conservatory. Rampal was chosen in the first round of the audition, but had his entrance to the Conservatory deferred for one year. When he discovered he would be deported to Germany on his return to his German outfit, he planned his escape. With his family's help, Rampal hid for a year in Marseilles before entering the Paris Conservatory.

Rampal knew he was safe under the director of the Conservatory, Claude Delvincourt, since Delvincourt never turned illegal students over to the authorities. Rampal decided on a career in music after five months of study, when he won first prize at the 1944 flute competition at the Conservatory.

Although he went home to Marseilles temporarily to continue his medical studies, a return to Paris in the spring of 1945 to play in a concert with the National Orchestra of France helped Rampal to make music his life. "I don't need another musician in the family. I want a doctor," his mother told him as he left, Rampal recounted in his autobiography. He did not want to disappoint his mother, but Paris was a ravaged city in need of entertainment when he arrived. Rampal found great success in the lucrative medium of French radio, as music lovers were discovering pieces of the Baroque

era, which showcased the flute. In the late 1940s, Rampal formed the musical relationships that were pivotal to his career. First, Robert Veyron-Lacroix joined Rampal as his piano accompanist in an association that would last the next thirty-five years. Then in 1946 Rampal organized the exemplary French Wind Quintet, and two years later, the Paris Baroque Ensemble. Both chamber ensembles existed simultaneously for fifteen years, but the Paris Baroque Ensemble outlasted the Quintet for fifteen more.

Library of Congress Debut

During the fifties Rampal's record sales earned him two Grand Prix du Disque Awards. Performances in concerts and recitals across Europe and Asia garnered him the 1956 Oscar du Premier Virtuose Francais. He became the principal flutist with the Paris opera in 1955, and remained in that position until 1962. His American debut at the Library of Congress in 1958 brought rave reviews. Rampal reported a sample, critical response in his autobiography from Day Thorpe in the *Evening Star,* who wrote: "Although I have heard many great flute players, the magic of Rampal still seems to be unique. In his hands, the flute is three or four music makers—dark and ominous, bright and pastoral, gay and salty, amorous and limpid. The virtuosity of the technique in rapid passages simply cannot be indicated in words."

In the seventies Rampal's work flourished in unexpected areas. Joined by the harpist Lily Laskine, who had played duets with him for thirty-five years, Rampal released an album of Japanese folk songs which was record of the year in Japan in 1970. Subsequently, Rampal became a successful crossover artist when his foray into a jazz/classical combo sold over a million records. In 1975 *The Bolling Suite* album with, French jazz artist Claude Bolling, gave Rampal such broad-based appeal that he was invited to appear on the popular television program *The Muppet Show,* where he performed "Ease on Down the Road" with Miss Piggy.

Fourteen-Carat Gold Flutes

In 1982 American pianist John Steele Ritter replaced Lacroix, who had retired due to ill health, as Rampal's accompanist. Despite this change and the diverse musical avenues Rampal has explored, the words "silvery," "sweet and pure," and "golden" to describe Rampal's play have remained constant throughout his lengthy concert career. Rampal only performs on his two fourteen-carat gold flutes; he is not interested in gimmicks, however, but prefers the sonority of the precious metal over that of silver. The artist who plays the delicate airs of Mozart and the rags of American Scott Joplin on the same program likes to balance Baroque music with contemporary pieces in the great concert halls of the world, including Theatre de Champs-Elysees, Carnegie Hall, and the Hollywood Bowl. In later years he has taken up conducting, frequently directing orchestras in accompaniment to his solo performances.

Rampal married Francoise Bacqueyrisse, the daughter of harpist Odette Le Dentu, on June 7, 1947. Rampal's home on the appropriately named Avenue Mozart is the gathering place for his family, including his daughter Isabelle, her husband Guillaume, his son Jean-Jacques and his wife Virginie, and three grandchildren, Caroline, Nicholas, and Elodie. An international superstar who discovered long-buried Baroque masterpieces, Rampal also promotes original works by contemporary composers like Poulenc and Joliet. As *Esquire* reported, one critic christened the phenomenal Rampal, with his successful, diverse career, "the Alexander of the flute, with no new worlds to conquer."

Selected discography

Vivaldi's Diverse Concertos, Columbia.
Tartini's Four Flute Concertos, CBS.
(With Claude Bolling) *The Bolling Suite*, CBS, 1975.
The Art of Rampal, RCA.
Classic Flute, RCA.

Classic Gershwin, Columbia.
18th Century Flute Duets.
Encores, Columbia.
Fantasies for Flute.
From Prague With Love, Columbia.
Japanese Folk Melodies for Flute and Harp (with harpist Lily Laskine), Columbia.
A Night at the Opera, Columbia.
Il Pastor Fido, RCA.
Picnic Suite, Columbia.
Portrait of Jean-Pierre Rampal, Columbia.
Sakura, Columbia.
Songs of Ravel & Debussy.
Yamanakabushi, Columbia.

Sources

Books

Rampal, Jean-Pierre, with Deborah Wise, *Music, My Love: An Autobiography*, Random House, 1989.

Periodicals

Esquire, September 1981.
Newsweek, January 1, 1968.
New Yorker, March 12, 1979.
New York Times Magazine, February 22, 1976.

—*Marjorie Burgess*

Marcus Roberts

Jazz pianist

Marcus Roberts is a young jazz musician who began his career as an apprentice to trumpeter Wynton Marsalis. Though blind, the pianist has taken his place among jazz masters with his albums *The Truth Is Spoken Here* and *Deep in the Shed*. He explained his motivating force to Philip Booth in a profile in *Down Beat,* "The only thing that I can do is play the music that I'm trying to get together and to pay homage to the musicians who I consider to be personally motivating forces behind the philosophy that I'm trying to develop."

When Booth questioned Roberts about his impairment, Roberts responded with the degree of insight which typifies his approach to jazz: "I never felt as a result of me being in a situation without sight that people owed me something or that they necessarily should cater to my situation, because if you talk to any person long enough you will find that their life dealt out many unexpected sets of circumstances that *they* had to deal with."

Roberts was born in Florida in 1964, and lost his vision to cataracts four years later. His mother was a gospel singer who had gone blind as a teenager, and his father was a longshoreman. Marcus was picking out notes on the piano at church when he was five. He was eight when he first found a center for his interests in his home in Jacksonville, after colliding with a new piano his parents bought. "I sat right down," Roberts told Jay Cocks in *Time,* "I thought, 'This, apparently, is for me. I could work on this all day.'"

Self-taught to play piano his first year, Marcus performed at church the next. At age twelve he began formal training, studying classical piano with Hubert Foster in St. Augustine. A year later while flipping the dial on a radio one afternoon, he heard Duke Ellington play. "I'd never heard piano played like that," Roberts recounted to *Esquire.* "I said to myself then and there, 'That's the kind of music I want to learn to play.'"

After attending a state school for the deaf and blind in St. Augustine, Marcus began study with Leonidas Lipovetsky at Florida State University in Tallahassee. He first encountered Marsalis when the 19-year-old Wynton performed at the Montreux Jazz Festival, while Roberts was on a tour abroad with some high-school jazz musicians. Another year passed before Roberts talked to the trumpeter in Chicago, at the National Association of Jazz Educators convention. Roberts and Marsalis began their fellowship by phone, when Wynton challenged the pianist to develop his philosophy of jazz. The young jazzman, whose concert appearances were limited to Jacksonville's Great American Competition in 1982, quit Florida State his senior year when

For the Record. . .

Born in 1964 in Florida. *Education:* Attended Florida State University.

Performer and recording artist, 1987—. Performed with high school jazz musicians at the Montreux Jazz Festival; toured and recorded with trumpet player Wynton Marsalis, 1985-1989; released first album as lead instrumentalist, *The Truth Is Spoken Here,* 1989.

Awards: Winner of the Thelonious Monk Piano Competition, 1987.

Addresses: *Record company*—Novus (Bertelsman Music Group), 1133 Ave. of the Americas, New York, NY 10036.

Marsalis asked Roberts to join him to tour and record in 1985.

Already gaining a reputation as a promising find in Marsalis's band with recordings like *J Mood, Live at Blues Alley,* and others, Roberts won the first Thelonious Monk Piano Competition in 1987. After four years with Marsalis, Roberts was ready to lead his own album. Released in 1989, *The Truth Is Spoken Here* featured "Blue Monk" and "Single Petal of a Rose." Marsalis joined Roberts along with John Coltrane's drummer, Elvin Jones, and Thelonious Monk's buddy Charlie Rouse, to pay homage to jazz standards and showcase Roberts's original work in a debut which topped *Billboard*'s jazz chart and sold well for a new arrival.

Some thought Roberts's approach too intellectual and his play scant in emotional warmth, but the majority of critics praised the album, hailing Roberts, as Chris Albertson did in *Stereo Review,* "decidedly star material."

In 1990, Roberts released his second album, *Deep in the Shed.* Chris Thomas, drummer Maurice Carnes, and trumpeters Scott Barnhart and E. Dankworth joined Roberts to produce an additional critical and financial success. Though Gary Giddins in *Entertainment Weekly* and a few other critics considered Roberts's cerebral approach "aloof," most seconded Philip Booth's opinion that Roberts "has arrived, or at the minimum, has established himself as one young jazz pianist with much to offer."

Highlighted on the album are Roberts's own improvisations which deal with the blues from differing perspectives. Roberts told Booth that his sources of inspiration were Jelly Roll Morton, Oscar Peterson, Art Tatum, and McCoy Tyner. He stated further, "One thing I like to work on, which is a Duke Ellington and Monk concep-

tion, is the whole idea of thematic conception, where you try to develop melodies throughout the entire solo—actual real, true melodies while you're playing, which are developed and extended. . . . This record was not nearly as difficult for me to deal with as the first one. The first one is the first one. It's like your first girlfriend. You don't know nothin' about girls."

The remarkable musical growth that Roberts has exhibited in his short career heightens expectations for his future. He told Booth that his immediate plans include a long-form video release to accompany *Deep in the Shed;* an unaccompanied solo album highlighting the music of Morton, Monk, and Ellington; and a solo and group-led set of dates to begin soon. His most pressing concern, he related to Booth, is his continued development: "The more active you are in the many aspects that the music allows you to participate in, the better chance you have as an artist to develop something original and special. I'm just starting to really see how complex dealing with art is, and the many variables that—especially when I was a kid—I had no idea were necessary, in order to play. Now it's becoming more apparent to me. What I'm starting to do in these next few years is just continue to work on my philosophy as a person, as well as a philosophy as an artist. Hopefully, if I'm doing that, I'll be able to come up with something with concrete substance for the people who check it out."

Selected discography

The Truth Is Spoken Here (includes "Blue Monk" and "Single Petal of a Rose"), RCA/Novus, 1989.
Deep in the Shed, RCA/Novus, 1990.
Alone With Three Giants, Novus, 1991.

With Wynton Marsalis

J Mood, Columbia, 1987.
Marsalis Standard Time, Vol. 1, Columbia, 1987.
Live at Blues Alley, Columbia, 1988.
The Majesty of the Blues, Columbia.
Crescent City Christmas Card, Columbia.

Sources

American Visions, October 1989.
Audio, May 1987.
Down Beat, January 1988; October 1988; June 1989; April 1990.
Ebony, May 1989.
Entertainment Weekly, July 6, 1990.
Esquire, September 1989.

High Fidelity, March 1987.
National Review, October 13, 1989.
People, April 10, 1989.
Stereo Review, December 1988; July 1989.
Time, July 17, 1989.
Variety, December 2, 1987.

—Marjorie Burgess

David Ruffin

Vocalist

David Ruffin made his sterling musical reputation as the lead singer for the Temptations on such smash 1960s hits as "My Girl," "Beauty Is Only Skin Deep," "Ain't Too Proud To Beg," and "I Wish It Would Rain." The Temptations scored large hits in 1967 and 1968 with Ruffin leading the way, propelling him toward a solo career with Motown records that began in 1969 and lasted throughout most of the 1970s. During the 1980s, Ruffin teamed up with former Temptations Eddie Kendricks and Dennis Edwards. Ruffin and Kendricks performed with Hall & Oates at the renovated Apollo Theatre in Harlem, then at the Live Aid concert for African famine victims and on the anti-apartheid record Sun City. Ruffin, Kendricks, and Edwards had just returned from a month-long tour of England when Ruffin died from a drug overdose on June 1, 1991.

David Ruffin was born in Meridian, Mississippi, on January 18, 1941, and was the younger brother of singer Jimmy Ruffin, who is perhaps best remembered for his hit, "What Becomes Of The Brokenhearted." The Ruffin family moved to Detroit in the 1940s, and during the late 1950s David Ruffin gained acclaim in Detroit as a solo performer. The Ruffin brothers lived near Temptation member Otis Williams and would engage in singing competitions at Williams's house. Ruffin began his professional career under the tutelage of producers Harvey Fuqua and Berry Gordy at Anna Records, a Detroit company. Ruffin's first solo release was "I'm In Love/One Of These Days," For the Anna label. He followed this up with two singles on another Detroit-based label, Check-Mate, that were written by noted rhythm and blues composer Billy Davis.

Joined Temptations

Although Ruffin possessed the ability to remain a solo artist, he ventured into other areas of the music industry. He found an opportunity with Motown's premier male vocal group, the Temptations. Although the group had released six singles by the mid-1960s, none had earned substantial success. Rumors began that Motown executive Berry Gordy was looking for a new lead singer for the group, and Ruffin capitalized on his past association with the Gordys while earning the position. Otis Williams, an original member of the Temptations, described Ruffin's audition in which the performer jumped onstage at one of the Temptations shows to the delight of the audience. Ruffin used a trick he would often perform: he threw the microphone into the air, caught it, and fell down into full splits.

The group realized immediate success with the first single Ruffin appeared on, "The Way You Do The Things You Do." The song became a national hit and climbed to number eleven on the charts. Eddie Kendricks sang lead on that Smokey Robinson song, and for the next five years Ruffin and Kendricks would alternate lead vocals for the Temptations. Smokey Robinson's writing and producing as well as the vocals by Kendricks and Ruffin contributed to the group's string of hits. Ruffin's "My Girl," which peaked at number one, stayed on the pop charts for the first three months of 1965. The next year Norman Whitfield and Eddie Holland teamed up to pen such hits for Ruffin and the Temptations as "Ain't Too Proud To Beg," "Beauty Is Only Skin Deep," "(I Know) I'm Losing You," and "I Wish It Would Rain."

Sought Personal Fame

Despite the Temptations's stellar accomplishments, Ruffin's craved greater recognition. As the group became more popular, Ruffin distanced himself from the other members—he rode in his own mink-lined limousine. In addition, by 1968, many of Motown's groups had been renamed to include the names of the lead singers. So it was perhaps natural that Ruffin was pushing for David Ruffin and the Temptations, but it was not to be. Some critics have suggested that during this period of soaring popularity Ruffin became dependent on the drugs that ultimately led to his death.

Ruffin left the Temptations in 1968 to pursue a solo career. His first solo release, "My Whole World Ended (The Moment You Left Me)," was a top ten pop hit. However, the follow-up bombed, and he would not have another top ten solo hit until late 1975 with "Walk Away From Love." Two follow-up singles, "Heavy Love" and "Everything Is Coming Up Love" reached the top ten on the rhythm and blues charts in 1976, but failed to achieve any crossover support on the pop charts.

After releasing two solo albums in 1969, Ruffin teamed with his brother Jimmy for the Ben E. King hit "Stand By Me," one of two singles Motown released from the album *I Am My Brother's Keeper* in 1970. It was the only album the two would record together. Motown released one album per year for Ruffin during the 1970s until the singer left the label for Warner Brothers. Ruffin produced two albums during his tenure at Warner Brothers. In 1982 Ruffin rejoined the Temptations for their reunion tour and album. Following the tour, Ruffin stopped performing for three years, living in southeastern Michigan on his horse farm. He also served four and one-half months in a low-security prison for failure to pay taxes.

Reunited With Former Group Members

Another turning point in Ruffin's career came at the end of 1984, when he attended a New Year's Eve show featuring Eddie Kendricks and Mary Wilson of the Supremes. Kendricks invited Ruffin up to the stage to perform, instigating a successful reunion of the two former lead singers of the Temptations. In May of 1985, Daryl Hall and John Oates invited Ruffin and Kendricks to join them at a benefit concert for the United Negro College Fund in Harlem's newly renovated Apollo Theatre benefit—a reunion that spawned a single and album. Later that year, Ruffin and Kendricks appeared in Philadelphia as part of the Live Aid concert and also performed on the anti-apartheid album *Sun City*. Ruffin and Kendricks continued to work on material for Hall & Oates' Empire label, and in 1988 RCA released an album entitled *Ruffin and Kendrick*—Kendrick had dropped the s from his name. The album featured new material that showed off the singers' smooth, soulful style.

Overdosed on Cocaine

By 1989, Ruffin, Kendrick, and former Temptations lead singer Dennis Edwards were performing together regularly. They had just returned from a month-long tour of England in May of 1991 when Ruffin suddenly died in Philadelphia from an apparent reaction to cocaine. Although Ruffin's drug use allegedly dated back to the 1960s, he was never arrested on drug charges until he was picked up in a 1987 Detroit drug raid. In 1988, he was found guilty of using cocaine and sentenced to two years probation on the condition he undergo drug rehabilitation and perform community service by singing and giving concerts. By the end of 1989, he was back in court for violating his probation, and at that time he admitted he was still using cocaine.

Ruffin's funeral was held at the Swanson Funeral Home

with services at Detroit's New Bethel Baptist Church. Pop star Michael Jackson paid for the funeral, and numerous celebrities attended, including Aretha Franklin, Stevie Wonder, Martha Reeves, Mary Wilson, and members of the Temptations, the Four Tops, and the Miracles. At the service Stevie Wonder told the audience: "We're confronted with a problem that touches every one of us. We're confronted with the most devastating slave owner of all times." The Reverand Louis Farrakhan, head of the Nation of Islam, told the mournful audience, "In David there is a lesson. We should not clap our hands and mourn, for he is out of trouble now. You are still in it."

Selected discography

Singles

"I'm In Love," Anna, 1961.
"Action Speaks Louder Than Words," Check-Mate, 1961.
"Knock You Out," Check-Mate, 1962.
"My Whole World Ended (The Moment You Left)," Motown, 1969.
"I've Lost Everything I've Ever Loved," Motown, 1969.
"I'm So Glad I Fell For You," Motown, 1969.
(By David and Jimmy Ruffin) "Stand By Me, Soul," 1970.
(By David and Jimmy Ruffin) "When My Love Hand Comes Down," Soul, 1971.
"Don't Stop Loving Me," Motown, 1971.
"You Can Come Right Back To Me," Motown, 1971.
"A Little More Trust," Motown, 1972.
"Blood Donors Needed (Give All You Can)," Motown, 1973.
"Common Man," Motown, 1973.
"Me And Rock 'n' Roll (Are Here To Stay)," Motown, 1974.
"Superstar (Remember How You Got Where You Are)," Motown, 1975.
"Walk Away From Love," Motown, 1975.
"Heavy Love," Motown, 1976.
"Everything's Coming Up Love," Motown, 1976.
"On And Off," Motown, 1976.
"Just Let Me Hold You For A Night," Motown, 1977.
"You're My Peace Of Mind," Motown, 1978.
"Break My Heart," Warner, 1979.

"I Get Excited," Warner, 1979.
"Slow Dance," Warner, 1980.
"Still In Love With You," Warner, 1980.
(By Daryl Hall and John Oates featuring David Ruffin and Eddie Kendrick) "A Nite At The Apollo Live! The Way You Do The Things You Do/My Girl," RCA, 1985.
(By Ruffin and Kendrick) "I Couldn't Believe It," RCA, 1987.
(By Ruffin and Kendrick) "One More For The Lonely Hearts Club," RCA, 1988.

Albums

My Whole World Ended, Motown, 1969.
Feelin' Good, Motown, 1969.
(As The Ruffin Brothers) *I Am My Brother's Keeper, Soul,* 1970, David Ruffin, Motown, 1973.
Me And Rock 'n' Roll Are Here To Stay, Motown, 1974.
Who I Am, Motown, 1975.
Everything's Coming Up Love, Motown, 1976.
In My Stride, Motown, 1977.
At His Best, Motown, 1978.
So Soon We Change, Warner, 1979.
Gentleman Ruffin, Warner, 1980.
(By Hall & Oates) *Live At The Apollo With David Ruffin and Eddie Kendrick,* RCA, 1985.
(By Ruffin and Kendrick) *Ruffin and Kendrick,* RCA, 1988.
At His Best, Motown, 1991.

Sources

Books

Bianco, David, *Heat Wave: The Motown Fact Book,* Pierian, 1988.
Williams, Otis, and Patricia Romanowski, *Temptations,* Putnam, 1988.

Periodicals

Detroit Free Press, June 2, 1991; June 3, 1991; June 11, 1991.
Detroit News, October 2, 1989; June 2, 1991; June 3, 1991; June 11, 1991.

—*David Bianco*

Mark Russell

Pianist, composer, political satirist

Mark Russell is one of the nation's foremost political comedians, a piano-pounding satirist who skewers the Washington scene with word and song. As Jeff Babineau put it in the *Akron Beacon Journal,* Russell has been a fixture in the capitol since 1961, "has monitored the pulse of the nation's political exploits . . . and has remained funny in doing so." Today Russell's brand of humor is a staple on the Public Broadcasting Service, where he performs six times a year in a half-hour musical comedy act. The affable comedian-songwriter also appears live in some 125 shows per year, a daunting schedule similar to that of the most popular professional musicians.

Russell's routine is essentially the same today as it was when he entered show business thirty-five years ago. He delivers a stand-up monologue, punctuated by short musical parodies of popular tunes. As he bashes the political pundits, Russell accompanies himself on a star-spangled grand piano in an exaggerated, joyfully sloppy style. What *does* change in Russell's act is the cast of characters—each new president, each new national scandal provides him with a wealth of material from which to draw humor. He told the Los Angeles *Daily News:* "We don't need comedians. We have politicians. There's a very thin line between satire and the original event. Sometimes there's no line at all."

Born Mark Ruslander in Buffalo, New York, Russell was a "class clown" from a very early age. His family moved to Washington, D.C. when he was a teen, and he became fascinated by the apparatus of national government in the capitol. In the early 1950s he served in the Marine Corps, principally as an entertainer in piano bars in Japan and Hawaii. He was discharged in 1956 and returned to Washington, where he continued to work the piano bar circuit.

Russell had begun to work comedy into his routine when he was in the service. As a professional performer he expanded the role of comedy in his act until he became more comedian than musician. He lists Mort Sahl and Tom Lehrer as early influences, along with black humorist Lenny Bruce. Music remained integral to his routine, however—in his early years he often made up songs on the spot about the customers in his audience.

Word of Russell spread quickly in the capitol, and soon he was attracting the very crowd he debunked so relentlessly. Politicians of every stripe took in the show. "Nobody in trouble would show up, of course, because they'd risk becoming part of the act," Russell told the *Arizona Republic.* "So I'd say, 'Here's Senator So-and-So. He's clean if he's here.'"

In 1961 Russell moved to the Shoreham Hotel. He and

For the Record. . .

Born Mark Ruslander, August 23, 1932, in Buffalo, NY; changed name, 1956; son of Marcus Joseph and Marie Elizabeth (Perry) Ruslander; married second wife, Alison Kaplan, December 17, 1978; children: (first marriage) Monica, John, Matthew. *Military service:* United States Marine Corps, 1953-56.

Comedian and political satirist, 1956—. Began performing stand-up comedy with piano accompaniment at Carroll Arms Bar, Washington, DC, 1956; comedian at Shoreham Hotel, Washington, DC, 1961-81. Star of bi-monthly television specials for PBS, 1975—; co-host of *Real People*, NBC, 1979-84; has provided political commentary during national nominating conventions for *Good Morning, America*, ABC. Syndicated columnist through the *Los Angeles Times*, 1975—.

Awards: Mark Twain Award for political comedy, 1980, 1986.

his bunting-draped piano became an institution there, performing regularly for twenty years. He might have remained a local celebrity had the Watergate scandal not broken in 1973—that shake-up in the halls of power proved president Nixon's undoing, but it made Russell's career. Reporters in town to cover the scandal relaxed at the Shoreham and caught Russell's comic rendition of the events. Word of his talents spread, and soon thereafter he moved to national television.

Since 1975, Russell has appeared in a comedy special every two months on the Public Broadcasting Service. The shows are produced by the affiliate in his hometown of Buffalo. The work for PBS spawned numerous requests for live performances, and by 1980 the comedian was logging 250,000 miles of air travel each year to every state in the nation. He also found time to co-host a network comedy show, *Real People,* and during presidential campaigns he served as a mock commentator on *Good Morning, America.*

Political comedians always tread a fine line where matters of taste and partisanship are concerned. Russell has ensured his continued popularity by lampooning both Democrats and Republicans with equal vigor. His humor is rarely nasty or vicious, and reflects a middle-class response to government foibles. Russell himself calls it "safe" comedy, a good-natured, equal-opportunity parody of current events. For this reason, Russell is most in demand during presidential campaigns. From the conventions to the inaugurations he finds masses of material in the daily posturing of candidates and their running mates.

Russell's silly songs—the signature of his act—are scripted in reaction to political personalities, scandals, and social concerns. He performs them with little regard for his voice or his piano skills—in fact, the very amateurism of his style heightens the humor. Topical in nature, few of them survive more than several performances. "Some of [my] jokes last 10 years. Some are gone in a week," Russell told the *Arizona Republic.* "If you do 90 minutes on stage, you don't do 90 minutes of what happened last week, you take little trips down Memory Lane." The comedian also delights in adding a local slant to his live shows. His motto, he says, is "know your audience."

When he is not on the road, Russell lives in the capitol with his second wife. He has three grown children by an earlier marriage. He likes to joke that he also keeps a "winter home" in Buffalo, where he is a major celebrity. Asked in the *Akron Beacon Journal* if he has any unfulfilled ambitions, the bespectacled comic replied: "I'd like to have a sandwich named after me at a Washington, D.C. restaurant."

Selected writings

Presenting Mark Russell, Everest House, 1980.

Sources

Books

Russell, Mark, *Presenting Mark Russell,* Everest House, 1980.

Periodicals

Akron Beacon Journal, June 16, 1987; December 20, 1987.
Arizona Republic, August 10, 1988; September 29, 1988.
Daily News (Los Angeles), September 16, 1988.
Phoenix Gazette, September 30, 1988; October 4, 1988.

—*Anne Janette Johnson*

Salt-N-Pepa

Rap trio

"We don't do hard-core rap music, because not everyone understands that. We're not just out to please our own crowd. Rap is for everyone," Salt-N-Pepa told David Denicolo in *Glamour*. Salt, also known as Cheryl James, and Pepa—nee Sandy Denton—are members of the first female rap group to cross over to the Billboard Pop Chart with the gold single "Push It," from their first album, *Hot, Cool & Vicious,* which went platinum in 1988. Regarded as something of a phenomenon in the record industry, Salt-N-Pepa put women in the forefront of male-dominated rap music with the critically and financially successful "Push It." The single got the serious airplay necessary to open the way for other female rappers like Finesse, who told Billboard, "In a way it's good that they came first because they had to go through a lot of interviews and speculation while people just pushed them off. It's made it easier for us."

Avoiding the old-fashioned, frivolous image of girl groups, Salt-N-Pepa call their particular brand of street poetry "pop-rap." Lyrics courtesy of their pro-

For the Record. . .

Group comprised of rapper **Cheryl James** (Salt), daughter of a bank manager and a transit worker; rapper **Sandy Denton** (Pepa), daughter of a nurse; and DJ **Dee Dee Roper** (Spinderella); James and Denton were raised in Queens, NY; both attended Queensborough Community College.

Rap performers and recording artists, 1985—. James and Denton worked as telephone customer-service representatives for Sears Roebuck until group was formed, c. 1985. Recorded first song, "The Showstopper," as a college project for lyricist and then-coworker Herby Azor; signed with Next Plateau Records; recorded "Push It," which went gold, 1988.

Addresses: *Record company*—Next Plateau Records, 1650 Broadway, Suite 1103, New York, NY 10019.

ducer—Herby "Hurby Love Bug" Azor—and borrowed "samples" from the music of Otis Redding, the Kinks, and Devo, to name a few, combine with a strong beat to create a mightily popular sound that earned rave reviews like this from *New Statesman* contributor Simon Reynolds: "Wholly inconsistent styles and ambiences, plucked from random points throughout pop history, are bolted together . . . affording the listener plenty of *jouissance,* ecstatic confusion." David E. Thigpen in *Time* nailed down Salt-N-Pepa's subject matter, reporting that they "punctuate soul-tinged R.-and-B. melodies with teasing, street-savvy raps about maturity, independence from men and sexual responsibility."

Met While Working at Sears

Salt-N-Pepa are middle-class young women from Queens, New York, who grew up in an urban environment. James's mother is a bank manager; her father is a transit worker. Denton's father died in 1983, leaving Sandy and her eight siblings in the care of her mother, a nurse. Although neither member of the group has a musical background, they are both natural performers who came together by chance.

In 1985 the duo attended Queensborough Community College, where one was in nursing, the other in liberal arts. Not long afterwards the two took jobs as telephone customer-service representatives for Sears Roebuck, where fellow employee Azor asked for help on his mid-term project. Azor, a student at New York City's Center for the Media Arts, needed to make a record to fulfill a class assignment. Encouraging James and Denton to

record a number to "answer" a big hit rap single at the time, "The Show" by Doug E. Fresh, Azor called the duo Supernature and their recording "The Showstopper." James and Denton made Azor a mid-term project that sold over 250,000 copies. When the rappers caught the attention of Next Plateau Records, Inc. they decided to quit their jobs at Sears. They launched a new career under the name Salt-N-Pepa, a phrase taken from a line in "The Showstopper."

"Push It" Broke Ground

Ironically, "Push It," the song that made their name and went gold on the same day Salt-N-Pepa's first album, *Hot, Cool & Vicious,* went platinum—March 23, 1988—was a fluke. Another chance happening for James, Denton, Azor, and by then, Spinderella (Dee Dee Roper)—the crucial DJ addition to the group—James said of "Push It" in *Essence:* "We recorded [the song] in Fresh Gordon's bathroom. We needed something quick for the B-side because we wanted to put out the single 'Tramp' the next day." The B-side became an A-side single after a California DJ concocted his own mix for "Push It" and sent the new version to Next Plateau Records.

Describing the group as "splendidly sexy," Marek Kohn in *New Statesman & Society* chimed in with other reviewers in their enjoyment of "Push It," which Kohn called "sex without smut." "'Push It''s lyrics, mostly a whispered refrain of the title, won't win any prizes, but the music, more melodic and complex than most rap, gives the record an irresistible twist," added Michael Small in *People.*

A Salt with a Deadly Pepa Soared

"Can the queens of rap make lightning strike twice?" asked Johnson about the group's million-selling second album, *A Salt with a Deadly Pepa*. Rob Hoerburger's review in *Rolling Stone* responded when the release went gold: "There's nothing as galvanizing as 'Push It' on S & P's new album, but Cheryl James, Sandy Denton, and Dee Dee Roper remain fixed on kicking rap in the pants. . . . In the best rap tradition, Salt-N-Pepa balance humor, arrogance and practicality."

"Their music is full of energy and invention—and their lyrics have real wit," stated Denicolo in *Glamour* after the group received a Grammy Award nomination in 1989 in the newly created rap category. The duo boycotted the show along with other rap groups, however, when the awards program did not televise the presentation of the award. That statement notwithstanding,

Salt-N-Pepa do not court controversy as some hardcore rappers do. Salt-N-Pepa, as Kohn further observed, "believe in doing their duty as role models."

Salt-N-Pepa's concert tours bring the performers onstage wearing black spandex body suits under oversize leather jackets. Choreographed dance routines accompany each song in a show that *People* described as "more sophisticated than the cliched finger popping and arm waving of their male counterparts." "You have to be strong on stage. You do things to hype up the crowd," Denton told Johnson; James added, "They want to see something visual."

Social and Political Commentary

With a song on the soundtrack of the controversial gang film *Colors* and a spot on rhythm and blues superstar Stevie Wonder's MTV special behind them, Salt-N-Pepa released their third album, *Blacks' Magic*—which had sold more than 500,000 copies by May of 1991—with an eye toward the business side of their careers. The future holds film prospects and new departures for the group. James, for instance, is interested in management, particularly as a producer. Both Denton and James would like to make political and social statements with their music, they told Kohn. "We're older now and more mature, and we just felt that it was time that we said something about what's going on in a positive way." In this intention, too, Salt-N-Pepa are considered pioneers who are leading the way to recognition and respect for women in the music industry mainstream. As Denicolo stated, "If Salt-N-Pepa . . . are the yardstick, then the future of rap looks bright."

Selected discography

Hot, Cool & Vicious (includes "Push It"), Next Plateau, 1986.
A Salt with a Deadly Pepa, Next Plateau, 1988.
Blacks' Magic, Next Plateau, 1990.
A Blitz of Salt-N-Pepa (greatest hits), Next Plateau, 1991.

Sources

Billboard, April 16, 1988; May 21, 1988.
Ebony, January 1989.
Essence, September 1988.
Glamour, May 1989.
Jet, February 26, 1990.
New Statesman, February 13, 1987.
New Statesman & Society, April 20, 1990.
People, April 18, 1988.
Rolling Stone, December 1, 1988.
Time, May 27, 1991.

—*Marjorie Burgess*

Diane Schuur

Jazz singer

Two-time Grammy winner Diane Schuur is considered one of contemporary jazz's leading vocalists. She has been compared to jazz greats Dinah Washington, Ella Fitzgerald, and Sarah Vaughan, and is noted for her expressive and powerful vocal deliveries. Blind from birth, the talented and effervescent singer, nicknamed "Deedles," has earned the admiration of many of jazz's greatest musicians. "Diane's got a great ear," saxophonist David Sanborn told Mary Huzinec in *People*. "She's a natural singer with an easy way of phrasing in the tradition of the great song interpreters." Fellow saxophone master Stan Getz concurred. "She can sing almost any style, from scat to country ballads that can tear your heart out," he told Huzinec. "In my opinion, Diane's got all the equipment to be one of the greats. She's the logical successor to Ella and Sarah."

Schuur grew up in suburban Seattle and was encouraged by both her parents to sing. Her early childhood music heroines were Vaughan and Washington, and Schuur's favorite song was the latter's "What a Difference a Day Makes." Teased by other children for singing like an adult, Schuur retreated to practicing in the closet to emulate her idols. Her mother heard her, as Schuur related to Paul Tough in *Savvy:* "One day my mom yanked me out of the closet and said 'Here's the microphone. I'm going to put on a record, and you're going to sing it.'" Schuur complemented her singing with a few music lessons and by the time she was ten had largely taught herself the piano and was performing in local clubs. One memorable performance of her early years was at the Tacoma (Washington) Holiday Inn. "I'll never forget it," she told Huzinec. "I forgot the words to 'Unforgettable.' I have it on tape with mother in the background saying, 'Oh, my God.'"

Schuur persisted with her singing and eventually was appearing at some of the top jazz clubs in the Pacific Northwest. A big break in her career came in 1979, when she sang a show-stopping rendition of "Amazing Grace" at the prestigious Monterey Jazz Festival. Getz, impressed with her performance, volunteered his services as mentor and helped her obtain future engagements. Schuur became a regular on the *Tonight Show,* and was a favorite at the Reagan White House. Regarding a 1986 performance by Schuur at New York City's famed Blue Note club, reviewer Stephen Holden of the *New York Times* called her "a vocalist of unusual warmth and power." Holden added that Schuur's "emotive directness and . . . unexpected shifts of intonation" recalled Phoebe Snow, while her "billowing warmth and optimism" recalled "the friendly embrace" of Kate Smith. Reviewing a Carnegie Hall 1987 concert with Mel Torme and Lonette McKee, Holden added other praises, lauding Schuur's "clear expansive delivery,"

For the Record. . .

B orn c. 1954; grew up in Auburn, WA; daughter of David (a police captain) and Joan Schuur. *Education:* Attended State School for the Blind, Vancouver, WA.

Awards: Grammy Awards for best female jazz performance, 1986, for *Timeless,* and 1987, for *Diane Schuur & the Count Basie Orchestra.*

Addresses: *Home*—Renton, WA. *Record company*—GRP Records, 555 West 57th St., New York, NY 10019.

her "sophisticated scat technique," and "phrases [that] roll out on a rich thrilling vibrato."

Schuur's debut album, *Deedles,* was released in 1984, the first of several recordings to showcase her vocal abilities. In 1986, she received her first Grammy, for the album *Timeless,* and the following year received another, for *Diane Schuur & the Count Basie Orchestra.* Schuur's recording with the Basie orchestra has been one of her most successful, topping *Billboard's* traditional jazz chart listing for an impressive 33 weeks. Schuur later branched out from her jazz approach to a more rhythm-and-blues-influenced style. Her 1988 album *Talkin' 'Bout You* demonstrated this new venture, and was more pop-orientated than her previous albums. Featuring Ray Charles's classics, including the title track, *Talkin' 'Bout You,* was well received by music critics. Alanna Nash commented in *Stereo Review:* "The sheer glory of Schuur's voice, captured here in an ultra-clean production, makes for one of the most engaging albums of the year—pop, jazz, or anywhere in between."

In person, Schuur maintains a positive, cheerful outlook on life, which carries through to her performances on stage. "Even though a song might be sad, I'll try not to drown it," she was quoted in the *New York Times.* "Like Johnny Mercer said, I always try to accentuate the positive." Regarding her Blue Note program, Holden commented on this aspect of Schuur as revealed through her performance of familiar jazz standards. "On all of them, the singer stamped her engaging, somewhat childlike musical personality. As an interpreter of lyrics, Ms. Schuur seems instinctively drawn toward whatever affirmative ideas can be gleaned from a song. In her hands, even a lament such as Irving Berlin's 'How About Me' becomes an expression of the singer's own resilience and eagerness to forgive." Holden called Schuur's singing "as sunny in spirit as it is voluminous."

Selected discography

Deedles, GRP, 1984.
Schuur Thing, GRP, 1985.
Timeless, GRP, 1986.
Diane Schuur & the Count Basie Orchestra, GRP, 1987.
(Contributor) *A GRP Christmas Collection,* GRP, 1988.
(Contributor) *GRP Super Live,* GRP, 1988.
Talkin' 'Bout You, GRP, 1988.
The Diane Schuur Collection, GRP, 1990.
Pure Schuur, GRP, 1991.

Sources

Down Beat, February 1987.
Jazz Journal International, April 1988.
Jazz Times, October 1987; November 1988; October 1989.
New York Times, November 24, 1986; June 28, 1987; September 5, 1990.
People, June 6, 1988; November 7, 1988.
Savvy, May 1989.
Stereo Review, February 1990.

—*Michael E. Mueller*

Andres Segovia

Classical guitarist

Andres Segovia, the most celebrated classical guitarist the world has ever known, is unquestionably acknowledged as the founding father of the modern classical guitar movement. Through his performances on concert stages worldwide, arranging and commissioning of new works for guitar, and teaching activities, Segovia gave the. guitar new stature. He changed the guitar from an instrument of popular entertainment into a vehicle of serious classical music, thus inscribing his name in the annals of music history.

Segovia was born February 21, 1893, in Linares, Jaen, in the region of Spain known as Andalusia. Because his father, a lawyer, found it difficult to support his large family, Segovia was sent to live with an aunt and uncle in Granada at age ten. It was the uncle who introduced Segovia to music, and the boy studied piano and violin at the Granada Musical Institute. While he was little interested in these instruments, he was attracted to the guitar upon hearing it played at a friend's home.

Because the guitar—used to accompany folk songs and dances in taverns—was not a well-respected instrument, Segovia had to learn to play on his own. Thus, he was largely self-taught, applying what he had learned of classical music theory and history in general to the guitar in particular. As a result he developed his own technique, which is characterized by a beautiful sonority, supreme expressivity, and the eliminating of extraneous sound and movement.

Made Debut at 16

In 1909 at age 16, Segovia made his public debut at the Centro Artistica in Granada. His recital was so well received that he began to perform throughout Spain, and in 1916 he made a successful tour of Latin America. From this early in his career, Segovia aspired to elevate the guitar from the noisy and disreputable realm of folkloric amusements, where it was held in contempt by serious composers of classical music. Throughout his career Segovia never lost sight of this goal, which he knew could only be realized by distinguished performances of serious pieces. Since the repertoire was extremely limited, Segovia looked to the works of the great composers for pieces suitable for transcription, and during his lifetime he produced dozens of transcriptions and editions of works.

Segovia's 1924 debut in Paris, France, was attended by many distinguished dignitaries of the music world and gave direct impetus to the composing of new guitar works by major composers of the era, such as Manuel de Falla and Manuel Ponce. Many composers did not know enough about the guitar's capabilities or limita-

He later resided in New York City for many years, before returning to southern Spain.

Segovia began recording works as early as 1925, eventually recording the majority of notable works for guitar, including pieces by Johann Sebastian Bach, Domenico Scarlatti, Enrique Granados, Isaac Albeniz, Manuel Ponce, Federico Moreno Torroba, and Heitor Villa-Lobos, among others. In his book *Segovia,* Graham Wade provides an extensive discography of Segovia's more than forty long-playing albums.

To perpetuate the playing of the guitar as he created it, Segovia aspired to provide a unifying medium for those interested in the guitar. He did so through his contributions to the international musicological journal, *Guitar Review,* in which he published many technical articles and in which his autobiography first appeared in serial form. He also tried to influence the authorities at conservatories, academies, and universities to include the guitar in their instruction programs on the same basis as the violin, piano, cello, and other instruments. By the late 1980s more than 1,600 schools of music in the United States offered guitar in their curricula.

While Segovia worked regularly at various universities, taught many master classes, and gave numerous private lessons, he never systematized his technique in guitar method. Views on such matters can be found in the numerous prefaces to editions of music or have been detailed by others, such as Vladimir Bobri's *Segovia Technique* or Charles Duncan's *The Art of Classical Guitar Playing.*

tions to compose works for it without Segovia's direct assistance. New pieces heard in concert inspired the writing of others, gradually building the body of literature for classical guitar.

Filled Concert Halls Worldwide

Throughout the 1920s and 1930s, Segovia's popularity rose with his repertoire, with country after country being captivated by his performances. While at first many thought that the guitar would not be able to be heard in a large concert hall, Segovia proved otherwise, demanding and getting complete silence from sell-out crowds of often more than a thousand. "The real music lover wants to hear the small instrument speaking straight to the heart of the people," he once said.

When civil war erupted in Spain in 1936, Segovia was forced to leave the country. He resettled in Montevideo, Uruguay, from where he made tours of South America.

Taught Numerous Contemporary Guitarists

A man of regular habits, Segovia practiced five hours daily in 1.25 hour increments, emphasizing with students the need to practice scales to maintain sound technique. Among his most notable students are John Williams, Christopher Parkening, Oscar Ghiglia, Julian Bream, and Michael Lorimer. Segovia was a purist and moderate in all aspects of his life. It is not surprising, therefore, that he disliked the use of amplification, because it distorts the true sound of the guitar, and he once denounced rock 'n roll as a "strange, terrible and dangerous disease." Segovia always scrupulously avoided any exhibitionism or sensationalism in his performing.

Segovia enjoyed an illustrious career that spanned seventy-eight years. In his nineties he continued to teach, maintain his regular practice regimen, and perform sixty concerts annually. In June of 1987 the maestro of the guitar succumbed to heart problems.

Selected discography

The EMI Recordings, 1927-1939, Vols. 1 and 2, Angel.
The Guitar and I, Vols. 1 and 2, MCA.
The Intimate Guitar, Vols. 1 and 2, RCA.
Mexicana, MCA.
My Favorite Spanish Encores, RCA.
On Stage, MCA.
Reveries, RCA.
Segovia and the Guitar, MCA.
The Segovia Collection, Vols. 1 through 4, MCA.
Three Centuries of the Guitar, MCA.
The Unique Art of Andres Segovia, MCA.

Selected writings

Segovia, Andres, *Andres Segovia: An Autobiography of the Years 1893-1920*, translation by W. F. O'Brien, Macmillan, 1976.

Sources

Bobri, Vladimir, *The Segovia Technique*, Macmillan, 1972.
Duncan, Charles, *The Art of Classical Guitar Playing*, Summy-Birchard Music, 1980.
Purcell, Ronald C., *Andres Segovia, Contributions to the World of Guitar*, Belwin Mills, 1975.
Wade, Graham, *Segovia: A Celebration of the Man and His Music*, Allison & Busby, 1983.

—*Jeanne M. Lesinski*

Sharon, Lois & Bram

Children's singing group

Children's entertainers Sharon, Lois, & Bram never dreamed they'd become the hottest act in their field when they teamed up in 1978. They simply wanted to make a record that would bring children and adults together in music. Today the trio has songbooks, videos, and records to their credit, as well as a popular cable television show and a succession of tours.

Sharon Hampson began her career as a folksinger in Toronto when she was just 17 years old. She toured Canada and the United States for four years before returning to her hometown to raise her two children. Family life certainly didn't put a stop to her involvement in music, however. She recorded two children's albums on her own, made radio and television appearances, and arranged, taught, and sang in children's music programs. She was also instrumental in founding Canada's innovative folk-artist program, Mariposa in the Schools.

Hampson was slightly acquainted with Bram Morrison from her Toronto coffeehouse days, but she came to know him better when he got involved with Mariposa in

For the Record. . .

Group comprised of **Sharon Hampson,** born in 1943, in Canada; married Joe Hampson (singer-composer); two children. **Lois Lilienstein,** born 1937, in Chicago; married; children: David. **Bram Morrison,** born 1941, in Canada; wife's name, Ruth; two children.

Began performing and recording as a group in 1978; first album, *One Elephant Deux Elephant,* became fastest-selling children's record in Canadian history; published songbook, *Elephant Jam,* in 1980; have appeared on television's *Sesame Street* and other shows, including their own program, *The Elephant Show.*

Awards: Juno Award from the Canadian Recording Industry for best children's album of the year, 1979, for *Smorgasboard,* and 1980, for *Singing and Swinging.*

Addresses: *Record company*—A&M, 1416 North La Brea Ave., Los Angeles, CA 90028.

the Schools. He had impeccable folksinging credentials, having left college to go on the road with Canada's respected folklorist/singer Alan Mills. For four years Morrison served as Mills's apprentice and guitar accompanist, building up an impressive repertoire of English, American, and French-Canadian songs on their many North American tours. Eventually he appeared as a solo artist on television and at the Mariposa folk festival. Later, he spent five years as an itinerant teacher in the Toronto school system. Through his involvement with Mariposa in the Schools and similar programs, he participated in workshops all over Ontario.

The third member of the trio, Lois Lilienstein, had studied music at the University of Michigan and worked as a classical and pop pianist in the United States before her husband's career led to a move to Toronto in 1966. Once there, Lilienstein gave up professional music to raise her son, but continued to sing as a volunteer leader of "music hour" at his nursery school. Eventually she became a professional preschool music teacher, utilizing a range of traditional and popular American songs. She was highly regarded in this field

and also as a collector of children's playground games and songs. She gave many seminars and workshops on these subjects, which led to her meeting with Hampson and Morrison.

Upon discovering that they shared many of the same feelings about children, music, and education, Hampson urged the formation of a partnership to make a record that would be fun for children and the adults in their lives. In 1978 they borrowed $22,000 from friends and relatives and formed Elephant Records with producer Bill Usher. Their first album, *One Elephant, Deux Elephants* was an instant success, becoming the fastest selling children's record in Canadian history. Since then, Sharon, Lois, & Bram have released many more records, published a songbook, appeared as guests on *Sesame Street* and other programs, appeared with symphony orchestras, and developed their own television program, *The Elephant Show.* All of this has put them in the ranks of the most successful of children's entertainers. The key to their appeal is simple, according to Morrison, who told *People:* "There are no three people with as much experience as us—on the floor, nose to nose with children. . . . we've really done our homework. We know kids and we respect them."

Selected discography

One Elephant, Deux Elephants, Elephant Records, 1978.
Smorgasboard, Elephant Records, 1979.
Singing and Swinging, Elephant Records, 1980.
Sing A to Z, A&M, 1991.
In the Schoolyard, Elephant Records.
One, Two Three, Four, Live!, Elephant Records.

Sources

Canadian Composer, November 1989.
Cinema Canada, September 1987.
Maclean's, December 1988.
People, May 1, 1989.
School Library Journal, March 1987.
Video Magazine, August 1989.

—Joan Goldsworthy

Jane Siberry

Singer, songwriter

Jane Siberry was described by Don Shewey in the *Village Voice* as "one of those rare artists who can crack brains and break hearts at the same time." Siberry came to the attention of American audiences in 1985 when her 1984 album, *No Borders Here,* was picked up and distributed by Open Air/A&M.

Her singular, slightly off-beat style makes her difficult to place; critics can only compare various aspects of her approach to that of other artists. Shewey, for instance, described her as a "garage band Laurie Anderson," and some critics have compared her quirky charm to that of Kate Bush. Her tendency to cram many words into a short space, and to use Eastern-ethnic rhythms liken her to fellow Canadian Bruce Cockburn. Like Rickie Lee Jones, Siberry employs frequent changes in time signatures; her vocal precision has been compared to Joni Mitchell's.

But Siberry is unique and inimitable. Her ethereal little-girl voice belies a perceptive, droll, black humor. She never hesitates to toss in weird little comments, verbal or musical. Her musical compositions, which are often first conceived by Siberry on paper as a drawing of shapes, has a highly visual quality. But, according to *Rolling Stone* critic Anthony DeCurtis, Siberry's most characteristic attribute, both on record and stage, is "her ability to infuse the everyday people and emotions she writes about with a stirring sense of wonder."

Her fascination with discovering the small wonders of the world is evidenced by her decision, while attending Ontario's University of Guelph, to switch her major from music to microbiology. "I used to leave the [science] class in heaven," she told DeCurtis, "because some little thing had been explained to me that I thought was a mystery. . . . I think it's a healthy thing about me—that openness to discovering something, that interest in everyday life."

The daughter of an investment dealer and a housewife, Siberry grew up in suburban Toronto, where, she says, "I was bored a lot, lived in my head." She has had piano training, french horn lessons, and taught herself to play the guitar. She was bored by the music courses at the University of Guelph and, since she essentially played by ear, learning the logistics of music seemed unnecessary to her. While still at Guelph, she hit Ontario's folk-club circuit—solo or as half of a female duo, doing original songs and tunes by the Ink Spots and Fats Waller. "I made people nervous enough of me to like me," she told DeCurtis.

Her first recording project, *Jane Siberry,* was independently released in 1981; Siberry financed the effort with tips she earned as a waitress, and sold the album off the stage. *No Borders Here* followed in 1984. It was

For the Record. . .

Born c. 1950 in Toronto, Ontario, Canada; daughter of George Siberry, an investment dealer. *Education:* University of Guelph (Ontario), B.Sc., 1980. *Politics:* "Apolitical."

Singer, songwriter, and recording artist, c. 1976—. Recorded album, *No Borders Here,* on Open Air, 1984. Also makes short feature films.

Addresses: Home—Toronto, Ontario, Canada. *Agent*—185 Frederick St., Suite 106, Toronto, Ontario M5A 4L4. *Manager*—Bob Blume, 2700 Rutherford Dr., Hollywood, CA 90068.

recorded on Duke Street Records, and earned her the hit "Mimi on the Beach." It was then that music critics began to take a serious look at this new artist. DeCurtis described the album as "a portrait gallery, filled with witty, carefully-drawn self-studies and probing explorations of character." Her attitude on writing music began to evolve and take shape with this album. As Siberry said in a *Canadian Musician* interview, "I seem to have written several songs about the same sort of fascination which is the idea of shifting boundaries. . . . of no borders here." *The Speckless Sky,* her third, more ambitious album, earned Canadian gold-record status and thoroughly established her as a major new recording and performing artist. With this album, said Siberry, she set out to open up "things that on *No Borders Here* seemed too rigid."

In 1987 Siberry won a U.S. recording contract with Warner Bros. (She remained on the Duke Street label in Canada, however.) The following year she recorded *The Walking,* a densely layered collection of impressionistic tone-poems. Making *The Walking* coincided with the breakup of her relationship with bassist and producer John Switzer. The songs evince much of the pain that Siberry was then experiencing. North American reception to this complex album was hesitant, and it failed to produce a hit. But her first European tour following its release earned her a large and enthusiastic response from European audiences.

Following the breakup with Switzer, she began a relationship with Toronto filmmaker Peter Mettler. *Bound by the Beauty,* her fifth album, was the result of a fresh perspective on the world. This more melodic and accessible album, full of joyful, ironic songs, was happily received by the public. With it, she had returned to her simpler, more folky roots. She told *Canadian Musician* that she worked out the final version of the songs for this album while on tour. "I like to go out with a half-baked idea, just wing it, and then have it find its own place."

Siberry's other passion is filmmaking. She has directed her own 12-minute movie, called *Bird in the Gravel.* And with Mettler, she is filming a 30-minute experimental work titled *Vladimir, Vladimir,* based on her 1985 song from *The Speckless Sky.* But it is Siberry's music that has earned her a growing reputation. Though she is unlikely to ever achieve superstar status, her single-minded adherence to the unique and fey qualities that make up Jane Siberry has earned her a devoted following and has established her as one of Canada's most innovative artists.

Selected discography

Jane Siberry, Street Records, Canada, 1981.
No Borders Here, Open Air Records, Canada, 1984.
The Speckless Sky, Open Air Records Canada, 1985.
The Walking, Duke Street Records, Canada, and Warner Bros., 1987.
Bound by the Beauty, Duke Street Records, Warner Bros., 1989.

Sources

Canadian Musician, March 1985, June 1990.
Maclean's, October 9, 1989.
Montreal Mirror, March 1990.
Rolling Stone, July 4, 1985; June 5, 1986; July 17, 1986.
Village Voice, June 10, 1986.

—Heather Rhodes

Soundgarden

Soundgarden is one of several new heavy metal acts to emerge from the Seattle area since 1985. After years of trial-and-error recording on independent labels, the four-member group found national success with the 1989 album, *Louder Than Love,* a major underground hit in 1990. Soundgarden's intriguing combination of psychedelic hard rock, speed-metal, and post-punk is admittedly not for sissies, but it is a step ahead of standard "party hearty" metal fare nonetheless. A favorite of college radio stations, the rebellious Soundgarden offers some of the hardest rock played on the planet today; as *Arizona Republic* columnist Salvatore Caputo put it, the music "isn't 'loud' as in a jackhammer, but 'loud' as in a 747 jetliner at full speed crashing into a skyscraper."

Lead guitarist Kim Thayil describes his band as "basically a bunch of punk rockers that kind of realized there [were] psychedelic and dynamic elements that could be dealt with if they slowed it down a bit. You tap into that sort of heartbeat, that sort of psychedelia. There is a reference point that is definitely visceral—you come

For the Record. . .

Band formed in 1984 in Seattle, Washington. Original members included **Kim Thayil** (guitar), **Chris Cornell** (vocals, drums), and **Hiro Yamamoto** (bass); drummer **Matt Cameron** joined group in 1986; Yamamoto left the group in 1989 and was replaced by **Jason Everman,** who was replaced c. 1990 by **Hunter "Ben" Shepherd**; songwriting is a collaborative effort.

Signed with Sub Pop Records, 1987, and released EP *Screaming Life.* Moved to SST label, 1988, and released album *Ultramega OK.* Moved to A&M Records, 1988, and released *Louder Than Love,* 1989.

Awards: Grammy Award nomination, 1990, for *Ultramega OK.*

Addresses: *Record company*—A&M Records, 1416 North La Brea Ave., Los Angeles CA 90028.

up with something that hits you in the heart, the head and the groin." With far-ranging influences, Soundgarden offers a crushing assault on the senses that still manages to avoid the usual metal-band bombast. *Houston Post* contributor John Voland observed that the group "manages to steer its sledgehammer intensity into some pretty interesting areas, like ambiguous sexuality, depersonalization and even . . . the environment."

Chicago Roots

Soundgarden was founded in Seattle in 1984, but its roots lie in Chicago. Two of its founders, Thayil and Hiro Yamamoto, grew up there and graduated from high school together. With a third friend, Bruce Pavitt, Thayil and Yamamoto moved to the Pacific Northwest in 1981. Pavitt started a rock 'n' roll fanzine while Thayil and Yamamoto studied philosophy at Evergreen State College. Eventually Thayil and Yamamoto found their way to Seattle, forming the band Soundgarden with drummer-vocalist Chris Cornell. Pavitt founded an independent label, Sub Pop Records, and by 1987 had recruited Soundgarden and several other local bands to make records with him.

Soundgarden's name is borrowed from a sculpture in a waterfront park north of Seattle. When the wind blows, pipes in the sculpture make a spooky, hooting noise. Thayil liked the sculpture and named his fledgling band after it. It is more or less a coincidence that Soundgarden's members began playing together at a time when the music scene in Seattle was beginning to attract attention. Although the group has often been lumped with other Seattle outfits such as Nirvana, Mudhoney, and Mother Love Bone, it bears little resemblance to those bands. Thayil told the *Chicago Tribune:* "We were a punk band with long hair, and we played with a punk attitude, but the music was slower, trippier." Cornell told the Los Angeles *Daily News:* "A lot of people hated us, which I dug a lot. Sometimes it's fun to be hated. When you're always liked, you become self-conscious."

Axl Rose a Fan

One person who did not hate Soundgarden was Axl Rose, frontman for the premiere quality-metal outfit Guns n' Roses. Rose attended his first Soundgarden concert in 1988 and was especially impressed by Cornell's keening vocals. By that time the group—with a new drummer, Matt Cameron—had pressed an EP on Sub Pop and were readying another album, *Ultramega OK,* for the SST label. Almost from the outset Soundgarden was courted by a number of major recording companies, including Capitol and Epic. "We didn't want to commit ourselves to someone else's ballgame," Thayil told the *Chicago Tribune.* "We wanted to learn about the industry ourselves, instead of being caught off-guard."

The group also wanted to make its music without being manipulated by profit-hungry producers. The hands-on style evident on *Ultramega OK* proved quite attractive to speed-metal fans, and the album earned a 1990 Grammy nomination in the metal category. Soundgarden finally moved to a major label in 1988, cutting *Louder Than Love* with A&M Records. Released late in 1990, *Louder Than Love* drew raves from critics *and* a sales-enhancing "explicit lyrics" sticker for a track entitled "Big Dumb Sex." The group promoted the album with a national tour through the summer of 1990.

In his *Rolling Stone* review of *Louder Than Love,* J. D. Considine wrote: "Soundgarden takes its cues from metal's new primitivism, eschewing virtuosity for the brutish efficiency of simple aggression. That's not to say these guys don't have chops. . . . But they do seem more inclined to beat a riff into submission than strut their stuff by playing rings around it. As a result, the songs on *Louder Than Love* are mean, lean, and fighting fit."

New and Improved Metal

The hurricane-force groove notwithstanding, Soundgarden's members reject what they call the "paint-by-numbers" sound of most metal music. Soundgarden has been known to parody its predecessors in songs like "Big Dumb Sex," but the band also tackles subjects rarely found in heavy metal such as pollution and power madness. "Like Metallica, Soundgarden ferrets out the best elements of metal while spitting out the cliches," wrote Greg Kot in the *Chicago Tribune*. "Even Soundgarden's hardest, loudest workouts have a subtle, sensual underpinning, an unlikely mix that makes 'Louder Than Love' one of the most innovative hard-rock records to come skateboarding down the pike."

Having achieved an international reputation, the members of Soundgarden are determined to keep the bite in their act. "We've come through a lot of buzz and hype," Thayil told the *Seattle Post-Intelligencer*. "You can't let it go to your head." The guitarist added: "I don't think we [have] prima donna attitudes. We've been at this five years. We'll take it in stride. Ultimately, you come home and eat dinner like anyone else."

Selected discography

Screaming Life, Sub Pop, 1987.
This Is Our Art, Sire, 1988.
Ultramega OK, SST, 1988.

Louder Than Love (includes "Big Dumb Sex"), A&M, 1989.
Badmotorfinger, A&M, 1991.
Flower (EP), SST.

Cornell and Cameron, with former *Mother Love Bone* members Jeff Ament and Stone Cossard, also released *Temple of the Dog*, 1991.

Sources

Arizona Republic, February 15, 1990.
Boston Globe, January 19, 1990.
Chicago Tribune, October 18, 1989.
Circus, October 31, 1989; May 31, 1990.
Elle, April 1991.
Daily News (Los Angeles), February 17, 1990.
Houston Post, November 28, 1989.
Philadelphia Inquirer, January 22, 1990; January 24, 1990.
Rolling Stone, March 23, 1989; October 19, 1989; January 11, 1990.
Rough Mix, August 1990.
Seattle Post-Intelligencer, October 6, 1989.
The State (Columbia, SC), August 24, 1990.
Washington Post, August 19, 1990.

—*Anne Janette Johnson*

Bruce Springsteen

Singer, songwriter, guitarist

ruce Springsteen has been something of a heroic figure since his arrival on the national music scene in the mid-1970s. In an era when music was dominated by flat, formulaic sounds, he embodied the pure, raw spirit of rock and roll in a way that Elvis or the Beatles had in earlier decades. Instead of mouthing Pop platitudes, Springsteen delivered characters and situations concerned with the struggle to maintain dignity and make sense out of life in a tarnished, troubled America. This outlook was a natural reflection of his own youth in a gritty New Jersey town where most people expected little more from life than a daily grind in a dead-end job. At a young age, Springsteen decided to avoid that fate by becoming a rock star.

At age thirteen he began playing guitar, and a year later he joined a band called Castile. They became quite popular locally, recording two of Springsteen's compositions in 1966 and playing a series of dates in 1967 at the Cafe Wha in New York City. Their success convinced the young guitarist to stay in New Jersey even when the rest of his family moved to California during his senior year in high school. He lived with various friends while finishing school and gigging in local clubs. After graduation, he moved to Asbury Park, New Jersey, where he formed Earth, a power trio inspired by Cream. He also attended Ocean County Community College for a short time but dropped out when a New York record producer offered him a contract. The contract never materialized and the producer vanished, but Springsteen decided to stay focused on music rather than return to college.

Child was Springsteen's next band, and it included two musicians who would be with him for years to come—drummer Vini Lopez and keyboardist Danny Federici. Soon renamed Steel Mill, the band gigged as far south as Virginia and developed a loyal following along the Atlantic seacoast. In 1969, Steel Mill played some club dates in San Francisco, which led to a contract offer from Fillmore Records. But the band members rejected the contract, saying that the advance offer was too small. Steel Mill returned to their home turf, where they remained popular until Springsteen disbanded them in 1971. He then formed Dr. Zoom and Sonic Boom, but that group lasted for just three gigs. Next he experimented with a band featuring several singers and a four-piece horn section. But by autumn the band had fallen apart and Springsteen was working solo.

Discovered by John Hammond

In 1972 Springsteen hired Mike Appel to manage his career. It was to be a double-edged association. On one hand, Appel's management did guide Springsteen

For the Record. . .

Born September 23, 1949, in Freehold, N.J.; son of Douglas (a bus driver) and Adele (a secretary; maiden name, Zirilli) Springsteen; married Julianne Phillips (an actress; divorced); married Patty Scialfa (a singer and guitarist), 1991; children: one son. *Education:* Attended Ocean City Community College.

Began playing guitar at age 13; performed in numerous local bands in New Jersey, including Castile, 1964-67, Earth, c. 1968, Child (renamed Steel Mill) c. 1969-71, Dr. Zoom and the Sonic Boom, 1971; performed and recorded as a soloist, 1971-72 (and for various brief periods during the late 1980s), and as featured performer with the E Street Band, 1972—.

Awards: Platinum Record from Recording Industry Association of America, 1978, for *Darkness on the Edge of Town*, and 1980, for *The River*; gold record from Recording Institute Association of America, 1975, for *Born to Run*, 1977, for *The Wild, the Innocent and the E Street Shuffle*, 1978, for *Darkness on the Edge of Town*, and 1978, for *Greetings from Asbury Park, N.J.*

Addresses: *Record company*—Columbia Records, 51 West 52nd Street, New York, NY 10019.

to the top, but disputes over their contract would eventually lead to a long, unwelcome hiatus in the musician's career. For the moment, however, their partnership seemed nothing but mutually beneficial. Appel arranged for his client to audition for John Hammond, artist and repertory manager at Columbia Records, whose notable feats included "discovering" Billie Holiday and Bob Dylan. As Hammond listened to Springsteen's word-packed songs and raspy voice, he wrote an enthusiastic evaluation concluding that he had heard "the greatest talent of the decade!"

In June 1972 Springsteen signed a ten-record contract with Columbia. Within a month, he had delivered his first album: *Greetings from Asbury Park, N.J.* Some of the music was set to the rhythm and blues stylings of his revitalized band, some to acoustic backing. The album was only a modest success by industry standards, selling mostly to springsteen's East Coast followers. Critical response was overwhelming, however; at the age of twenty-four, Bruce Springsteen was lionized as a powerful new force and frequently compared to the early Bob Dylan. Writing in *Crawdaddy*, Peter Knobler and Greg Mitchell announced that he had written "individual lines worth entire records." *Melody Maker's* Richard Williams called *Asbury Park* "staggeringly good," and declared: "Whatever happens next in mu-

sic, I have a strong suspicion that Bruce Springsteen will be a big part of it. He may even be it."

Extensive tours of the Northeast followed the release of the record, and Springsteen began developing the stage show that would become his trademark: a marathon event filled with epic tales, long narratives leading into songs, and emotionally exhausting performances. He tried to capture the unique qualities of his show on his second album, *The Wild, The Innocent and the E Street Shuffle.* Lyrics and instrumentals were interwoven with extended narratives, producing another album that was lauded by critics but only a modest commercial success. On the road again (this time with the original E Street Band), Springsteen developed and tightened his show even further.

Lionized by Critics

It was about this time that Boston critic Jon Landau wrote in the *Real Paper:* "I saw rock and roll future and its name is Bruce Springsteen. . . . On a night when I needed to feel young, he made me hear music like I was hearing it for the first time." That quote was used as the centerpiece of a massive publicity campaign launched by Columbia before the release of *Born to Run.* The album, jointly produced by Springsteen, Appel, and Jon Landau, underscored the singer's histrionics with dramatic arrangements and production techniques. During the final phases of production, Springsteen expressed dissatisfaction with the sound that had been developed and urged the release of a live album instead. But Columbia's promotional campaign had already reached a fever pitch, and *Born to Run* was released in October of 1975, just as Springsteen appeared on the covers of both *Time* and *Newsweek* in the same week.

The intensity of the hype generated a good deal of skepticism among those who were unfamiliar with Springsteen's music, and he was himself dismayed by all the media attention. He believed that it trivialized his artistry and made him appear to be an invention of the record company's publicity department—a manufactured product to be packaged, promoted, and foisted off on the public. In a *Chicago Tribune* interview, he told Lynn Van Matre: "You know what I thought right after that *Time* and *Newsweek* thing? All I could see ahead for me was 'Celebrity Bowling.' It was funny. I'm talking in an extreme way, I know, but I knew things were going to be rough—and they *were* rough." But he weathered the hostility and the skepticism, and as the first reviews were published it became apparent that critics almost without exception felt that, if anything, Springsteen had exceeded the claims of the advance publicity. His first national tour, in 1975, was a sellout wherever it went.

Contract Dispute Forced Hiatus

Springsteen was perfectly poised to release a followup album that would cement his critical acceptance and further his fame, but legal difficulties brought his career to a grinding halt. He had fired his manager, who retaliated by blocking the release of the next album. Suits and countersuits dragged on, and an injunction prohibited Springsteen from recording again until May 1977. During 1976 and early 1977 he toured at a grueling pace to maintain the momentum of his hard-earned success. The very fact that he was unavailable on records gave his live concerts (and bootleg recordings of them) an almost mythical status. He also wrote prolifically at this time, both for his upcoming albums and for other artists.

Darkness on the Edge of Town, finally released in 1978, reflected the bitterness and disillusionment Springsteen felt during that period. The songs on it were marked by a more adult, somber tone than his earlier compositions, and this starkness was matched by a stripped-down production style. He began work on *The River* in April of 1979 and during the extended period he took to complete it he appeared onstage only two times. One of those appearances was at the Musicians United for Safe Energy (MUSE) concert in New York City (released on film as *No Nukes*). Reviewing the movie, Janet Maslin wrote in the *New York Times:* "Springsteen, who steals the show . . . proves that in performance he is indeed a thing of beauty. . . . When 'No Nukes' cuts away from him to another backstage planning session, the comedown is considerable."

Prior to the release of *The River,* Springsteen embarked on another marathon tour, crossing the United States twice, and performed in Japan, Australia, and Europe as well. Every one of his four-hour shows was a sellout. When *The River,* a two-record set, was released, sales swiftly topped two million, in part because of all the anticipation that had built up regarding the album, but also because of its crowd-pleasing mix of brief, uptempo songs along with those colored in the darker tones. Asked about the dichotomy within the album by Dave DiMartino in *Creem,* Springsteen said: "When I did *The River,* I tried to accept the fact that . . . the world is a paradox and that's the way it is. And the only thing you can do with a paradox is live with it."

After the runaway sales of *The River,* the obvious move would have been to release a very similar album. Instead, Springsteen heeded an inner feeling that his studio work had lost its vitality, and he accordingly released a solo, acoustic album whose sound quality was not far removed from that of a typical demo tape. *Nebraska* was, in fact, recorded on a four-track machine in his home. The simple treatment seemed appropriate for the stark, gloomy themes of fear, loneliness, and despair that dominated the album. *Rolling Stone* reviewer Steve Pond applauded Springsteen's decision to assert his "right to make the records *he* wants to make. . . . *Nebraska* comes as a shock, a violent, acid-etched portrait of a wounded America that fuels its machinery by consuming its people's dreams."

Achieved Pop Legend Status

If *Nebraska* was somewhat inaccessible, its followup, *Born in the U.S.A.,* was all a record company executive could dream of. It also covered bitter themes of disillusionment and tragedy, yet many seemed to embrace it as a flag-waving anthem. The album was in the Top Ten for more than a year, and became the best-selling album in Columbia's history. It spawned another epic tour, with audiences on their feet singing and screaming throughout the entire show. The *Born to Run* phenomenon established Springsteen once and for all as "the Boss," a genuine rock legend. It seemed appropriate, then, for Columbia to canonize him by releasing a monumental collection of his work, the five-record set *Bruce Springsteen and the E Street Band Live, 1975-1985.*

Included in the collection were spoken sections in which Springsteen discussed his music and the influence of Woody Guthrie. Robert Palmer discussed the connection between the two musicians in the *New York Times:* "Springsteen gives the people who attend his concerts some food for thought, along with plenty of celebratory music that involves the crowd in call-and-response and sing-along routine. . . . He is a kind of latter day Woody Guthrie, singing about America—not the major cities or the enclaves of the rich, but small-town, working-class America, where young people frustrated by dead-end jobs, factory shut-downs and the sounds of shattering hopes and dreams are as much a part of the picture as the more traditional rock and roll imagery of fast cars and summertime romances."

Tunnel of Love, released in 1987, turned to a quieter, more intimate tone than Springsteen had dealt with previously. Its songs depicted the pitfalls, tensions, and misunderstandings of love. This was perhaps a reflection of his courtship and marriage to actress Julianne Phillips—a doomed union that dissolved shortly after the album was released. Springsteen told Bill Barol in a *Newsweek* interview: "For 10 or 14 years I wrote songs about the man in the car. . . . This record is about the man in the house. One of the things I wanted the record to be about is, we live in a society that wants us to buy illusion everyday. . . . You just can't live like that and people shouldn't be asked to."

In 1991 Springsteen married Patty Scialfa, a guitarist and vocalist in his backup band and the mother of his son.

Selected discography

On Columbia

Greetings from Asbury Park, N.J., 1973.
The Wild, the Innocent and the E Street Shuffle, 1973.
Born to Run, 1975.
Darkness on the Edge of Town, 1978.
The River, 1980.
Nebraska, 1982.
Born in the U.S.A., 1984.
Bruce Springsteen and the E Street Band, 1975-1985, 1985.
Tunnel of Love, 1987.

Sources

Books

Contemporary Authors, Volume 111, Gale, 1984.
Contemporary Literary Criticism, Volume 17, Gale, 1981.
Gambaccini, Peter, *Bruce Springsteen,* Quick Fox, 1979.
Marsh, Dave, *Born to Run: The Bruce Springsteen Story,* Doubleday, 1979.
Swartley, Ariel, *Stranded: Rock and Roll for a Desert Island,* edited by Greil Marcus, Knopf, 1979.
Williams, Paul, *Right to Pass and Other True Stories,* Berkeley Publishing, 1977.

Periodicals

America, February 6, 1988.
Atlantic, September 1978.
Business World, December 1, 1975.
Chicago Sun-Times, October 6, 1985.

Chicago Tribune, November 2, 1980.
Crawdaddy, March 1973; March 1974; October 1975; August 1978; October 1978.
Creem, November 1975; January 1981.
Detroit News, February 15, 1983.
Down Beat, October 19, 1978; February 8, 1979.
Esquire, December 1985; December 1988.
Grooves, June 1979.
Harper's, April 1988.
Houston Post, May 26, 1974.
Maclean's, November 18, 1978.
Melody Maker, March 31, 1973; October 12, 1974; June 10, 1978; November 10, 1979.
Musician, November 1982.
New Republic, March 23, 1987.
Newsweek, September 8, 1975; October 27, 1975; August 5, 1985; November 3, 1975; June 5, 1978; November 2, 1987.
New Times, September 5, 1975; October 17, 1975; August 7, 1978.
New Yorker, November 4, 1974.
New York Times, August 29, 1975; October 5, 1975; October 22, 1976; May 26, 1978; August 7, 1984; August 6, 1985; November 9, 1986; October 4, 1987; February 27, 1988; June 12, 1988.
People, August 10, 1981; October 19, 1987; March 14, 1988; June 27, 1988; August 22, 1988; September 26, 1988; October 10, 1988; January 11, 1990.
Playboy, December 1975.
Pulse, March 1989.
The Real Paper, May 22, 1974.
Record World, October 2, 1975.
Rolling Stone, July 13, 1978; August 24, 1978; September 6, 1979; November 15, 1979; November 27, 1980; February 5, 1981; August 10, 1981; October 14, 1982; October 28, 1982; October 10, 1985; September 10, 1987; November 5, 1987; May 5, 1988; September 8, 1988.
Stereo Review, August 1978; December 1982.
Super Rock Awards, Winter 1978.
Teen, September 1981.
Thunder Road, Spring 1979.
Time, April 1, 1974; October 27, 1975; August 7, 1978; January 29, 1990.
Village Voice, October 10, 1974; June 12, 1978; June 19, 1984; September 3, 1985.

—Joan Goldsworthy

The Supremes

Pop vocal group

More than any other Motown group or artist, the Supremes achieved Motown's goal of appealing to audiences of all races. The group's widespread popularity began in the 1960s and resulted in twelve number-one hits on *Billboard*'s pop charts. That puts them third on the all-time list, behind only the Beatles and Elvis Presley.

Although the Supremes employed various line-ups, the group achieved their greatest success with Diana Ross as lead singer and Mary Wilson and Florence Ballard as backing vocalists. Their greatest hits were all written by Motown's songwriting/production team—and fellow Rock and Roll Hall of Famers—of brothers Eddie and Brian Holland and Lamont Dozier (known as Holland-Dozier-Holland).

The Supremes began in Detroit in the late 1950s as a quartet known as the Primettes. As young teenagers in junior high and high school, they attempted to audition for Berry Gordy at Motown, but he considered them too young at the time. As the Primettes, they recorded for Lupine Records, a local Detroit label, both as a featured

group and as backing singers. These recordings are now available as reissues on various specialty labels.

The group persisted in their attempts to land a contract with Motown, however, and by the time they graduated from high school, they had become a trio, signed a contract with Motown, and released several singles. According to the liner notes from their first album, *Meet the Supremes,* the girls had just graduated from high school when the album was released. None of the songs on the album were very popular.

Scored First Hit Single

The group's first six singles were produced either by Berry Gordy or Smokey Robinson. At that time, Robinson had been generating hits for Mary Wells in addition to his duties as singer-songwriter for the Miracles. None of these early singles performed very well, and the group really didn't click until their seventh single, released late in 1963. Although the group reportedly didn't like the song, they went ahead and recorded "When the Lovelight Starts Shining Through His Eyes." It was their first Holland-Dozier-Holland recording, and the beginning of a remarkable collaboration that would yield twelve number-one hits.

The Supremes' first string of consecutive top pop hits— all written and produced by the Holland-Dozier-Holland team—began in July 1964 with "Where Did Our Love Go," which was followed by "Baby Love," "Come

See About Me," "Stop! In The Name of Love," and "Back in My Arms Again." Led by Ross's vocals, the Supremes captured the attention of American teenagers with a brand of pop/rock that had a good beat for dancing, complemented by striking melodies and lyrics that stood up to repeated listening. Within a few years, the group would also be playing the nightclub circuit and singing for more mature audiences.

By the fall of 1965, the Supremes were in great demand for television appearances, which included variety shows hosted by Ed Sullivan, Dean Martin, Sammy Davis, and Red Skelton, and several "Hullabaloo" shows. The group toured the Far East, and upon their return to the states made their first Las Vegas appearance at the Flamingo Hotel. By the end of the year, "I Hear a Symphony" was added to their list of chart-topping hits. The song featured a lush musical background provided by members of the Detroit Symphony Orchestra.

With the help of Holland-Dozier-Holland, the Supremes began another string of top hits in 1966 that would take them into the next year. "My World Is Empty Without You" and "Love Is Like an Itching in My Heart," their first two songs of the year, "only" reached the top ten. Those songs were followed by four straight number ones, "You Can't Hurry Love," "You Keep Me Hangin' On," "Love Is Here and Now You're Gone," and "The Happening."

Changed Emphasis and Personnel

In retrospect, what happened next to the Supremes may have marked the beginning of their decline in popularity. They were Motown's most popular singing group of the time, and their schedule of live appearances had become very demanding by mid-1967. In live performances, the group was now being billed as "Diana Ross and the Supremes," a change in nomenclature that was adopted by other Motown groups as well, to feature the names of lead singers like Smokey Robinson and Martha Reeves.

It was at this juncture that one of the Supremes, Florence Ballard, was removed from the group and replaced by Cindy Birdsong. Birdsong was a talented backup singer from Patti LaBelle's group, the Blue Belles. Depending on the perspective, Ballard was either a victim of Berry Gordy's greed and Diana Ross's ambition, or she brought about her own downfall through her own behavior and unrealistic expectations. Motown would explain her departure from the group by saying she was "exhausted from the girls' demanding schedule." In a lawsuit she would later charge Motown, as well as present and future Supremes, with a conspiracy to oust her from the group. Sadly, she was unable to mount her own solo career, and she died in 1976 of cardiac arrest.

Ross Featured

Most casual fans of the group were probably unaware of the personnel change. Indeed, Motown promoted the group in such a way as to downplay the individuality of the group's members, at least until the Supremes became a launching pad for Ross's rise to individual stardom. With Ross clearly featured as the group's lead singer, the Supremes achieved two more top pop hits, "Love Child" in 1968 and "Someday We'll Be Together" in 1969. The group joined the Temptations to host Motown's first television special, *T.C.B.: Taking Care of Business,* in the Christmas season of 1968. In addition to several albums, the collaboration resulted in a number-two pop hit, "I'm Gonna Make You Love Me," that featured the lead vocals of Ross and Eddie Kendricks.

"Reflections," the first song released by the Ross-Wilson-Birdsong lineup, also reached number two, and their next song, "In and Out of Love," made the top ten. Again reflecting Motown's lack of concern with the group's individual members, "Reflections" was recorded when Ballard was still a member of the group, according to Mary Wilson. Indeed, Wilson points to other substitutes being used as unidentified backup vocalists on records and in live performances when necessary.

Farewell Shows

Motown had always groomed the Supremes for the posh nightclub circuit as well as for the charts. It was appropriate, then, that the Supremes' farewell shows would be held at the Frontier Hotel in Las Vegas in January, 1970. Highlights from these performances can be found on the double-album set, *Farewell.* In addition to a medley of their mid-sixties hits, Ross led the group through a variety of show tunes and pop songs. Reflected on the *Farewell* album is Wilson's statement that Ross, who was leaving the group, "really wanted to upstage us that night."

The Ross decade was over for the Supremes. She would go on to even greater heights as a solo artist and film star, not leaving Motown until the end of the 1970s. As for the Supremes, a succession of personnel changes would finally leave the group with little or no audience, and they would be out of existence before the end of the decade.

Jean Terrell replaced Ross as the group's lead singer. She had been discovered in 1968 by Berry Gordy, who heard her singing at Miami's Fountainbleau Hotel with her brother's group, Ernie Terrell & The Heavyweights. The Terrell-Wilson-Birdsong edition of the Supremes was the most popular post-Ross combination. They recorded such hits as "Stoned Love," which charted in the top ten in 1970; "Nathan Jones" in 1971, which reached the top twenty; and "Floy Joy" in 1972. The latter two songs were also top ten rhythm & blues hits.

Final Breakup in 1977

When Terrell left the group in 1973 to get married, the Supremes didn't release any albums until her replacement Scherrie Payne joined the group in 1975. The Supremes disbanded in 1977, although Wilson toured the United Kingdom in 1978 with Karen Ragland and Karen Jackson performing as the Supremes.

The fame of the Supremes still lives on, however. In 1988 the group, featuring the lineup of Ross, Wilson, and Ballard, was inducted into the Rock and Roll Hall of Fame for their achievements. Their most popular songs are still heard on radio today—indeed, superstar Ross still performs them in her solo concerts—and they are recalled fondly as a major part of the celebrated "Motown Sound." As *Rolling Stone* stated in elevating the group to the Rock and Roll Hall of Fame: "The Supremes embodied the 'Motown sound' that kept America dancing throughout the Sixties." With their many great singles, the citation concluded, the Supremes "set a gorgeous new standard for Top Forty pop."

Selected discography

Singles; as the Supremes

"When the Lovelight Starts Shining Through His Eyes," Motown, 1963.
"Run, Run, Run," Motown, 1964.
"Where Did Our Love Go," Motown, 1964.
"Baby Love," Motown, 1964.
"Come See About Me," Motown, 1964.
"Stop! In the Name of Love," Motown, 1965.
"Back in My Arms Again," Motown, 1965.
"I Hear a Symphony," Motown, 1965.
"Children's Christmas Song," Motown, 1965.
"My World Is Empty Without You," Motown, 1965.
"Love Is Like an Itching in My Heart," Motown, 1966.
"You Can't Hurry Love," Motown, 1966.
"You Keep Me Hangin' On," Motown, 1966.
"Love Is Here and Now You're Gone," Motown, 1967.
"The Happening," Motown, 1967.

Singles; as Diana Ross and the Supremes

"Reflections," Motown, 1967.
"In and Out of Love," Motown, 1967.
"Love Child," Motown, 1968.
(With the Temptations) "I'm Gonna Make You Love Me," Motown, 1968.
"Someday We'll Be Together," Motown, 1969.

Later singles; as the Supremes

"Stoned Love," Motown, 1970.
(With the Four Tops) "River Deep, Mountain High," Motown, 1970.
"Nathan Jones," Motown, 1971.
"Floy Joy," Motown, 1971.

Albums; as the Supremes

Meet the Supremes, Motown, 1963.
Where Did Our Love Go, Motown, 1964.
A Bit of Liverpool, Motown, 1964.
Supremes Sing Country, Western and Pop, Motown, 1965.
We Remember Sam Cooke, Motown, 1965.
More Hits by the Supremes, Motown, 1965.
Merry Christmas, Motown, 1965.
Supremes at the Copa, Motown, 1965.
I Hear a Symphony, Motown, 1966.
Supremes a Go Go, Motown, 1966.
Supremes Sing Holland, Dozier, Holland, Motown, 1967.

Albums; as Diana Ross and the Supremes

Supremes Sing Rodgers and Hart, Motown, 1967.
Diana Ross and the Supremes Greatest Hits, Motown, 1967.
Reflections, Motown, 1968.
Diana Ross and the Supremes Sing and Perform "Funny Girl," Motown, 1968.
Diana Ross and the Supremes "Live" at London's Talk of Town, Motown, 1968.
Diana Ross and the Supremes Join the Temptations, Motown, 1968.
Love Child, Motown, 1968.
(With the Temptations) *TCB*, Motown, 1968.
Let the Sunshine In, Motown, 1969.
(With the Temptations) *Together*, Motown, 1969.
Cream of the Crop, Motown, 1969.

(With the Temptations) *On Broadway*, Motown, 1969.
Diana Ross and the Supremes Greatest Hits, Volume 3, Motown, 1970.
Farewell, Motown, 1970.

Later albums; as the Supremes

Right On, Motown, 1970.
(With the Four Tops) *The Magnificent Seven*, Motown, 1970.
New Ways but Love Stays, Motown, 1970.
(With the Four Tops) *The Return of the Magnificent Seven*, Motown, 1971.
Touch, Motown, 1971.
(With the Four Tops) *Dynamite*, Motown, 1971.
Floy Joy, Motown, 1972.
The Supremes, Motown, 1972.
Anthology, Motown, 1974.
The Supremes, Motown, 1975.
High Energy, Motown, 1976.
Mary, Scherrie & Susaye, Motown, 1976.
At Their Best, Motown, 1978.

Sources

Books

Betrock, Alan, *Girl Groups: The Story Of A Sound*, Delilah Books, 1982.
Bianco, David, *Heat Wave: The Motown Fact Book*, Pierian Press, 1988.
Hirshey, Gerri, *Nowhere To Run*, Times Books, 1984.
Turner, Tony, with Barbara Aria, *All That Glittered: My Life With The Supremes*, Dutton, 1990.
Wilson, Mary, *Dreamgirl: My Life As A Supreme*, St. Martin's, 1986.
Wilson, Mary, *Supreme Faith: Someday We'll Be Together*, Harper & Row, 1990.

Periodicals

Rolling Stone, November 11, 1988.

—David Bianco

Taj
Mahal

Singer, songwriter, composer

Singer and songwriter Taj Mahal is a musician for whom origins are everything. An avid musicologist, particularly of traditional "country" blues, Mahal combines an extensive knowledge of black folk music with his own distinct musical interpretations. Mahal rose to prominence in the late 1960s and 1970s as a performer and recording artist of both traditional blues standards and his own authentic-sounding blues compositions. During that time, he became well-known for his trademark buoyant and energetic stage performances, and for a string of albums which, as a *Village Voice* reviewer once wrote, "always exhibited a roving intelligence and refreshing humor." Throughout his career, Mahal has been acclaimed as a leading modern purveyor of traditional blues and, despite the trends of popular music, has continually adhered to his own distinct style—one steeped in, and respectful of, black folk tradition. "Raw, bone-deep funk and sweetness flow naturally from Mahal's fingers and mouth or lathers on teasing licks that have nothing to do with virtuosity and everything to do with taste," wrote Josef Woodard in a 1991 *Down Beat* profile. "Mahal is unmistakable, a musician without precedent or peers."

Mahal was born Henry Saint Clair Fredericks in New York City—the name Taj Mahal came to him in a dream; he chose it because of its sound. Early musical influences included his father, who was a West Indian jazz pianist and arranger, and his mother, a schoolteacher and gospel singer from South Carolina. Mahal's involvement with the blues, however, was inspired from within. While working towards an agricultural degree at the University of Massachusetts during the early 1960s, he discovered traditional blues—such as that performed by legendary artists Lightnin' Hopkins and Leadbelly—and absorbed himself in researching the roots of black folk music. It was a direction that went against the grain of much black music, which at the time was more intent on breaking with the past. "That was a choice on my part," he recalled to Dimitri Ehrlich in a 1991 *Pulse!* interview. "There was something about the blues that just full and wholly knocked me out. . . . Instead of popular music creating me, I programmed myself for what I'm interested in." What particularly attracted him to the blues, as he explained to Ehrlich, was how—as in African musical tradition—music functioned as "part of the whole of life."

Explored Black Folk Music

Originally a bass player, Mahal became familiar with the acoustic guitar, piano, harp, banjo, mandolin, harmonica, dulcimer, and a variety of fifes and whistles. In addition to the blues, he delved into other black folk music, including that of Africa and reggae. Disenchant-

For the Record. . .

Born Henry Saint Clair Fredericks, May 17, 1942, in New York, NY; son of Henry Saint Clair (a jazz musician) and Mildred (a schoolteacher; maiden name, Shields) Fredericks; married Inshirah Geter, January 23, 1976; children: Aya, Taj, Gahmelah, Ahmen, Deva, Nani. *Education:* University of Massachusetts, B.A., 1964.

Performing artist, 1964—; played with group Rising Sons, late 1960s; recording artist, 1967—. Composer of scores for films *Sounder, Sounder II,* and *Brothers;* television programs *Ewoks, The Man Who Broke a Thousand Chains,* and *Brer Rabbit;* and the play, *Mule Bone,* produced on Broadway, 1991. Actor in films *King of Ragtime, Sounder,* and *Sounder II.*

Awards: Best Ethnic Music Award, Bay Area Music Awards, 1979, for *Brothers* soundtrack.

Addresses: *Office*—c/o Folklore Productions, 1671 Appian Way, Santa Monica, CA 90401.

ed with what he felt was too constricted a folk scene on the East Coast, Mahal moved to California in 1965. He joined guitarist Ry Cooder to form a band called Rising Sons, which, despite showing great promise, broke up after a record deal folded. "Ry was one person I connected big-time with because he always heard the music," Mahal explained to Woodard. "It wasn't the swagger or the stagger or the dark glasses or the pork pie hat or the look or the way you held your saxophone." Mahal then set out on a solo career, and in 1967 released the first of what would be several successful albums for Columbia Records. Throughout the rest of the 1960s and 1970s Mahal was a leading performer of blues and other black folk music at concerts and music festivals across the country. A reviewer for the *Village Voice* wrote in 1974 that "Taj Mahal has pursued black traditional music, particularly blues, with single-mindedness, probity, and originality. . . . He has become our preeminent modern traditionalist."

Overflowed With Personality *and* Authenticity

Mahal has been acclaimed throughout his career for his dynamic stage performances. A contributor to *Newsweek* wrote in 1972: "[Mahal's] on a journey into the heart of black music from the moment he appears on stage in jeans and a colorful dashiki, 6 feet 4 inches, smiling through his bearded face, and says, 'We're gonna start out real smooth and take it to where we can't hardly stand it.'" Often holding his steel guitar or

banjo while seated on a straight-backed chair, or engaging his audience in foot-stomping and hand-clapping, Mahal infuses old blues standards, as *Newsweek* noted, "with a burlesque style that caricatures the grin-and-bear-it blues tradition, or with a vocal inflection that's West Indian." John Rockwell in the *New York Times* described Mahal on stage as "an outwardly laconic blues singer and scholar who makes simply wonderful music. . . . Many blues specialists, black or white, either sound studiously antiquarian or distort the purity of the music in a search for personality. Taj Mahal overflows with personality, . . . yet the end effect remains one of authenticity."

Composed *Sounder* Soundtrack

Mahal's albums reflect his predominant pursuit of old-style country blues, yet they also display a wide-ranging interest in preserving black music of all origins, including reggae, gospel, and the folk music of Western Africa. "To me the music is sacred," he told Ehrlich. "Blues, gospel, jazz, Latin music, whatever the style, this stuff should flourish from generation to generation." Woodard suggested that Mahal's 1969 album, *Giant Step/Ole Folks at Home,* is one of his most important, consisting of "stark, lustrous renditions of traditional songs on guitar, banjo, and voice." Mahal commented to Woodard that "some of the roots of [*Ole Folks*] went back in a lot of different directions." Of the numerous albums Mahal released in the late 1960s and 1970s, particularly notable is the soundtrack he composed for the 1972 movie *Sounder,* in which he also played the role of Ike. After a relatively dry recording spell during the 1980s, Mahal returned in 1991 with *Like Never Before,* a collection that displays him singing a variety of music, including blues, reggae, and scat, on such playful tunes as "Squat That Rabbit," "Cakewalk Into Town," and "Big Legged Mommas Are Back in Style." *Like Never Before* features both simple arrangements of typical Mahal material, in addition to cuts employing large instrument and vocal ensembles; contributing artists include Hall & Oates, the Pointer Sisters, Dr. John, and Eric Clapton. According to Ehrlich, "Mahal's voice sounds better than ever for all his experience, burnished and aglow," and the album is "one of his finest efforts in years."

Also in 1991, Mahal composed the musical score for the Broadway production of *Mule Bone,* a stage play originally written during the 1920s Harlem Renaissance by poet Langston Hughes and novelist Zora Neale Hurston, but never produced because of a dispute between the authors. Set in a small black Florida town in the early part of the 1900s, the play depicts a conflict between two men in the community and gives insight into the society of southern black rural life at the turn of the century. Mahal was chosen by the play's producers to compose the musical score—which included setting Hughes's poems to music—because of his stature as a black musicologist and, as *Mule Bone*'s dramaturge Anne Cattaneo told Ehrlich, he "was the best person who could understand and reclaim this musical tradition." Mahal commented to Ehrlich on capturing the essence of Hughes's and Hurston's love of black heritage: "I wanted to pay homage to both of these wonderful people by representing them a generation and a half later—and at the same time have it loose enough to still be me. The music had to be in touch with the old timers, and the new timers as well."

Selected discography

Taj Mahal, Columbia, 1967.
Natch'l Blues, Columbia, 1969.
Giant Step/Ole Folks at Home, Columbia, 1969.
The Real Thing, Columbia, c. 1970.
Happy Just to Be Like I Am, Columbia, 1971.
Recycling the Blues and Other Related Stuff, Columbia, 1972.
Sounder (film soundtrack), Columbia, 1972.
Oooh So Goodn' Blue, Columbia, 1973.

Mo' Roots, Columbia, 1974.
Music Keeps Me Together, Columbia, 1975.
Satisfied 'n Tickled Too, Columbia, 1976.
Music Fuh Ya' (Music Para Tu), Warner Bros., 1977.
Brothers (film soundtrack), Warner Bros., 1977.
Evolution (the Most Recent), Warner Bros., 1978.
The Best of Taj Mahal, Columbia, 1981.
Taj, Gramavision, 1986.
Brer Rabbit and the Wonderful Tar Baby, Windham Hill.
Like Never Before (includes "Squat That Rabbit," "Cakewalk Into Town," and "Big Legged Mommas Are Back in Style"), Private Music, 1991.
Mule Bone, Gramavision, 1991.

Sources

Down Beat, February 1991.
Interview, April 1991.
Newsweek, February 28, 1972.
New York Times, March 15, 1970; November 18, 1973; November 23, 1973; October 18, 1974.
Pulse!, June 1991.
Rolling Stone, January 4, 1969; June 24, 1971.
Village Voice, December 6, 1973; October 24, 1974.

—Michael E. Mueller

Take 6

Christian singing group Take 6 burst onto the music scene in 1988 with their critically acclaimed debut album *Take 6*. The a capella sextet, with voices emulating the sounds and rhythms of musical instruments, has since awed both jazz and gospel listeners with immaculate harmonies and stirring vocal arrangements. Featuring original gospel songs by group members, in addition to jazzed-up renditions of traditional hymns, Take 6 boasts an uplifting, sophisticated sound that recalls the music of spirituals, doo-wop groups, and classic jazz combos. "Like their stylish clothes, the a capella music of Take 6 is performed with style—always in time, in tune," wrote Michael Handler in *Down Beat*. "It might be another reworking of a classic gospel tune, or an original, up-tempo number, but every song sounds fresh, clean, and full of joy."

Take 6 originated in 1980 at Oakwood College, a small Seventh-Day Adventist school in Huntsville, Alabama, and began as a gospel quartet named Alliance (later called Gentleman's Estate Quartet). Expanded into a sextet, the group held early rehearsals within the re-

For the Record. . .

Group formed in 1980 in Huntsville, AL, as quartet Alliance, later called Gentlemen's Estate Quartet; current sextet includes **Claude V. McKnight III**, born c. 1963; **Mark Kibble**, born c. 1965; **Mervyn Warren**, born c. 1965; **David Thomas**, born c. 1967; **Cedric Dent**, born c. 1963; and **Alvin "Vinnie" Chea**, born c. 1968. *Education:* All attended Oakwood College, Huntsville. *Religion:* Seventh-Day Adventist.

Recording and performing act, 1988—. Released album *Take 6* on Reprise, 1988.

Awards: Grammy Awards for best jazz vocal, duo or group, for single "Spread Love," and best soul gospel, Duo, or Group, for album *Take 6*, both 1989; and best contemporary soul gospel album, 1991, for *So Much 2 Say*; Grammy Award nomination for best new artist, 1989; four Gospel Music Dove Awards, 1989; named vocal group of the year by *Down Beat* magazine, 1989.

Addresses: *Home*—Group members live in the Nashville, TN, area. *Record company*—Reprise Records, 1815 Division St., Nashville, TN 37203-2736; 3300 Warner Blvd., Burbank, CA 91505-4696; 75 Rockefeller Plaza, New York, NY 10019-9608.

sounding walls of their college dormitory bathrooms, where they worked to develop their unique six-part gospel harmonies and arrangements. Each member was an accomplished music instrumentalist before becoming a vocalist, and most had jazz backgrounds. "It just seemed natural to have extended jazz chords throughout the music," recalled original member Claude V. McKnight III to Leonard Pitts, Jr., in *Musician*. "To make a capella music really fresh and exciting, you really have to get into a lot of the intricate rhythms and things that characterize jazz."

In 1987 Take 6 held an exclusive performance for gospel recording company executives, yet many refrained from attending, considering the group's sound too controversial. Fortunately, an uninvited representative of Warner Bros. showed up who was impressed with a tape he'd received of the group. "When I first played their tape," Jim Ed Norman told *Ebony*, "I heard the most enchanting, wonderful sound in music coming from the human voice that I had heard in the longest time." Warner Bros. signed Take 6 to a recording contract, and their self-titled debut album was released the following year on the company's Reprise label. Although the group had originally hoped to sign with a gospel label, they later realized the evangelistic

opportunity to reach wider audiences with their jazzed-up gospel music. "We are purposely styling our music the way we do so that we can take our message of the gospel to people who don't always listen to Christian music," explained group member Mervyn Warren to *Ebony*. "We have a message that is appropriate for everybody."

Take 6 received wide critical acclaim upon its release, and went on to earn 1988 Grammy Awards in both jazz and gospel categories, The sextet also became the first-ever gospel group nominated for a "Best New Artist" Grammy Award. Take 6's broad appeal was further evident in the variety of other honors accumulated after their debut album: four Gospel Music Dove Awards, an award from the television program *Soul Train*, and a first-place finish in jazz magazine *Down Beat*'s 1989 readers' poll for Vocal Group of the Year. At their first-ever performance at the Monterey Jazz Festival in 1989, Take 6 electrified the audience and was called back for a rare curtain call. Music industry giants were quick to enlist the group's talents. Take 6 was invited to perform with Stevie Wonder, an ardent fan, at New York's Radio City Music, and recorded with artists such as Quincy Jones, Johnny Mathis, Stephanie Mills, and Smokey Robinson, in addition to maintaining a solid string of concert appearances in the United States and abroad.

In 1990, Take 6's second album, *So Much 2 Say*, was released to further acclaim. Take 6 "combines the heartfelt devotion of the church with . . . audacious wit," wrote reviewer Will Friedwald in the *New York Times*. "In leavening their voices with passion, intelligence and musicianship, Take 6 has breathed new life into a musical genre dormant for generations." Robin Tolleson proclaimed in *Down Beat:* "There's nobody 2 really compare Take Six 2. They outsoul Manhattan Transfer in a minute and are far more adventurous than the Nylons. . . . There's never been any question about these guys' abilities since they strutted on the scene, but here the soul is catching up and starting to go right along with the talent." Reviewing the group's 1990 Carnegie Hall performance, *New York Times* music critic Stephen Holden wrote: "The Christian music group from Alabama has developed a vocal blend of such extraordinary precision and harmonic richness [that] . . . one is left awestruck at the level of technical perfection."

Although the music of Take 6 has a strong jazz following, their "message," Handler notes, "never strays from their common goal of spreading the good news through song." Devout Seventh-Day Adventists, the group is serious about their role as non-traditional Christian evangelists. "We present the message in an attractive package, and hopefully the folks will leave the show humming a tune," McKnight told Handler. "We let the Holy Spirit take it from there." In accordance with their strict religious beliefs, the group abstains from performing on Saturdays, in observance of the traditional Sabbath, unless specific contractual obligations require them to do so. Take 6 has been criticized by some of the more conservative elements of their Seventh-Day Adventist religion, yet are resolved in their mission. "We've accomplished what we set out to do, and that's to reach people in all walks of life," McKnight told Yanick Rice Lamb in the New York Times. "It has never made sense to just sing in church or to people who supposedly already have the message. You take it out into the world and into the streets to the people who really need it." Group member Alvin Chea told Lamb that their music is a natural extension of their talents: "We're just trying to share what makes us happy."

Selected discography

Take 6 (includes "Spread Love" and "Mary Don't You Weep"), Reprise, 1988.
So Much 2 Say (includes "So Much 2 Say" and "I L-O-V-E- U"), Reprise, 1990.

Contributors to Quincy Jones's album Back on the Block; background vocalists on Stephanie Mills's single "Home"; song arrangers for the Winans' album Heaven; co-wrote "U-Turn" for Joe Sample's album Spellbound; sang "Don't Shoot Me" for film Do the Right Thing; performed theme song for television movie The Women of Brewster Place.

Sources

Christianity Today, July 14, 1989.
Down Beat, February 1990; March 1990; November 1990; December 1990.
Ebony, March 1989.
Esquire, March 1989.
Essence, October 1990.
Musician, October 1988.
New York Times, August 26, 1988; January 23, 1989; May 24, 1990; May 27, 1990; October 14, 1990.
Stereo Review, January 1989.
Time, March 20, 1989.

—Michael E. Mueller

Toru Takemitsu

Composer

Western art music from the mid-twentieth century onward has often greatly benefitted from Eastern influences. Various composers have featured traditional Asian instruments, used Eastern compositional and improvisational techniques, and attempted to transfer aesthetics of the East to Western music. While often the result is an interesting juxtaposition of Eastern and Western features, one may well wonder whether the complete integration of Eastern and Western musical traditions is indeed possible or even desirable. British author Rudyard Kipling once wrote that "East is East and West is West, and never the twain shall meet." Nonetheless, it would seem that the music of Japan's leading composer, Toru Takemitsu, achieves precisely this, a thorough integration of materials from both the East and West that results in a new and different world of sound, a music whose coherency is derived equally from both traditions.

Takemitsu was born in Tokyo, Japan, in 1930. He first decided to pursue a career in music when he was in his teens at the end of World War II. Recalling this time in an interview for the *Los Angeles Herald Examiner,* Takemitsu said that he was "very negative about everything Japa-

nese. During the war it was forbidden to listen to anything but Japanese music, and we were thirsty to hear music of the West and wanted to learn just that music. Only afterwards could I find my own way to Japanese tradition."

At age 18 Takemitsu studied composition privately with Yosuji Kiyose, but otherwise is self-taught and holds no degrees in music. He told Edward Downes, program annotator for the New York Philharmonic Orchestra, that his teacher was "his daily life, including all of music and nature." It is probably this lack of formal musical education and prolonged study with no particular composer that in part accounts for Takemitsu's highly original style—and this in spite of his experimenting with every new musical method and current among other contemporary composers since World War II.

"A Gardener, Not a Composer"

Takemitsu's compositions demonstrate the entire gamut of compositional features current in the West: In addition to conventional features, he uses improvisation, non-musical notation, electro-acoustic means of composition on tape, unusual instrumentation, and instrumental passages of such difficulty that they challenge the ability of even the most seasoned performers. Yet, all of Takemitsu's compositions have some added quality—which the composer says is their bicultural nature—which distinguishes them from the rest of Western music that uses these same techniques. He told Downes, "Maybe it can be said that I am rather a gardener, not a composer. I don't like to construct sounds as great architecture the way Beethoven did. My music is different. I set up a place where sounds meet each other. I don't construct but create some order which makes my music quite close to the idea of a Japanese garden. In the garden there are different cycles, short and long; there is mobility and immobility. The growing of trees and the growing of grass is different you know."

Integrated Eastern and Western Styles

Takemitsu has not always been able to use the word "bicultural" to describe his music. In the 1950s his music was entirely in the style of the Western avant-garde; only in the 1960s did he become seriously interested in traditional Japanese instruments, such as the lute-like biwa, and begin to combine them with Western instruments. By the 1970s his integration of Eastern and Western elements was nearly complete. While the ensembles and compositional technique are for the most part Western, the spirit of Takemitsu's music is Eastern and almost always evokes natural phenomena. His greatest artistry lies in creating timbres and textures, and the titles of his compositions most frequently allude to sound or sound color as it occurs in nature, for example, *Garden Rain, Waves, In an Autumn Garden.*

As Bernard Rands pointed out in the *Musical Times,* such titles are quite different from "abstract or technological ideas contained in the thousands of titles that dominate contemporary music publishers' catalogues: *Fragments, Formants, Phonics, Prisms, Variants, Collage, Projections* etc. The complexity of experience implied in Takemitsu's titles is universal human experience whereas the complexity of technical abstract ideas implied in the others is Western, local, culturally conditioned in its cerebral, esoteric concern with process."

Audience Defines Technique

Rather than having an all-consuming interest in the process of composing or in abstract musical problems, Takemitsu is intrigued by the contemplation of natural phenomena. Thus he has not written extensively about his own compositional procedure as the overwhelming majority of contemporary composers have, and what writing and lecturing he has done do not include any particular terminology to explain his compositional techniques. Instead, Takemitsu tends to focus on the listener's potential response.

Aside from his talent in the realm of sound and sound colors, Takemitsu's music is also unique in its pacing. The listener may get the impression that the music evolves on its own, a characteristic that is directly related to Takemitsu's evocation of natural phenomena. The structure and climax of his works are often strictly non-Western and thus the aspect of his music the most often misunderstood by Western listeners. Ellen Pfeifer, writing for the *Boston Herald,* said that there is an "unfortunate sameness about [Takemitsu's] writing—unvarying dynamic level (quiet) and pace (slowish)." The Japanese critic Hidekazu Yoshida, writing for a Japanese recording of Takemitsu's works, observed that "in Japanese music, however, it is not unusual for one to bring out the climax, which is supposed to be the cardinal element in the work concerned, very abruptly and without any preparation, or suddenly to cut it. . . . This traditional sense of beauty of the Japanese has been revived in a very vivid way in Takemitsu's work. I do not think it was done unconsciously. This is the reason why a piece which at first may sound monotonous and lacking in compactness of structure leaves one with a generally fresh memory after one has listened to it."

Takemitsu gained his greatest international acclaim as a result of the immediate success of his 1967 work, *November Steps,* commissioned and performed by the New York Philharmonic as part of its 125th anniversary celebration. He continues to be an active and successful composer with a large catalog of published works for all media, including cinema, radio, and television. He is also a frequent lecturer and composer-in-residence at music schools and festivals throughout the world.

Selected compositions

Orchestral

Ikiru yorokobi [The joy to live] (ballet), 1951.
Shitsunai kyosokyoku [Chamber concerto], 1955.
Requiem (for strings), 1957.
Solitude sonore, 1958.
Ki no kyoku [Tree music], 1961.
Arc (piano and orchestra), 1963-66.
Chiheisen no doria [Dorian horizon], 1966.
November Steps, 1967.
Green (November Steps II), 1967.
Asterism (piano and orchestra), 1968.
Crossing, 1969.
Cassiopea (percussion and orchestra), 1971.
Gemeaux, 1972.
Aki [Autumn], 1973.
Gitimalya, 1975.
Quatraine, 1975.
Marginalia, 1976.

Vocal

Kuroi kaiga [Black painting], 1958.

Kansho [Coral island], 1962.
Kaze no uma [Horse in the wind], 1962.

Textures, Odyssey.
Toward the Sea, for Alto Flute and Guitar, Bridge.

Selected discography

Arc, for Piano and Orchestra (contains "Solitude," "Your Love and the Crossing," "Textures," "Reflection," and "Coda"), Varese/Sarabande.

Asterism for Piano and Orchestra; Requiem for String Orchestra; Green for Orchestra (November Steps II); Dorian Horizon for Seventeen Strings, Victor.

In an Autumn Garden, Varese/Sarabande.

Coral Island for Soprano and Orchestra; Water Music for Magnetic Tape; Vocalism A I for Tape, RCA.

Corona; Far Away; Piano Distance; Undisturbed Rest, London.

Dorian Horizon, Columbia.

Miniature: Stanza No. 1—Sacrific-Ring-Valeria, DG.

Munari by Munari, for Percussion, RCA.

November Steps, RCA.

Piano Distance; Uninterrupted Rests.

Piano Music, RCA.

Quatrain; A Flock Descends into the Pentagonal Garden, DG.

Quatrain II; Water Ways; Waves, RCA.

Seasons for Glass Trombone, Metal Instruments and Tape, Oiseau.

Selected writings

Oto, chinmoku to hakariaeru hodo ni (Translated as "As much as can be measured with sounds and silence"), Tokyo, 1971.

Sources

Boston Herald, November 23, 1984.
Classical Guitar, May 1988.
Guitar Player, October 1987.
Los Angeles Herald Examiner, January 11, 1985, January 12, 1985.
MLA Notes, vol. 43, no. 1, 1986; vol. 44, no. 2, 1987.
Musical Opinion, August 1988.
Musical Times, September 1987.
Neue Zeitschrift fur Musik, July/August 1988.
Nutida Musik, vol. 3/2, 1988/1989.
Orchester, April 1987, September 1987.
Record geijutsu, September 1973.

—*Margaret Escobar and Jeanne M. Lesinski*

John Michael Talbot

Composer, performer

"**M**y music changed radically when I became Catholic. . .," John Michael Talbot, a Third Order Franciscan friar who has sold more than two million records, told L. Katherine Cook in the *Christian Century*. "That experience . . . put me in touch with a broader spectrum of artistic experience." When the singer, who in his teens had played guitar and banjo with the country-rock band Mason Proffit, donned St. Francis's traditional brown robe, he wanted to make one more record. Assuming the album would be his last, Talbot released *The Lord's Supper* in 1979. The irony is that this recording was only the beginning for the rich tenor's contemplative, inspirational music. "I had a definite call on my life," the monk Talbot related to Carol Azizian in a *People* profile. "They say you are born a Franciscan and later you find out where you belong."

Talbot's spiritual journey began in the sixties when Mason Proffit was an opening act for singer Janis Joplin. "I saw her drinking Southern Comfort like soda pop," he disclosed to Azizian. The drug and party scene dismayed Talbot, whose searing social consciousness eventually would lead him, after his conversion, to found a hermitage in the Arkansas Ozarks. In the twenty-year pilgrimage since he played a fundraiser concert for Jerry Rubin, one of the notorious "Chicago Seven," Talbot divulged to Evelyn Bence in *Publisher's Weekly* that he felt "God wanted him to use the gift of music as a tool of reconciliation." Reviewing Talbot's albums in *Christianity Today,* Michael G. Smith wrote, "I no longer give away books. Instead, I pass on the records of John Michael Talbot. His music conveys the vision of the kingdom of God better than some of the best prose of the theologians."

Born in Oklahoma City, Oklahoma, on May 8, 1954, to musically talented parents, Talbot grew up in Indianapolis, Indiana. His father, Dick Talbot, had performed the violin in the Oklahoma City Orchestra. His mother, Jimmie Margaret, played the piano and raised her three children on stories about her father, the Reverend James Cochran, an itinerant singing Methodist minister. John, along with his older brother Terry, and sister Tanni, played several instruments, including banjo, guitar, cello, and tambourine. "There was, shall we say," related Talbot in his biography *Troubadour for the Lord,* "a not quite active, but not really passive drive toward music—it was just part of our family life—it was simply there."

A musical prodigy, Talbot began playing in regional bands with Terry when he was ten years old. Two years later, he was a seasoned vocalist and rhythm guitarist. In 1968 Terry and John, veterans of a series of well-received regional bands, decided their latest group was ready for national exposure. Changing the band's name to Mason Proffit, they dressed like American woodsmen in buckskin and leather and let their hair grow. Their "message" music, laden with social commentary, fit the nature of the Vietnam era. Audience response to their albums, including *Two Hangmen* and *Last Night I Had the Strangest Dream,* induced Warner Bros. to sign them to a contract. The members of a very good band, Terry and John Talbot, Tim Ayres, Art Nash, and Ron Scheutter, were on their way to becoming a great band when drugs and artistic differences split the group.

When the band broke up, Talbot, who had married at age seventeen in 1971, had a wife and daughter to support. Tutored through his high school years while on concert tours with the band, he had never received a high school diploma. Life was rough when his savings ran out, but Talbot's embrace of extreme fundamental religion was more a factor in the breakup of his marriage in 1977. When the former Methodist sought spiritual guidance at Alverna, a Catholic retreat center in Indiana, he discovered peace in the 800-year-old teachings of St. Francis of Assisi.

Although Talbot had ventured into Christian music with his brother Terry prior to his conversion to Catholicism as a Third Order Franciscan lay brother, he assumed his vow of chastity and poverty would end his musical career. Over the years, his release *The Last Supper* has sold 300,000 albums and garnered critical praise from theological circles. "His rendition of the Apostle's Creed is one of the strongest affirmations of faith set to music— some would say it rivals even the conviction and power of the "Credo" in Beethoven's *Missa Solemnis,"* Smith's review stated. In 1980 his brother Terry joined him with the London Chamber Orchestra to make *The Painter.*

Troubadour of the Great King (1982), *Light Eternal* (1982), *Empty Canvas,* and *Few Be the Lovers* (1987), among other recordings, captured Talbot's Franciscan contemplative tone and medieval leaning. The *Christian Century,* noting that his music does not fit the rock-oriented, contemporary Christian music scene, stated: "In every case, though, the music constitutes worship."

Earnings, including over $2 million from his previous albums, go into the various charities and the maintenance of The Little Portion, a Franciscan hermitage Talbot founded at Eureka Springs, Arkansas, in 1982. Built near the site of the 1973 Ozark Mountain Folk Fair, where Mason Proffit had performed a hit act for over 10,000 people, the religious community of more than a dozen men and women consecrate their efforts toward renewal and reform through a prayerful life. Talbot performs concert tours one week out of the month and spends the rest of his time at the retreat working for "the gentle revolution," an awakening transformation of spiritual identity. Talbot told Cook that "his role as a musician" was "to bring people into an authentic relationship with Christ." "I don't do the challenging myself," he confessed in the *Christian Century.* "I just present Jesus to them as real, and Jesus challenges the socks off them. The music just prepares the way for that to happen."

Selected discography

Reborn, Sparrow, 1972.
John Michael Talbot, Sparrow, 1976.
Firewind, Sparrow, 1976.
The New Earth, Sparrow, 1976.
The Lord's Supper, Sparrow, 1979.
Come to the Quiet, Sparrow, 1980.
The Painter, Sparrow, 1980.
Beginnings, Sparrow, 1980.
For the Bride, Sparrow, 1981.
Troubadour of the Great King, Sparrow, 1982.
Light Eternal, Sparrow, 1982.
Songs for Worship, Vol. 1, Sparrow, 1983.
No Longer Strangers, Sparrow, 1983.
The Quiet.
Be Exalted.
Empty Canvas.
Few Be the Lovers, 1987.
Heart of the Shepherd, 1987.

With Mason Proffit

Two Hangmen.
Moving toward Happiness.
Last Night I Had the Strangest Dream.
Rockfish Crossing.

Bareback Rider.
Come and Gone.

Sources

Books

O'Neill, Dan, *Troubadour for the Lord,* Crossroad, 1983.

Periodicals

Christian Century, March 18, 1987.
Christianity Today, February 1, 1985.
People, June 8, 1987.
Publishers Weekly, September 30, 1983.

—*Marjorie Burgess*

Tears
for
Fears

Rock band

Representatives of "moody, introverted British pop," according to John Rockwell in the *New York Times,* the rock group Tears for Fears combines weighty lyrics of self-exploration with a compelling and sensual pop sound. Composed of founders Roland Orzabal and Curt Smith, Tears for Fears rose to prominence with their multi-platinum second album, *Songs From the Big Chair,* followed in 1989 by the equally-successful *Sowing the Seeds of Love.* Although some detractors originally likened the group to what Rick G. Karr in *Stereo Review* called "overzealous college freshmen who have read too much and understood too little," several critics have lauded Tears for Fears as accomplished and innovative pop musicians. Rockwell claimed that *Songs From the Big Chair,* produced predominantly with synthesizers, "knits several strands of introspective English art-rock into an exquisitely textured, often haunting expression of youthful angst." Four years later, *Sowing the Seeds of Love,* featuring a revamped, more politically-directed Tears for Fears, was praised by Ira Robbins in *Rolling Stone* as "a challenging, ambitious album" with "forays into jazz pop, blues and soul—plus delicious Beatles parody."

Orzabal and Smith both hail from Bath, in southwestern England. They began playing music together when they were two unhappy thirteen-year-olds from broken homes. Their first recording, "The Sounds of Silence," was made at a Bath music center when they were fifteen, and three years later the duo was playing gigs in local clubs, experimenting with various forms of rock 'n' roll and folk music. Shortly thereafter, Orzabal and Smith formed their first band, Graduate, with three other musicians, specializing in what David Fricke in *Rolling Stone* called "Beatlesque power pop." Constrained by the group, however, Orzabal and Smith broke away in the early 1980s to focus on their own sound, and explore their interest in the theories of psychotherapist Arthur Janov and his concept of the primal scream. Janov's theories hold that emotional disorders stem from painful early recognition of parental abandonment, and that direct confrontation like rage—the "primal scream"—is essential for adult mental health. Like John Lennon in his album, *Plastic Ono Band,* Orzabal and Smith found musical inspiration in Janov's theories, which also provided the basis for their name, Tears for Fears.

Lyrics Called Depressing

Joined by keyboardist Ian Stanley, another ex-Graduate member, Tears for Fears began writing songs and experimenting with synthesizers, releasing a demo of "Pale Shelter" which landed the group a recording contract. Together with drummer Manny Elias, the group

For the Record. . .

Band formed in Bath, England, in 1982; founding members include **Roland Orzabal** (guitar, keyboard, vocals), born c. 1961, **Curt Smith** (bass, vocals), born c. 1961, **Ian Stanley** (keyboards), and **Manny Elias** (drums).

Orzabal and Smith previously performed with the band Graduate, late 1970s and early 1980s; released one album on PYE Records; Orzabal produced Oleta Adams's album, *Circle of One*, 1991.

Addresses: *Office*—Tears for Fears World Service, P.O. Box 4ZN, London WIA 4ZN, England.

began working in London recording studios, and in 1983 their first album, *The Hurting,* was released. Despite mixed reviews, *The Hurting* enjoyed respectable sales, was popular in dance clubs, and spawned three top-five singles in England. A number of reviewers complained that the album, with cuts such as "Mad World," "Suffer the Children," and "Pale Shelter," was too depressing or, as Orzabal told Dave DiMartino in *Creem,* "too stoic, too reflective." While Fricke, writing in *Musician* praised the music of *The Hurting* as "an artful compromise between pure electronics and classic pop instrumentation, blending slick synthesizer gimmickry with hypnotic staccato guitar effects and sensitive piano figures," he added that the lyrics made the group seem too "obsessed with their own troubled youth, dissecting with almost masochistic glee their sundered romances and smallest psychological tremors like transistorized James Taylors and Jackson Brownes."

"Everybody Wants to Rule the World"

A follow-up Tears for Fears single, "The Way You Are," was unsuccessful, and in 1984 producer Chris Hughes suggested the group leave recording studios and retreat to Stanley's home to work. The suggestion proved valuable as over the course of the year Tears for Fears wrote the songs that would constitute the hugely successful album, *Songs From the Big Chair.* Achieving a more commercial sound, the album—bolstered by the hit singles "Everybody Wants to Rule the World" and "Shout"—became one of 1985's biggest-sellers in both the United States and England. Suddenly Orzabal and Smith found themselves internationally famous music stars. Reviewer Freff in *Musician* commented on the appeal of *Songs From the Big Chair,* calling it "a significant advance over *The Hurting:* bigger and

stronger in all ways, and considerably more cheerful, for all the continued intensity of its lyrical content." Although Orzabal remarked in *Rolling Stone* that the album represented "watered-down Tears for Fears," reviewers were nonetheless impressed with the accomplishment. Rockwell, commenting about the group's "haunting expression of youthful angst," described "Shout" as an "exhortatory anthem deploring mindless conformism," and "Everybody Wants to Rule the World," an "airy blues shuffle, [which] talks indirectly about personal power, responsibility and nuclear peril."

Third Album Continued Success

Four years would pass before Tears for Fears would release another album and, judging from critical response, the result was worth the wait. Relying on their financial independence gained from the success of *Songs From the Big Chair,* Orzabal and Smith set out to explore a new creative direction, wanting to, in Robbins words, "expand their stylistic and emotional range." They enlisted the services of more live musicians, including songwriter Nicky Holland, former musical director for Fun Boy Three, and Oleta Adams, a rhythm and blues singer who Orzabal and Smith discovered in 1985 at a Kansas City night club. Released in 1989, *Sowing the Seeds of Love,* according to Stephen Holden in the *New York Times* possessed a "sound . . . much warmer, more spacious and more acoustical than its predecessor, whose chilly textures were electronically produced." The album's title track, a top ten hit on U.S. charts, recalls the Beatles's "Sgt. Pepper's Lonely Hearts Club Band" and "I Am the Walrus" and, according to Holden, "lovingly imitates the treadmill rhythms, trumpet-laced textures and exhortatory mood" of the former. Other cuts on the album like "Woman in Chains" and "Standing on the Corner of the Third World" show the group's concern with political issues such as feminism and poverty. A reviewer in *People* praised Tears for Fears's new direction, calling the album "warmly human" and "more soulful."

Orzabal explained to Karr the direction of *Sowing the Seeds of Love:* "When we first started, technology was very anti-rock-establishment. Now it's the dominant force in pop music. Meanwhile, the unreal element of recording and video is increasing. To maintain our stance—outside the mainstream—we've had to move away from our roots, go back to a more organic sound." Future Tears for Fears should display even further evolution. Orzabal told Karr that their next album should "be a bit more forward-looking. . . . We borrowed heavily from the Seventies and Sixties: the Beatles, Little Feat, Steely Dan. I'd like to take that further but introduce some more innovative things."

Selected discography

(With Ian Stanley and Manny Elias) *The Hurting* (includes "The Pale Shelter," "Suffer the Children," and "Mad World"), Mercury, 1983.

(With Stanley and Elias) "The Way You Are" (single), 1984.

(With Stanley and Elias) *Songs From the Big Chair* (includes "Everybody Wants to Rule the World," "Shout," "I Believe," and "Head over Heels"), Polygram, 1985.

(With Nicky Holland, Oleta Adams, and others) *Sowing the Seeds of Love* (includes "Sowing the Seeds of Love" and "Woman in Chains"), Fontana, 1989.

Sources

Creem, May 1985.

Melody Maker, March 9, 1985; October 19, 1985; August 19, 1989; August 26, 1989; November 25, 1989.

Musician, November 1983; September 1985.

New York Times, August 4, 1985; October 7, 1985; February 9, 1986; September 27, 1989; February 21, 1990.

People, November 13, 1989.

Rolling Stone, June 6, 1985; November 2, 1989; November 16, 1989; December 14, 1989; April 5, 1990.

Stereo Review, October 1990.

—*Michael E. Mueller*

Conway Twitty

Singer, songwriter

Speaking strictly in terms of Number One hits, Conway Twitty is the most successful recording artist in the history of country music. Twitty has reached the top of the charts with country singles no less than 50 times in a career spanning more than three decades. While other superstars have come and gone, he has maintained solid fan support and shown an almost uncanny ability to choose the most appealing material to record. As Alanna Nash put it in *Behind Closed Doors: Talking with the Legends of Country Music,* Twitty "staked his claim at the pinnacle of the music business thirty years ago, and one way or another, he's held it ever since."

Twitty's success in country music is all the more remarkable because he came to country from rock 'n' roll. For almost ten years in the late 1950s and early 1960s, Twitty was a teen idol who released hit after hit on the pop charts. His switch to country was a dramatic mid-career move, a decision he made against all advice simply because he had always loved country music. The singer-songwriter was quoted in *The Country Music Encyclopedia* about his dramatic switch in styles: "After I'd been [performing] for about eight years, I felt like I had lived long enough and had experienced enough of the things that a country song is all about to compete with the different country singers that I thought were great. Not taking anything away from the rock thing, but I feel like I started off with rock and worked my way up to country music, and I really feel that way. I don't mean that to put rock-and-roll music down. But I love country music so much and I think it's so much a part of everybody's everyday life that it's like Coke—it's the real thing."

Huckleberry Finn Childhood

Twitty was born Harold Lloyd Jenkins in the tiny Mississippi town of Friars Point. His father was a riverboat pilot and the family lived in a houseboat. Twitty told Nash that his early years were "kind of a Huckleberry Finn type of childhood. . . . My dad was a pilot on a Mississippi River boat. I used to sit up in the pilothouse and practice on the guitar and sing songs. Growing up there really helped make me turn out the way I am." Twitty was picking guitar by the time he was five and had formed his first band at ten.

Twitty loved music, but saw performing strictly as a hobby. He had another profession in mind—baseball. At 18 he was offered a contract by the Philadelphia Phillies, but before he could sign he was drafted into the service. He spent most of his Army years in Japan,

Born Harold Lloyd Jenkins, September 1, 1933, in Friars Point, MS; son of a riverboat pilot; married first wife, Georgia, c. 1955 (divorced, 1985); married Dee Henry (a secretary and record producer), 1987; children: (first marriage) Conway, Jr., Cathy.

Singer, songwriter, guitar player, 1951—. Recorded rock songs with Mercury and MGM Records, 1957-65; had first Number One hit, "It's Only Make Believe," 1958. Moved to country music in 1965, signed with Decca Records and released more than 50 Number One country singles between 1968 and 1986. Has made numerous live tours in the United States, Canada, and Europe, and has appeared as guest star on television variety shows. Star of syndicated television program, *The Conway Twitty Show*, 1966. Appeared in films *Platinum High, Sex Kittens Go to College,* and *College Confidential.*

Awards: With Loretta Lynn, named vocal duo of the year by the Country Music Association, 1972-78, and 1980.

Address: *Record company*—UNI Distribution Corp. (formerly MCA records), 70 Universal City Plaza, Universal City, CA 91608.

where he performed in a country band to entertain the furloughed troops. When he returned to the States, Twitty was astonished by the first music he heard on the radio, Elvis Presley's "Mystery Train." Later he was thrilled by the Carl Perkins hit "Blue Suede Shoes." Twitty said in the *Country Music Encyclopedia:* "I thought this was a young type of music and I thought I could do this. . . . So I got a little group together . . . and we started playing in nightclubs and on street corners and under shade trees—anywhere they'd let us play down in Arkansas and Tennessee and the Mississippi area."

Twitty auditioned at Sun Records for Sam Phillips—the legendary producer who signed Presley, Jerry Lee Lewis, and Roy Orbison—but Phillips did not offer Twitty a contract. Instead, the singer found himself at Mercury Records with a producer who urged him to change his name. He was reluctant at first, because he wanted the folks in his hometown to see that "Harold Jenkins" had made the big time. Eventually, though, he became convinced that only a distinctive name would assure his singles air time in the competitive pop market. He used maps of the South to come up with his stage name—Conway, from Conway, Arkansas, and Twitty, from Twitty, Texas.

"It's Only Make Believe"

A Mercury single, "I Need Your Lovin'," was Twitty's first chart-making song. In 1958 the artist moved to MGM Records and released "It's Only Make Believe," a song he wrote himself. The record—a powerful vocal performance featuring Twitty's trademark growl—became one of the biggest singles of the 1950s, selling in excess of eight million copies and topping record charts in 22 countries. In America "It's Only Make Believe" reached Number One on the country, pop, and blues charts and made a star of its author. From 1958 until 1965 Twitty rode a crest of popularity as a rock 'n' roll performer. He was such a phenomenon that he inspired the character of Conrad Birdie in the Broadway musical *Bye Bye, Birdie.*

Twitty's young fans, however, were unaware of his discontent with rock music. In his spare time he wrote country songs and sold them to other artists; gradually he became determined to move into country himself. "I was thirty-two years old and still playing the rock shows," he said in the *Country Music Encyclopedia.* "I wanted to get in the country thing so bad." For a while Twitty was stymied by his contract with MGM and extensive entourage of agents and managers. Finally, he let his MGM deal expire and presented himself to Decca producer Owen Bradley in Nashville. Bradley signed Twitty as strictly a country performer, and the two men worked together for the next 20 years.

Goodbye Rock, Hello Country

Twitty took a hefty pay cut when he decided to go country. He soon recouped his losses, though, scoring 36 consecutive Top Five hits between 1968 and 1977. Both as a solo singer and in duet with country superstar Loretta Lynn, Twitty was almost always represented somewhere on the country charts. His biggest hits include "Guess My Eyes Were Bigger Than My Heart," "Next in Line," "Hello Darlin'," "She Needs Someone to Hold Her," "The Games That Daddies Play," and "Play Guitar, Play." Occasionally he released songs featuring suggestive lyrics—"You've Never Been This Far Before" and "Slow Hand"—that sold all the more for the controversy they engendered. Remarkably, Twitty never won an award from the Country Music Association for his solo work, even though he and Lynn won best duo almost constantly throughout the 1970s.

Carefully Guarded Image

Today Twitty is still one of the most popular country stars and is arguably *the* most popular in his age group.

The duration of his success is a result of his inspired choice of recording material and his extremely wise manipulation of the limelight. Twitty is not uncommonly handsome or vocally dynamic; but he recognizes the fact that country fans want good, meaningful songs, and a fantasy world into which they can slip, however briefly, during concerts. He has shunned interviews and television appearances over the years and does little talking on stage. "There may be ten thousand different people that think Conway Twitty is ten thousand different things," he told Nash. "As long as you don't get on some talk show and blow all that—say things that you shouldn't say, and destroy that fragile little image in that one country music fan's mind—then you *can* be all things to all people. . . . I respect that image that each fan out there creates individually. I try to never do anything that will destroy that image."

Twitty knows it is the song, not the singer, that appeals to country fans. Women in particular love his work

---

My dad was a pilot on a Mississippi River boat. I used to sit up in the pilothouse and practice on the guitar and sing songs. Growing up there really helped make me turn out the way I am.

---

because his lyrics acknowledge both sensuality *and* the desire for respect and affection. Twitty feels that his deep love for country music gives him a charmed ear for hit songs; he will listen to as many as 3,000 tunes before choosing ten to record. "If there's any so-called secret to my success and longevity in this business, it is that talent," Twitty told the *Philadelphia Inquirer*. "I can just tell [a hit] when I write one or when I hear one. That's the one thing that's sustained me down through the years."

Selected discography

Hello Darlin', MCA, reissue, 1985.
Chasin' Rainbows, Warner Bros., 1985.
Fallin' for You for Years, Warner Bros., 1986.
Borderline, MCA, 1987.
Number Ones: The Warner Bros. Years, Warner Bros., 1988.
House on Old Lonesome Road, MCA, 1989.
Greatest Hits, MCA, 3 Volumes; Volume 3, 1990.

Crazy in Love, MCA, 1990.
25th Silver Anniversary Collection, MCA, 1990.
Number Ones, Capitol Nashville, 1991.
Hits of Conway Twitty, MGM.
Hit the Road, MGM.
Conway Twitty, MGM.
Honky Tonk Angels, MCA.
I'm Not through Loving You, MCA.
To See My Angel Cry, MCA.
Shake It Up, Pickwick.
Linda on My Mind, MCA.
You've Never Been This Far, MCA.
High Priest of Country, MCA.
Now and Then, MCA.
Twitty, MCA.
Play Guitar, Play, MCA.
Cross Winds, MCA.
Heart and Soul, MCA.
A Night with Conway Twitty, MCA.
Number Ones, MCA.
Songwriter, MCA.
By Heart, Warner Bros.
Conway's #1 Classics, 2 Volumes, Warner Bros.
Don't Call Him a Cowboy, Warner Bros.
Dream Maker, Warner Bros.
Lost in the Feeling, Warner Bros.
Southern Comfort, Warner Bros.

With Loretta Lynn

Twenty Greatest Hits of Loretta Lynn and Conway Twitty, MCA, 1987.
The Very Best of Conway Twitty and Loretta Lynn, MCA, 1988.
Louisiana Woman, Mississippi Man, MCA.
We Only Make Believe, MCA.
Country Partners, MCA.
Feelin's, MCA.
United Talent, MCA.
Never-Ending Song of Love, Coral.
Diamond Duet, MCA.
Dynamic Duo, MCA.
Lead Me On, MCA.
Two's a Party, MCA.

Sources

Books

Brown, Charles T., *Music U.S.A.: America's Country and Western Tradition*, Prentice-Hall, 1986.
The Illustrated Encyclopedia of Country Music, Harmony, 1977.
Malone, Bill C., *Country Music U.S.A.*, revised edition, University of Texas Press, 1985.
Nash, Alanna, *Behind Closed Doors: Talking with the Legends of Country Music*, Knopf, 1988.

Shestack, Melvin, *The Country Music Encyclopedia*, Crowell, 1974.

Stambler, Irwin, and Grelun Landon, *The Encyclopedia of Folk, Country, and Western Music*, St. Martin's, 1969.

Periodicals

Philadelphia Inquirer, July 22, 1990.

—*Anne Janette Johnson*

Vanilla Ice

Rap singer

Vanilla Ice, the white boy who recorded the first rap single to hit Number One on Billboard's Hot 100 pop chart, was controversial from the moment he arrived on the music scene. Accused of inventing his image as an urban rapper, the Iceman, whose real name is Robby Van Winkle, lowered his pants on Rick Dees's TV show to display scars he claims he received in a knife fight. He informed his critics in his acceptance speech as favorite new artist at the 1991 American Music Awards Ceremony that they could kiss his white posterior. With a hit single, "Ice, Ice Baby," that catapulted sales of his first album, *To The Extreme,* to five million in three months, Vanilla Ice is a hot new performer who seems to defy categorization. "So who is he," questioned *People,* among others, "fibber or phenom, street kid or star. . .?" Ice answered them all in *Newsweek:* "I'm 100 percent original."

Robert Matthew Van Winkle was born on Halloween in 1967 in Miami, Florida. His father left his mother, Beth Mino, a music teacher and classical pianist, while she was pregnant with Van Winkle. "I will not say anything about my father. Period," Ice told *People.* "I don't have a dad." His mother raised him and an older half-brother in culturally and ethnically mixed neighborhoods of Miami. When Van Winkle was five years old he became interested in music and dance. "I picked up the dance steps from what I saw the black kids doing in the streets," he related in his autobiography *Ice By Ice.* "The streets of Miami—that was my dance school." As a youngster Van Winkle shunned formal music lessons, never learning to play an instrument. His childhood dream was to become a motocross champion. Eventually he won a few amateur regional motocross titles; at one point in late adolescence he broke his ankles in a race.

Not a Model Child

Van Winkle was a difficult child, moody and temperamental, who used to play truant from grade school. His mother tried in vain to modify his behavior by seeking counseling and changing addresses frequently. When Van Winkle was eight his mother married Ecuadorean Byron Mino, whom she met when he sold her a car. Although family economics improved, the marriage broke up after three years. The couple got back together for a time after the divorce, but did not remarry. In his teens Van Winkle moved with his family, which now included a younger sister, to a middle-class suburb of Dallas where Mino had landed a better auto sales position. Van Winkle continued to rap and dance; he was also hanging out on weekends with gang members who took joy rides and picked fights. At a hospital after one skirmish in which he was stabbed several times,

Born Robert Matthew Van Winkle, October 31, 1967 (one source says 1968), in Miami, FL; son of Beth Mino (a music teacher and classical pianist). *Education:* Attended R. L. Turner High School; received high school diploma through correspondence course from the American School.

Discovered in 1987 at the City Lights Talent Show, Dallas, TX; opened for City Lights opening acts, including Tone-Loc, Public Enemy, and Paula Abdul; City Lights owner Tommy Quon became his talent manager in 1988; formed Vanilla Ice Posse (VIP) with City Lights disc jockey Earthquake (Floyd Brown) and dancers Hi-Tec (Jay Huffman), E-Rock (Everett Fitzgerald), and Juice (Marc Grinage). Recording artist and touring performer; film appearances include cameo role in *Teenage Mutant Ninja Turtles: The Secret of the Green Ooze;* television appearances include *Into the Night with Rick Dees, Friday Night Videos, Saturday Morning Videos, MTV's Hot Seat, Saturday Night Live, American Music Awards, The Arsenio Hall Show,* and *MTV Tailgate Party for the Superbowl;* has made endorsements for Nike and Coke.

Awards: Favorite new artist award from the American Music Awards, 1991.

Addresses: *Record company*—SBK Records (distributed by CEMA), 1750 North Vine St., Hollywood, CA 90028. *Fan Club*—Vanilla Ice Fan Club, P.O. Box 261117, Plano, TX 75026-1117.

Van Winkle found God and gave up gang life. Dropping out of suburban R. L. Turner High School in his second year, he worked as a lot attendant at the car dealership where his stepfather was employed.

An IROC Camaro Z28 became Van Winkle's next obsession. When he parked his car under the marquee one evening in 1987 at City Lights, a 2,000-seat club in Dallas, the owner of the club, Tommy Quon, went out to tell Van Winkle to park elsewhere. "He looked like a rich white kid—and he looked like a star," Quon told Dave Handelman in *Rolling Stone.* After Van Winkle convinced Quon to let him keep his parking place, he won the club's talent show. Quon confessed to Handelman, "He wasn't that great as a rapper, but he had that charisma, style." Quon signed him to a contract at City Lights where he performed before the club's opening acts, which included rap and pop acts Tone-Loc, Public Enemy, and Paula Abdul. When Quon became the rapper's talent agent in 1988 he backed Van Winkle with all black, male dancers to make him stand out.

Dubbed "Vanilla" in seventh grade because he was the only white boy around rapping with blacks, Van Winkle became Vanilla Ice—purportedly because he was smooth as ice—and named his back-up group VIP, or Vanilla Ice Posse.

Mix Up Sent "Ice, Ice Baby" to the Top

The group included Ice, writer-DJ Earthquake (Floyd Brown), and dancers Hi-Tec (Jay Huffman), E-Rock (Everett Fitzgerald), and Juice (Marc Grinage). When Quon could not interest record companies, he independently made the album *Hooked,* which featured "Ice, Ice Baby." To promote the group Quon released the single "Play That Funky Music" with "Ice, Ice Baby" on the B-side. DJ Darrell Jaye in Columbus, Georgia, meant to air Ice's "Play That Funky Music" when he flipped the record over accidentally. Overnight the song went to Number One on Southern channels and became a top request on pay-per-view *Video Jukebox.* Consequently the album was remixed and reissued by SBK Records in October of 1990 under its new title, *To the Extreme.* Ice had unprecedented success with the single "Ice, Ice Baby." When the song topped Billboard's pop chart, SBK executives made the single available only on the album. The strategy worked; *To the Extreme* was the first album to reach all five certification levels in one month, and Ice was handed gold, platinum, double-platinum, and triple-platinum album awards on November 19, 1990. The next day he received a quadruple-platinum award, and subsequently, a multi-fold persona problem with his SBK bio.

Accused of Faking "Street" Credentials

A skeptical press hooted at the discrepancies in his stories—especially over those concerning the loss of half his blood when he was stabbed five times and resultant religious conviction. When they discovered that Ice had given three different locales for the incident, they intimated that the singer—with his Z28 and home in a Texan suburb—was a rich kid who fibbed. Critics of *To the Extreme* wrote scathing reviews accusing the model-handsome rapper of creating a streetwise background to more effectively appropriate a black art form. "Rap lite," *Newsweek* called Ice's work, summing up reviewers' response to the lack of profanity and political substance in his lyrics. The magazine questioned whether a black rapper "with little vocal technique or rhythmic sense, largely inarticulate and devoid of wit" could sell millions of records, unless like Ice, he had "the right clothes, the right look and the right moves, and the right recycled hits to rap to." *People* reported that the album "mostly thumps on mindlessly," but John Rockwell defended "the looker with attitude" in the *New York Times*. Interpreting *To the Extreme* as a new, mainstream musical style, Rockwell called the album "a triumph for Vanilla Ice, a triumph for rap." Proof of Ice's "street" past and some vindication came with the warrant issued for his arrest in 1991 by Dallas police—which dated back to a 1988 unpaid fine for a parking lot incident where Ice had maced a kid and beat him over the head—and the publication of his autobiography *Ice By Ice*.

Despite that legal entanglement, the future is bright for the star who maintains that he allowed the press to be misled to protect his family's privacy. His cameo role in the sequel to the movie *Teenage Mutant Ninja Turtles* has led to a film project about a motorcycle gang, entitled *Cool as Ice*. Though he opened the M. C. Hammer 1990 fall tour, he went solo on his own world tour in 1991. A new album, *Ice Capades*, is in the works for the bad-boy-turned-role-model, who will be endorsing Coke and Nike. "I always set new goals," Vanilla Ice told Sanders, emphasizing that his success is no novelty, "and that's my new goal, to be here, keep it goin'! The media can try and break me all they want, but the bottom line is it's *up . . . to . . . me.*"

Selected writings

Ice by Ice, Avon, 1991.

Selected discography

To the Extreme, SBK Records, 1990.
Extremely Live, SBK Records, 1991.

Sources

Billboard, November 3, 1990; December 15, 1990; December 22, 1990.
Entertainment Weekly, March 15, 1991.
Newsweek, December 3, 1990.
New York Times, November 18, 1990.
People, November 26, 1990; December 3, 1990.
Rolling Stone, January 10, 1991.
Variety, November 12, 1990.

—*Marjorie Burgess*

Sippie Wallace

Singer, songwriter, pianist, organist

Sippie Wallace, "The Texas Nightingale," was one of the major blues artists of the 1920s, whose renown as a performer carried well into the 1980s. Wallace was respected as both a blues singer and songwriter. Jon Pareles in the *New York Times* described her original songs "Mighty Tight Woman" and "Women Be Wise"—which found a new audience with younger listeners in the 1970s—as "earthy and self-assertive blues songs." She is best remembered, however, as one of the foremost interpreters of the blues. Paul Oliver in *Jazz on Record* called Wallace "one of the major singers in the Classic blues idiom. . . . Possessing a mellow and tuneful voice, [she] had the qualities of shading and inflection in her singing that marked the classic blues artist."

One of Wallace's specialties was the "shout," a precursor to the modern blues, in which the singer repeats two lines of a song, and improvises a third. Wallace, who frequently sang without a microphone, was influenced by blues great Ma Rainey, yet developed a style all her own. A contributor to *The New Grove Dictionary of Jazz* wrote: "In her earliest work she attempted to project a vocal weightiness similar to that of Ma Rainey. Later she sang in a manner better suited to the lighter, prettier qualities of her voice, which may be heard to advantage on [the album] *I'm a Mighty Tight Woman*. . . . Wallace composed most of her own songs, which are notable for the shapeliness and dignity of their melodies."

Wallace learned music in her father's Baptist church in Houston, where she played the organ and sang gospel music. She was nicknamed "Sippie" because, as Pareles quoted her, "my teeth were so far apart and I had to sip everything." Around 1910 she moved with her family to New Orleans, where Wallace's brother George W., Jr., a professional musician and composer, lived. The family later returned to Houston and while Wallace was in her late teens she began performing with traveling tent shows. She learned blues and ragtime in the shows, in addition to performing in chorus lines and acting in comedy skits. These experiences influenced her contributions as a blues artist. As LeRoi Jones commented in *Blues People: Negro Music in White America*, Wallace was of a line of distinguished performers who "brought a professionalism and theatrical polish to blues that it had never had before."

In the 1920s Wallace gained a national reputation as a recording artist, working with Okeh Records in Chicago. She recorded a number of solo albums and also worked with jazz greats Louis Armstrong and Sidney Bechet. She continued theatrical touring in the 1920s and frequently worked with another brother, Hersal, a respected jazz pianist. In 1929 Wallace settled in Detroit. In the 1930s she became active again in gospel music, playing the organ and singing for the Leland Baptist Church. Wallace recorded only ocassionally in the 1940s through early 1960s.

Wallace revived her blues career in the mid-1960s at the urging of fellow blues singer Victoria Spivey. In the autumn of 1966 Wallace traveled to Europe with the American Folk Blues Festival, and throughout the rest of the 1960s frequently performed at various blues and jazz festivals in the United States. "Visiting Europe in 1966, . . . Wallace astonished by the breadth of her singing and a delivery recalling Bessie Smith," noted Oliver. The same year, her album *Sippie Wallace Sings the Blues* likewise demonstrated that she still had her touch. A contributor to *The New Grove Dictionary of Jazz* remarked: "The importance of the present disc . . . is that she can still sing these blues. . . . Her wide range of material and masterful reinterpretations are clearly shown in the efforts 'I'm a Mighty Tight Woman,' 'Shorty George Blues,' and 'Special Delivery Blues.'"

Singer and guitarist Bonnie Raitt broadened interest in Wallace's music when she featured two of the blueswoman's songs on her 1971 debut album. Wallace toured and recorded with Raitt in the 1970s and eighties while continuing to perform on her own. In 1980 Wallace was featured at New York City's Avery Fisher Hall in a salute to prominent blueswomen. *New York Times Magazine* contributor Ariel Swartley said that Wallace, at 81 the show's oldest participant, offered "her own, still-fresh remedies for heartache." Swartley commented on Wallace's popularity with a new generation of music lovers. "It's one of the program's bittersweet ironies that, of all the performers, it's probably the aging Sippie Wallace who's best known to audiences under 30. . . . And yet it shouldn't be surprising that a young audience appreciated her—the blues, after all, is the root of both jazz and rock and roll."

Selected discography

(With C. Williams) *Caldonia Blues*, Okeh, 1924.
Special Delivery Blues, Okeh, 1926.
The Flood Blues, Okeh, 1927.
I'm a Mighty Tight Woman, Victor, 1929.
Bedroom Blues, Mercury, 1945.
(With L. B. Montgomery and R. Sykes) *Sippie Wallace Sings the Blues*, Storyville, 1966.
Sippie, Atlantic, 1982.

Sources

Books

Harris, Sheldon, *Blues Who's Who*, Arlington House, 1979.
Jones, LeRoi, *Blues People: Negro Music in White America*, Morrow, 1963.
McCarthy, Albert, Alun Morgan, Paul Oliver, and Max Harrison, *Jazz on Record: A Critical Guide to the First 50 Years, 1917-1967*, Hanover Books, 1968.
The New Grove Dictionary of Jazz, edited by Barry Kernfeld, Macmillan, 1988.

Periodicals

New York Times, November 4, 1986.
New York Times Magazine, June 29, 1980.

—*Michael E. Mueller*

Was
(Not Was)

Rhythm-and-Blues/pop duo

"Was (Not Was)'s shtick is unconventionality, from the enigmatic name to the mix of dance rhythms and dada lyrics," David Gates wrote in *Newsweek*. Founded by "brothers" Don and David Was (real names, Donald Fagenson and David Weiss, respectively), Was (Not Was) is an eclectic funk band that combines hard-driving soul and rock music—sung by lead vocalists Sweet Pea Atkinson and Sir Harry Bowens—with wacked-out absurdist lyrics that revel in the flip side of modern life and love. A brief sampling of Was (Not Was) songs displays such left-field scenarios as the transatlantic transport of Elvis Presley's Rolls Royce to Graceland, the selling-out of Havana by Fidel Castro in exchange for Kentucky Fried Chicken franchises, and a tender ballad recounting the near strangulation of a lover. The band's accomplished music and one-of-a-kind lyrics have been critically acclaimed since their inception in the early 1980s, though commercial success did not arrive until their 1988 album *What Up, Dog?,* which spawned dance chart hits in Europe and the United States. Don Was, who has also become a much-sought-after record producer,

For the Record. . .

Group formed in early 1980s; founding members include **Don Was** (composer, instrumentalist, and producer), born Donald Fagenson c. 1952, in Detroit, MI, and **David Was** (instrumentalist and lyricist), born David Weiss c. 1952, in Detroit; group also includes **Sweet Pea Atkinson** (vocals), born c. 1945, and **Sir Harry Bowens** (vocals), born c. 1951.

Don Was: son of Harriet and Bill Fagenson (both teachers); David Was: son of Elizabeth and Rubin Weiss (both entertainers); both grew up in Oak Park, MI; Don Was married in 1972 (divorced) and has one son, Anthony; David Was married in the mid-1970s and has two children, Nicholas and Phoebe. *Education:* Both attended the University of Michigan.

Don Was produced Bonnie Raitt's *Nick of Time,* the B52s' *Cosmic Thing,* and Iggy Pop's *Brick by Brick;* has also produced recordings for Dion, David Crosby, Leonard Cohen, Elton John, Ozzy Osbourne, Paula Abdul, and Bob Seger; David Was was a jazz critic for the *Herald Examiner* (Los Angeles); Was and Was coproduced Sweet Pea Atkinson's *Don't Walk Away,* Christina's *Sleep It Off,* and Bob Dylan's *Under the Red Sky.*

Addresses: *Recording company*—Chrysalis Records, 645 Madison Ave., New York, NY 10022.

explained the intent of Was (Not Was) to Andrea Sachs in *Time:* "We would like to sound like the Motown revue on acid."

The Was brothers' eclectic musical influences began in their hometown of Detroit, where they grew up among the soulful Motown sounds of the 1960s, and where such acts as funk frontrunner George Clinton and the hard-rock MC5 played concerts at their high school. Friends from childhood, Fagenson and Weiss (as they were known then), grew up in a suburban middle-class Jewish neighborhood, and their flair for the offbeat was evident at a young age. They began writing songs in Weiss's parent's basement, in a room they called the "Humor Prison." "[David] wore a Colonel Sanders mask and I wore a President Kennedy mask," Fagenson told Michael Goldberg in *Rolling Stone.* "This was because it was tough to reject the other one's ideas and look him in the eyes at the same time." One of their early recordings, Goldberg reports, was "(My Oh My) I Forgot My Wallet," in which the song's narrator shops around town accompanied by a German shepherd dog, which growls on cue to each of the narrator's orders to "Charge it." The pair also published a humor magazine, led a neighborhood comedy troupe, and once staged a

show at their high school entitled "You Have Just Wasted Your Money." Weiss's mother told Goldberg: "Everyone thought they were strange, including their parents. They were always weird. Both of those kids marched to a different drummer."

Needed Money: Made a Record

Both attended the University of Michigan, and Weiss went on to Los Angeles, where he became a jazz critic for the *Herald Examiner.* Fagenson stayed in Detroit, where he worked as a record producer, studio musician, and played gigs with local bands. Was (Not Was)—the name originated with a word game of Fagenson's young son—was created when Fagenson, nearly broke, called Weiss for help, and the two decided they should make a recording. With money borrowed from Weiss's parents, they recruited Atkinson and Bowens, two Detroit singers, and recorded *Wheel Me Out* in a Detroit studio (the song also featured a rap vocal supplied by Weiss's mother). The single was released by Ze Records in New York, and gained Was (Not Was) enough positive recognition in Great Britain and the United States to spur the duo onwards. They began a long-distance songwriting collaboration between California and Michigan, with Weiss supplying lyrics to Fagenson over the phone or through the mail.

Lauded for Offbeat Approach

The Was brothers' debut album, *Was (Not Was),* was released by Ze in 1981, and displayed "a lively fusion of jokey lyrics and hard-edged white-boy funk," according to Christopher Connelly in *Rolling Stone.* Two years later, *Born to Laugh at Tornadoes* was picked up by Geffen Records and initiated an ongoing Was (Not Was) tradition of including appearances by unlikely guest vocalists. *Tornadoes* featured rocker Marshall Crenshaw singing the mournful pop standard "Feelings," heavy metal Ozzy Osbourne crooning a seductive "Shake Your Head (Let's Go to Bed"), and jazz scat impresario Mel Torme rendering a torch, "Zaz Turns Blue," which recounts a lover nearly being strangled. Connelly called *Tornadoes* "a superb example of what smart rock & roll can be: tuneful, toe tapping, refreshingly irreverent." Critical respor e was overwhelmingly positive, yet the album found a limited listening audience and only sold 50,000 copies. Geffen Records, in what Don Was says was not a racist move but reflective of the "reality of the music business," put pressure on the group to, as he told Sachs, "get rid of the black guys" and make the band more marketable as a one-color group. Was (Not Was) staunchly refused, and soon found themselves looking for another record company.

Their contract with Geffen was eventually purchased by an English label, Fontana, which in 1988 released the group's next album, *What Up, Dog?* Two cuts off the album, "Walk the Dinosaur" and "Spy in the House of Love," were Top Ten hits in Europe, and the album was later released in the United States under the Chrysalis label. The same two cuts became top hits on Billboard's dance charts. Guest vocalist this time around was Frank Sinatra, Jr., singing "Wedding Vows in Las Vegas," and, as Steve Dougherty and Jim McFarlin noted in *People,* "laughs flood most of the grooves, and such titles as "Out Come the Freaks" and "Dad, I'm in Jail" extend—most often with a dance-happy beat—the Wasmological view that life is a terrifying absurdity." Lyricist Dave Was commented on his songwriting philosophies to an interviewer in *Melody Maker:* [A pop song] gives people a momentary forgetfulness so they can be just like a child playing with a mobile above a crib. They can have this little pattern of rhythm and rhyme and colour and vibration to keep them mesmerized. . . . It's a fundamental, primitive appeal and it's why, maybe, so much irony infects my work as a writer, because what I believe we're dealing with, in the end, is a trifle."

"Papa Was a Rolling Stone" Redux

The group's next album, *Are You OK?,* continued to display their knack for the absurd, yet also displayed more serious tones. Among the cuts is a rap-infused cover of the Temptations' classic "Papa Was a Rolling Stone," which, according to Rob Tannenbaum in *Rolling Stone,* "turns a tale of victimization into a statement of determination." Larry Katz in *Boston* magazine, citing the power of the remake, noted that Was (Not Was) "brings out the full measure of hurt and anger in the Temptations' tale of a louse of a father." The song also showcases the vocal talents of Atkinson and Bowens who, according to Tannenbaum, are "as vintage a pair of soul singers as still exists." While *Are You OK?* shows Was (Not Was) capable of writing more straightforward songs, the variation seems to be another addition to their eclectic bag of music. Tannenbaum wrote: "From their be-bop-to-hip-hop perspective and their sarcasm to their careful musicianship . . . Don and David Was want nothing less than to weave together the multiple discrete strands of American culture. Not since Talking Heads' heyday has there been such a wonderfully contrary dance band."

Don Was Acclaimed as Top Producer

In recent years, Don Was has made a singular name for himself as one of the top producers in the record industry. In 1989 he produced Bonnie Raitt's multiple Grammy Award-winning *Nick of Time,* and also co-produced (with Nile Rodgers), the B-52's multi-platinum comeback album, *Cosmic Thing.* Other artists who have sought out Was include Bob Dylan, Bob Seger, Iggy Pop, and Paula Abdul. Was's strength as a producer, according to Seger in *Newsweek,* is that "he's very true to the music itself" and does not "put something on your record just to fit some formula." Don Was commented to *Rolling Stone* on his philosophy: "I wouldn't take a gig if I had to figure out how to embellish it. I only want to work with people who have an existing point of view and an ability to express it. I should just be there to channel it. Like in photography, turning on all the lights and pointing right in someone's face."

Selected discography

"Wheel Me Out" (single), Ze/Antilles, 1980.
Was (Not Was), Ze/Island, 1981.
Born to Laugh at Tornadoes, Ze/Geffen, 1983.
What Up, Dog? (includes "Spy in the House of Love" and "Walk the Dinosaur"), Chrysalis, 1988.
Are You OK? (includes "Papa Was a Rolling Stone"), Chrysalis, 1990.

Sources

Boston, October 1990.
Creem, January 1984; July 1984.
High Fidelity, April 1984.
Melody Maker, May 12, 1990.
Musician, November 1983.
Newsweek, August 20, 1990.
People, December 12, 1988.
Rolling Stone, October 13, 1983; December 18, 1983; October 6, 1988; November 17, 1988; May 17, 1990; June 14, 1990; September 6, 1990.
Stereo Review, February 1984.
Time, January 30, 1989.

—*Michael E. Mueller*

Kitty Wells

Singer

"**K**itty Wells opened the door for Patsy [Cline], Loretta [Lynn], Dolly [Parton] and every other female country singer since," *Country Music* magazine neatly concluded in 1988. With her 1952 hit "It Wasn't God Who Made Honky Tonk Angels," Wells became the first female vocalist to have a Number One record on the country charts. Throughout the 1950s and 1960s, she continued to score successful singles, including "Making Believe," "I Can't Stop Loving You," and "Love Makes the World Go 'Round." Wells also released acclaimed duets with country artists Roy Acuff, Red Foley, Webb Pierce, and her husband, Johnny Wright, with whom she toured Canada and Europe during the heyday of her stardom. She is widely hailed as *the* influence on female country singers from Cline to Canadian upstart k. d. lang, who invited Wells to lend her famous voice to "Honky Tonk Angels Medley" on lang's 1988 release, *Shadowland.*

Wells was born Muriel Deason on August 30, 1919, in Nashville, Tennessee. She showed an early preference for country music, singing along with the radio as a child. By the age of 15, she had honed her skills on the guitar sufficiently to become a popular performer at local dances. By 1936 Wells was playing on Nashville radio station WSIX. In 1938, however, her career took an important turn when Wells married Johnny Wright, half of the country duo Johnny and Jack. Presented with her stage name by Wright—from an old song called "Sweet Kitty Wells"—she began to perform on radio stations throughout the South with Johnny and Jack.

Despite the opportunities provided her through her husband's act, Wells did not concentrate on her career during the late 1930s and early 1940s, opting instead to devote her full time to raising children. When the youngsters got older, however, Wells redoubled her previous efforts to gain fans' attention; she cut some country and gospel records for RCA, and in 1947 made a guest appearance on the famed Grand Ole Opry. Also during that year Wells, Wright, and Wright's partner Jack Anglin became a regular feature of the radio show *Louisiana Hayride*. These appearances meant that Kitty Wells had arrived as a force in country music.

The year Wells left *Hayride*, 1952, was also the one during which she was catapulted to country stardom with "It Wasn't God Who Made Honky Tonk Angels." At the time, Wells was under contract to Decca Records, with which she stayed through its transition to MCA. "Honky Tonk Angels"—an answer to Hank Thompson's hit, "The Wild Side of Life"—quickly sold 800,000 copies, eventually reaching the million-seller mark. Shortly after Wells's single topped the country charts, she and Johnny and Jack were invited to become regular performers at the Grand Ole Opry.

Born Muriel Deason, August 30, 1919, in Nashville, TN; married Johnny Wright (a musician), 1938; children include son, Bobby.

Played guitar at local dances in the Nashville area during the early 1930s; began appearing on Nashville radio station WSIX, 1936; appeared on radio stations, including WCHS, Bluefield, West Virginia, WNOX, Knoxville, Tennessee, WPTF, Raleigh, North Carolina, and WEAS, Decatur, Georgia, with country act Johnny and Jack, during the late 1930s and 1940s; appeared on the Grand Ole Opry, 1947; appeared with Johnny and Jack on the radio show *Louisiana Hayride,* 1947-52; regular performer with Johnny and Jack on the Grand Ole Opry, beginning 1952; solo and duet performer and recording artist, beginning 1952. Appeared on syndicated television show *The Kitty Wells/Johnny Wright Family Show,* beginning 1969.

Awards: Named Outstanding Tennessee Citizen by Governor Frank Clement, 1954; elected to the Country Music Hall of Fame, 1976; Lifetime Achievement Award from the National Academy of Recording Arts and Sciences, 1991.

Addresses: *Home*—Nashville, TN. *Record company*—UNI Distribution Corp. (formerly MCA Records, Inc.), 70 Universal City Plaza, Universal City, CA 91608.

she and Johnny and Jack were invited to become regular performers at the Grand Ole Opry.

Meanwhile, Wells continued to produce hits. She followed up "Honky Tonk Angels" with 1953's "I'm Paying for That Back Street Affair." In 1954 two duets with Foley, "One by One" and "As Long as I Live," as well as the solo singles "Making Believe" and "Lonely Side of Town" became chart-toppers. Wells's later 1950s releases included "Searching Soul," "I Can't Stop Loving You," and "Amigo's Guitar," which she wrote with John Loudermilk. Wells also entered the 1960s on top with songs like "Heartbreak U.S.A.," "Day into Night," "You Don't Hear," and "Love Makes the World Go 'Round." But, as *Newsweek* reported, after achieving 22 Number One country songs, "her churchy, four-square singing fell from favor in the mid-'60s and new country queens like Loretta Lynn and Tammy Wynette won even larger followings."

Nevertheless, Wells was popular enough to start her own syndicated television program with her husband in 1969. *The Kitty Wells/Johnny Wright Family Show* also featured appearances by their children, including actor

Bobby Wright, and stayed on the air for several years. At the same time, Wells continued recording, until the 1970s, when her contract with MCA expired. She attempted a comeback with a smaller record label, but slow sales proved prohibitive.

Despite her waning popularity, Wells remained a successful concert attraction at smaller venues throughout the country and was still performing on the summer resort circuit as late as the mid-1980s. Unforgotten by her millions of fans, Wells was elected to the Country Music Hall of Fame in 1976. In her seventies, she received a lifetime achievement award from the National Academy of Recording Arts & Sciences, appearing in fine form on the international telecast of the 1991 Grammy Awards presentation. *Newsweek* attested in 1985 that "these days, as in 1952, [Wells's] voice is clear and tart, her delivery without a hint of artifice," qualities that made her a pioneering female vocalist and one of the true giants of country music.

Selected discography

Singles; on Decca/MCA

"It Wasn't God Who Made Honky Tonk Angels," 1952.
"I'm Paying for That Back Street Affair," 1953.
(With Red Foley) "One by One," 1954.
(With Foley) "As Long As I Live," 1954.
"Making Believe," 1954.
"Lonely Side of Town," 1954.
"Searching Soul," 1956.
"I'll Always Be Your Fraulein," 1957.
"Repeating," 1957.
"I Can't Stop Loving You," 1958.
"Amigo's Guitar," 1959.
"Mommy for a Day," 1959.
"Left to Right," 1960.
"Heartbreak U.S.A.," 1961.
"Day into Night," 1962.
"Unloved, Unwanted," 1962.
"We Missed You," 1962.
"Will Your Lawyer Talk to God," 1962.
"Password," 1964.
"The White Circle on My Finger," 1964.
"You Don't Hear," 1965.
"Love Makes the World Go 'Round," 1966.

Also released "Cheatin's a Sin," "I Don't Claim to Be an Angel," "God Put a Rainbow in the Cloud," and "How Far to Heaven."

Albums; on Decca/MCA except where noted

Lonely Street, 1958.
After Dark, 1959.
Dust on the Bible, 1959.

Kitty's Choice, 1960.
Seasons of My Heart, 1960.
Golden Favorites, 1961.
Heartbreak U.S.A., 1961.
Queen of Country Music, 1962.
Singing on Sunday, 1963.
Especially for You: The Kitty Wells Story, 1963.
Country Music Time, 1964.
Burning Memories, 1965.
Lonesome, Sad, and Blue, 1965.
Family Gospel Sing, 1965.
Songs Made Famous by Jim Reeves, 1966.
All the Way, 1966.
Kitty Wells Show, 1967.
Love Makes the World Go 'Round, 1967.
(With Foley) *Together Again*, 1967.
Queen of Honky Tonk, 1967.
Greatest Hits, 1968.
The Golden Years: 1949-1957, Rounder, 1988.

Selected writings

Favorite Songs and Recipes, 1973.

Sources

Books

Stambler, Irwin, and Grelun Landon, *The Encyclopedia of Folk, Country, and Western Music*, St. Martin's, 1984.

Periodicals

Country Music, May/June 1988.
Newsweek, August 12, 1985.
Rolling Stone, November 17, 1988.

—Elizabeth Wenning

Barry White

Singer, songwriter, composer, arranger, record producer

During the mid-1970s singer/songwriter Barry White was the undisputed maestro of sensual soul music. Growling seductive lyrics in a deep, husky voice backed by lush orchestration, White produced a string of hit songs during the decade, with titles such as "I'm Gonna Love You Just a Little Bit More, Baby," "I'll Do Anything You Want Me To," and "I'm Qualified to Satisfy." His repetitive melodies and danceable rhythms were major influences on the disco music that emerged later in the decade; with his 41-piece Love Unlimited Orchestra he produced the prognostic disco hit "Love's Theme" in 1973. The multifaceted White frequently wrote, arranged, and produced for other performers as well as himself; by the time his popularity as a singer had waned in the late seventies, his musical talents had earned him more than one hundred million dollars in worldwide record sales. "Before Teddy Pendergrass's snarl, Luther Vandross's arpeggios and Michael Jackson's hiccups, there was Barry White's deep, smooth moan," *High Fidelity* writer Havelock Nelson recalled. "He promised his baby virtually everything," Dave Marsh remarked in the *New Rolling Stone Record Guide,* "in a way still acceptable to the FCC."

White grew up in poverty and, like many poor black performers, got his musical start at a local church. At eight he began singing in the choir and two years later he played the organ and assisted the choir director. By the time he was 16 White had joined a rhythm and blues band, the Upfronts, as a singer and pianist performing in small clubs in the Los Angeles area. He next joined Rampart Records and started composing and producing. During this time he met performers Bob and Earl and wrote their 1963 hit "The Harlem Shuffle." In 1966 White became head of A & R (artists and repertoire) for Mustang/Bronco Records, where he wrote, produced, and unsuccessfully recorded as a solo vocalist. While there he met three female singers—Diane Taylor, Linda James, and Glodean James. Naming them Love Unlimited, he produced their first single, "Walkin' in the Rain with the One I Love" which turned gold. In 1973 White and his female associates signed recording contracts with Twentieth Century-Fox Records. His initial release, "I'm Gonna Love You Just a Little Bit More, Baby," topped the charts, the first in a succession of million-selling singles and albums which included "Never, Never Gonna Give You Up," "You're My First, My Last, My Everything," *Can't Get Enough,* and *Just Another to Say I Love You.* White's easy-listening soul appealed to both pop and rhythm and blues audiences and was described as "sophistisoul." In 1973 White formed the Love Unlimited Orchestra to accompany him on his concert tours. The performer and his entourage left Twentieth Century-Fox when he founded his own recording company, Unlimited Gold, in 1979.

Born September 12, 1944, in Galveston, TX (one source says Los Angeles, CA), raised in Los Angeles; married Glodean James (a singer), July 4, 1974; children: Kevin, Bridgett, Barry, Jr.

Sang in Galveston church choir at age eight; became church organist and part-time choir director at ten; professional debut at age 11 playing piano on Jesse Belvin's recording of "Goodnight My Love"; joined Los Angeles rhythm and blues band the Upfronts as singer/pianist at 16; worked as arranger for Rampart Records under name Lee Barry and as road manager for Bob and Earl; songwriter and producer for Mustang/Bronco Records, beginning 1966; producer for Love Unlimited singing trio, beginning 1972; signed recording contract with Twentieth Century-Fox, 1973; conductor, composer, and arranger for Love Unlimited Orchestra, beginning 1973; founded recording company, Unlimited Gold, 1979; other business interests include Sa-Vette Music, Soul Unlimited, and Barry White, Inc.

Awards: 20 gold singles and 103 gold albums; 10 platinum singles and 38 platinum albums.

Addresses: *Record company*—A&M Records Inc., 1416 North La Brea Ave., Hollywood, CA 90028.

Although White's appeal declined in the 1980s, he continued to compose, produce, and perform. His 1982 album *Chance* sold particularly well. Marsh quipped that the singer's "corpulent frame" and "cluster of huge rings" sabotaged his reign as "a black matinee idol." In a 1990 *Jet* interview White deemed many current love songs "blatant and . . . vulgar." "Making love is one thing," he related, "having sex is another . . . I've always advocated loving, sharing, giving, understanding, making love, making time for each other, making time to communicate, stimulate." While critics have noted more uptempo tunes and less heavy orchestration in later White albums, a *People* critic wrote in a review of *Change* that "the product seems to be the same basic White bread: a little change, and a lot of status quo." Still, in his *High Fidelity* critique of the 1988 album *The Right Night and Barry White*, Nelson concluded: "During any quiet storm, underneath White satin is still a pretty good place to be."

Selected discography

Compositions

Has written numerous songs, including "The Harlem Shuffle," recorded by Bob and Earl and The Rolling Stones; "I Feel Love Coming On," recorded by Felice Taylor; and the instrumental "Love's Theme," recorded by the Love Unlimited Orchestra.

Albums

I've Got So Much to Give, Twentieth Century-Fox, 1973.
Stone Gon', Twentieth Century-Fox, 1973.
Rhapsody in White, Twentieth Century-Fox, 1974.
Can't Get Enough, Twentieth Century-Fox, 1974.
Just Another to Say I Love You, Twentieth Century-Fox, 1975.
Barry White's Greatest Hits, Twentieth Century-Fox, 1975.
Let the Music Play, Twentieth Century-Fox, 1976.
Is This Whatcha Want?, Twentieth Century-Fox, 1976.
Barry White Sings for Someone You Love, Twentieth Century-Fox, 1977.
The Man, Twentieth Century-Fox, 1978.
The Message Is Love, Unlimited Gold, 1979.
I Love to Sing the Songs I Sing, Twentieth Century-Fox, 1979.
Sheet Music, Unlimited Gold, 1980.
Best of Our Love, Unlimited Gold, 1981.
Beware, Unlimited Gold, 1981.
Barry White's Greatest Hits, volume 2, Twentieth Century-Fox, 1981.
Change, Unlimited Gold, 1982.
Dedicated, 1983.
The Right Night, A&M, 1987.
The Man Is Back, A&M, 1989.
Put Me in Your Mix, A&M, 1991.

Also contributed to Quincy Jones's Grammy Award-winning "The Secret Garden (The Seduction Suite)" from the album *Back on the Block,* and to rapper Big Daddy Kane's "All of Me Wants All of You," 1990.

Sources

Books

The Encyclopedia of Rock, edited by Phil Hardy and Dave Laing, Schirmer Books, 1988.
The New Rolling Stone Record Guide, edited by Dave Marsh and John Swenson, Random House, 1983.
The Rolling Stone Encyclopedia of Rock and Roll, edited by Jon Pareles and Patricia Romanowski, Summit Books, 1983.

Periodicals

Daily News (New York), May 20, 1990.
Ebony, March 1990.
Elle, December 1989.
High Fidelity, March 1988.

Jet, July 9, 1990.
Newspaper, June 7, 1990.
People, August 18, 1980; October 4, 1982; September 26, 1983.
Washington Times, June 21, 1990.

—Nancy Pear

Tony Williams

Drummer, composer

"I wouldn't change anything that I've done, because it's all brought me to where I am," Tony Williams, jazz drummer and composer, told John Ephland in *Down Beat*. "And where I am is a good place to be." Throughout a turbulent three decades, Williams has drummed with such superstars of jazz as Miles Davis, Sonny Rollins, and Wynton Marsalis, among others. The ups and downs of this child prodigy are a stellar, textbook entry in the history of jazz.

Anthony Williams was born in Chicago, Illinois, on December 12, 1945. His family moved to Boston when Williams was a toddler. His father, Tillman Williams, introduced Tony to music at the various jazz clubs around Boston, where Tillman played saxophone on the weekends. "I would sit in the audience when I was a kid," Williams recalled to Ephland, "and just watch the drummer." Williams asked his father if he could sit with the band in one of the clubs. He played his first set of drums that night in front of an audience at age nine. As an 11-year-old, he was drumming in the Boston clubs on his own. The next year Williams was performing with

Art Blakey, and the following year, with Max Roach. He took private lessons from Alan Dawson, who was a teacher at the Berklee College of Music, but never got on campus. At age 15, he had a reputation as one of the best drummers in Boston. His adolescence was spent gigging with key jazzmen Sam Rivers, Gil Evans, Eric Dolphy, Cecil Taylor, and Jackie McLean. McLean discovered Williams in Boston and took the sixteen-year-old to New York to perform. "So Jackie was the reason for me to really get to where I am," Williams recounted to Ephland. "He was the link."

Miles Davis Offered an Invitation

Williams had not been playing with McLean more than a few months when McLean invited Miles Davis, who was in town from California, to hear his band. Williams had met Davis before when he was guesting at a Boston club. He had gone backstage after one of Davis's sets to ask Davis if he could sit in with his band. Musicians around Boston often let the young Williams join them, but Davis was not as casual. Williams told Ephland he was rebuffed at age 14 when he approached Davis. "Miles turned around and said, "Go back, sit down, and listen."" Their second meeting fared much better in New York. One month later, Williams received a call to join Davis. "Tony Williams erupted onto the jazz scene in 1963, a 17-year-old prodigy with a full-blown, volcanic style of drumming that would blow hard-bop tastiness out the door," wrote *Down Beat,* describing Williams's debut in California. The Jazz Workshop, a club in San Francisco, waived its liquor license to have the underage Williams perform. The grouping of trumpeter Miles Davis, saxophonist Wayne Shorter, pianist Herbie Hancock, bassist Ron Carter, and drummer Tony Williams in the sixties was one of the outstanding jazz quintets in the archives of jazz history.

After recording eight records with Davis, including *Nefertiti* and *In a Silent Way,* Williams left Davis and acoustic jazz in December of 1988. The twenty-two-year-old Williams formed his own group, Lifetime, and turned the volume up in his entry to electric jazz-rock fusion with *Emergency, Turn It Over,* and *Ego.* "I like it," Williams told *Newsweek* when he put microphones to his drums to record. "Like hearing a car go by at night or a refrigerator suddenly turned on. It's to us what the sounds of horses and birds were to Beethoven." His fans did not respond, and subsequent recordings bombed. He left his role as a leader from 1972 to 1975. When Williams was motivated to lead again from 1975 to 1976, his albums, like *Million Dollar Legs,* were pop-oriented. Critics accused him of trying to turn a profit in the more lucrative rock market. He resigned his role as a leader once more from 1976 to 1979.

For the Record. . .

Born Anthony Williams, December 12, 1945, in Chicago, IL; son of Tillman Williams. *Education:* Studied classical composition at the University of California, Berkeley, 1979.

Drummer, composer. Played clubs in the Boston area while still a child; at age 12, performed with Art Blakey, at age 13, with Max Roach; at age 15, considered among the best drummers in Boston; gigged with saxophonist Sam Rivers; joined Miles Davis quintet, 1960s; debuted with his own group, Lifetime, in 1969; performed with V.S.O.P., 1970s; has played with Herbie Hancock, Sonny Rollins, and Wynton Marsalis, among others; contributed music and performace to the film *'Round Midnight,* Warner Bros., 1986.

Addresses: Record company—Blue Note Records, 810 Seventh Ave., Fourth Floor, New York, NY 10019.

Therapy Revitalized Career

"I could deal with drums. I could deal music. But my business and personal relations were totally fogged," Williams confessed to Lee Underwood in *Down Beat* about this period. After entering group therapy in 1976, Williams's outlook improved. A year later, he moved from New York to Marin County, California. The end of the seventies saw his reemergence as drummer extraordinaire. "With the 1979 release of *The Joy Of Flying,* 33-year-old Tony Williams is back in the arena," raved *Down Beat.* Ironically, Williams had never left the arena. His record flops were more the result of improper management, poor promotion, and the shortsightedness of critics, than Williams's personal failure.

From the later years of the seventies to the present, Williams has continued to compose, perform, and record with the prestigious jazz quintet V.S.O.P., whose members have included Freddie Hubbard and Wynton Marsalis. He has played in trios with Ron Carter and Hank Jones, and gigged with Sonny Rollins. In 1985 he contributed to and performed in the movie *'Round Midnight,* by the French director Bertrand Tavernier. The film about jazz players in Paris starred jazz legends Dexter Gordon, Billy Higgins, Herbie Hancock, and John McLaughlin, along with Williams and others. That same year he formed his own quintet, which showcased his writing and production talents in straight-ahead jazz, a format he maintains to date. "Tony Williams has shown himself to be a key figure in the revival of the contemporary jazz mainstream," wrote Josef Woodard in a review of Williams's album *Native Heart* in 1990. "With his able band, Williams is going after a striking,

familiar-but-fresh sound here. . .," continued Woodard, "but informed by the peregrinations of a different drummer who can go home again."

Emphasis on Rock Rhythms

Once slighted as a sell-out, the unmarried Williams is now viewed as a pioneer in the move from acoustic jazz to electronic funk and fusion. His controversial emphasis on rock rhythms and electric music is heralded as setting the standard for the new sounds in seventies fusion. His studies in classical composition, begun in 1979 with Robert Greenberg at the University of California at Berkeley, have brought Williams back to his traditional jazz roots without foregoing his tumultuous approach to jazz drumming. "Perhaps more than any drummer over the past 30 years," wrote Ephland, summarizing the jazzman's impact, "Tony Williams has epitomized that incessant drive towards newness of expression on his chosen instrument, the drums."

Selected discography

Lifetime, Blue Note, 1964.
Once in a Lifetime, Verve.
Spring, Blue Note, 1965.
Emergency, Polydor, 1969.
Turn It Over, 1970.
Ego, Polydor, 1971.
The Old Bum's Rush, Polydor, 1972.
Believe It, Columbia.
Million Dollar Legs, Columbia.
The Joy of Flying, Columbia, 1979.
Foreign Intrigue, Blue Note, 1986.
Civilization, Blue Note, 1986.
Angel Street, Blue Note.
Native Heart, Blue Note.

With Herbie Hancock

My Point of View, Blue Note, 1963.
Empyrean Isles, Blue Note.
Maiden Voyage, Blue Note, 1965.

With Miles Davis

Seven Steps to Heaven, Columbia, 1963.
In Europe, Columbia, 1963.
Four and More, Columbia.
Heard Round the World, Columbia.
Live at the Plugged Nickel, Columbia.
Cookin' at the Plugged Nickel, Columbia.
My Funny Valentine, Columbia, 1964.
Miles Smiles, Columbia, 1966.

E.S.P., Columbia, 1967.
Sorcerer, Columbia, 1967.
Nefertiti, Columbia, 1967.
Miles in the Sky, Columbia, 1968.
Filles De Kilimanjaro, Columbia, 1968.
In a Silent Way, Columbia, 1969.
Water Babies, Columbia, 1978.

With V.S.O.P.

Live under the Sky, Columbia.
Quintet, Columbia, 1977.
Third Plane, Milestone.

With Hank Jones and Ron Carter

Milestones, Inner City.
New Wine in Old Bottles, Inner City.
At The Village Vanguard, Inner City.

Has also recorded albums with Erich Dolphy (*Out to Lunch,* Blue Note, 1964), Sam Rivers *(Fuchsia Swing Song,* Blue Note, 1964), Gil Evans (*There Comes a Time,* RCA/Bluebird), Jackie McLean (*One Step Beyond,* Blue Note, 1963), Sonny Rollins (*Easy Living,* Milestone, 1977; *Don't Stop The Carnival,* Milestone, 1978), Mulgrew Miller (*The Countdown,* Landmark), Andrew Hill (*Point Of Departure,* Blue Note), Kenny Dorham (*Una Mas,* Blue Note), Wayne Shorter (*The Soothsayer,* Blue Note), Chet Baker (*You Can't Go Home Again,* A&M Horizon), Carlos Santana (*The Swing of Delight,* Columbia), and Wynton Marsalis (*Wynton Marsalis,* Columbia, 1981). Performed on the soundtrack of the film *'Round Midnight* (Columbia, 1985).

Sources

Down Beat, June 1979; November 1983; February 1986; June 1986; December 1988; May 1989; July 1990; September 1990.
Newsweek, February 9, 1970.
People, July 9, 1990.
Rolling Stone, August 23, 1979.

—*Marjorie Burgess*

Bob Wills

Fiddler, bandleader, songwriter

Known as "the king of western swing," Bob Wills left an indelible mark on country-and-western music across five decades, and has been an influence to numerous modern country artists. A top-notch fiddler, songwriter, and the bandleader of his Texas Playboys, Wills blazed a trail from the 1920s onward with his innovative style of up-tempo, dance-beat swing music, which combined elements of bluegrass, jazz, blues, and Texas folk music—all tinged with the distinct aura of the American West. A popular performer at dancehalls and concerts across the Southwest and West, and an equally popular recording and radio artist throughout the United States, Wills wrote such classic songs as "San Antonio Rose," "Texas Two Step," "Take Me Back to Tulsa," and "Texas Playboy Rag." Open to whatever music made for good dance rhythms, Wills introduced instruments that had never been used in country-and-western bands before—such as horns, reeds, and drums—and produced a fiddle-based swing sound that brought him national recognition. According to Bill C. Malone in *Country Music U.S.A.,* Wills was "an influence for change that has seldom been equaled in country music history."

Wills, who was born in East Texas and moved to West Texas when he was eight, came from a very musical family. Both his father's and mother's sides had many experienced fiddle players, and as a boy he played backup to his father at local ranch and square dances. Although the mandolin was his first instrument, he became adept at the fiddle, and learned a vast repertoire of songs from his father and other fiddle-playing relatives. He performed solo for the first time when he was fifteen, after his father was late for a dance they were to perform at. Growing up in Texas, Wills was exposed to the various music of the region, including Spanish music, cowhand songs, and the folk music of blacks; he was especially fond of blues and once rode fifty miles on horseback to see the "Empress of the Blues," Bessie Smith, perform. In *Stars of Country Music,* Charles R. Townsend noted that "the blues idiom contributed to the distinctiveness of Wills's fiddle style and helped give his music the 'heat of jazz' that was so necessary in the popular music of his generation."

Doughboys on KFJZ

In 1929 Wills moved to Fort Worth and, with guitarist Herman Arnspiger, formed the Wills Fiddle Band. Vocalist Milton Brown, guitarist Durwood Brown, and banjoist "Sleepy" Johnson joined the following year, and the band became known as Aladdin Laddies after their radio sponsor, Aladdin Lamps. They later were sponsored by Burrus Mills Flour Company and became

For the Record. . .

Born James Robert Wills, March 6, 1905, near Kosse, Limestone County, TX; moved to Hall County, TX, 1913; died May 13, 1975, in Fort Worth, TX; son of John and Emmaline (Foley) Wills; married Edna Posey, 1926 (divorced, 1935); married Ruth McMaster, 1936 (divorced, 1936); married Mary Helen Brown, 1938 (divorced, 1938; remarried, 1938; divorced, 1939); married Mary Louise Parker, 1939 (divorced, 1939); married Betty Anderson, 1942; children: (first marriage) Robbie Jo, (fifth marriage) Rosetta, (sixth marriage) James Robert II, Carolyn, Diane, Cindy.

Fiddler, beginning 1915; bandleader, beginning 1929. Formed Wills Fiddle Band, 1929 (later became Aladdin Laddies and then Light Crust Doughboys); formed Bob Wills and the Texas Playboys, 1934. Appeared in several movies, 1940-46. *Military service:* U.S. Army, 1942-43.

Awards: Gold record, 1940, for "New San Antonio Rose"; elected to Country Music Hall of Fame, 1968; Pioneer Award, Academy of Country and Western Music, 1969; recognized by the Texas state legislature for his contributions to American music, May 30, 1969; inducted into Songwriters Hall of Fame, Nashville Songwriters Association, 1970; citation from American Society of Composers, Authors and Publishers (ASCAP), 1973, for lifelong contributions to American music.

known as the Light Crust Doughboys. In 1931, the Doughboys appeared on their own radio show on Fort Worth's KFJZ; their announcer, manager, and spokesman at the time was W. Lee Daniel, president of Burrus Mill and later, governor of Texas. The show became extremely popular and was eventually broadcast on stations throughout Texas and Oklahoma. However, after a dispute with Daniel, who did not want the Doughboys to also perform at dances, Brown left the group in 1933 to form his own band—Milton Brown and his Brownies—and was replaced by singer and pianist Tommy Duncan. Wills also left in 1933, and moved to Waco where he began forming the group that would become the renowned Texas Playboys.

Texas Playboys Enjoyed Popular Success

Joined by Duncan, trumpeter Everett Stover, guitarist brothers June and Kermit Whalin, and Wills's own banjo-playing brother Johnny Lee, the Texas Playboys were successful performers in Waco, but moved to Oklahoma in 1934 where they got their own radio program on Tulsa's KVOO. Based in Tulsa for the rest of the 1930s and into the early 1940s, Wills and the Texas Playboys reached their greatest popularity. They played an extensive road schedule to packed dancehalls in Texas and Oklahoma, and their radio program became a fixture for music listeners throughout the Southwest. During his Tulsa years, Wills put together what is considered his greatest band. In addition to the previous members, the Playboys were joined by bass player Son Lansford, saxophonist and clarinetist Robert McNally, guitarist Herman Arnspiger, trombonist and fiddler Art Haines, fiddler Jesse Ashlock, guitarist and banjoist Clifton Johnson, drummer William Eschol Dacus, steel guitarist Leon McAuliffe, and pianist Al Stricklin. With this large set-up—which would see various musicians come and go over the years—Wills popularized what came to be known as western swing, combining, as Townsend describes, "traditional jazz instruments with string instruments, and all of them performing in a jazz or swing style. . . . A key to Bob Wills's success was the fact that he felt free to add instruments, songs, and stylistic innovations that were foreign to traditional string bands."

"New San Antonio Rose"

"The second half of the 1930s and the early 1940s amounted to a golden era for the Playboys," noted Irwin Stambler and Grelun Landon in the *Encyclopedia of Folk, Country & Western Music.* They played to sold-out concerts throughout the Southwest and as far away as California. Wills became famous for his entertaining performances, playing his fast-paced fiddle as he skirted around the stage, smoking a cigar, engaging the audience and his band members in playful banter, and letting out his trademark cries of "Ah, ha, San Antone!" or "Take it away, Leon!" The Playboys' radio program was broadcast across the United States, and by the 1940s their recordings appeared on jukeboxes nationally. They had their biggest hit single in 1938 with Wills's composition, "San Antonio Rose"; however, a subsequent 1940 version entitled "New San Antonio Rose," with lyrics cowritten by Wills and vocals by Duncan, became an even bigger hit for the Playboys, and earned them a gold record. "New San Antonio Rose" remains Wills's best-known song and has been recorded by numerous other artists, including Bing Crosby who also had a hit with it in the 1940s. Other hits by Wills during this time included "Texas Playboy Rag," "Mexicali Rose," "Take Me Back to Tulsa," and "Faded Love," the latter cowritten with his father. Also in the 1940s, Wills and the Playboys began a movie career, and performed their songs in several western films.

After World War II, the demand waned for dance music by swing bands, and Wills moved to California in 1943 where he formed a new, smaller Playboys band. (He enlisted in the army in 1942, but was discharged shortly thereafter for health reasons.) During the rest of the 1940s and 1950s, Wills and the Playboys never reached their previous level of popularity, yet they continued to command sold-out concerts of loyal fans and sell many records. Heart attacks suffered by Wills in 1962 and 1964, in addition to other health problems, seriously reduced his output during the 1960s, yet his earlier recordings were released as sets by various record companies.

Influenced a Generation of Musicians

Wills's influence was beginning to show during the early 1960s on a new generation of country performers. Emerging artists such as Roger Miller, Willie Nelson, and Merle Haggard all cited Bob Wills as the primary influence in their country careers. Later, in the 1970s and into the 1980s, the "Austin musicians," comprised of folk and country musicians centered in Austin, Texas, and featured on the music program "Austin City Limits," frequently referred to Wills as their figurehead. Malone wrote that "the Texas mystique clearly affected the imagery that Austin musicians used to describe themselves. The name and music of Bob Wills were often invoked because they supposedly embodied the spirit of liberation and innovation that Texas had contributed to music and on which the Austin musicians now drew."

In 1968, Wills was inducted into the Country Music Hall of Fame for his lifelong contributions to country music. Among other honors late in his life Wills received a special citation from the American society of Composers, Authors and Publishers (ASCAP) in 1973 for his lifelong contributions to American country music. In 1973, Wills and several of the Playboys were reunited for what would be his last recording session, a collection of 27 selections of Wills's standards which were released in the mid-1970s by United Artists as a multi-disc set, *For the Last Time*. Wills suffered a stroke in 1973, from which he never recovered, and died in 1975 in Fort Worth, where he had lived for the last 12 years.

Selected discography

Wills recorded over 550 records in his lifetime, and numerous collections of his recordings have been issued.

The Best of Bob Wills and His Texas Playboys, MCA.
Bob Wills and His Texas Playboys, MCA.
Bob Wills and His Texas Playboys in Concert, Capitol.
Bob Wills Anthology, Columbia.
Bob Wills and His Texas Playboys: The Golden Era, Columbia.
Bob Wills in Person, MCA.
Bob Wills Keepsake, Longhorn.
Bob Wills Plays the Greatest String Band Hits, MCA.
Bob Wills Sings and Plays, Liberty.
Bob Wills Special, Harmony.
(With Asleep at the Wheel) *Fathers and Sons*, Epic.
For the Last Time, United Artists.
Hall of Fame, United Artists.
Here's That Man Again, Kapp.
Home in San Antone, Harmony.
King of the Western Swing, MCA.
Living Legend, Liberty.
Mr. Words and Mr. Music, Liberty.
Time Changes Everything, MCA.
Together Again, Liberty.
A Tribute to Bob, United Artists.
A Tribute to Bob Wills, MGM.
Western Swing Along, RCA.
Western Swing Along with Bob Wills and His Texas Playboys, Vocalion.
Anthology, Rhino, 1991.

Sources

Malone, Bill C., *Country Music U.S.A.*, revised edition, University of Texas Press, 1985.

Malone, Bill C., and Judith McCulloh, editors, *The Stars of Country Music*, Avon Books, 1975.

Marschall, Rick, *The Encyclopedia of Country & Western Music*, Exeter Books, 1985.

Shestack, Melvin, *The Country Music Encyclopedia*, Crowell, 1974.

Stambler, Irwin, and Grelun Landon, *Encyclopedia of Folk, Country & Western Music*, 2nd edition, St. Martin's, 1983.

Stricklin, Al, with Jon McConal, *My Years with Bob Wills*, Naylor Company, 1976.

Townsend, Charles R., *San Antonio Rose: The Life and Music of Bob Wills*, discography and filmusicography by Bob Pinson, University of Illinois Press, 1976.

White, Timothy, *Rock Lives: Profiles and Interviews*, Henry Holt, 1990.

—*Michael E. Mueller*

Subject Index

Volume numbers appear in **bold.**

Zukerman, Pinchas **4**

Composers
Anka, Paul **2**
Atkins, Chet **5**
Bacharach, Burt **1**
Bernstein, Leonard **2**
Clarke, Stanley **3**
Coleman, Ornette **5**
Cooder, Ry **2**
Cooney, Rory **6**
Copland, Aaron **2**
Davis, Chip **4**
Davis, Miles **1**
de Grassi, Alex **6**
Ellington, Duke **2**
Enya **6**
Gillespie, Dizzy **6**
Glass, Philip **1**
Guaraldi, Vince **3**
Hamlisch, Marvin **1**
Hartke, Stephen **5**
Jarre, Jean-Michel **2**
Jarrett, Keith **1**
Jones, Quincy **2**
Jordan, Stanley **1**
Kitaro **1**
Lloyd Webber, Andrew **6**
Mancini, Henry **1**
Metheny, Pat **2**
Monk, Meredith **1**
Monk, Thelonious **6**
Nascimento, Milton **6**
Newman, Randy **4**
Ott, David **2**
Parker, Charlie **5**
Satriani, Joe **4**
Schickele, Peter **5**
Shorter, Wayne **5**
Solal, Martial **4**
Story, Liz **2**
Summers, Andy **3**
Sun Ra **5**
Takemitsu, Toru **6**
Talbot, John Michael **6**
Washington, Grover Jr. **5**
Zimmerman, Udo **5**

Conductors
Bacharach, Burt **1**
Bernstein, Leonard **2**
Copland, Aaron **2**
Domingo, Placido **1**
Fiedler, Arthur **6**
Jarrett, Keith **1**
Mancini, Henry **1**
Rampal, Jean-Pierre **6**
Schickele, Peter **5**
von Karajan, Herbert **1**
Zukerman, Pinchas **4**

Contemporary Dance Music
Abdul, Paula **3**
B-52s **4**
The Bee Gees **3**
Brown, Bobby **4**
Brown, James **2**
Cherry, Neneh **4**
Depeche Mode **5**
Eurythmics **6**
Expose **4**
Fox, Samantha **3**
Hammer, M.C. **5**
Harry, Deborah **4**
Idol, Billy **3**
Jackson, Janet **3**
Jackson, Michael **1**
James, Rick **2**
Madonna **4**

Pet Shop Boys **5**
Prince **1**
Queen Latifah **6**
Salt-N-Pepa **6**
Technotronic **5**
Was (Not Was) **6**
Young M.C. **4**

Country
Acuff, Roy **2**
Alabama **1**
Anderson, John **5**
Asleep at the Wheel **5**
Atkins, Chet **5**
Auldridge, Mike **4**
Black, Clint **5**
Buffett, Jimmy **4**
Campbell, Glen **2**
Carpenter, Mary-Chapin **6**
The Carter Family **3**
Cash, Johnny **1**
Cash, June Carter **6**
Cash, Rosanne **2**
Clark, Roy **1**
Cline, Patsy **5**
Coe, David Allan **4**
Cooder, Ry **2**
Cowboy Junkies **4**
Crowe, J.D. **5**
Daniels, Charlie **6**
Denver, John **1**
Desert Rose Band **4**
Dylan, Bob **3**
Flatt, Lester **3**
Ford, Tennessee Ernie **3**
Gayle, Crystal **1**
Griffith, Nanci **3**
Haggard, Merle **2**
Hall, Tom T. **4**
Harris, Emmylou **4**
Hartford, John **1**
Hay, George D. **3**
Healey, Jeff **4**
Highway 101 **4**
Jennings, Waylon **4**
Jones, George **4**
The Judds **2**
Kentucky Headhunters **5**
Kristofferson, Kris **4**
Lang, K.D. **4**
Lee, Brenda **5**
Little Feat **4**
Loveless, Patty **5**
Lovett, Lyle **5**
Lynn, Loretta **2**
Lynne, Shelby **5**
Mandrell, Barbara **4**
Mattea, Kathy **5**
Miller, Roger **4**
Milsap, Ronnie **2**
Monroe, Bill **1**
Murray, Anne **4**
Nelson, Willie **1**
The Nitty Gritty Dirt Band **6**
Oak Ridge Boys **4**
O'Connor, Mark **1**
Oslin, K.T. **3**
Owens, Buck **2**
Parton, Dolly **2**
Pearl, Minnie **3**
Pride, Charley **4**
Rabbitt, Eddie **5**
Raitt, Bonnie **3**
Rich, Charlie **3**
Rodgers, Jimmie **3**
Rogers, Kenny **1**
Scruggs, Earl **3**
Skaggs, Ricky **5**
Strait, George **5**

Tubb, Ernest **4**
Tucker, Tanya **3**
Twitty, Conway **4**
Van Shelton, Ricky **5**
Watson, Doc **6**
Wells, Kitty **6**
Williams, Don **4**
Williams, Hank Jr. **1**
Williams, Hank Sr. **4**
Wills, Bob **6**
Wynette, Tammy **2**
Yoakam, Dwight **1**

Dobro
Auldridge, Mike **4**
Burch, Curtis
   See New Grass Revival **4**
Knopfler, Mark **3**

Drums
See **Percussion**

Dulcimer
Ritchie, Jean **4**

Fiddle
See **Violin**

Film Scores
Anka, Paul **2**
Bacharach, Burt **1**
Bernstein, Leonard **2**
Cafferty, John
   See the Beaver Brown Band **3**
Copland, Aaron **2**
Ellington, Duke **2**
Guaraldi, Vince **3**
Hamlisch, Marvin **1**
Harrison, George **2**
Hedges, Michael **3**
Jones, Quincy **2**
Knopfler, Mark **3**
Lennon, John
   See the Beatles **2**
Mancini, Henry **1**
McCartney, Paul
   See the Beatles **2**
Metheny, Pat **2**
Nascimento, Milton **6**
Richie, Lionel **2**
Robertson, Robbie **2**
Sager, Carole Bayer **5**
Schickele, Peter **5**
Taj Mahal **6**
Waits, Tom **1**
Williams, Paul **5**
Young, Neil **2**

Flute
Galway, James **3**
Rampal, Jean-Pierre **6**
Wilson, Ransom **5**

Folk/Traditional
Baez, Joan **1**
Blades, Ruben **2**
The Carter Family **3**
Chapin, Harry **6**
Chapman, Tracy **4**
Childs, Toni **2**
Cohen, Leonard **3**
Collins, Judy **4**
Crosby, David **3**
de Lucia, Paco **1**
Dylan, Bob **3**
Elliot, Cass **5**
Enya **6**
Estefan, Gloria **2**
Galway, James **3**

Griffith, Nanci **3**
Guthrie, Arlo **6**
Guthrie, Woodie **2**
Harding, John Wesley **6**
Hartford, John **1**
Iglesias, Julio **2**
Indigo Girls **3**
Ladysmith Black Mambazo **1**
Lavin, Christine **6**
Leadbelly **6**
Lightfoot, Gordon **3**
Los Lobos **2**
Mitchell, Joni **2**
Morrison, Van **3**
Nascimento, Milton **6**
N'Dour, Youssou **6**
Near, Holly **1**
O'Connor, Sinead **3**
Paxton, Tom **5**
Peter, Paul & Mary **4**
The Pogues **6**
Redpath, Jean **1**
Ritchie, Jean, **4**
Rodgers, Jimmie **3**
Santana, Carlos **1**
Seeger, Pete **4**
Snow, Pheobe **4**
Sweet Honey in the Rock **1**
Taj Mahal **6**
Vega, Suzanne **3**
Watson, Doc **2**

French Horn
Ohanian, David
See Canadian Brass **4**

Fusion
Beck, Jeff **4**
Clarke, Stanley **3**
Coleman, Ornette **5**
Corea, Chick **6**
Davis, Miles **1**
Jarreau, Al **1**
Metheny, Pat **2**
O'Connor, Mark **1**
Reid, Vernon **2**
Shorter, Wayne **5**
Summers, Andy **3**
Washington, Grover, Jr. **5**

Gospel
Brown, James **2**
The Carter Family **3**
Charles, Ray **1**
Cleveland, James **1**
Cooke, Sam **1**
Ford, Tennessee Ernie **3**
Franklin, Aretha **2**
Houston, Cissy **6**
Knight, Gladys **1**
Little Richard **1**
Oak Ridge Boys **4**
Presley, Elvis **1**
Redding, Otis **5**
Take 6 **6**
Watson, Doc **2**
Williams, Deniece **1**
Womack, Bobby **5**

Guitar
Ackerman, Will **3**
Allman, Duane
See the Allman Brothers **6**
Atkins, Chet **5**
Baxter, Jeff
See the Doobie Brothers **3**
Beck, Jeff **4**
Belew, Adrian **5**
Berry, Chuck **1**

Betts, Dicky
See the Allman Brothers **6**
Buck, Peter
See R.E.M. **5**
Buckingham, Lindsey
See Fleetwood Mac **5**
Campbell, Glen **2**
Clapton, Eric **1**
Clark, Roy **1**
Collins, Albert **4**
Cooder, Ry **2**
Daniels, Charlie **6**
de Grassi, Alex **6**
de Lucia, Paco **1**
Diddley, Bo **3**
Earl, Ronnie **5**
The Edge
See U2 **2**
Flatt, Lester **3**
Frampton, Peter **3**
Frehley, Ace
See Kiss **5**
Garcia, Jerry **4**
George, Lowell
See Little Feat **4**
Gibbons, Billy
See ZZ Top **2**
Gilmour, David
See Pink Floyd **2**
Green, Peter
See Fleetwood Mac **5**
Guy, Buddy **4**
Haley, Bill **6**
Harrison, George **2**
Healey, Jeff **4**
Hedges, Michael **3**
Hendrix, Jimi **2**
Hillman, Chris
See Desert Rose Band **4**
Holly, Buddy **1**
Hooker, John Lee **1**
Howlin' Wolf **6**
Jardine, Al
See the Beach Boys **1**
Johnson, Robert **6**
Jones, Brian
See the Rolling Stones **3**
Jordan, Stanley **1**
Kantner, Paul
See Jefferson Airplane **5**
King, Albert **2**
King, B.B. **1**
Knopfler, Mark **3**
Leadbelly **6**
Lindley, David **2**
Marr, Johnny
See the Smiths **3**
May, Brian
See Queen **6**
Metheny, Pat **2**
Montgomery, Wes **3**
Nugent, Ted **2**
Owens, Buck **2**
Page, Jimmy **4**
Also see Led Zeppelin **1**
Perry, Joe
See Aerosmith **3**
Prince **1**
Raitt, Bonnie **3**
Ray, Amy
See Indigo Girls **3**
Reid, Vernon **2**
Richard, Keith
See the Rolling Stones **3**
Robertson, Robbie **2**
Robillard, Duke **2**
Santana, Carlos **1**
Saliers, Emily
See Indigo Girls **3**

Satriani, Joe **4**
Segovia, Andres **6**
Skaggs, Ricky **5**
Slash
See Guns n' Roses **2**
Springsteen, Bruce **6**
Stewart, Dave
See Eurythmics **6**
Stills, Stephen **5**
Summers, Andy **3**
Taylor, Mick
See the Rolling Stones **3**
Townshend, Pete **1**
Tubb, Ernest **4**
Vai, Steve **5**
Vaughan, Jimmie
See the Fabulous Thunderbirds **1**
Vaughan, Stevie Ray **1**
Walker, T-Bone **5**
Walsh, Joe **5**
Also see the Eagles **3**
Watson, Doc **2**
Weir, Bob
See the Grateful Dead **5**
Wilson, Nancy
Winter, Johnny **5**
Yamashita, Kazuhito **4**
Yarrow, Peter
See Peter, Paul & Mary **4**
Young, Angus
See AC/DC **4**
Young, Malcolm
See AC/DC **4**
Young, Neil **2**

Harmonica
Dylan, Bob **3**
Guthrie, Woodie **2**
Waters, Muddy **4**
Wilson, Kim
See the Fabulous Thunderbirds **1**

Heavy Metal
AC/DC **4**
Aerosmith **3**
Def Leppard **3**
Guns n' Roses **2**
Led Zeppelin **1**
Mötley Crüe **1**
Nugent, Ted **2**
Osbourne, Ozzy **3**
Petra **3**
Reid, Vernon **2**
Roth, David Lee **1**
Soundgarden **6**
Stryper **2**
Whitesnake **5**

Humor
The Coasters **5**
Jones, Spike **5**
Pearl, Minnie **3**
Russell, Mark **6**
Schickele, Peter **5**

Inventors
Paul, Les **2**

Jazz
Armstrong, Louis **4**
Bailey, Pearl **5**
Basie, Count **2**
Belle, Regina **6**
Berigan, Bunny **2**
Calloway, Cab(ell) **6**
Canadian Brass **4**
Carter, Benny **3**
Carter, Betty **6**
Charles, Ray **1**

Clarke, Stanley **3**
Cole, Nat King **3**
Coleman, Ornette **5**
Coltrane, John **4**
Connick, Harry Jr. **4**
Corea, Chick **6**
Davis, Miles **1**
Eckstine, Billy **1**
Ellington, Duke **2**
Fitzgerald, Ella **1**
Galway, James **3**
Gillespie, Dizzy **6**
Goodman, Benny **4**
Guaraldi, Vince **3**
Hampton, Lionel **6**
Hedges, Michael **3**
Hirt, Al **5**
Holiday, Billie **6**
Jarreau, Al **1**
Jarrett, Keith **1**
Jones, Quincy **2**
Jordan, Stanley **1**
Kirk, Rahsaan Roland **6**
Kronos Quartet **5**
Mancini, Henry **1**
Marsalis, Wynton **6**
McFerrin, Bobby **3**
Metheny, Pat **2**
Monk, Thelonious **6**
Montgomery, Wes **3**
Nascimento, Milton **6**
Parker, Charlie **5**
Paul, Les **2**
Professor Longhair **6**
Rampal, Jean-Pierre **6**
Reid, Vernon **2**
Roberts, Marcus **6**
Robillard, Duke **2**
Sanborn, David **1**
Santana, Carlos **1**
Schuur, Diane **6**
Severinsen, Doc **1**
Shorter, Wayne **5**
Solal, Martial **4**
Summers, Andy **3**
Sun Ra **5**
Take 6 **6**
Torme, Mel **4**
Vaughan, Sarah **2**
Waits, Tom **1**
Walker, T-Bone **5**
Washington, Dinah **5**
Washington, Grover, Jr. **5**

Keyboards, Electric
Corea, Chick **6**
Davis, Chip **4**
Emerson, Keith
    See Emerson, Lake & Palmer/Powell **5**
Jackson, Joe **4**
Jarre, Jean-Michel **2**
Kitaro **1**
Manzarek, Ray
    See the Doors **4**
McDonald, Michael
    See the Doobie Brothers **3**
McVie, Christine
    See Fleetwood Mac **5**
Pierson, Kate
    See B-52s **4**
Sun Ra **5**
Wilson, Brian
    See the Beach Boys **1**
Winwood, Steve **2**
Wonder, Stevie **2**

Liturgical music
Cooney, Rory **6**
Talbot, John Michael **6**

Mandolin
Bush, Sam
    See New Grass Revival **4**
Duffey, John
    See the Seldom Scene **4**
Hartford, John **1**
Lindley, David **2**
Monroe, Bill **1**
Rosas, Cesar
    See Los Lobos **2**
Skaggs, Ricky **5**

Musicals
Andrews, Julie **4**
Bacharach, Burt **1**
Bailey, Pearl **5**
Buckley, Betty **1**
Burnett, Carol **6**
Channing, Carol **6**
Chevalier, Maurice **6**
Crawford, Michael **4**
Crosby, Bing **6**
Curry, Tim **3**
Davis, Sammy Jr. **4**
Garland, Judy **6**
Hamlisch, Marvin **1**
Lloyd Webber, Andrew **6**
Patinkin, Mandy **3**
Sager, Carole Bayer **5**

New Age
Ackerman, Will **3**
Davis, Chip **4**
de Grassi, Alex **6**
Enya **6**
Hedges, Michael **3**
Jarre, Jean-Michel **2**
Kitaro **1**
Kronos Quartet **5**
Story, Liz **2**
Summers, Andy **3**

Opera
Battle, Kathleen **6**
Cotrubas, Ileana **1**
Domingo, Placido **1**
Pavarotti, Luciano **1**
Price, Leontyne **6**
Sills, Beverly **5**
Te Kanawa, Kiri **2**
von Karajan, Herbert **1**
Zimmerman, Udo **5**

Percussion
Bonham, John
    See Led Zeppelin **1**
Collins, Phil **2**
    Also see Genesis **4**
Densmore, John
    See the Doors **4**
Dunbar, Aynsley
    See Jefferson Starship **5**
    Also see Whitesnake **5**
Fleetwood, Mick
    See Fleetwood Mac **5**
Hart, Mickey
    See the Grateful Dead **5**
Henley, Don **3**
Jones, Kenny
    See the Who **3**
Jones, Spike **5**
Kreutzman, Bill
    See the Grateful Dead **5**
Mason, Nick
    See Pink Floyd **2**
Moon, Keith
    See the Who **3**
N'Dour, Youssou **6**
Palmer, Carl

    See Emerson, Lake & Palmer/Powell **5**
Powell, Cozy
    See Emerson, Lake & Palmer/Powell **5**
Sheila E. **3**
Starr, Ringo
    See the Beatles **2**
Watts, Charlie
    See the Rolling Stones **3**

Piano
Arrau, Claudio **1**
Bacharach, Burt **1**
Basie, Count **2**
Bronfman, Yefim **6**
Bush, Kate **4**
Charles, Ray **1**
Clayderman, Richard **1**
Cleveland, James **1**
Cole, Nat King **3**
Collins, Judy **4**
Collins, Phil **2**
    Also see Genesis **4**
Connick, Harry Jr. **4**
Domino, Fats
Ellington, Duke **2**
Feinstein, Michael **6**
Flack, Roberta **5**
Frey, Glenn **3**
Glass, Philip **1**
Guaraldi, Vince **3**
Hamlisch, Marvin **1**
Hornsby, Bruce **3**
Horowitz, Vladimir **1**
Jackson, Joe **4**
Jarrett, Keith **1**
Joel, Billy **2**
John, Elton **3**
Kissin, Evgeny **6**
Lewis, Jerry Lee **2**
Little Richard **1**
Manilow, Barry **2**
McDonald, Michael
    See the Doobie Brothers **3**
McVie, Christine
    See Fleetwood Mac **5**
Milsap, Ronnie **2**
Monk, Thelonious **6**
Newman, Randy **4**
Professor Longhair **6**
Rich, Charlie **3**
Roberts, Marcus **6**
Russell, Mark **6**
Schickele, Peter **5**
Sedaka, Neil **4**
Solal, Martial **4**
Story, Liz **2**
Waits, Tom **1**
Winwood, Steve **2**
Wonder, Stevie **2**
Wright, Rick
    See Pink Floyd **2**

Piccolo
Galway, James **3**

Pop
Abdul, Paula **3**
Adams, Bryan **2**
Aerosmith **3**
Armatrading, Joan **4**
Astley, Rick **5**
Atkins, Chet **5**
Avalon, Frankie **5**
B-52s **4**
Bacharach, Burt **1**
Bailey, Pearl **5**
Basia **5**
The Beach Boys **1**
The Beatles **2**

Musicians Index

Volume numbers appear in **bold**.

Fadden, Jimmie
  See the Nitty Gritty Dirt Band
Fagan, Don
  See Steely Dan
Falconer, Earl
  See UB40
Farrell, Perry
  See Jane's Addiction
Farriss, Andrew
  See INXS
Farriss, Jon
  See INXS
Farriss, Tim
  See INXS
Fearnley, James
  See the Pogues
Feinstein, Michael **6**
Felder, Don
  See the Eagles
Ferguson, Keith
  See the Fabulous Thunderbirds
Ferry, Bryan **1**
Fiedler, Arthur **6**
Finer, Jem
  See the Pogues
Fisher, Roger
  See Heart
Fitzgerald, Ella **1**
Flack, Roberta **5**
Flatt, Lester **3**
Flavor Flav
  See Public Enemy
Fleck, Bela
  See New Grass Revival
Fleetwood, Mick
  See Fleetwood Mac
Fleetwood Mac **5**
Fletcher, Andy
  See Depeche Mode
Flynn, Pat
  See New Grass Revival
Fogelberg, Dan **4**
Fogerty, John **2**
Ford, Tennessee Ernie **3**
Fossen, Steve
  See Heart
Fox, Samantha **3**
Fox, Oz
  See Stryper
Frampton, Peter **3**
Francis, Mike
  See Asleep at the Wheel
Franklin, Aretha **2**
Franklin, Larry
  See Asleep at the Wheel
Franklin, Melvin
  See the Temptations
Frantz, Chris
  See Talking Heads
Frehley, Ace
  See Kiss
Freiberg, David
  See Jefferson Starship
Frey, Glenn **3**
  Also see The Eagles
Gabriel, Peter **2**
  Also see Genesis
Gahan, Dave
  See Depeche Mode
Gaines, Timothy
  See Stryper
Gallup, Simon
  See The Cure
Galway, James **3**
Garcia, Jerry **4**
  Also see Grateful Dead
Gardner, Carl
  See the Coasters
Garfunkel, Art **4**

Garland, Judy **6**
Gaye, Marvin **4**
Gayle, Crystal **1**
Genesis **4**
    Also see Collins, Phil
    Also see Gabriel, Peter
Gentry, Teddy
  See Alabama
George, Lowell
  See Little Feat
Gibb, Barry
  See the Bee Gees
Gibb, Maurice
  See the Bee Gees
Gibb, Robin
  See the Bee Gees
Gibbons, Billy
  See ZZ Top
Gibson, Debbie **1**
Gift, Roland **3**
Gillespie, Dizzy **6**
Gilmour, David
  See Pink Floyd
Gingold, Josef **6**
Gioia
  See Exposé
Glass, Philip **1**
Godchaux, Donna
  See the Grateful Dead
Godchaux, Keith
  See the Grateful Dead
Golden, Bill
  See Oak Ridge Boys
Goodman, Benny **4**
Gordy, Berry, Jr. **6**
Gore, Martin
  See Depeche Mode
Gradney, Ken
  See Little Feat
Gramolini, Gary
  See the Beaver Brown Band
The Grateful Dead **5**
Gray, Ella
  See Kronos Quartet
Gray, Tom
  See the Seldom Scene
Gray, Walter
  See Kronos Quartet
Grebenshikov, Boris **3**
Green, Karl Anthony
  See Herman's Hermits
Green, Peter
  See Fleetwood Mac
Green, Susaye
  See the Supremes
Green, Willie
  See the Neville Brothers
Greenspoon, Jimmy
  See Three Dog Night
Griffin, Bob
  See BoDeans
Griffith, Nanci **3**
Guaraldi, Vince **3**
Guns n' Roses **2**
Gunther, Cornell
  See the Coasters
Gustafson, Steve
  See 10,000 Maniacs
Guthrie, Arlo **6**
Guthrie, Woodie **2**
Guy, Billy
  See the Coasters
Guy, Buddy **4**
Hackett, Steve
  See Genesis
Haggard, Merle **2**
Haley, Bill **6**
Hall, Daryl
  See Hall & Oates

Hall, Tom T. **4**
Hall, Tony
  See the Neville Brothers
Hall & Oates **6**
Hamilton, Tom
  See Aerosmith
Hamlisch, Marvin **1**
Hammer, M.C. **5**
Hammond, John **6**
Hampson, Sharon
  See Sharon, Lois & Bram
Hampton, Lionel **6**
Hanna, Jeff
  See the Nitty Gritty Dirt Band
Harding, John Wesley **6**
Harrell, Lynn **3**
Harrington, David
  See Kronos Quartet
Harris, Damon Otis
  See the Temptations
Harris, Emmylou **4**
Harris, Evelyn
  See Sweet Honey in the Rock
Harrison, George **2**
  Also see The Beatles
Harrison, Jerry
  See Talking Heads
Harry, Deborah **4**
Hart, Mickey
  See the Grateful Dead
Hartford, John **1**
Hartke, Stephen **5**
Hartman, Bob
  See Petra
Hartman, John
  See the Doobie Brothers
Hassan, Norman
  See UB40
Hay, George D. **3**
Haynes, Warren
  See the Allman Brothers
Hayward, Richard
  See Little Feat
Headon, Topper
  See the Clash
Healey, Jeff **4**
Heart **1**
Hedges, Michael **3**
Helm, Levon
  See the Nitty Gritty Dirt Band
Hendrix, Jimi **2**
Henley, Don **3**
  Also see The Eagles
Herman's Hermits **5**
Herndon, Mark
  See Alabama
Hewson, Paul
  See U2
Hidalgo, David
  See Los Lobos
Highway 101 **4**
Hill, Dusty
  See ZZ Top
Hillman, Chris
  See Desert Rose Band
Hirt, Al **5**
Hoffman, Guy
  See BoDeans
Holiday, Billie **6**
Holland, Brian
  See Holland-Dozier-Holland
Holland, Eddie
  See Holland-Dozier-Holland
Holland, Julian "Jools"
  See Squeeze
Holland-Dozier-Holland **5**
Holly, Buddy **1**
Hooker, John Lee **1**
Hopwood, Keith

Sun Ra **5**
The Supremes **6**
    Also see Ross, Diana
Sutcliffe, Stu
    See the Beatles
Sweet, Michael
    See Stryper
Sweet, Robert
    See Stryper
Sweet Honey in the Rock **1**
Sykes, John
    See Whitesnake
Taj Mahal **6**
Take 6 **6**
Takemitsu, Toru **6**
Talbot, John Michael **6**
Talking Heads **1**
Taylor, Andy
    See Duran Duran
Taylor, Dick
    See the Rolling Stones
Taylor, James **2**
Taylor, John
    See Duran Duran
Taylor, Mick
    See the Rolling Stones
Taylor, Roger
    See Duran Duran
Taylor, Roger Meadows
    See Queen
Tears for Fears **6**
Technotronic **5**
Te Kanawa, Kiri **2**
Tennant, Neil
    See Pet Shop Boys
The Temptations **3**
10,000 Maniacs **3**
Terminator X
    See Public Enemy
Terrell, Jean
    See the Supremes
Thayil, Kim
    See Soundgarden
Thomas, David
    See Take 6
Thomas, Mickey
    See Jefferson Starship
Thompson, Les
    See the Nitty Gritty Dirt Band
Thompson, Porl
    See The Cure
Three Dog Night **5**
Tiffany **4**
Tilbrook, Glenn
    See Squeeze
Timbuk 3 **3**
Timmins, Margo
    See Cowboy Junkies
Timmins, Michael
    See Cowboy Junkies
Timmins, Peter
    See Cowboy Junkies
Tolhurst, Laurence
    See The Cure
Toller, Dan
    See the Allman Brothers
Tone-Lōc **3**
Torme, Mel **4**
Tosh, Peter **3**
Townes, Jeffery
    See DJ Jazzy Jeff and the Fresh Prince
Townshend, Pete **1**
    Also see The Who
Travers, Brian
    See UB40
Travers, Mary
    See Peter, Paul & Mary
Trucks, Butch
    See the Allman Brothers

Tubb, Ernest **4**
Tucker, Tanya **3**
Turner, Tina **1**
Twitty, Conway **6**
Tyler, Steve
    See Aerosmith
Tyson, Ron
    See the Temptations
UB40 **4**
U2 **2**
Vai, Steve **5**
    Also see Whitesnake
Vandenburg, Adrian
    See Whitesnake
Vandross, Luther **2**
Vanilla Ice **6**
Van Shelton, Ricky **5**
Vaughan, Jimmie
    See the Fabulous Thunderbirds
Vaughan, Sarah **2**
Vaughan, Stevie Ray **1**
Vega, Suzanne **3**
Vicious, Sid
    See the Sex Pistols
Vincent, Vinnie
    See Kiss
Virtue, Michael
    See UB40
Vito, Rick
    See Fleetwood Mac
Volz, Greg
    See Petra
von Karajan, Herbert **1**
Vox, Bono
    See U2
Wahlberg, Donnie
    See New Kids on the Block
Waits, Tom **1**
Walker, Ebo
    See New Grass Revival
Walker, T-Bone **5**
Wallace, Sippie **6**
Walsh, Joe **5**
    Also see the Eagles
Warnes, Jennifer **3**
Warren, Mervyn
    See Take 6
Warwick, Dionne **2**
Was, David
    See Was (Not Was)
Was, Don
    See Was (Not Was)
Was (Not Was) **6**
Washington, Dinah **5**
Washington, Grover, Jr. **5**
Waters, Muddy **4**
Waters, Roger
    See Pink Floyd
Watson, Doc **2**
Watts, Charlie
    See the Rolling Stones
Watts, Eugene
    See Canadian Brass
Weaver, Louie
    See Petra
Webber, Andrew Lloyd
    See Lloyd Webber, Andrew
Weir, Bob
    See the Grateful Dead
Welch, Bob
    See Fleetwood Mac
Wells, Cory
    See Three Dog Night
Wells, Kitty **6**
Welnick, Vince
    See the Grateful Dead
Weymouth, Tina
    See Talking Heads
Whitesnake **5**

Whitford, Brad
    See Aerosmith
Whitwam, Barry
    See Herman's Hermits
The Who **3**
    Also see Daltrey, Roger
    Also see Townshend, Pete
Wilder, Alan
    See Depeche Mode
Wilkinson, Keith
    See Squeeze
Williams, Andy **2**
Williams, Boris
    See The Cure
Williams, Cliff
    See AC/DC
Williams, Deniece **1**
Williams, Don **4**
Williams, Hank Jr. **1**
Williams, Hank, Sr. **4**
Williams, Lamar
    See the Allman Brothers
Williams, Otis
    See the Temptations
Williams, Paul
    See the Temptations
Williams, Paul (Hamilton) **5**
Willis, Pete
    See Def Leppard
Wills, Bob **6**
Wilson, Anne
    See Heart
Wilson, Brian
    See the Beach Boys
Wilson, Carl
    See the Beach Boys
Wilson, Carnie
    See Wilson Phillips
Wilson, Cindy
    See B-52s
Wilson, Dennis
    See the Beach Boys
Wilson, Jackie **3**
Wilson, Kim
    See the Fabulous Thunderbirds
Wilson, Mary
    See the Supremes
Wilson, Nancy
    See Heart
Wilson, Ransom **5**
Wilson, Ricky
    See B-52s
Wilson, Wendy
    See Wilson Phillips
Wilson Phillips **5**
Winter, Johnny **5**
Winwood, Steve **2**
Womack, Bobby **5**
Wonder, Stevie **2**
Wood, Danny
    See New Kids on the Block
Wood, Ron
    See the Rolling Stones
Woods, Terry
    See the Pogues
Woodson, Ollie
    See the Temptations
Woody, Allen
    See the Allman Brothers
Wright, Rick
    See Pink Floyd
Wright, Simon
    See AC/DC
Wyman, Bill
    See the Rolling Stones
Wynette, Tammy **2**
Ya Kid K
    See Technotronic
Yamamoto, Hiro